D1488528

Amphibians and Reptiles
of the Great Lakes Region

 GREAT LAKES ENVIRONMENT

Matthew M. Douglas, Series Editor

Amphibians and Reptiles
of the
Great Lakes Region

by James H. Harding

Series Editor
Matthew M. Douglas

Ann Arbor

THE UNIVERSITY OF MICHIGAN PRESS

Copyright © by the University of Michigan 1997
All rights reserved
Published in the United States of America by
The University of Michigan Press
Printed in Hong Kong
⊛ Printed on acid-free paper

2000   1999   1998   1997   4   3   2   1

A CIP catalog record for this book is available from the British Library

Library of Congress Cataloging-in-Publication Data

Harding, James H., 1949–
    Amphibians and reptiles of the Great Lakes Region / James H.
    Harding.
        p.   cm. — (Great lakes environment)
    Includes bibliographical references and index.
        ISBN 0-472-09628-1 (clth : acid-free paper). — ISBN 0-472-06628-5
    (pbk : acid-free paper)
        1. Reptiles—Great Lakes Region.   2. Amphibians—Great Lakes
    Region.   I. Title.   II. Series.
    QL653.G74H37   1996
    597.6'0978—dc20   96-25343
                                                              CIP

Preface

This book is a guide to the identification, distribution, and life history of the amphibians and reptiles of the Great Lakes drainage basin. Included in this area is nearly all of the state of Michigan and portions of Ohio, Indiana, Illinois, Wisconsin, Minnesota, New York, Pennsylvania, and the province of Ontario. Emphasis is placed on the recognition and general distribution of species and subspecies known to occur in this region, along with a discussion of their habitats, seasonal cycles, behavior, reproduction, and interrelationships with other organisms, including humans. Notes on relative abundance, population trends, and conservation are also included. This book is intended as a reference for the nonspecialist, although the summaries of life history information should prove useful to professional herpetologists as well.

Amphibians and reptiles have historically been held in lower public esteem than their fellow vertebrates, the fishes, birds, and mammals. When asked to rank their greatest fears, many people put snakes near the top of the list. Broad public sympathy for preserving rare species of birds and mammals is rarely extended to scaly or slimy creatures. Prior to the mid–twentieth century, amphibians and reptiles were frequently assumed to be comparatively insignificant members of most North American wildlife communities, even by some biologists. Not surprisingly, these animals were often ignored or even persecuted by wildlife managers in the Great Lakes region and elsewhere. Research over the last several decades has led to a better understanding of the important ecological roles that these animals play in nature. We now realize that preserving amphibian and reptile species and populations is an essential and worthy conservation goal. It is hoped that this volume will assist citizens and private and government resource managers in making wise decisions affecting the future of the Great Lakes herpetofauna.

Acknowledgments

In compiling the information presented in this book, an extensive and growing literature on the herpetology of the Great Lakes area was consulted. The results of ecological, distributional, and taxonomic studies on amphibians and reptiles are reported in a variety of professional journals, and have been summarized in various popular, semipopular, and regional publications. Published sources of information consulted during the writing of this book are listed in the "Resources" section. Major herpetological organizations and their publications are also listed in that section.

Many colleagues familiar with the regional herpetofauna were consulted during the preparation of this book, and I am grateful for their assistance and advice. Special thanks go to J. Alan Holman, who offered constant encouragement as well as stimulating discussion on paleoherpetology and postglacial amphibian and reptile distributions, to James Fowler, who freely shared his vast field experience and knowledge of herpetological literature, and to Peter Wilson, for companionship and critical assistance during many memorable field forays. Many people kindly shared unpublished distributional or biological data; these include Tom Anton, Ellin Beltz, Alvin Breisch, Kevin Brewster, Gary Casper, Craig Campbell, Philip Cochran, David Good, Lisa Hallock, Dennis Herman, Kenneth Mierzwa, Sherman Minton, John Moriarty, Michael Oldham, Alan Resetar, Douglas Rossman, Al Sandilands, Frederick Schueler, Mark Sellers, and Leni Wilsmann.

Valued correspondence and advice concerning amphibian and reptile biology and taxonomy was provided by John Behler, Ronald Brooks, Joseph Collins, Roger Conant, Bob Johnson, John Kaufmann, Michael Klemens, the late C. J. (Jack) McCoy, Kenneth Storey, and Gordon Ultsch. Kraig Adler, Charles Cleland, S. Blair Hedges, Margaret Holman, and Ronald Richards provided information on paleontological and archeological questions. Supplemental information on laws and regulations for their respective states was supplied by Al Breisch (New York), Ned Fogle (Michigan), Bob Hay (Wisconsin), David Ross (Ohio), Clark Shiffer (Pennsylvania), and Catherine Smith (Indiana). William Brown, Justin Congdon, Michael Ewert, James Gillingham, and Al Holman reviewed portions of the manuscript and offered valuable suggestions that greatly improved the text. Advice on photographing amphibians and reptiles was given by Larry West and Bill Leonard, and Kristine Morrissey assisted with word-processing and computer problems. Russ Burke, Jim McGrath, and Wayne VanDevender provided specimens for photography. To the friends and colleagues noted above, and to any I might have inadvertently missed, please accept my heartfelt thanks for your many kindnesses.

A number of people kindly provided photographic materials, and these individuals are credited adjacent to each photograph. Photographs not otherwise credited were taken by the author. Cover art and line illustrations were prepared by Gijsbert van Frankenhuyzen.

Distribution descriptions and range maps in the species accounts are broadly based on information in Conant and Collins (1991) and previously published regional works noted under "Resources." These have been modified to reflect personal field notes as well as published range extensions or corrections and verified survey information provided by biologists noted above.

Classification and common names of amphibians and reptiles used in this book are based on the "Checklist of Vertebrates of the United States, the U.S. Territories, and Canada" (Banks, et al., 1987) except where superseded by published taxonomic revisions.

I am grateful to the editors and staff of the University of Michigan Press for their patience and enthusiasm for this project. A special note of appreciation must go to my parents for their toleration and support during my herpetologically oriented childhood, and to my wife Shirley and daughters Alissa and Laura for their love, understanding, and tolerance during the preparation of this book.

Inevitably in a book of this nature, information will become outdated or be superseded by continued research, and also as inevitably, errors of interpretation, omission, or transcription will occur. Readers are encouraged to bring any errors or new information to the attention of the author.

How to Use This Book

This book is divided into three parts. First is an introduction to herpetology. Here we consider the defining attributes, paleohistory, and taxonomy of amphibians and reptiles, and present a classification and checklist of all Great Lakes species. Special focus is placed on the role of amphibians and reptiles in the ecosystem, their interactions with humans, and factors involved in making prudent decisions about their conservation. The climatic and vegetational history of the Great Lakes region during and since the Pleistocene epoch ("Ice Age") is discussed in an attempt to explain the present distribution of amphibians and reptiles in the area.

The second part presents an account of each species and subspecies known to occur within the Great Lakes basin. Species occurring close to the accepted boundaries of the basin, and those that have been reported therein only as isolated specimens, but are not yet known to breed within the basin, are briefly described under "Marginal and Questionable Species." Each account includes at least one photograph of a representative specimen and a range map showing the species' or subspecies' Great Lakes distribution. Also included is a smaller map showing the overall North American distribution of the species concerned. Note that each species can be expected to occur only in specific habitats, which usually occupy a very small portion of the indicated range. The range maps are provided as a guide to the recent distribution of amphibian and reptile species in the Great Lakes basin, and should be interpreted in conjunction with the comments under "Distribution and Status" in each account. They are not intended to be used as the basis for publishing new distributional records.

Each species account is divided into sections providing the following information:

Description: Identifying characteristics are given for adults of each species, and for juveniles if they differ from adults. Notable differences between the sexes are also given. The breeding calls and certain other vocalizations of frogs and toads are described. Identifying characteristics are noted for many amphibian eggs and larvae, although identification of larval amphibians can be difficult. Watermolen (1995) has published a key to eggs and egg masses of Wisconsin amphibians, and technical keys to amphibian larvae can be found in the books by Minton (1972), Vogt (1981), Watermolen and Gilbertson (1996), and (salamanders only) Pfingsten and Downs (1989).

Each species' size is given as a range, usually the minimum size at sexual maturity to the maximum known size, based on published sources. All measurements are expressed in metric units, with English equivalents in parentheses. (Standard abbreviations are used.) Unless stated otherwise, sizes are expressed as total length (tip of the snout to the tail tip). Frogs and toads are measured from the snout to the vent (anal opening), which is equivalent to the total head-body length. Turtle size is the length of the carapace, as measured in a straight line down the middle (not following the curve) from front to back. Because lizards frequently lose portions of their tails, the maximum head-body length (measured from snout to the vent) is included along with the total length measurements.

If the species has been divided into named subspecies, those known to occur in the Great Lakes drainage basin are described in detail; if only one subspecies occurs in the region, the account is listed under the subspecies name.

Confusing Species: Characters are given to distinguish the species in question from other species that are similar in appearance.

Distribution and Status: The historical geographic range is described and relative abundance and recent population trends are noted. In general, no attempt is made to describe the precise legal status of amphibian or reptile species for states or provinces in the Great Lakes basin; such information would soon be outdated, since endangered species lists and other wildlife regulations are subject to frequent revision. Persons needing such information should contact the wildlife resource agency for the state or province in question; addresses for regulatory agencies are listed in "Resources."

Note: The term *local* is used to describe a species that tends to occur in isolated populations or special habitat types surrounded by areas that are either lacking in suitable habitat or where the species has been extirpated. A *locally common* species is one that may exist in fairly large numbers within small and/or isolated geographical areas. A species described as *uncommon and local* or *rare and local* tends to exist in low or very low numbers within very small and/or isolated geographical areas.

Habitat and Ecology: The preferred habitat of each species or subspecies is described, and its general behavior, feeding habits, predators, and defenses are discussed.

Reproduction and Growth: This section discusses courtship behavior, egg laying, hatching or birth, early growth, age at maturity, and life span, if known.

Conservation: Here the animal's relationship to humans is discussed, with comments on economic importance, population trends, threats posed by human activities, and possible management strategies.

The third part, "Resources," includes a bibliography of books, articles, and other important information sources on Great Lakes amphibians and reptiles, many of which were consulted during the preparation of this book. Readers wishing additional information on Great Lakes area amphibians and reptiles can consult these works and the literature cited therein. Key references to assist in literature reviews are given at the end of the introduction for each order or suborder. A selection of commercially available recordings of frog and toad vocalizations follows the bibliography. Additional sections list the major international and larger regional herpetological societies, as well as state and provincial governmental agencies concerned with regulation and management of amphibians and reptiles.

A glossary of selected terms is included at the end of the book.

Contents

Introduction to Herpetology

Definitions and Origins

Herpetology (from the Greek word *herpeton,* meaning "something that crawls") is the branch of biology concerned with the study of amphibians and reptiles. A biologist who specializes in the study of these animals is a *herpetologist,* while the word *herpetofauna* refers to the amphibians and reptiles living in a particular geographical area. The word *herps* is sometimes used as a shortened, informal way of saying "amphibians and reptiles." Amphibians (class Amphibia) include the frogs and toads (collectively called anurans), salamanders, and the legless, tropical caecilians. The reptiles (class Reptilia) include the turtles and tortoises, crocodilians, lizards, worm-lizards, snakes, and the tuatara of New Zealand. Both classes also traditionally include a large number of extinct forms known only from fossils. That these two classes of animals are grouped together in the same scientific discipline is more a product of tradition than of biology. Certain amphibians and reptiles may display a superficial resemblance to one another (especially salamanders and lizards), but there are significant differences between the two groups. In their physical structure and reproductive biology, the reptiles are more similar to birds and mammals than they are to amphibians.

Amphibians and reptiles are vertebrates and, like other vertebrate groups (i.e., fishes, birds, and mammals), have backbones and an internal bony skeleton. (Some fishes, such as sharks, have a skeleton that is mostly cartilage.) Amphibians and reptiles are ectothermic, a word meaning "outside heat" and used to denote animals that lack internal temperature regulation and depend on outside sources of heat (such as sunlight) to warm their bodies. Such animals are often called "cold-blooded," but this can be a misleading term—a turtle or lizard basking in the sun on a warm day is not "cold." Birds and mammals are considered endothermic ("inside heat"), since they can produce heat within their bodies and usually maintain a relatively constant body temperature.

Amphibians are characterized by moist skins that may be smooth or warty, but not covered with scales, feathers, or hair. They do not have claws on their feet. Amphibian skin contains numerous mucous glands that secrete substances to protect the animal from desiccation. Some species possess glands that produce distasteful or toxic substances to repel predators. Although most adult amphibians have lungs, much of their respiration is through the skin, and water is readily absorbed or lost through the skin as well. For this reason, the great majority of amphibian species live in moist or wet environments.

The word *amphibian* comes from Greek words that mean "double life." This refers to the fact that typical amphibians lay small, unshelled eggs that are fertilized externally under water. These hatch into aquatic larvae that breathe with gills (fig. 1). After a variable period of time living under water, the larvae metamorphose into air-breathing adults capable of moving about on land. There are many exceptions to this "standard" mode of reproduction. Many salamanders have a form of internal fertilization in which the males deposit packets of sperm that the females pick up and store in their cloacas. Some frogs and salamanders (such as our native Red-backed Salamander) lay eggs in damp places on land; larval development is completed within the egg, and their young hatch out as tiny versions of the adults. Several salamander species are permanently aquatic and rarely or never leave the water; most of these retain their gills into adulthood (as in the Mudpuppy). Some frogs are also totally aquatic, although these are mostly found in the tropical regions; a well-known example is the African Clawed Frog *(Xenopus laevis)* often used as a laboratory animal for research.

The first amphibians evolved in the late Devonian period of the Paleozoic era, about 370 million years ago. They were a pioneering group of vertebrates that had evolved adaptations allowing them to leave the water and exploit terrestrial habitats. Most paleontologists (scientists who study fossils) agree that the direct ancestors to the amphibians are to be found among the crossopterygian ("lobe-finned") fishes. One of the most ancient amphibians known is *Ichthyostega,* fossils of which have been found in Devonian-age rocks in Greenland. *Ichthyostega* retained a number of features found in its fish ancestors, such as the structure of the skull and teeth, a streamlined body, and a tail fin. This animal undoubtedly spent much of its time in water, but the robust feet, limbs, and ribs, and the strong interlocking backbones suggest that it was quite capable of moving about on land.

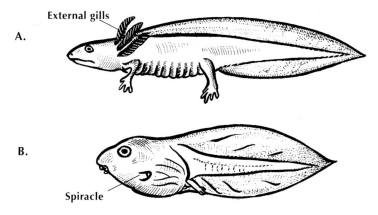

Fig. 1. Amphibian larvae. *A*, salamander larva (*Ambystoma*). Note external gills and presence of four limbs during majority of larval period. *B*, typical frog larva, or tadpole (*Rana*). Gills are internal, except in newly hatched larvae.

During the latter third of the Paleozoic era (about 350 to 245 million years ago), amphibian evolution produced a variety of adaptive forms, but most remained dependent on the water and near-shore environments for feeding and reproduction. Many were small aquatic creatures, although a group called the temnospondyls included some large creatures that grew to over 1.5 meters (5 feet) long and somewhat resembled chunky alligators with short legs and flattened skulls. Living amphibian groups probably originated within the temnospondyls, and are placed in a single subclass, the Lissamphibia, but it is not yet certain that frogs, salamanders, and caecilians share a close common ancestor. Additional fossil discoveries may be needed to clarify the matter.

One important lineage of ancient amphibians, known as anthracosaurs, had some members that became better adapted for moving, feeding, and probably reproducing, on land. Paleontologists consider it likely that one or more of the anthracosaur amphibians eventually evolved into the first reptiles. But what makes an animal a reptile?

A typical reptile is an ectothermic, air-breathing vertebrate with a dry, scaly skin and clawed feet (if it has feet). Most reptiles hatch from shelled eggs that are fertilized internally and laid on land. Some lizards and snakes do not lay eggs, but instead give birth to young that have developed within the female's body. A young reptile, whether hatched or "born alive," breathes with lungs immediately and is essentially a small version of its parents. This classical definition is based on the living reptile groups, such as turtles, lizards, snakes, and crocodiles. Many extinct groups traditionally considered reptiles, such as the dinosaurs and the therapsids ("mammal-like reptiles"), actually differed in many ways from present-day reptiles.

At the present time, the earliest known undisputed fossil reptiles are known from sedimentary rocks deposited during the mid-Carboniferous period, about 335 million years ago. These were small, agile, lizardlike animals well adapted for terrestrial life. Their tiny sharp teeth suggest a diet of insects. They probably laid shelled *amniotic* eggs on land, a radical departure from their water-breeding amphibian ancestors. An amniotic egg has special membranes that protect the embryo and allow for respiration and waste storage (fig. 2). The amniotic membranes form a special fluid-filled sac, called the amnion, that has been likened to a private pond for the developing embryo. This feature is also found in vertebrates in which the embryos develop in the female's body until birth, including certain lizards and snakes and nearly all living mammals. Thus, all of the descendants of those earliest reptiles, including the living reptiles, dinosaurs, birds, and mammals, form a natural group—the amniotes.

By the late Carboniferous period there were already three distinct lineages of reptiles, primarily defined by the structure of the skull and other skeletal features. The first of these, the anapsids, are characterized by a primitive skull structure; the earliest members of this "stem" group may have been ancestral to all later amniotes. The turtles and tortoises are considered to be the only living anapsids. The second lineage, the synapsids, included the therapsids, which are often called "mammal-like reptiles." The synapsids were quite successful late in the Paleozoic era but ultimately became extinct, except for one group that ultimately led to the true mammals (and thus to you!). The third lineage, the diapsids, branched into two main groups—the lepidosaurs and the archosaurs. Lizards, worm-lizards, snakes, and the tuatara (*Sphenodon*) of New Zealand are surviving lepidosaurs. The archosaurs include the dinosaurs, pterosaurs, and crocodilians. Birds can be considered archosaurs, since they either descended from dinosaurs or shared a close common ancestor with the dinosaurs.

The Mesozoic era, which began about 245 million years ago, is often called the "Age of Reptiles," due largely to the ecological dominance of the dinosaurs. However, all living amniote groups, including the turtles,

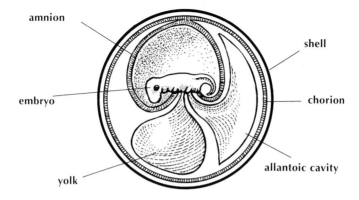

Fig. 2. Amniotic egg

lizards, snakes, crocodiles, birds, and mammals, had evolved by the middle of the Mesozoic, as had the "modern" amphibians (frogs, salamanders, and caecilians).

Many biologists do not consider the class Reptilia to be a truly "natural" taxonomic group, since it includes animals that descended from several evolutionary lineages, unlike the class Aves (birds) and class Mammalia (mammals), each of which can be clearly defined and undoubtedly derived from a common ancestor. The word *reptile* is useful, however, when applied to living vertebrates and defined using the typical characters noted above. In any case, we can simply state that a reptile is any amniote that is not a bird or a mammal.

Incidentally, we can also define the class Amphibia with equal simplicity, since an amphibian is any tetrapod (four-footed vertebrate) that is not an amniote. Although the tropical caecilians are legless amphibians, and sirens have only two legs, these undoubtedly descended from four-footed ancestors and thus qualify as "honorary" tetrapods. (Among reptiles, the legless snakes are also "honorary" tetrapods, thanks to their lizard ancestry.)

Classifying Amphibians and Reptiles

Biologists classify living things using a system devised by the Swedish naturalist Carolus Linnaeus in the mid–eighteenth century. Linnaeus grouped organisms into categories according to how similar or different they appeared, but today we can also incorporate information about their evo-lutionary relationships. The basic unit of classification is the species, but defining what we mean by "species" is not a simple task. Traditionally biologists have said that a species is a genetically distinct group of organ-isms that normally breeds within, but not outside, the group. (That is, they share a common gene pool—genes being the units of heredity within each organism's cells.) This is called the "biological species concept."

The development of new species probably occurs most often when a small population (or even a few individuals) becomes geographically iso-lated from a larger parent population. An isolated population may even-tually begin to change genetically in response to new environmental con-ditions. A population that changes enough so that, under natural conditions, its members can no longer successfully reproduce with mem-bers of its "parent" species (should they come back into contact) can be considered a new species. Such reproductive incompatibility may be due to physical or behavioral differences, or both.

In recent years, a new definition of *species* has been proposed that takes into account the presumed evolutionary history of each named species. Under this "evolutionary species concept," all members of a species are assumed to share specific characteristics and habits because they are the result of a single line of descent from an ancestral species. Thus, any population of amphibians or reptiles that is completely isolated from related or ancestral populations and has some uniquely evolved morphological characters would be considered to be a true species with its own separate evolutionary history and future.

Under the Linnaean system, a species is assigned a unique name made up of two parts: a genus name, and a species name. (The species name is often an adjective describing or modifying the genus name.) These names are either derived directly from Latin, or are Latinized forms of Greek or another language. For example, in the scientific name of the Painted Tur-tle, *Chrysemys picta,* the genus name translates into "golden turtle" (from Greek *chrysos,* gold, and *emys,* a freshwater turtle) while the species name is from the Latin *pictus,* meaning "painted." Note that the genus name is always capitalized, while the species name is not, and that both are either italicized or underlined in text.

In formal texts, the two-word name (genus and species) is usually fol-lowed by the name of the person who first named the species and pub-lished its description in the scientific literature; this may be followed by the date of publication. For example the Ring-necked Snake's scientific name would be written as *Diadophis punctatus* (Linnaeus, 1766). In this case, the parentheses indicate that the species was placed in a different genus sometime after the original description was published.

Latin is used because it was once the universal language of science and, more importantly, it offers a stable system of naming that stays the same wherever in the world it is used. One species might have several common names that change from region to region and country to country. For example, the Painted Turtle is locally called "mud turtle," "pond turtle," or "painter" in different parts of its range. A French Canadian would call it "tortue peinte," while in western Tennessee it is sometimes called the "painted lady turtle." But herpetologists throughout the world recognize *Chrysemys picta* as a specific species of freshwater turtle.

While there is only one species currently recognized in the genus *Chrysemys,* many genera (the plural form of genus) contain more than one species; thus we can define a genus as a group of very closely related species. Further, in the Linnaean system a group of closely related genera is called a family, and a group of related families is an order. Continuing into still broader categories, a class encompasses a group of related orders, while related classes are placed in a phylum, and, finally, a grouping of related phyla is a kingdom. Here is how the Common Garter Snake would be classified in the Linnaean system.

KINGDOM Animalia (animals)
  PHYLUM Chordata (vertebrates and some invertebrate relatives)
    CLASS Reptilia (amniote vertebrates that are not birds or
      mammals)
      ORDER Squamata (lizards, worm-lizards, and snakes)
        FAMILY Colubridae ("typical," mostly harmless, snakes)
          GENUS Thamnophis (striped snakes; literally,
            "bush snake")
            SPECIES *Thamnophis sirtalis* (Common Garter Snake)

To further refine the classification system, new categories may be added, and the seven major categories are sometimes broken into subgroups. For example, the order Squamata contains three suborders: Lacertilia (lizards), Serpentes (snakes), and Amphisbaenia (worm-lizards).

Wide-ranging species of reptiles and amphibians frequently exhibit regional differences in size, coloration, or other characteristics. If these differences are particularly distinct and separable by geographical area, a species may be divided into two or more subspecies. Subspecies are designated by adding a third name to the species name. *Chrysemys picta,* the Painted Turtle, has four recognized subspecies, of which two are found in the Great Lakes area—the Midland Painted Turtle, *Chrysemys picta marginata,* and the Western Painted Turtle, *Chrysemys picta belli.* In this book, only subspecies native to our area are included in the checklist and described in the species accounts.

To save space and avoid redundancy, a genus name may be abbreviated by its first letter if it is repeated one or more times in a paragraph or article. In some circumstances the species name may also be abbreviated. For example, we might list the four subspecies of the Painted Turtle as *Chrysemys picta belli, C. p. marginata, C. p. picta,* and *C. p. dorsalis.* Here only the first name was written in full, and in the following names the "*C. p.*" clearly refers to *Chrysemys picta.* When using this shortcut, care must be taken to assure that names are written out in full if there is any chance of confusion, such as when different genus or species names begin with the same letter.

The identification of certain species of amphibians and reptiles can be complicated by the existence of hybrid populations, which result from the interbreeding of two different species. Climatic changes and other ecological factors can occasionally disrupt the physical, behavioral, and geographic barriers that normally prevent hybridization. Hybrid offspring are often sterile, but hybrids between related species can sometimes reproduce with each other and their parents, leading to unique populations and even the development of new species.

One example of the "hybrid problem" is the rather complicated taxonomy of certain salamanders in the genus *Ambystoma,* especially the Jefferson and the Blue-spotted Salamanders (*Ambystoma jeffersonianum* and *A. laterale* respectively). Prior to the early 1950s these two species were generally combined under the former name. It has been suggested that a single parent species was split into two or more geographically separate populations at some time in the last few million years. These were isolated long enough to become separate species, which then came back into contact. However, the new species retained similar breeding habits, and males of one species would occasionally court females of another species. The resulting hybrid offspring were often triploids, meaning that they carried two sets of chromosomes from one parent and one set from the other. (Chromosomes are structures in the nucleus of body cells that carry hereditary information. Normal individuals of vertebrate species are diploid, with one set of chromosomes from their father and one set from their mother.) The hybrids, which are all females, are often difficult to distinguish in the field. However, biologists can identify them in the laboratory by examining blood cells (triploid hybrids have red blood cells that are almost a third larger than those of normal diploid females) or genetic material (e.g., chromosomes).

It was once thought that the all-female triploid salamanders represented new species, since they were believed to reproduce without fertilization of eggs by males and were assumed to be genetically isolated from the "parent species." The name Tremblay's Salamander ("*Ambystoma tremblayi*") was given to triploid salamanders with two sets of chromosomes from *A. laterale* and one set from *A. jeffersonianum*. Salamanders with two chromosome sets from *A. jeffersonianum* and one from *A. laterale* were given the name Silvery Salamander ("*A. platineum*"). Most herpetologists no longer recognize these hybrids as species. Recent studies have shown that hybrid egg development often involves contact with male sperm from one of the parent species and that actual fertilization may occur, particularly at higher water temperatures.

It seems the more this hybridization phenomenon is studied, the more complicated it appears. We now know that hybrids between *Ambystoma laterale* and *Ambystoma texanum,* the Small-mouthed Salamander, occur in parts of Ohio and southern Michigan, and that some of these turn out to be tetraploids (with four sets of chromosomes). The situation can get even more complicated, as specimens have been found in the same area (notably Kelleys Island in western Lake Erie) that have genetic material from three or even four species, with some combinations including the Tiger Salamander, *Ambystoma tigrinum.* Persons trying to identify *Ambystoma* salamanders in formerly glaciated parts of North America should be aware that many specimens and populations will be of hybrid origin and will be difficult or impossible to assign to a particular species. The habits and life history of hybrid salamanders are usually most similar to the "parent species" with which they share the most genetic material. (For a summary of the "*Ambystoma*" problem, along with some recent literature references, see Klemens 1993, 25–26.)

A Classification and Checklist of Great Lakes Amphibians and Reptiles

Ongoing research into the biology, physiology, and fossil history of amphibians and reptiles often leads to new ideas about their classification. The checklist below is based on information current at time of publication, but advances in taxonomy (the science of plant and animal classification) will almost certainly necessitate changes in the future. In species with named subspecies, only those subspecies found in the Great Lakes drainage basin are listed.

CLASS AMPHIBIA

Order Caudata (Salamanders)

Family Proteidae (Mudpuppies and Waterdogs)
Necturus maculosus maculosus . . . . .Mudpuppy
Family Sirenidae (Sirens)
Siren intermedia nettingi . . . . .Western Lesser Siren
Family Salamandridae (Newts)
Notophthalmus viridescens viridescens . . . . .Red-spotted Newt
Notophthalmus viridescens louisianensis . . . . .Central Newt
Family Ambystomatidae (Mole Salamanders)
Ambystoma maculatum . . . . .Spotted Salamander
Ambystoma laterale . . . . .Blue-spotted Salamander
Ambystoma jeffersonianum . . . . .Jefferson Salamander
Ambystoma texanum . . . . .Small-mouthed Salamander
Ambystoma opacum .Marbled Salamander
Ambystoma tigrinum tigrinum . . . . .Eastern Tiger Salamander
Family Plethodontidae (Lungless Salamanders)
Desmognathus fuscus fuscus . . . . .Northern Dusky Salamander
Desmognathus ochrophaeus . . . . .Mountain Dusky Salamander
Plethodon glutinosus . . . . .Northern Slimy Salamander
Plethodon cinereus .Red-backed Salamander
Plethodon richmondi . . . . .Ravine Salamander
Hemidactylium scutatum . . . . .Four-toed Salamander
Gyrinophilus porphyriticus porphyriticus Northern Spring Salamander
Pseudotriton ruber ruber . . . . .Northern Red Salamander
Eurycea bislineata . . . . .Northern Two-lined Salamander

Order Anura (Frogs and Toads)

Family Bufonidae (True Toads)
Bufo americanus americanus . . . . .Eastern American Toad
Bufo fowleri . . . . .Fowler's Toad
Family Hylidae (Treefrogs and relatives)
Acris crepitans blanchardi . . . . .Blanchard's Cricket Frog
Hyla versicolor . . . . .Eastern Gray Treefrog
Hyla chrysoscelis . . . . .Cope's Gray Treefrog
Pseudacris triseriata triseriata . . . . .Western Chorus Frog
Pseudacris triseriata maculata . . . . .Boreal Chorus Frog
Pseudacris crucifer crucifer . . . . .Northern Spring Peeper
Family Ranidae (Typical Frogs)
Rana catesbeiana . . . . .Bullfrog
Rana clamitans melanota . . . . .Green Frog
Rana septentrionalis . . . . .Mink Frog
Rana sylvatica . . . . .Wood Frog
Rana pipiens . . . . .Northern Leopard Frog
Rana palustris . . . . .Pickerel Frog

CLASS REPTILIA

Order Testudines (Turtles and Tortoises)

Family Chelydridae (Snapping Turtles)
Chelydra serpentina serpentina . . . . .Common Snapping Turtle
Family Kinosternidae (Mud and Musk Turtles)
Sternotherus odoratus . . . . .Common Musk Turtle
Family Emydidae (Pond and Box Turtles)
Clemmys guttata . . . . .Spotted Turtle
Clemmys insculpta . . . . .Wood Turtle
Clemmys muhlenbergii . . . . .Bog Turtle
Terrapene carolina carolina . . . . .Eastern Box Turtle
Emydoidea blandingii . . . . .Blanding's Turtle
Graptemys geographica . . . . .Common Map Turtle
Chrysemys picta marginata . . . . .Midland Painted Turtle
Chrysemys picta belli . . . . .Western Painted Turtle
Trachemys scripta elegans . . . . .Red-eared Slider
Family Trionychidae (Softshell Turtles)
Apalone spinifera spinifera . . . . .Eastern Spiny Softshell Turtle

Order Squamata (Lizards, Amphisbaenians, and Snakes)

Suborder Lacertilia [= Sauria] (Lizards)

Family Scincidae (Skinks)
Eumeces fasciatus . . . . .Five-lined Skink
Eumeces anthracinus anthracinus . . . . .Northern Coal Skink
Family Teiidae (Whiptails and Racerunners)
Cnemidophorus sexlineatus . . . . .Six-lined Racerunner
Family Anguidae (Glass Lizards and Alligator Lizards)
Ophisaurus attenuatus attenuatus . . . . .Western Slender Glass Lizard

Suborder Serpentes (Snakes)

Family Colubridae (Typical Snakes)
Nerodia sipedon sipedon . . . . .Northern Water Snake
Nerodia sipedon insularum . . . . .Lake Erie Water Snake
Nerodia erythrogaster neglecta . . . . .Copper-bellied Water Snake
Regina septemvittata . . . . .Queen Snake
Clonophis kirtlandii . . . . .Kirtland's Snake
Thamnophis sirtalis sirtalis . . . . .Eastern Garter Snake
Thamnophis sirtalis semifasciatus . . . . .Chicago Garter Snake
Thamnophis butleri . . . . .Butler's Garter Snake
Thamnophis brachystoma . . . . .Short-headed Garter Snake
Thamnophis radix radix . . . . .Eastern Plains Garter Snake
Thamnophis sauritus septentrionalis . . . . .Northern Ribbon Snake
Thamnophis proximus proximus . . . . .Western Ribbon Snake
Storeria dekayi dekayi . . . . .Northern Brown Snake
Storeria dekayi wrightorum . . . . .Midland Brown Snake
Storeria occipitomaculata occipitomaculata . . . .
. . . . Northern Red-bellied Snake
Opheodrys vernalis . . . . .Smooth Green Snake
Coluber constrictor constrictor . . . . .Northern Black Racer
Coluber constrictor foxii . . . . .Blue Racer
Elaphe obsoleta obsoleta .Black Rat Snake
Elaphe vulpina . . . . .Western Fox Snake
Elaphe gloydi . . . . .Eastern Fox Snake
Lampropeltis triangulum triangulum . . . . .Eastern Milk Snake
Diadophis punctatus edwardsii . . . . . . .Northern Ring-necked Snake
Heterodon platirhinos . . . . .Eastern Hog-nosed Snake

Family Viperidae (Pit Vipers and Vipers)
Sistrurus catenatus catenatus . . . . .Eastern Massasauga
Crotalus horridus . . . . .Timber Rattlesnake

Amphibians and Reptiles in the "Age of Mammals"

By the middle of the Mesozoic era, the amphibians had been reduced from their former prominence to the three living groups, the anurans (frogs and toads), salamanders, and caecilians, possibly due to competition from the reptiles. The "Age of Reptiles" lasted for about 175 million years and ended some 65 million years ago with the extinction of the dinosaurs and several other orders of reptiles. The following (and present) era, the Cenozoic, has been called the "Age of Mammals." A popular view presumes that the supposedly superior warm-blooded mammals and birds took over the world after the dinosaurs' demise, leaving the surviving amphibians and reptiles to play only minor roles in the ecosystem. This idea is now known to be largely erroneous.

It is true that mammals now occupy most of the ecological niches for large terrestrial animals, but the amphibians and reptiles fill many niches for small and medium-sized animals in temperate and tropical climates. There are about the same number of amphibian species as mammal species in existence (roughly about 4,000 in each class), while reptiles (with about 6,500 species) greatly outnumber the mammals in species diversity.

Reptiles and amphibians seem better suited for some habitats than birds or mammals. Reptiles species often outnumber their endothermic counterparts in arid desert regions, and amphibians are more diverse than mammals in humid neotropical forests. The ectotherms hold their own in temperate climates as well. For example, a study in a New Hampshire forest revealed that salamanders outnumbered the birds and mammals combined and had a biomass (living weight) 2.6 times greater than the birds and roughly equal to that of the resident small mammals. Over 100,000 salamanders were found in one 36-hectare test plot, of which 93 percent (95,000) were Red-backed Salamanders, a species common in the Great Lakes area as well (Burton and Likens 1975).

Being endothermic does give mammals and birds certain advantages.

Compared to terrestrial ectotherms, most can remain active at lower environmental temperatures and maintain higher levels of activity over longer time periods. But these abilities come at a cost, for endotherms must take in a lot of energy (food) to produce heat (or, in hot weather, to lose heat) and to fuel the muscles and the large brain needed to control their fast-paced lifestyle. (To "eat like a bird or a mouse" is to really shovel in the calories!)

In comparison, a lizard or salamander may require less than 5 percent of the food calories used by a mammal of equal size over a given time period. Ectothermic amphibians or reptiles require less energy in part because their body heat comes directly or indirectly from the sun. (In our area, amphibians are generally active at lower temperatures than reptiles). On a warm, sunny spring day, a frog or a garter snake has all the "free" heat it needs to carry out its life processes, such as eating or breeding. If the weather turns cold and rainy for a few days, it simply stops feeding and remains inactive. A robin or a rabbit under the same circumstances would soon have to leave shelter to find food.

In the Great Lakes area, most amphibians and all reptiles hibernate (i.e., become dormant) in winter, while most mammals and all resident birds remain active and continue to feed. A few completely aquatic amphibians, such the Mudpuppy, are active all winter. Some mammals sleep for extended periods during severe weather, but only a few native mammals (e.g., woodchucks, ground squirrels, and some bats) are true hibernators. Hibernation presents many hazards for an animal, including possible attacks by predators and the risks of freezing, flooding, or oxygen depletion in the hibernaculum. Mammal hibernation differs in some ways from hibernation in amphibians or reptiles, particularly in details of energy storage and metabolism. For this reason some herpetologists prefer to use the term *brumation* instead of hibernation when referring to winter dormancy in amphibians or reptiles; in this book the latter, more familiar term is used.

Amphibians and Reptiles in the Ecosystem

Amphibians and reptiles are consumers that feed on living or dead plant or animal material and convert it into energy for movement, growth, and reproduction. The great majority of Great Lakes area species are carnivorous. Salamanders, frogs, and toads eat mostly invertebrates (e.g., insects, spiders, earthworms). Large frogs (especially Bullfrogs and Green Frogs) also eat smaller vertebrates such as snakes, mice, birds, and other frogs (including their own offspring). The aquatic larvae of terrestrial salamanders often feed on smaller amphibian larvae, although invertebrates make up the largest proportion of the diet of most species.

When abundant, amphibians can consume substantial quantities of favored prey organisms, perhaps serving to limit prey populations. The smaller woodland salamanders may have large populations, as noted above, with obvious impacts on their invertebrate prey. It has been estimated that an average American Toad could eat about 26 insects in one day, or over 3,200 insects per season (Pope 1947). A tiny Blanchard's Cricket Frog was estimated to eat about 4,800 insects in one year—thus a population of a thousand Cricket Frogs distributed around a lake could potentially consume at least 4.8 million insects annually (Johnson and Christiansen 1976).

The only herbivorous Great Lakes area amphibians are frog and toad tadpoles, most of which feed largely on algae and other aquatic plant material. However, tadpoles also consume small planktonic animals and frequently supplement their diets by scavenging the remains of larger animals. Wood Frog tadpoles, in particular, have carnivorous tendencies, and often consume amphibian eggs and larvae, including those of their own species. Lesser Sirens and some salamander larvae are known to ingest plant material, but it is likely that most or all of this vegetation is swallowed accidently during the capture of small animal prey.

Most reptiles are carnivores, although many turtles are omnivorous, feeding on both plants and animals. In some species, including Box Turtles, Wood Turtles, Painted Turtles, and Sliders, the hatchlings and juveniles prefer animal food and gradually add more vegetable matter to their diets as they mature. Animal foods are higher in protein than plants, and undoubtedly facilitate rapid growth in the young turtles.

A few turtle species specialize in certain foods. Blanding's and Spiny Softshell Turtles show a preference for crayfish. Map Turtles, particularly the larger females, favor mollusks such as snails and small clams, and Musk Turtles also feed heavily on mollusks. Other turtle species will accept a variety of food items, with choices influenced by opportunity and seasonal abundance. Box and Wood Turtles readily exploit strawberries, raspberries, and other fruits when available, and may, like birds, assist in seed dispersal of food plants.

Common Snapping Turtles, the largest reptiles in the Great Lakes basin, feed on a variety of aquatic animals and plants. By consuming carrion, they play a part in recycling dead organisms. They will also take vertebrate prey such as fish and young ducks, which has given them a poor reputation among wildlife managers. In reality, snappers take few game fish and have a minimal effect on waterfowl populations in natural situations, although control might be warranted in managed waterfowl-breeding facilities and fish-rearing ponds. Snapping Turtles can accumulate chemical pollutants in their body tissues, a tendency that may be enhanced by the species' tolerance for polluted waters and their ability to feed at several levels of the "food chain."

Although a number of herbivorous lizard species inhabit tropical regions, Great Lakes area lizards are almost entirely carnivorous, feeding on insects and their larvae, spiders, and other small invertebrates. Large individuals of some species (e.g., Slender Glass Lizards and Five-lined Skinks) may occasionally eat small vertebrates, including smaller reptiles and their eggs.

All snakes are carnivorous throughout their lives. The larger species, such as Black Rat Snakes, Western and Eastern Fox Snakes, Bullsnakes, Milk Snakes, and Racers, have a preference for rodents and other endothermic prey; the latter two also eat other reptiles. Eastern Hognosed Snakes are specialized toad-eaters. Garter, ribbon, and water snakes tend to eat ectothermic vertebrates such as fish and amphibians, though many garter snakes and the secretive Brown, Red-bellied, and Kirtland's Snakes feed heavily on earthworms. The Smooth Green Snake is the only Great Lakes area snake with a primary diet of arthropods, mainly insects, insect larvae, and spiders.

In nature the consumers often become the consumed, and this is certainly true of amphibians and reptiles, which are eaten by a great variety of natural predators. Frogs are a much-favored prey item for a long list of predators, including mink, otters, foxes, raccoons, skunks, shrews, herons, bitterns, hawks, many snakes and turtles, larger frogs, and fish, especially bass and pike. Salamanders, though readily eaten by the same predators, may be less accessible since most species remain underground or beneath logs and rocks except when breeding. Frog tadpoles and salamander larvae are eaten by many of these predatory vertebrates, as well as by a number of carnivorous invertebrates, including giant water bugs, diving beetles, dragonfly nymphs, and water scorpions.

Frogs typically produce great numbers of eggs, which serves to balance the high losses to predators. For example, a female Spring Peeper might lay a thousand eggs each spring, a Green Frog perhaps 5,000 eggs, and a Bullfrog up to 20,000 eggs. It has been estimated that less than one frog egg in a hundred ultimately produces a new frog that survives to breed. Clearly, a major contribution of frogs in the ecosystem is providing energy for other animals. Many salamanders (and the smaller frogs) breed in temporary ponds that lack fish and other large aquatic predators. They seem able to maintain their numbers by laying eggs by the hundreds rather than thousands, but typically over 90 percent of eggs and larvae will still be lost to predators. There are numerous other threats to survival in addition to predation. For example, in drought years the breeding ponds can disappear before the larvae metamorphose, resulting in a total loss of new young for that season.

Amphibians do have defenses against predators. Most depend on avoidance, rapid escape, or concealment, but American and Fowler's Toads, Pickerel Frogs, Mink Frogs, and many adult salamanders can secrete irritating or toxic substances from skin glands. These defenses are described in more detail in the species accounts.

Reptiles also suffer high rates of predation. The buried eggs of turtles are a favorite seasonal food for many small mammals, particularly raccoons and skunks. Numerous studies show that these nest predators often destroy between 60 percent and 90 percent of all turtle nests at the described sites, and in certain years and locations the destruction can reach 100 percent. Hatchling turtles are bite-sized snacks for the same mammalian carnivores, as well as crows, ravens, gulls, and wading birds, and the remains of young turtles are often found in the stomachs of game fish such as pike and bass. Turtles have fewer natural predators once they mature and are notably long-lived compared to other similar-sized vertebrates. Most turtle species have potential life spans of several decades; Eastern Box Turtles are known for their ability to reach the century mark. It is this potentially long adult reproductive life that allows turtle populations to persist despite heavy losses of their eggs and young.

Lizards and snakes contribute to the food supply of numerous predators, particularly birds. A hawk flying off with a snake dangling from its talons or a heron spearing a water snake are routine sightings for Great Lakes area naturalists. Young snakes and lizards are vulnerable even to smaller birds such as thrushes, jays, and blackbirds. Many mammals, including raccoons, opossums, foxes, badgers, and skunks, also eat these reptiles. Shrews are significant, if often unsuspected, predators on the eggs and young of many species, and also attack adult reptiles that are immobilized during winter dormancy.

Amphibians, Reptiles, and People

There was a time when wildlife conservation had to be justified in economic terms. Sadly, the questions "what good is it?" and "how much is it worth?" are occasionally still heard in discussions about preserving wild species. Amphibians and reptiles do provide a number of direct benefits to the human economy, even though these values are often difficult to quantify. Many species have feeding habits that make them potentially beneficial to human interests. Bullsnakes, Western and Eastern Fox Snakes, Black Rat Snakes, Racers, and Milk Snakes consume mice, rats, and other potential agricultural pests. The vast numbers of insects eaten by amphibians and small reptiles surely includes many pest species. A toad in the garden has long been considered a symbol of good fortune, a reputation no doubt well deserved.

The commercial harvest of amphibians and reptiles has contributed more directly to human economic interests, although there is legitimate concern about the long-term sustainability of this exploitation. Larger frogs are harvested for edible frog legs, and great numbers of frogs, Mudpuppies, and other salamanders have been collected by biological supply companies for use in high school and college science classes. In some places, frogs and salamanders and their larvae are collected and sold as fish bait.

Commercial trappers supplying turtle meat for human consumption usually concentrate their efforts on the two largest Great Lakes species, the Common Snapping Turtle and the Eastern Spiny Softshell. Substantial numbers are also taken for personal consumption. Smaller species have less value as human food but are occasionally collected and sometimes sold for this purpose. Biological supply companies have collected and sold turtles in large numbers for educational and research use, notably in Wisconsin. Certain species have been in great demand in the commercial pet trade, particularly Wood Turtles, Spotted Turtles, and Box Turtles; this exploitation has severely reduced many populations. Several species of snakes and lizards have also been collected for the biological supply and pet trade.

Of course, the intangible values of amphibians and reptiles should not be overlooked. Springtime choruses of toads and frogs are a joyful sound to many northerners seeking signs of winter's end, while basking turtles can add a feeling of tranquility to a day of fishing or canoeing. Many hikers now react with pleasure, not fear, at seeing a snake glide across the trail. Yet in the end, the conservation of amphibians and reptiles can be justified simply because they are active participants in the ecosystem and an important part of our wildlife heritage.

Conservation of Amphibians and Reptiles

The degradation, fragmentation, and destruction of natural habitats due to human activities are undoubtedly the greatest threats to amphibian and reptile populations in the Great Lakes region. Vast areas have been converted to agricultural use, while urban and suburban developments consume more habitat each year. The draining and filling of wetlands has obvious deleterious implications for many species. Terrestrial and wetland habitats that are still available (including those "protected" in parks or wildlife areas) may be degraded by air and water pollution, bisected by roadways, or ruined by the irresponsible use of off-road vehicles.

As amphibian and reptile populations are restricted to smaller and smaller "islands" of habitat, they become increasingly vulnerable to threats such as road mortality and direct exploitation. Not surprisingly, those species with historically restricted ranges or with specialized habitat requirements are the first to appear on endangered and threatened species lists. However, even some wide-ranging, so-called common species appear to be declining in parts of the Great Lakes region. Examples of these, including the Spotted Salamander, Blanchard's Cricket Frog, Northern Leopard Frog, and Common Garter Snake, are discussed in the species accounts.

The direct exploitation of amphibians and reptiles, until recently largely unregulated, has resulted in population declines and even localized extirpation of some species. This situation resulted both from traditional neglect of these animals by resource managers, and ignorance of their habits and populations. Government conservation agencies willing to consider their management were often faced with a lack of basic biological data needed to guide regulatory decisions. Concerns about declining amphibian and reptile numbers have spurred new efforts to survey populations and study life cycles and habitat needs, but there is still much to be learned. Sufficient information now exists to support general recommendations on the conservation and management of amphibians and reptiles.

Many frog species are potentially very prolific and appear to have a fairly rapid turnover in their populations. But the larger species most in demand for human use, particularly the Bullfrog, may take several years to reach a size worthy of harvesting, which is also prime breeding size. Frog populations in colder climates, including the Great Lakes basin, are subject to shorter growing seasons and greater climatic stresses than those to the south. Amphibians in general are vulnerable to natural disasters, such as drought and floods, and various human-caused problems (e.g., industrial pollution, farm chemical runoff, acid precipitation). Many frog and salamander species congregate for breeding purposes and are especially vulnerable to exploitation at these times. Standard wildlife management tools such as minimum sizes, possession limits, and closed seasons may be useful in preserving viable populations of hunted species. Regulations on amphibians should be modified when needed to accommodate changes in habitats and populations, as they are with fish, waterfowl, and other game species.

Many turtle species have a relatively low rate of recruitment of young individuals into the breeding population, due to typically high egg and hatchling mortality and the long time periods needed to reach reproductive size. These factors are normally balanced by comparatively low adult mortality and long adult life spans. Any factor that removes mature adult turtles from the population faster than they can be replaced will cause the population to decline. Research has demonstrated that several turtle species have virtually no "harvestable surplus" of mature animals in their populations. If a primary goal of game management is to maintain stable or increasing numbers of a harvested species, then it is unlikely that turtle populations anywhere in the Great Lakes area are prolific enough to tolerate a continuous or systematic harvest by humans (Congdon et al. 1993, 1994).

Some populations of species with wide habitat tolerances, such as Common Snapping Turtles, may be able to sustain a modest, well-dispersed harvest on a "personal use" basis. On the other hand, Snapping Turtle populations in the northern part of their range are known to have lower annual rates of recruitment and slower growth rates than those farther south, making them more likely to decline if adult animals are removed by humans (Brooks et al. 1988). Species with narrow habitat requirements and/or particularly slow growth or recruitment rates, such as Wood, Spotted, Bog, Blanding's, and Box Turtles, will predictably experience population declines if subjected to even low levels of exploitation.

Based on what is known (and not known) about amphibian and reptile populations in the Great Lakes area, it would seem reasonable to manage them conservatively, in much the same way that we manage wild birds. The great majority of species should be protected as nongame wildlife, as are songbirds, wading birds, and birds of prey. A few species, perhaps Snapping Turtles and the larger frogs, could be carefully managed as game species, similar to waterfowl, grouse, and pheasants. The collection of small numbers of common species for classroom observation and nature study purposes could also be permitted. As has been long recognized for birds, commercial exploitation of amphibians and reptiles appears to be incompatible with prudent conservation goals.

Within the Great Lakes basin, all states and the province of Ontario have protective laws and regulations that affect amphibians and reptiles. State and provincial wildlife regulatory agencies throughout the region are also charged with maintaining lists of rare, threatened, or endangered species, though precise categories and definitions vary. Listed species are usually given special protection and management consideration. Recent publications have attempted to summarize state and federal laws and regulations affecting amphibians and reptiles (e.g., Levell 1995); however, these statutes are subject to frequent revision and modification. Persons wishing to study or collect any amphibian or reptile species should contact the responsible governmental agency in their state or province for current legal information and permit requirements. A list of addresses for these agencies, current at time of publication, is given in "Resources."

Effects of Glaciation on Amphibian and Reptile Distribution in the Great Lakes Region

Twenty thousand years ago there were no amphibians or reptiles in the Great Lakes basin. The Great Lakes as we know them did not exist. Several massive lobes of glacial ice, spreading south from Canada, had converged over the region, obliterating practically all life. Reaching a mile or more in height, the glaciers at one time extended as far as central Ohio,

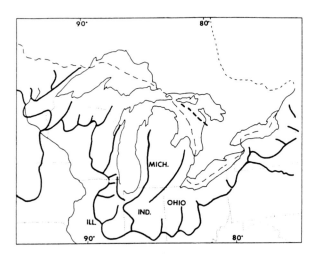

Fig. 3. Maximum Wisconsinan glacial advance in the Great Lakes area, about 20,000 years ago. Lines represent end moraines. (Reprinted from *Quaternary Science Reviews* 11, J. A. Holman, Late Quaternary Herpetofauna of the Central Great Lakes Region, U.S.A.: Zoogeographical and Paleoecological Implications, 345–51, Copyright 1992, with kind permission from Elsevier Science Ltd, The Boulevard, Langford Lane, Kidlington OX5 1GB, UK.)

Indiana, and Illinois (fig. 3). Known to geologists as the Late Wisconsinan glaciation, this was the latest climatic assault on a region that had, during the previous two million years, already experienced a number of advances and retreats of glacial ice. Some scientists believe that we are now in an interglacial period, and that someday glaciers may once again spread over parts of Canada and the northern United States. However, by definition the "ice age" (properly called the Pleistocene epoch) began about 1.8 million years ago and ended 10,000 years ago, by which time the ice had retreated from most of the Great Lakes area. The time period from the end of the Pleistocene to the present is called the Holocene.

Glaciers have had a profound effect on the land and living organisms in the Great Lakes area. The Great Lakes themselves were created by glaciers scouring out ancient pre-Pleistocene river valleys. Soil, sand, boulders, and trees were picked up by the advancing glaciers and deposited hundreds of miles away. During times of glacial retreat, buried blocks of ice would become lakes and bogs, and raging meltwater flows would carve new river courses. Plant and animal species displaced by advancing glaciers would survive in suitable habitats, called refugia, to the south and west, only to reinvade formerly occupied areas during times of glacial recession (interglacial periods). To understand the present distribution of amphibians and reptiles and their habitats in the Great Lakes area, it is helpful to briefly review what is known about the regional environment during and after the last glaciation.

We know very little about conditions and life in the Great Lakes region during the early and middle parts of the Pleistocene, since later glaciations tended to destroy much of the evidence of earlier ones. The latest (Wisconsinan) glacial advance began about 110,000 years ago and reached its maximum southern extent about 20,000 years ago. Prior to that time there was a warmer interglacial period called the Sangamonian, during which time amphibians, reptiles, and other organisms had undoubtedly reinhabited the proto–Great Lakes area. Fossils of giant land tortoises *(Geochelone crassiscutata)* have been discovered in Sangamonian sediments of south-central Illinois and in southern Indiana, suggesting that the climate must have been even milder than today, or at least had warmer winters, since giant tortoises cannot survive in areas with prolonged freezing temperatures. However, a fairly mild climate may have persisted in parts of the continent even at the height of the Wisconsinan glaciation. Studies of fossil amphibians and reptiles have provided much of the evidence for this idea.

During late Wisconsinan times, as the converging glaciers readvanced over the Great Lakes region, conditions near the ice front were presumably quite severe. An analysis of pollen samples taken from sites that were dated by the carbon 14 method suggests that a tundralike vegetation, chiefly grasses, sedges, and scattered coniferous trees, predominated in a narrow band adjacent to the glacier. Beyond this tundra zone a mixture of different habitats existed, depending on local environmental conditions. Large areas of the eastern and central United States may have been covered with spruce forest or open savanna (mixed grassland and woodland) dominated by grasses and spruce, pine, oak, and birch trees. Open oak woodlands existed in the lower midwest, and deciduous woodlands and swamp forests survived in lowlands and southern river valleys. But where were our Great Lakes herps during this time?

Many fossil sites dating to the late Wisconsinan contain mixes of plants and animal species that would not be found together today. The climate in the central and southern United States during the glacial maximum may have been, at least locally, rather mild, with cooler summers, warmer winters, and perhaps more precipitation than today. This equable climate allowed an unusual mixture of northern and southern species to coexist. A late Wisconsinan fossil site in Mississippi yielded both the extinct giant tortoise and the living Blanding's Turtle, while a site in northern Georgia has produced the remains of many amphibians and reptiles that live there today, as well as giant tortoises and an assortment of species that do not presently occur in the area. Warm-adapted Southern Toads *(Bufo terrestris)* and Florida Red-bellied Turtles *(Pseudemys nelsoni)* were then living alongside such cold-adapted Great Lakes species as the Wood Turtle and a Fox Snake. The strange Pleistocene climate allowed our northern herps to survive well south of their modern ranges, while southern species were able to move north. Similarly, intermixes of eastern and western species are known from the present Great Plains area, which is thought to have been at least partially forested during much of the Wisconsinan glaciation. (For further discussion on Pleistocene climatic equability see Wright and Porter 1983 and Holman 1995a.)

Responding to warmer temperatures and perhaps lower precipitation, the Wisconsinan glaciers began a slow, vacillating retreat about 18,000 years ago. As the ice receded, plants and animals began to disperse back into the Great Lakes area. By 15,000 years before present (B.P.) there was already a fairly diverse herpetofauna in south-central Indiana, including several species of frogs, turtles, and snakes found in the area today. Between 12,000 and 11,000 B.P., with glacial ice still covering portions of northern Lower Michigan, Leopard and Green Frogs, American Toads, and Painted Turtles were sharing southeastern Michigan habitats with mastodonts, mammoths, and giant beavers. Spruce woodlands gave way to pine forests, and then to deciduous hardwood forests, and vast new areas of marsh and bog habitats became accessible.

By 9,500 B.P. the Great Lakes region was ice free, but it took several thousand more years for the climate, the vegetation, and the herpetofauna to take on a modern aspect. The levels of the Great Lakes fluctuated considerably during the glacial retreat, as drainages changed in response to melting rates and the rebounding of the land newly free of its ice burden. During times of low lake levels, amphibians and reptiles were able to disperse over dry land to places that are now offshore islands; this probably explains why many Great Lakes islands have a surprisingly diverse herpetofauna.

The climate during the early and middle Holocene was highly variable; the earliest Holocene appears to have been warmer and more moist than today. This so-called climatic optimum allowed southern species to disperse rapidly northward. Relict Great Lakes populations of certain "southern" species, such as the Western Lesser Siren, Marbled Salamander, and Copper-bellied Water Snake, may be remnants of a northern dispersal during this warm period.

A time of reduced precipitation, called the xerothermic period, is thought to have occurred in the midwest from about 8,000 to 6,000 years ago. This allowed prairie-type vegetation (grasses and associated herbaceous plants) to spread eastward at the expense of forest in the lower Great Lakes region. This so-called prairie peninsula at one point extended well into Illinois, Indiana, and southern Michigan, and probably (at least on a spotty basis) to Pennsylvania and points eastward.

Relict prairie and savanna habitats still exist in Indiana, Ohio, and southwest Michigan, and much more existed at the time Europeans first entered the region. Fire, whether caused by lightning or set by humans, may have promoted the spread of prairie habitat, or at least helped to maintain it. A number of reptile species have modern ranges that strongly suggest that they followed the prairie peninsula into the Great Lakes area (Schmidt 1938; Smith 1957). For example, the Ornate Box Turtle *(Terrapene ornata),* Six-lined Racerunner, Western Slender Glass Lizard, and Plains Garter Snake are characteristic grassland reptiles of the west-central United States with range extensions or relict populations in or near this area. Kirtland's Snake exists today almost entirely within the presumed prairie peninsula, while the Eastern Massasauga Rattlesnake, an inhabitant of marshes, bogs, and wet prairie, may fit the pattern as well.

Woodland species could have been displaced by the spread of drier grassland habitats during the xerothermic period. The apparent absence of the Wood Turtle in southern Michigan and Ohio and the scarcity of Eastern Box Turtles in northeastern Ohio may be the result of forest decline in the early Holocene. The Northern Ring-necked Snake is another woodland reptile conspicuously absent from the prairie peninsula. However, an alternate explanation in the absence of fossil evidence is that these species failed to invade (or reinvade) these areas postglacially.

The effects of Pleistocene glaciation and the resulting faunal displacements and dispersals in the Great Lakes area are reflected in the distribution of many native amphibians and reptiles. In addition, the changing glacial and interglacial climates may have contributed to the development of new species and subspecies.

The Eastern Gray Treefrog *(Hyla versicolor)* is one species that may owe its existence to Pleistocene climatic disruption. This species is practically identical in outward appearance to Cope's Gray Treefrog *(Hyla chrysoscelis),* but the two species can be distinguished by their spring mating calls. The male *H. chrysoscelis* typically gives a fast, rather high-pitched trill, with a sound pulse rate of about 38 to 70 pulses per second (as measured by a sonograph, an audio analyzing device). At like temperatures, the male *H. versicolor* has a slower, more musical trilled call with a pulse rate of about 15 to 29 pulses per second. The two species can be most readily identified when they are calling at the same time, allowing a direct comparison. A laboratory test may also be used to distinguish the species. *Hyla versicolor,* a genetic tetraploid, has red blood cells that are considerably larger and fewer in number than those of the diploid *H. chrysoscelis,* its probable ancestor. It has been suggested that *Hyla chrysoscelis* was split into at least two populations during a glacial advance, and that these underwent genetic changes during this separation. *Hyla versicolor* was probably produced as glaciers receded and the now slightly different populations came back into contact.

The Painted Turtle is a wide-ranging species consisting of four intergrading subspecies, two of which are found in the Great Lakes area. It appears likely that a single ancestral species was split into several populations during a glacial advance. These isolated populations would have begun the evolutionary transition toward becoming new species but were not separated long enough to complete the transformation. Once the ice retreated and the populations came again into contact, they were still genetically similar enough to interbreed and produce fertile offspring.

Butler's Garter Snake and the Short-headed Garter Snake are closely related species that probably evolved due to shifting habitats and isolation during glacial times. It has been suggested that the common ancestor of these two snakes evolved from the Plains Garter Snake in the eastern part of its range, perhaps early in the Pleistocene. This ancestral population was possibly split again during a later glaciation, with the ancestral Butler's Garter Snake population forced south of the ice front below the proto–Great Lakes, and the ancestral Short-headed Garter Snake population isolated on the unglaciated Allegheny plateau in Pennsylvania. In a similar example, the ancestral Fox Snake was apparently forced into at least two separate refugia during the Wisconsinan glaciation (perhaps earlier), and two separate populations remain today, one largely west and north of Lake Michigan, and another along the Lake Huron and Lake Erie shorelines. Some biologists, noting the complete geographic and reproductive isolation of the two populations, as well as differences in color pattern and habitat preference, recognize these two forms as separate species, the Western Fox Snake and the Eastern Fox Snake, a view adopted here.

It is interesting to note that despite the drastic climatic changes of the last two million years, the North American herpetofauna appears to have been quite taxonomically stable when compared to mammals and birds (Holman 1995b). During the late Pleistocene and the early Holocene, at least 19 genera of birds and 46 genera of mammals became extinct in North America, but only one reptile (the giant tortoise, *Geochelone*) disappeared. Eastern North America lost mammoths, mastodonts, horses, ground sloths, saber-tooth cats, short-faced bears, and many other mammals, but apparently no frogs, salamanders, aquatic turtles, lizards, or snakes. Amphibians and reptiles may have benefited from relatively small body size, an ectothermic metabolism (and the ability to hibernate), and more flexible and prolific reproductive habits. It is also likely that they were less intensively or less effectively exploited by early human hunters than were the larger mammals.

Environments for Great Lakes Amphibians and Reptiles

The suitability of an area as habitat for amphibians and reptiles is closely related to the type of vegetation growing there, which in turn depends on a combination of factors, including seasonal temperatures, precipitation, soils, drainage, and the contours of the land. Figure 4 illustrates the primary vegetation types that are thought to have existed in the Great Lakes basin prior to European settlement. The actual plant communities growing in any particular place within a mapped vegetational region will depend on local conditions. It should be kept in mind that these mapped vegetation categories are based largely on dominant forest tree species. Relatively few amphibians and reptiles are true forest animals per se; many species occupy ecotones (edge habitats) between dense woodlands and open grasslands, and many others live in wetlands or open-water habitats.

It is obvious that human activities have drastically altered the natural plant communities. Agricultural fields, orchards, roads, and cities now occupy vast areas of former forests and wetlands, and plant species intro-

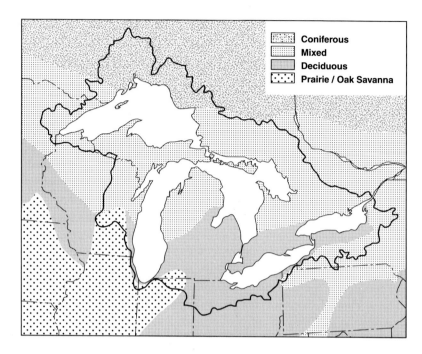

Fig. 4. Map of major plant communities in the Great Lakes basin. (From Kurta 1995.)

duced from Europe and elsewhere often crowd out native species. Even in existing natural areas the mix of trees, shrubs, and herbaceous plants may be quite different from that which greeted the first European settlers, due in part to accidental or intentional introductions of nonnative species.

The Great Lakes region is a transition zone between the boreal coniferous forests north of Lake Superior, the mixed-hardwood forests to the south, and the drier prairie and savanna to the west. A glance at the range maps in the species accounts will reveal that many amphibian and reptile species reach their distributional limits in the region, and that the number of species increases from north to south. These trends are largely related to seasonal temperatures, though precipitation may be a limiting factor on the western edge of the drainage basin.

Large bodies of water such as the Great Lakes have a moderating effect on both winter and summer temperatures. The number of frost-free days each year ranges from as few as 100 in northern Minnesota and Wisconsin to two hundred days or more along the southern shores of Lake Michigan. This factor is undoubtedly reflected in the ranges of several "southern" species that reach their northern limits along Great Lakes shorelines; examples include the Marbled Salamander, Fowler's Toad, Spotted Turtle, and Eastern Box Turtle. Winter survival of terrestrial amphibians and reptiles is also enhanced by the greater snow depths along the lakeshores (particularly the leeward sides), which offer increased insulation and thus reduce penetration and duration of ground frost.

Some hardy amphibian and reptile species can survive in a variety of habitat types and may occupy a very broad geographical range. The Northern Spring Peeper, American Toad, Painted Turtle, and Common Garter Snake are examples of adaptable, often abundant species found throughout the Great Lakes region. Many other species have more specialized habitat requirements and are associated with specific aquatic or terrestrial plant communities.

The major vegetation regions (and the special habitats they encompass) are summarized below, along with notes on some of the characteristic species of amphibians and reptiles that are found within them. The species mentioned as "typical" for certain plant associations are not necessarily restricted to those regions, nor are they necessarily found throughout the region. Many aquatic species are associated with wetland and open-water habitats that are represented in several vegetation regions.

True **boreal (coniferous) forest** is found in the Great Lakes basin north of Lake Superior, but it grades into the northern transitional forest in a broad band from the western edge of Lake Superior to the Maine coast. The dominant boreal forest trees are the balsam fir and white spruce, along with varying mixtures of paper birch, aspen, poplar, maple, white pine, white cedar, and eastern hemlock. Long, cold winters and short, cool summers contribute to a sparse herpetofauna. Wood Frogs, Blue-spotted Salamanders, and Red-backed Salamanders are found in the moister forests, while Mink Frogs and Northern Leopard Frogs inhabit pond and lake edges.

The **northern transitional (mixed) forest** is the most variable forest type in the Great Lakes and extends from Minnesota and northern Wisconsin across the Upper and northern Lower Peninsulas of Michigan, through central Ontario to upper New England. Sugar maple is the most characteristic tree species where soils are moderately moist, along with hemlock, beech, and yellow birch. Stands of oak and pine trees are common where soils are dry and sandy. As noted above, this forest type blends with the fir-spruce forest in the northern parts of the region. Typical species of the mixed-hardwood forest include the Spotted Salamander, Eastern Gray Treefrog, Wood Turtle, Northern Red-bellied Snake, and Northern Ring-necked Snake. The Eastern Hog-nosed Snake and Smooth Green Snake inhabit open oak/ pine woods and associated grassy clearings and edges.

The **deciduous forests** of the southern Great Lakes are also quite variable, depending on soil moisture levels and elevation. Here the climate is milder, with ample precipitation. Forests of sugar maple and American beech occupy the moist lowland sites with rich soils, while oak-hickory forests may dominate in slightly higher, drier areas. Spotted, Blue-spotted, Jefferson, Red-backed, and Dusky Salamanders, Black Rat Snakes, and Eastern Box Turtles are characteristic species of deciduous woodlands.

The true **prairie,** dominated by grasses and herbaceous flowering plants, approaches the Great Lakes drainage basin in northern Illinois and southern Wisconsin. As previously noted, prairie habitats also extend (at least in relict form) into Indiana, Ohio, and southern Michigan. This eastern "prairie peninsula" exists (or existed) largely in the form of a mixture of tallgrass prairie and oak-hickory woodland, with elevation and moisture levels determining the local vegetative type. Oak savannas are grasslands with scattered clumps of trees (especially the bur oak). Other grassland habitats occur where the soil is dry and sandy, for example in the dune areas along the southern Great Lakes shoreline. Most of the original prairie is now under cultivation. Characteristic grassland and savanna herps include the Eastern Tiger Salamander, Plains Leopard Frog, Ornate Box Turtle, Six-lined Racerunner, Western Slender Glass Lizard, Plains Garter Snake, and Bullsnake.

Aquatic communities offer habitat to many amphibians and reptiles. Large, permanent bodies of water (inland lakes and rivers) are homes to Mudpuppies, Bullfrogs, Common Map Turtles, Eastern Spiny Softshell Turtles, Common Snapping Turtles, and Northern Water Snakes. Few species enter open Great Lakes waters, but Mudpuppies and Snapping Turtles inhabit the shallower bays, and the peripheral marshes and weedy inlets support Bullfrogs, Green Frogs, Northern Leopard Frogs, Blanding's Turtles, Painted Turtles, Northern Water Snakes, and Northern Ribbon Snakes. These same species also occur in or around inland marshes, ponds, and weedy lakes.

Some amphibians and reptiles depend on unique aquatic habitats. Temporary (vernal) ponds in both woodlands and open grassland are important breeding places for many species of anurans and salamanders. The lack of fish and other aquatic predators in these sites may compensate for the risk of premature drying and loss of larvae in drought years. Spring-fed bog ponds, fens, and flooded sedge meadows are preferred habitats for Pickerel Frogs and Spotted and Bog Turtles. Small ponds and seepages fringed with moss are breeding sites for the Four-toed Salamander, while woodland brooks and springs are utilized by the Northern Red, Two-lined, Spring, and Dusky salamanders. Permanent streams with rocky bottoms and overhanging shrubbery are favored by Queen Snakes.

Adaptable species with broad habitat tolerances are usually the most successful species in human-altered environments. For example, Painted and Snapping Turtles can be common in moderately polluted rivers and lakes in urban areas. Tiger Salamanders, Spring Peepers, Gray Tree Frogs, American Toads, and Green Frogs often breed in farm stock ponds and ornamental pools in suburban gardens. Common, Butler's, and Short-headed Garter Snakes and Brown Snakes may be found in suburban yards and vacant urban lots and parks, while these and Red-bellied Snakes, Eastern Milk Snakes, Western Fox Snakes, and Racers will inhabit abandoned or fallow farm fields, grassy-edged hedgerows, and lightly grazed pastures. Kirtland's Snake is another species known to inhabit vacant city lots and moist pasture, but it is now scarce or absent in many places where it was once common.

Observing and Studying Great Lakes Amphibians and Reptiles

"Herp watching" is not yet as popular a hobby as bird watching, but amphibians and reptiles offer similar opportunities for "nonconsumptive" outdoor recreation. Finding and observing amphibians and reptiles is much like "birding"—you must learn the habits of the creatures you seek and be in the right place at the right time. Relevant habitat and behavioral information is noted for each species in the second part of this book. What follows are some general notes on discovering amphibians and reptiles in the wild. For readers interested in more systematic studies or surveys of Great Lakes amphibians and reptiles, the publications by Karns (1986) and Heyer et al. (1994) offer useful information on commonly used techniques.

The majority of salamanders spend most of their lives underground, or hidden beneath forest debris or in aquatic vegetation. Woodland species may sometimes be discovered by carefully turning (and then replacing) logs and rocks, but the surest way to find them is to venture out in early spring and investigate potential breeding ponds or streams. For many of the "mole" salamanders in the genus *Ambystoma,* this can be the only reliable way of observing them. Breeding activity is greatest at night, often during rainy weather. When wading after dark, take a good flashlight or headlamp and be alert for deep spots and underwater debris. Respect the habitat and the animals—get only as close as is necessary for observation, and avoid disturbing breeding salamanders or their egg masses. While it is unwise to go out alone at night, large groups of people will inevitably cause damage to fragile habitats. A deep footprint in the mud at the edge of a pond can be a significant obstacle to a migrating salamander.

Frogs and toads are usually easier to locate and observe than the secretive salamanders. Like birds, breeding anurans vocally announce their presence with characteristic calls. With practice, breeding calls can be used to identify which species are present and to estimate the size of the frog population. Learning to identify frog and toad vocalizations is not difficult, and recorded calls are commercially available to help the beginner (see the listing in "Resources"). Frog breeding activity tends to be greatest on warm, damp evenings; the calling males can often be spotted with a flashlight. After the breeding season, some anurans stay close to breeding areas, while others disperse to new habitats. Green Frogs, Mink Frogs, and Bullfrogs tend to remain in or near ponds and lakes, while Northern Leopard Frogs often move into surrounding fields and uplands. Toads, Wood Frogs, Gray Treefrogs, and Spring Peepers prefer moist woodlands but sometimes wander into fields and yards.

Amphibians should be handled only when necessary for positive identification or study, and captured specimens should be released as quickly as possible where they were found. Smaller individuals and species are quite delicate and sensitive to the heating and drying effects of human hands. Never handle an amphibian if your hands have insect repellent, sunscreen, or other chemical substances on them, as these can be harmful or fatal to the specimen. The skin secretions of Great Lakes amphibians are not generally harmful to humans who handle them, but it is wise to avoid getting secretions in your mouth or eyes, and to wash your hands after handling any animal.

Aquatic turtles are most easily observed and identified as they bask on logs and along shorelines. They are usually wary and ready to dive into the water at any disturbance, but a careful approach and a good pair of binoculars will allow ample opportunities to see important field marks and behavior. Lizards and snakes can be encountered by walking slowly and carefully through likely habitats, or by examining likely hiding places. If you carefully turn logs, flat rocks, boards, or other debris, small secretive species may be revealed. (Use special caution in areas where venomous snakes are found.) Always respect the habitat—return cover objects to their original positions and leave critical habitats like rotting logs and rock formations intact and undisturbed if they cannot be explored without their destruction.

Reptiles are more tolerant of handling than amphibians, but it is always a good idea to observe them from a distance to avoid disrupting their normal behavior. Specimens that are captured should be released where they were found. **Only well-trained people should ever approach or handle venomous snakes.** Remember that even nonvenomous reptiles may bite if they feel threatened. Avoid the temptation to take herps home as pets or vacation souvenirs. All amphibians and reptiles have special environmental and nutritional needs that are often difficult to meet in captivity, and most children (and their parents) soon tire of the day-to-day maintenance. Amphibians and reptiles have no need for play and are not suitable pets for small children, who often view live animals as animated toys. Remember that all states and provinces have regulations that protect certain species from capture or disturbance.

There are scientific and educational benefits to be gained from studies or exhibition of captive amphibians and reptiles, and many useful books on the care, husbandry, and breeding of these animals are now available (e.g., Mattison 1992; Murphy, Adler, and Collins 1994). Many regional herpetological societies offer captive care information to their members and the public. Captive-breeding programs for rare or endangered species can be important conservation tools when integrated into well-planned and officially sanctioned restoration efforts. But studies of amphibians and reptiles in their natural habitats are far more enlightening and valuable. Each year thousands of amateur ornithologists derive much enjoyment from seeking, observing, and photographing birds in the wild, and much useful scientific information is often gathered at the same time. Amateur herpetologists, on the other hand, have been largely concerned with the keeping and breeding of captive amphibians and reptiles. Refocusing some of the interest and enthusiasm of "herp hobbyists" toward the observation and study of wild amphibians and reptiles would add a new recreational dimension to herpetology that would benefit both science and conservation.

Venomous Snakes and Snakebite

Of the 23 species of snakes found in the Great Lakes region, only 2 are potentially dangerous to humans. The Timber Rattlesnake is extremely rare and possibly extirpated from the region, while the Eastern Massasauga Rattlesnake can be locally common in ideal habitat. There are no venomous species reported from Michigan's Upper Peninsula, the northern third of Wisconsin, or north of Lake Superior.

Both rattlesnake species tend to avoid confrontation with potential predators, including humans, if given the chance. Rattlesnake venom probably evolved as an aid to capturing food rather than as a defensive weapon. It is produced in modified salivary glands and delivered by hollow fangs mounted at the front of the mouth. Bites from rattlesnakes are very rare in the Great Lakes area, and many of those that do occur are provoked by attempts to handle, prod, or kill the snakes. It bears repeating that rattlesnakes should be approached and handled only by trained persons involved in legitimate research.

There is no reason to let a fear of these snakes interfere with enjoyment of the outdoors. The great majority of people that hunt, fish, camp, or hike in the Great Lakes region will never encounter a venomous snake. Anyone planning activities in or near natural habitats should familiarize themselves with the snake species of the area, including harmless species that could be mistaken for venomous ones. Wear protective clothing, such as sturdy, high-topped footwear and long, loose pant legs and sleeves, when hiking off cleared trails. (However, staying on established trails is not only safer, but helps to preserve vegetation and habitats.) A little common sense goes a long way—the very small chance of accidental snakebite is reduced even further by simply watching where you put your feet and hands.

Should a venomous snakebite occur, the victim should be kept calm and transported as quickly as possible to a hospital or other emergency medical facility. Traditional first-aid measures, such as cutting and sucking the bite wound and use of tight tourniquets, have fallen into disfavor, as these can lead to severe complications. The use of antivenin serum, administered by a medical professional, is the accepted way to treat snake envenomation, although in cases of mild envenomation or allergy to antivenin serum, a physician might opt for symptomatic treatment and observation. Because of the rarity of snakebite in our area, many physicians will not have firsthand experience with its treatment, but information should be available from poison control centers located in major cities.

In all snakebite cases it is critical that the snake be properly identified, since treating a bite from a harmless snake as though it were a venomous bite would expose the patient to needless risk and worry. If doubt exists, it is reasonable to kill the snake for later identification, providing it can be done safely and without undue delay. Rattlesnake bites typically produce pain and swelling, sometimes accompanied by faintness and nausea. Marks left by the two enlarged fangs are usually visible, although occasionally only one fang will penetrate. It has been estimated that perhaps a quarter of all bites from venomous snakes are "dry" (that is, no venom is injected). A bite from a nonvenomous snake will show scratches or pinpoint wounds (from the numerous tiny recurved teeth), and often bleeds freely. It can be treated as one would any minor scratch or skin puncture, taking care to avoid infection. Seek professional medical advice if any doubt exists as to the severity of the wound.

Accounts of Species

Amphibians (Class Amphibia)

Salamanders (Order Caudata)

There are about 380 species of salamanders worldwide, grouped into 60 genera. A large majority of these are native to the Western Hemisphere, and the eastern and the far western (Pacific coastal) regions of the United States appear to be centers of salamander evolution and diversity. Salamanders are tailed amphibians that generally have four legs of roughly equal size, though sirens have only two legs. Their lack of scales and claws and a preference for cool, moist surroundings distinguishes them from the scaled, warmth-loving lizards, with which they are often confused. Most species have a characteristic number of vertical creases (costal grooves) between the front and hind legs that may be helpful in identification (fig. 5).

A majority of Great Lakes salamanders are largely terrestrial as adults but lay eggs in or near water and have aquatic larvae. Species in the genus *Plethodon* live and reproduce entirely on land. Some species, such as the Mudpuppy and Western Lesser Siren are permanently aquatic and retain external gills throughout their lives. Under certain conditions, some species of salamanders that normally are terrestrial when sexually mature can remain in the water and reproduce as mature "larvae." Amphibians that can breed while retaining gills and other larval characters are said to be *neotenic*. Neotenic populations of the Tiger Salamander have been found in the Upper and northern Lower Peninsulas of Michigan.

Most salamanders have a unique method of internal egg fertilization. During or after courtship (which may be simple or elaborate, and take place on land or in water, depending on species) the male salamander deposits one or more spermatophores, which are cylindrical or cone-shaped globs of gelatinous (jellylike) material capped with sperm. The female then crawls over the spermatophore and takes up the sperm through her vent, where it is stored in the cloaca until the eggs are laid. The period of sperm storage may range from a few hours to a year or

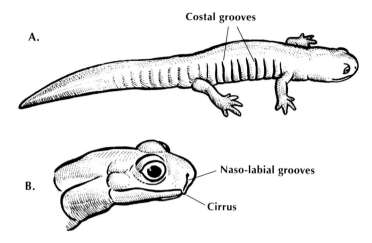

Fig. 5. Salamander characteristics. *A,* typical salamander showing costal grooves. *B,* head of Plethodontid salamander showing naso-labial groove and cirrus

more, again depending on the species. This fertilization method differs greatly from the external fertilization of most frogs and toads. A few salamanders, such as the Hellbender *(Cryptobranchus alleganiensis)* and, probably, the Western Lesser Siren, also have external fertilization.

Selected references for salamanders: Bishop 1941, Conant and Collins 1991, Duellman and Trueb 1986, Pfingsten and Downs 1989, and Stebbins and Cohen 1995.

Mudpuppies
Family Proteidae

The family Proteidae includes two genera of permanently aquatic, neotenic salamanders. Inhabiting lakes and streams of eastern North America are at least five species of "mudpuppies" and "waterdogs" in the genus *Necturus*. Only one species is found in the Great Lakes area. The only other member of the family is the blind, cave-dwelling Olm *(Proteus anguinus)* of the European Adriatic coast.

Mudpuppy *Necturus maculosus maculosus*

Description: A Mudpuppy is a large aquatic salamander with bushy reddish gills behind its head. The gills are larger and bushier in warm, oxygen-poor water, and smaller in cooler waters with higher oxygen content. The Mudpuppy's body, sides, and tail are brown or grayish brown with scattered bluish black spots or blotches. Dark pigment tends to increase in older specimens, and some may appear almost black. The head is broad and flattened, and the eyes are small; an irregular dark stripe runs through each eye. The belly is usually pale gray or yellow, often with dark spots. The tail is vertically flattened, and there are four toes on each foot. Mudpuppies have slimy skins and are difficult to hold in the hand. Adult length: 20 to 48.6 cm (8 to 19.1 inches).

The sexes are similar, but the male Mudpuppy's vent has wrinkled margins and appears swollen during the breeding season; behind the vent is a curved groove with two backward pointing papillae. In contrast, the female has a simple slitlike vent.

Larval Mudpuppies usually have a yellowish or cream-colored stripe running down each side, from nose to tail.

Confusing Species: Larvae of the "mole" salamanders (genus *Ambystoma*) have five toes on each hind foot; Mudpuppies have four toes. The Western Lesser Siren has external gills but is eel-like and lacks hind legs.

Distribution and Status: Mudpuppies range from New England west through the Ohio valley to southern Manitoba and south along the Mississippi valley to Missouri, Tennessee, and northern Georgia. They are found throughout most of the Great Lakes region but appear to be rare or

Mudpuppy, (Photo by R. D. Bartlett.)

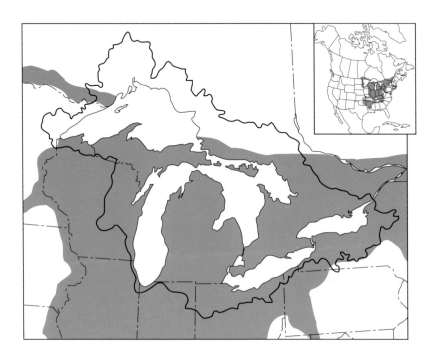

absent along much of the western shore of Lake Superior and in the boreal forest region north of the lake. (A related subspecies, *Necturus maculosus louisianensis,* is restricted to the Arkansas River drainage.) Mudpuppies can be locally abundant but have declined or even disappeared from many places where they were once common.

Habitat and Ecology: Mudpuppies inhabit permanent waters, including rivers, reservoirs, inland lakes, and Great Lakes bays and shallows. In clear waters they tend to be nocturnal, remaining hidden beneath rocks and other objects during the day. They can be active both night and day in shallow inlets and coves with thick aquatic vegetation. Mudpuppies are primarily bottom-walkers, but can swim with a fishlike motion, their legs folded against the body. These salamanders tend to move into shallower waters in spring and fall but seek deeper water in winter and summer. They have been recorded at depths of nearly 30 meters (100 feet) in Lake Michigan. Young Mudpuppies usually occupy habitats separate from the adults.

Mudpuppies are active throughout the year and are often caught on baited hooks in winter by people ice fishing. They feed mostly at night and eat a wide variety of aquatic animal life, including crayfish and other crustaceans, insect larvae, worms, mollusks, fish eggs, small fish, and other amphibians (including smaller Mudpuppies). Carrion is readily consumed and is probably located by a well-developed sense of smell. Mudpuppies are often caught in traps baited with dead fish.

Enemies of the Mudpuppy include fish, water snakes, and herons. These salamanders (and many other aquatic amphibians) have sense organs in the skin, equivalent to the lateral-line system in fish, which can detect motion and pressure changes in the surrounding water. These epidermal sensors probably help Mudpuppies avoid predators and locate prey.

Reproduction and Growth: Mudpuppies often form aggregations in shallow water in the fall (late September–November), when the normally solitary males join the females in their shelters beneath submerged rocks and wood. During courtship, the male may swim or crawl under, around, and over the female. Eventually, the male deposits spermatophores, which are gelatinous, sperm-capped globs about 1 cm (0.4 in) high. The female picks up a spermatophore with her vent, and stores the sperm in her cloaca until spring.

Egg laying usually occurs in late May or June. Female Mudpuppies typically locate or excavate a nest cavity under a rock, log, board, or other flat object, in water from about 10 cm to 3 m (4 in to 10 ft) deep. In rivers and streams, the opening of the nest tends to face downstream. From 18 to over 100 eggs are attached to the roof of the cavity, where they hang suspended by gelatinous stalks. Egg laying may extend over several days, and the female usually remains with her eggs at least until hatching. Incubation takes from one to two months, with warmer water temperatures speeding up the process.

At hatching the larvae range from 2.0 to 2.5 cm (0.8 to 1 in) long. They grow rapidly, more than doubling their length by the end of their first year. Maturity is reached in 4 to 6 years, at a length of about 20 cm (8 in). Mudpuppies may live 20 years or more.

Conservation: Mudpuppies are often persecuted due to their odd appearance, slimy skins, and undeserved reputation as a menace to game fish. Ice fishers who catch Mudpuppies on their lines frequently throw the hapless creatures out on the ice to die, in the mistaken belief that the salamanders are worthless or even dangerous. The Mudpuppy is harmless to humans and an important contributor to the aquatic ecosystem. While they may occasionally eat fish eggs or small fish, there is no evidence that these salamanders significantly reduce natural game fish populations.

Mudpuppy numbers have reportedly fallen in parts of the Great Lakes region, including southern Lake Erie and many inland lakes and rivers in Wisconsin, Michigan, Indiana, and Ohio, but information on populations and trends is lacking for most areas. In some places these salamanders have been harvested in large numbers for the biological supply trade, with collectors often targeting breeding aggregations. Since Mudpuppies accomplish most of their respiration through their skin and exposed gills, they may predictably be vulnerable to various pollutants and changes in water quality. They are reportedly sensitive to certain chemicals used in Great Lakes lamprey control programs.

Sirens
Family Sirenidae

The Sirenidae is a North American family of aquatic, eel-like salamanders consisting of three mostly southern species. All have external gills and lack hind feet. The Dwarf Siren *(Pseudobranchus striatus)* is a tiny southeastern species, while the Greater Siren *(Siren lacertina),* of Florida and the lower Atlantic coastal plain, is one of the largest salamanders, with a record length of over 3 feet (97.8 cm). The range of the Lesser Siren *(Siren intermedia)* is centered in the deep South but extends up the Mississippi, Ohio, and Wabash drainages into Illinois and Indiana, barely reaching the Great Lakes basin.

Western Lesser Siren   *Siren intermedia nettingi*

Description: Western Lesser Sirens are aquatic salamanders with bushy reddish gills, elongate, eel-like bodies, and vertically flattened tails. The front legs are tiny, with four toes on each foot, and there are no hind legs. The head is wider than the neck, the snout is rounded, and the eyes are small. Sirens are dark gray, brown, or olive in color, usually with scattered dark spots or flecks, though some specimens may appear almost black. There may be a light stripe on the upper lip. The belly is grayish, often with light spotting. Sirens, like Mudpuppies, have very slimy skins and are difficult to hold. Adult length: 18 to 50 cm (7 to 19.7 in).

The sexes are similar, though males may be larger than females in some populations. Very young larvae have red, orange, or yellow markings on the head, a yellowish stripe down each side of the body, and a dorsal tail fin (though occasional larvae are unmarked).

Confusing Species: Mudpuppies also have bushy external gills, but are not eel-like and have four legs (sirens have only front legs).

Distribution and Status: The Western Lesser Siren ranges from eastern Texas and the lower Mississippi valley north to central Illinois and the Wabash and Kankakee drainages of Indiana. There are records for Porter County, Indiana, and for single sites in Allegan and Van Buren Counties in southwestern Michigan. Based on the scarcity of recent records, the species can be considered extremely rare, and possibly even extirpated, within the Great Lakes drainage basin.

Western Lesser Siren, (Photo by R. W. Van Devender.)

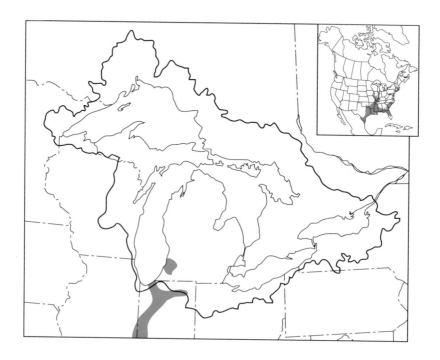

Habitat and Ecology: Western Lesser Sirens are found in ponds, ditches, backwater sloughs, sluggish streams, and shallow lake inlets. Habitats with muddy bottoms and an abundance of aquatic plants are preferred. They are largely nocturnal, remaining hidden in clumps of thick vegetation or beneath submerged debris during daylight hours. Sirens are well adapted for an aquatic existence but can presumably move overland on occasion, as they will colonize artificial ponds unconnected to natural habitats. They are able to survive drought and the drying of their habitat by retreating into crayfish tunnels or by burrowing into the mud. If the surrounding mud begins to dry, a siren can conserve water by producing a protective cocoon, which covers its body except for the mouth. The cocoon is probably derived from skin gland secretions and layers of epidermal skin.

Sirens eat a variety of invertebrate prey, including small crustaceans, insect larvae, snails, and worms. Quantities of algae and other aquatic plants have been found in their stomachs, but this material is probably swallowed accidently when these salamanders feed on small animals in thick vegetation.

Few salamanders are known to make noises of any kind, but Lesser Sirens reportedly make a variety of hisses, squeaks, whistles, and other sounds. A siren may "yelp" if seized by a predator or taken in hand and can produce clicking sounds if approached by another siren.

Reproduction and Growth: Courtship has not been observed in this species, although fertilization is presumably external, since there are no sperm storage areas in the female's cloaca and males appear to lack cloacal glands needed for producing spermatophores. The eggs are laid in spring in small depressions in the bottom mud, and in some cases may be attended by the female. The number of eggs produced in a season is highly variable, ranging from about 200 to 500 or more, although individual clutches may contain fewer than a dozen eggs. Upon hatching, the larvae are about 1.1 cm (0.4 in) long. Western Lesser Sirens reach maturity in about 2 years after hatching and may live for 20 years or more.

Conservation: Lesser Sirens are harmless to humans and human interests. They are at the periphery of their range in the Great Lakes region and were perhaps never well established north of the Kankakee River in Indiana. It has been suggested that the Michigan populations could have been introduced by humans, but it seems equally likely that the species dispersed there naturally. Sirens are secretive and inconspicuous, and it is possible that undetected populations still exist in the lower Lake Michigan drainage basin. It is noteworthy that both disjunct Michigan populations were reportedly discovered when rotenone, a pesticide used to kill fish, was applied to the shallow inlets of two lakes for fish management purposes. While the use of rotenone revealed the presence of Western Lesser Sirens, it could presumably have eliminated them as well.

Newts
Family Salamandridae

The family Salamandridae includes 53 species in 15 genera found in Europe, northern Africa, Asia, and North America. Of the two North American genera, *Taricha* contains three species restricted to the Pacific coast region, while *Notophthalmus,* also with three species, occurs in the eastern United States and Canada. The Eastern Newt, *Notophthalmus viridescens,* is the Great Lakes representative.

Newts lack costal grooves and slimy skins that are typical of most other salamanders. Their rather rough skins are well supplied with poison glands that help discourage predators. Some species can be deadly if swallowed. Reproduction in the Salamandridae involves internal fertilization with spermatophores, but the family shows diverse breeding strategies. Most species have aquatic larvae, but the female Alpine Salamander *(Salamandra atra)* retains the developing larvae in her body and gives birth to fully formed baby newts. Several species have aquatic adults, eggs, and larvae, with an intervening terrestrial juvenile stage. The Eastern Newt follows this pattern.

Eastern Newt *Notophthalmus viridescens*

Description: The Eastern Newt is unique among Great Lakes salamanders in that the gilled aquatic larvae usually metamorphose into a nonbreeding terrestrial stage called an eft. After a variable time on land, the eft undergoes another metamorphosis as it changes into an aquatic breeding adult.

The aquatic adults are olive, greenish brown, or reddish brown above, with small black dots scattered over the back and tail. Depending on subspecies, there may be a row of red spots along each side, and sometimes the spots are bordered with black. There is usually a dark stripe through the eye. The throat and belly are yellow, with scattered tiny black dots. The dull-looking skin is soft to the touch but not slimy. Neoteny can occur in some populations, in which the breeding adults will retain at least remnants of external gills. Adult length: 6.4 to 14 cm (2.5 to 5.5 in).

Males in breeding condition develop very high, rounded tail fins that extend to a point above the front of the hind legs. The females have straight tail fins that extend only to a point above the back of the hind

Eastern Newt

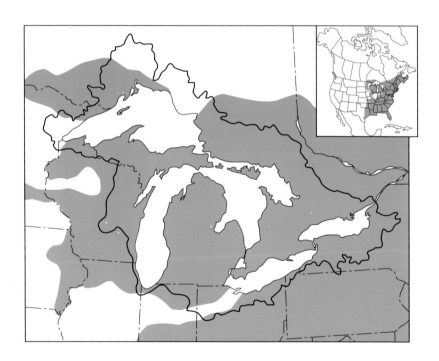

legs. In addition, the hind legs of males are thicker than those of the females and develop rough, black ridges on the inner thighs and black nubbins on the toe tips during the breeding season.

Terrestrial efts are usually red, orange, or reddish brown above and light yellow on the belly. In populations where adults are typically red-spotted, the spots are visible on the eft as well. Efts have a rough, bumpy-textured skin that feels dry to the touch. Their tails are round in cross section, unlike the flattened tails of adults. Efts that are in the process of changing to the aquatic form are darker and may appear intermediate in skin texture and body shape as well as color. Complicating the picture is the fact that adult newts that leave drying ponds to hibernate or aestivate will darken in color, lose the tail fin, and regain a rough skin texture, and thus can be confused with transforming efts. Efts are smaller than the adults, ranging in length from 3.5 to 8.6 cm (1.4 to 3.4 in).

Larval Eastern Newts are typically grayish or olive brown with black speckling, one or two rows of light yellowish spots on each side, and a black stripe running through the eye. When viewed from above, the head narrows toward the nose, appearing wedge-shaped. Larvae have tail fins that extend well up the back.

Note: Four subspecies of the Eastern Newt have been recognized, of which two are found in the Great Lakes region. Red-spotted Newts (Notophthalmus viridescens viridescens) usually have two rows of black-bordered red or orange spots on the back, both as efts and adults. In the slightly smaller Central Newt (Notophthalmus virisdescens louisianensis), the red spots either lack the black borders or are entirely absent.

Confusing Species: All other potentially confusing salamanders have costal grooves and slimy skins.

Distribution and Status: Eastern Newts are found throughout most of southeastern Canada and the eastern United States west to the edge of the Great Plains. They appear to be absent from the prairie peninsula in Illinois, Indiana, and Ohio. Newts occur throughout the Great Lakes region, with the Red-spotted Newt occupying the eastern part (Lake Erie and Lake Ontario drainages) and the Central Newt the western part (Lake Michigan and southern Lake Superior drainages). There is a broad zone of intergradation across Michigan's Lower Peninsula and into Indiana; specimens from this area can display coloration intermediate between the two subspecies.

Population densities of Eastern Newts in the Great Lakes basin appear to be generally lower than those often observed to the east and south of the region. Newts can be locally abundant in good habitat but decline or disappear where ponds are drained or polluted, or when the surrounding area is deforested.

Habitat and Ecology: Small, permanent ponds with ample aquatic plant life are preferred habitats for adult Eastern Newts, although they also occur in temporary ponds, the shallows of large lakes, and in river sloughs and backwaters. The terrestrial efts are usually found in wooded areas near the breeding ponds, taking refuge under rotting logs, boards, and other natural and unnatural objects. They can tolerate drier habitats than other woodland salamanders, but are most active on the surface during and after rain.

Adult Eastern Newts may remain active all year in the deeper ponds, while those in shallow waters that become dry in summer or freeze solid in winter are able to aestivate or hibernate on land, becoming darker and regaining an eftlike skin texture. In some areas, newts join other woodland salamanders in the late winter and early spring migration back to the breeding ponds. Once in the water, the characteristics of the aquatic form (e.g., skin texture, color, and tail fins) redevelop.

Adult Eastern Newts eat many types of small aquatic invertebrates, including crustaceans (e.g., fairy shrimp, cladocerans, copepods), insect larvae (such as mosquito and midge larvae), and mollusks (fingernail clams, snails). They will readily consume the eggs and larvae of other amphibians when available. Newt larvae feed largely on small invertebrates. The land-living efts eat insects, worms, snails, and other small animals of the leaf litter.

All life stages of the Eastern Newt have toxic skin secretions that can discourage certain predators. Adults are seemingly distasteful to some predatory fish. The terrestrial eft appears to have the greatest concentration of poison glands, and it is believed that the eft's bright red or orange color may serve to warn potential enemies that it is distasteful or even dangerous to eat. When attacked by a bird or small mammal, an eft may arch its back, raise its head and tail, and become immobile. This stiff posture, called the Unken reflex, occurs in a number of amphibians and may serve as a warning as well as eliminate movement that could stimulate the predator to attack.

Reproduction and Growth: Courtship in Eastern Newts can occur both in late fall and in spring, but eggs are laid only in spring. Courtship behavior can be quite complex, and usually begins with the male nudging the female's cloaca and displaying by twitching and undulating his body. She may repeatedly swim away, only to be reapproached by the persistent male. The male will eventually crawl over the female and move forward until he can clasp her at the neck or just behind her front feet using his hind feet. While in this embrace, called amplexus, the male uses a rippling movement of the end of his tail to "fan" the female, probably to spread stimulating secretions from his cloaca toward her head. He may also rub the side of his head on her snout, again to spread glandular secretions. The female may also raise her own tail and produce the fanning motion.

Amplexus can last for several minutes or hours, after which the male releases the female and crawls forward, often with tail still raised and with continued body undulations. The female then follows while nudging the male's tail and cloaca, stimulating him to deposit a spermatophore. The female may then pick up the sperm packet at the tip of the spermatophore with her cloaca, though the male may deposit several more spermatophores before sperm transfer is completed.

Most egg laying occurs in April and May. Females deposit from a few dozen to 300 or more eggs over a period of several days or weeks, usually attaching them singly (rarely in small clusters) to plants or other objects. The incubation period lasts from two to five weeks, depending on water temperature; at hatching the tiny larvae measure about 0.7 to 0.9 cm (0.3 to 0.4 in) long. The larvae grow quickly, and in late summer they leave the water, transforming into efts. An eft can remain on land for two to seven years before undergoing a second metamorphosis into an aquatic breeding adult. In some populations, particularly in the western part of the Great Lakes area, newts may skip the terrestrial stage and metamorphose directly into adults. They can live for 10 or more years.

Conservation: Eastern Newts are harmless to humans, and their habit of feeding on mosquito larvae and pupae is certainly a desirable trait. This species is frequently collected for the pet and biological supply trade, although data on the volume or effect of this collection in the Great Lakes region is lacking. Using Eastern Newts as fish bait is ill-advised for several reasons, including the fact that many fish would be repelled by this amphibian's skin secretions.

Eastern Newts have declined or disappeared in many areas where habitats have been destroyed or degraded. Populations at the northern periphery of their range might be expected to be more sensitive to disturbance than those farther south or east, where densities are often initially higher. Newts are best conserved by protecting or creating ponds that are close to woodland habitats.

Red eft

Mole Salamanders
Family Ambystomatidae

Members of the family Ambystomatidae are generally medium to large salamanders with prominent costal grooves, robust limbs and bodies, and broad heads. The common family name "mole" salamander comes from the habit of usually staying underground or beneath objects except when breeding. Fertilization is internal, and eggs hatch into typical aquatic gilled larvae that transform into terrestrial adults, though neoteny can occur in some species. There are 30 species in two North American genera; the genus *Ambystoma* is represented in the Great Lakes region with 6 species. Species identification can be confounded by hybridization between certain members of this genus; this problem is discussed in the introduction and in the pertinent species accounts.

Spotted Salamander   *Ambystoma maculatum*

Description: These are fairly stout salamanders with broad heads and rounded snouts. They are black, dark gray, or dark brown above, with two irregular rows of yellow spots running from the back of the head onto the tail. Spots may also be present on the legs and snout; sometimes the head spots are bright orange. Occasional specimens have whitish or tan spots, or (rarely) may lack spots altogether. The normally unspotted sides and belly are gray or purplish gray. Costal grooves: 11–13. Adult length: 10.8 to 24.8 cm (4.3 to 9.8 in).

The sexes are quite similar, but male Spotted Salamanders generally have slimmer bodies than the females, and the area around the male's vent is greatly swollen during the breeding season.

The older larvae (greater than 4 cm in length) are usually greenish gray to brown above with small yellowish spots or flecks along the side. Their tail fins are often grayish, mottled with light yellow. Newly transformed Spotted Salamanders tend to be dark gray or brown with scattered greenish yellow flecks or patches and dull yellow or tan bellies. The characteristic rounded spots can develop fairly quickly, usually by the time the young salamanders are around 6 cm (2.4 in) long.

Spotted Salamander

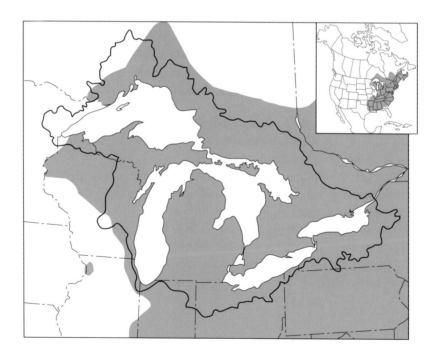

Confusing Species: The larger Tiger Salamander has irregularly shaped spots or blotches that extend onto the sides and belly. Newly transformed Blue-spotted Salamanders may have yellow spotting on the sides and belly; in Spotted Salamanders the spots are usually restricted to the upper surfaces.

Distribution and Status: Spotted Salamanders occur throughout the eastern United States and southeastern Canada, with the exception of Florida and portions of the Atlantic coastal plain. They have been recorded in all parts of the Great Lakes region, excepting the western shore of Lake Superior.

This species can be locally abundant where forested habitat remains intact, but they quickly decline or disappear when woodlands are cleared or disturbed by cutting or grazing.

Habitat and Ecology: Moist closed-canopy deciduous or mixed woodlands are the preferred habitats for the Spotted Salamander. They usually avoid swamp forests subject to flooding, and are uncommon or absent in disturbed forests that have been recently grazed, burned, or harvested for timber. Temporary or semipermanent ponds, either within or adjacent to the woods, are critical habitat elements for this species.

Spotted Salamanders are rarely seen after the spring breeding season. They spend much of their time in burrows underground and have been recorded at a depth of 1.3 meters (4.3 feet). They are occasionally found under or within rotting logs, leaf litter, and other moist places. These salamanders probably do not dig their own burrows but use or modify tunnels dug by other animals, such as rodents or large earthworms, or follow cracks and root systems. Hibernation occurs on land, usually close to the breeding ponds but sometimes up to 800 meters (2,600 ft) away.

Adult Spotted Salamanders eat worms, snails, slugs, insects, millipedes, spiders, and other invertebrates. The larvae feed on small aquatic invertebrates such as crustaceans (especially copepods and cladocerans), insect larvae, and mollusks, as well as tiny fish and larvae of other amphibians (including newt larvae). In turn, Spotted Salamander eggs and larvae are eaten by aquatic insects (e.g., diving beetles, giant water bugs, caddisfly larvae, and dragonfly nymphs), fish, Eastern Newts, and the larvae of other *Ambystoma* salamanders, particularly Tiger and Marbled Salamanders. Both the adults and larvae fall prey to snakes, turtles, herons, and raccoons.

Spotted Salamanders have granular ("poison") glands that produce secretions capable of repelling some predators. When confronted with a predator, a Spotted Salamander may extend its forelegs and lower its head, or raise and lash its tail, depending on the direction of the attack. This behavior presumably presents the predator with the greatest concentrations of poison glands, which are located behind the eyes and on the tail. These secretions may be irritating to humans if rubbed into the eyes or mucous membranes.

Reproduction and Growth: In the Great Lakes area, Spotted Salamanders usually migrate to their breeding ponds from late March to mid-April, depending on local weather conditions. Migration is stimulated by the thawing of the ground and high humidity, and often begins on a relatively warm night with heavy rain. Individual salamanders do not always breed every year but tend to return to the same pond each time they breed—probably the pond in which they hatched. Spotted Salamanders often arrive in the ponds a few days later than Blue-spotted or Jefferson Salamanders or their hybrids, perhaps because the latter species overwinter closer to the ponds and thus have a lesser distance to travel. Spotted Salamanders appear to use established routes when traveling to and away from the breeding ponds, even entering and leaving the pond at about the same point each time.

Once in the breeding pond, the males (which often arrive a day or two ahead of the females) congregate in groups and begin moving in circles, swinging their heads back and forth and nudging other salamanders in the sides and vent region with their snouts. When females approach the courting area, the activity increases, as males frantically mill about, trying to identify potential mates. From time to time each salamander will swim rapidly to the surface to get a breath of air and then sink back to the bottom to continue courtship; the frenzied courting and air gulping can cause a noticeable disturbance on the water's surface.

Upon contacting a female, the courting male may continue nudging her vent, as well as walking under her lower jaw ("chin") and rubbing his own chin on her back and tail. The female also joins in the nudging and chin lifting, and the two may continue circling in this odd "dance" for some time. Eventually, the male crawls under the female's chin and then moves away, undulating his body and tail. If the female follows, he will place his vent against the pond bottom or a twig and deposit a spermatophore. As the female moves from side to side, her vent may contact the spermatophore, at which time she can take the sperm into her cloaca. The male may return to nudging and chin rubbing and deposit additional spermatophores. In crowded situations, a female can be courted by several males at the same time and will pick up sperm from any spermatophore that she encounters. In addition, if a male happens upon another male's spermatophore, he often covers it with one of his own.

Eggs are laid from one to several days after courtship and sperm transfer. Each female can lay from 50 to over 250 eggs, in one large globular gelatinous mass or several smaller clusters, attached to sticks or vegetation. Fresh egg masses expand to a diameter of 4 to 10 cm (1.5 to 4 inches) and are quite dense in consistency, often retaining their shape even if lifted from the water. The stiffness of the surrounding mass offers the eggs extra protection against some predators.

Spotted Salamander egg masses can be transparent or an opaque milky color that obscures the eggs. Additionally, many masses take on a greenish color due to the growth of a harmless and possibly symbiotic species of algae within the egg membranes. The algae could provide the developing salamander embryos with additional oxygen, while benefiting from the carbon dioxide given off by the embryos.

The eggs hatch in 20 to 60 days, with the shorter incubation periods occurring at higher water temperatures. The newly hatched larvae average about 1.3 cm (0.5 in) in length. They metamorphose in late summer, at lengths of 4.0 to 7.5 cm (1.6 to 3 in). Larvae living in drying ponds can hasten their development but will transform at a smaller size than those completing development in more stable aquatic environments. The minimum larval period appears to be about 60 days, while occasional larvae living in cold, permanent waters may not metamorphose until spring of the following year. Male Spotted Salamanders can breed when two or three years old, females when three to five years old. Approximately equal numbers of males and females transform, but males usually outnumber females in breeding aggregations. Spotted Salamanders may live for over 20 years.

Conservation: The future of the Spotted Salamander is tied to the continued presence of relatively undisturbed woodlands and associated temporary and semipermanent ponds. Any human activity that opens the forest canopy, such as selective logging, can lower humidity and create conditions unsuitable to their survival. The construction of roads running between wooded uplands and lowland breeding sites can lead to mass mortality of migrating salamanders.

Spotted Salamanders are sometimes collected for the biological supply and pet trade; the animals are usually trapped or seined when they are concentrated in breeding ponds. Persistent exploitation could threaten local populations, particularly if collecting pressure was focused on a few scarce breeding sites. Acid precipitation may also be a threat to Spotted Salamanders, although the sensitivity of their eggs and larvae to the effects of pond acidification reportedly varies among populations.

Blue-spotted Salamander *Ambystoma laterale*

Description: This is a black or grayish black salamander with blue spots and flecks on the sides, limbs, belly, and tail, occasionally extending onto the back. The color of the belly may be either black or slightly lighter than the upper surfaces, but the vent area is usually black. Costal grooves: 12–14. Adult length: 7.6 to 14 cm (3 to 5.5 in).

The sexes are similar, though males average slightly smaller than females and have relatively longer, more flattened tails. During the breeding season the males have swollen vents.

The larvae vary in appearance, but older individuals (those with all four legs present) tend to be dark brown, olive, or gray above with dark mottling on the tail fins. Some may have dull yellow dorsal blotches and/or a yellowish stripe down each side of the back. The belly is usually unmarked and lighter than the back.

This species hybridizes with other species of *Ambystoma* throughout much of the Great Lakes region. Blue-spotted/Jefferson Salamander hybrids are most common, but hybridization with Small-mouthed and Tiger Salamanders occurs in the Lake Erie drainage area. Hybrids are usually intermediate in form and color between the two parent species but will look more like the species from which they received the most inherited genetic material. It is often difficult or impossible to confirm the identity or parental origin of a hybrid *Ambystoma* without laboratory analysis.

Confusing Species: The Jefferson Salamander is larger and is brown or gray, not black, on the back and paler on the belly, with gray color around the vent. Bluish flecking, if present, is confined to the sides and limbs. The

Blue-spotted Salamander

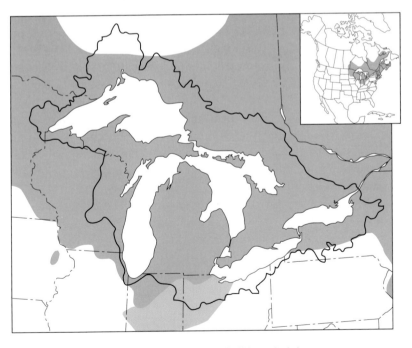

Note: Pure *Ambystoma laterale* may be absent from the lightest shaded area.

Jefferson also has longer limbs and toes and a relatively longer, broader snout.

The Small-mouthed Salamander has a very short snout, with a slightly protruding lower jaw, and its markings are usually grayish, not blue. The Slimy Salamander has white markings on the back and has a groove between each nostril and the lip. The dark phase of the Red-backed Salamander has a much narrower body, tiny legs, and small black and white spots on the belly.

Distribution and Status: The Blue-spotted Salamander is a cold-tolerant species occurring from New England and northern New Jersey west through the Great Lakes basin and north to southeastern Manitoba, then east across southern Ontario and Quebec to Labrador. A zone of hybridization with the Jefferson Salamander covers much of the southern part of this range, from Nova Scotia west to northern Wisconsin.

Blue-spotted Salamanders can be common in woodlands with the required breeding ponds. They seem to more tolerant of human habitat disturbance than the Spotted Salamander, persisting in fragmented and cutover woods long after the latter species has disappeared.

Habitat and Ecology: These salamanders inhabit both deciduous and coniferous forests, from moist bottomlands to dry uplands. They are perhaps most abundant in moist woodlands with sandy soils but turn up in a variety of places, including open fields and suburban backyards. The presence of ponds that retain water into midsummer is an essential element of their habitat.

Blue-spotted Salamanders spend much of their time hidden beneath logs, rocks, and leaf litter and will use or enlarge the burrows of other small woodland animals. Unlike most other *Ambystoma* species, however, they are often found above ground throughout the warmer months and may move about in the open during rain showers.

These salamanders eat many types of small invertebrates, including earthworms, spiders, snails, slugs, centipedes, and various insects and their larvae. Adults in and around breeding ponds in spring will reportedly eat aquatic insect larvae and nymphs. The salamander larvae feed on aquatic invertebrates, particularly cladocerans (water fleas), copepods, and insects. Where abundant, larval *Ambystoma* may be significant predators on mosquito larvae.

The skin of this species contains granular glands that produce a whitish, presumably toxic substance. These glands are especially concentrated on the upper surface of the tail. If gently prodded by a curious human, a Blue-spotted Salamander may raise and undulate its tail; poking or grasping the animal's body can lead to a lashing of the tail accompanied by greater production of the noxious secretions. The head may be protected by tucking it beneath the tail. Presumably these defensive behaviors would also be elicited by the probing nose of a hungry shrew or raccoon.

Reproduction and Growth: Migration of Blue-spotted Salamanders to their breeding ponds occurs in late March or early April, often spurred by warm evening rains, though warming temperatures and rapid snow melt may be enough to trigger movement. This species generally arrives at the ponds a day to several days before the other spring-breeding *Ambystoma* salamanders.

Courtship can involve an often brief phase where the male nuzzles and nudges the female with his snout. He then crawls above the female, grasps her behind the front legs with his own front legs, and begins rubbing his chin on her head and snout. The pair may stay in this position for several hours, occasionally rising to the surface for air and then sinking slowly to the bottom. If approached by a rival male, a clasped male will attempt to carry his mate away with vigorous swimming motions of his tail. Eventually, after much thrashing and chin rubbing, the male releases the female and moves forward, depositing a spermatophore in front of her. She may then move over the spermatophore and take the sperm into her cloaca. The male often deposits several spermatophores during one mating sequence and can produce from about 10 to 40 or more during the breeding season.

Female Blue-spotted Salamanders normally lay their eggs within two days of mating, attaching the rather flimsy gelatinous egg masses to sticks, rocks, leaves, and other submerged objects. There are one to a dozen or so eggs per cluster, with the total egg complement per female ranging from 35 to over 500, probably averaging about 225. The larvae hatch after three to five weeks (depending on water temperature), at a length of 0.8 to 1.2 cm (0.3 to 0.5 in).

In late summer, the larvae metamorphose into land-dwelling salamanders at a length of about 5.5 to 7.5 cm (2.2 to 3 in). If a breeding pond begins to dry up prematurely , the larvae can transform earlier but at a smaller size than usual. Newly transformed Blue-spotted Salamanders may have yellowish instead of bluish spotting on the sides and tail but usually attain the adult coloration over a period of several weeks. These salamanders mature in about two years.

Conservation: Blue-spotted Salamanders and their hybrid kin require wooded habitats adjacent to fishless ponds and other still, shallow waters. They are fairly tolerant of selective logging and low-density residential development, as long as the critical parts of the habitat remain intact. Local populations of this species are threatened by clear-cutting of woodlands and the building of roads between breeding ponds and terrestrial habitats.

Jefferson Salamander *Ambystoma jeffersonianum*

Description: This salamander is dark brown, brownish gray, or slate gray above, with a paler belly, and a grayish vent region. Many specimens have light bluish flecks scattered along the sides and tail, sometimes extending onto the back. This flecking is most conspicuous in younger salamanders and may virtually disappear in older adults. Compared to other *Ambystoma*, Jefferson Salamanders have relatively long, wide snouts and long toes. Costal grooves: 12–14. Adult length: 10.7 to 21 cm (4.2 to 8.3 in).

Breeding males have swollen vents, and their tails are relatively longer and more compressed and bladelike than those of females; they also appear more slender than egg-carrying females. Both sexes reportedly become darker and less conspicuously marked after the breeding season.

Newly hatched larvae are usually yellowish green with darker blotches on the back and a tail fin that is mostly uncolored except toward the tip. Older larvae are mottled greenish gray above, sometimes with small yellowish spots along the sides, and have a pale, mostly unmarked belly.

The Jefferson Salamander hybridizes with the Blue-spotted Salamander throughout the central and southern Great Lakes basin, forming populations of mostly female triploid hybrids. A hybrid specimen may appear more like one or the other of the parent species, depending on which species contributed the majority of its inherited genetic material.

Jefferson Salamander

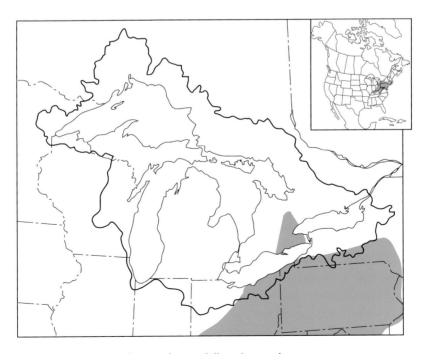

Note: Maps shows range of pure *Ambystoma jeffersonianum* only.

Confusing Species: A Blue-spotted Salamander is smaller and darker (usually black) with conspicuous bluish spots on the sides; its vent area is usually black. Small-mouthed Salamanders have very short snouts, short toes, and grayish markings. The Slimy Salamander has white markings and a groove running from each nostril to the lip.

Distribution and Status: Jefferson Salamanders are found from southern New England, New York, and Pennsylvania, west to southern Indiana and northern Kentucky. The hybrid zone with the Blue-spotted Salamander extends from the Maritime Provinces west through the southern and central Great Lakes region to Indiana and Wisconsin. Within the Great Lakes region, pure populations of Jefferson Salamanders are most likely to occur in the drainages south of Lake Erie and Lake Ontario, and in southwestern Ontario west of Lake Ontario. They can be locally common in suitable habitat.

Habitat and Ecology: Jefferson Salamanders prefer relatively undisturbed deciduous woodlands. They are most common in moist, well-drained upland forests, and usually avoid lowland areas prone to flooding. Like other *Ambystoma,* this species breeds in ponds within or adjacent to their woodland habitats. Ideal breeding ponds are fishless but must hold water at least into midsummer. They frequently share habitat and breeding sites with the Spotted Salamander and Wood Frog.

For much of the year these salamanders remain hidden underground or beneath or within rotting logs or leaf litter. They often use or modify burrows of other small woodland animals. Most Jefferson Salamanders spend the summer–winter period within 400 m (0.25 mi) of their breeding ponds, although a few specimens may travel up to 1,600 m (1 mi). Surface activity and migration occurs at night or, occasionally, on overcast rainy days.

Adult Jefferson Salamanders are known to eat insects and snails, and probably take an assortment of small invertebrates. The larvae consume aquatic invertebrates, as well as smaller siblings and Spotted Salamander larvae.

Like their relatives, this species has skin glands that produce noxious secretions; these are particularly concentrated on the upper base of the tail. Defensive behaviors include tail waving and lashing, and tucking the head under the tail. Skin secretions of these salamanders may cause irritation if rubbed into eyes or mucous membranes.

Reproduction and Growth: Jefferson Salamanders migrate to breeding ponds in late winter or very early spring, often while snow still covers much of the ground and ice has barely begun to retreat from the pond edges. A day or two of rain or rapid snow melt appears to trigger the movement. If cold weather returns, the migrating salamanders take cover and wait for more favorable conditions; thus the salamanders may arrive at the ponds in "waves" over a period of several days or weeks. The first contingent of males usually precedes the arrival of the first females, and Jefferson Salamanders are often well into breeding before Spotted Salamanders arrive at shared breeding sites.

Courtship behavior of this species closely resembles that of the Blue-spotted Salamander. The male grasps the female behind her front legs with his own forelimbs and rubs her head with his snout and chin. The pair may remain clasped together for several hours. Eventually the male releases the female and crawls ahead of her while wriggling his body and waving his tail. If she follows and nudges his tail and vent, he will deposit a spermatophore on a leaf or twig on the pond bottom. The female may move over the spermatophore and pick up the sperm, or perhaps the whole spermatophore, with her cloaca. The last part of the sequence is often repeated when necessary, and the male can release one or more additional spermatophores during the courtship.

The females deposit their eggs in small, elongate gelatinous clusters attached to underwater sticks and vegetation. Anchoring the eggs below the surface assures their survival if the pond should refreeze during a cold period. The number of eggs per mass varies from 1 to 60 (usually 20 to 30), and the total number of eggs produced per female ranges from 100 to about 280.

The length of incubation varies with the water temperature. Eggs removed to a warm (21°C) indoor tank can hatch in about two weeks, but under natural conditions up to 45 days may be required. Newly hatched larvae range in length from 1.0 to 1.4 cm (0.4 to 0.55 in). Hatching success can be quite high, but the survival rate of larvae is normally very low (often less than 1 percent), due mostly to predation. Surviving larvae transform into terrestrial salamanders in two to three months, with metamorphosis occurring sooner, and at a smaller size, if the breeding pond begins to dry prematurely. In a dry summer, however, many larvae will die if the ponds dry too quickly. New metamorphs are from 4.8 to 7.5 cm (1.9 to 2.9 in) long. They can breed in two to three years, and individual Jefferson Salamanders may live for six years or longer.

Conservation: This species can persist as long as relatively undisturbed woodland habitats adjacent to suitable, fishless breeding ponds are preserved. The construction of roads between terrestrial winter habitats and breeding sites can have disastrous consequences, as large numbers of salamanders are often destroyed during the brief spring migration.

Small-mouthed Salamander   *Ambystoma texanum*

Description: As its name implies, this species has a relatively small head and a very short, blunt snout. The head often looks somewhat swollen behind the eyes. When viewed from the side, the lower jaw barely protrudes beyond the upper jaw. The dorsal coloration varies from light gray to brownish gray or black. Most specimens have an irregular pattern of grayish or whitish blotches and flecks on the upper surfaces, becoming heaviest on the sides and extending onto the otherwise dark belly. Small-mouthed Salamanders in their breeding ponds may appear paler and have more conspicuous light markings than those found on land after the breeding season. Costal grooves: 14–16. Adult length: 11 to 17.8 cm (4.3 to 7 in).

Male Small-mouthed Salamanders have swollen vents during the breeding season and tend to be smaller than females, but with longer and more compressed tails.

Newly hatched larvae are dark brown or olive green with light bars or crossbands on the back. Larger larvae may still show crossbands and have a light stripe down each side of the back, but those nearing metamorphosis often have the light markings obscured by dark pigment.

Small-mouthed Salamanders hybridize with other *Ambystoma* species, particularly in the region south and west of Lake Erie. These hybrid individuals may be intermediate in form and color or may resemble one or the other of the parent species. Hybrids between this species and the Blue-spotted Salamander are most common, but combinations with Jefferson Salamanders and the various Blue-spotted/Jefferson hybrid populations are also known. Individual salamanders possessing genetic material from the Small-mouthed, Blue-spotted, and Tiger Salamander are known from Kelleys Island in southern Lake Erie.

Confusing Species: Both Blue-spotted and Jefferson Salamanders have longer snouts and bluish markings on the sides. Marbled Salamanders

Small-mouthed Salamander

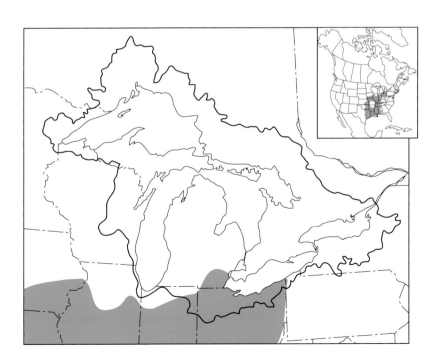

have a bold pattern of whitish bands on a black background. The Slimy Salamander and the dark phase of the Red-backed Salamander both have a groove running from each nostril to the lip.

Distribution and Status: This species is found from northeastern Ohio west to Missouri and eastern Nebraska and south through western Kentucky and Tennessee to the Gulf Coast. It occurs in southeast Michigan and on several of the islands in southern Lake Erie.

These salamanders are common in many parts of this range, and they are reported to be fairly tolerant of human environmental disturbance, persisting even in some agricultural and suburban areas. Small-mouthed Salamanders are considered an endangered species in Michigan, where they reach the northern limit of their range.

Habitat and Ecology: Small-mouthed Salamanders are most abundant in lowland floodplain woods, but they also occur in areas where the forest cover has been fragmented or largely removed and seem quite at home in open habitats such as prairie and farmlands. Shallow bodies of water are required for breeding purposes, and they often share woodland vernal ponds with other *Ambystoma*. However, Small-mouthed Salamanders also breed in runoff ponds, floodings, river backwaters, and roadside ditches, where there is less competition from forest-dependent species.

At times other than the spring breeding season, these salamanders generally remain hidden beneath rotting logs, rocks, or natural leaf litter. They also use the burrows dug by crayfish and small mammals. Evening rain showers may stimulate them to wander above ground, perhaps seeking food or alternative cover.

Insects, slugs, and earthworms are favored foods of adult Small-mouthed Salamanders, while the larvae eat a variety of small aquatic invertebrates and occasionally smaller larvae of their own and other salamander species. The larvae are, in turn, eaten by crayfish, predaceous aquatic insects, birds, and snakes, while adults are consumed by garter and water snakes and other vertebrate predators.

This species, like other *Ambystoma,* has concentrations of granular ("poison") glands on the upper surface of the tail. Secretions of these glands are probably toxic or at least repellent to some predators. When confronted with a potential enemy, a salamander will raise and undulate its tail, while curling the head underneath the tail. At times the tail may be lashed at the attacker, and if grasped by a limb the salamander may roll toward the attacker. Some Small-mouthed Salamanders may also use a defensive posture (the Unken reflex) in which the body is curled up with head and tail arched upward and limbs held tightly to the side. It is thought that the attack response of a predator may be inhibited when the prey becomes stiff and motionless.

Reproduction and Growth: Small-mouthed Salamanders often migrate to their breeding ponds very early in the year, seemingly at the first hint of springlike weather. A couple of days of rain in late winter may stimulate movement, frequently while ice still covers portions of the ponds. This salamander typically appears to remain closer to the aquatic breeding sites in summer and winter than related species and thus may not have as far to travel for reproduction.

Courtship behavior in the Small-mouthed Salamander is quite similar to that of the Spotted Salamander. They may gather in courting groups with males bumping and nudging the females and each other. Now and then a male will move off and deposit several spermatophores on sticks or leaves or the bottom substrate, often in the presence of one or more females. They will also cover the spermatophores of other males with their own. Females walk over the spermatophores and take up the sperm into their cloacas; each female may receive sperm from several different males. Courting male Small-mouthed Salamanders sometimes clasp the females behind the front legs, as occurs in Blue-spotted and Jefferson Salamanders, but clasping appears to be the exception rather than the rule in this species.

Each female can produce from 300 to 700 eggs annually, deposited in small, rather loose gelatinous masses containing 3 to 30 eggs each. The masses are usually attached to sticks, leaves, or plant stems. Hatching may occur in three to eight weeks, with incubation period dependent on water temperature. Newly hatched larvae are about 1 cm (0.4 in) in length. They grow quickly and transform into terrestrial salamanders in two to three months, when about 5 cm (2 in) long, and probably reach breeding size in the second year after metamorphosis.

Conservation: Small-mouthed Salamanders are common in many parts of their range, due no doubt to their wide habitat tolerances. On the northern edge of their range, where they can be uncommon or rare, management would include the preservation of woodlands with known populations, along with maintenance of adjacent shallow, fish-free ponds that hold water into midsummer.

Marbled Salamander *Ambystoma opacum*

Description: The Marbled Salamander is a stout, thick-bodied salamander with white or gray markings on a black to dark brown-black background color. The light markings usually occur as bands across the head and back; sometimes these merge into an irregular stripe along each side of the back and neck. The tail is banded with black and white, and the belly may be black or brownish black, occasionally with some light speckling. Costal grooves: 11–13. Adult length: 8.5 to 12.7 cm (3.4 to 5 in).

In males the light dorsal markings are pure white, while in females they are gray. The male's vent appears more swollen than the female's. Both of these sexual characters are more pronounced during the breeding season.

The larvae are usually brown or gray-brown with light spots or blotches on the sides and tail fins. Newly transformed juveniles are brown or black with scattered light markings that are often quite dense on the head and more diffuse on the back and tail. These markings may start out yellowish and become bluish to silvery white during the first few days out of water. The crossbanded pattern of the adult develops gradually over a period of several weeks or months.

Confusing Species: These stocky and boldly marked salamanders are unlikely to be confused with other species in the Great Lakes area. Small-mouthed Salamanders are slimmer, with light markings scattered along the sides and not arranged in crossbands. Spotted Salamanders have rounded yellow spots that do not merge on the sides. Tiger Salamanders are much larger, with irregular yellowish or brownish spots and blotches.

Distribution and Status: Marbled Salamanders are found from southern New England to northern Florida, west to eastern Texas and north to southern Indiana and Ohio. Disjunct populations occur in northern Ohio (including Kelleys Island in western Lake Erie) and in Indiana and the southern edge of the Lake Michigan basin. These latter localities may be

Marbled Salamander

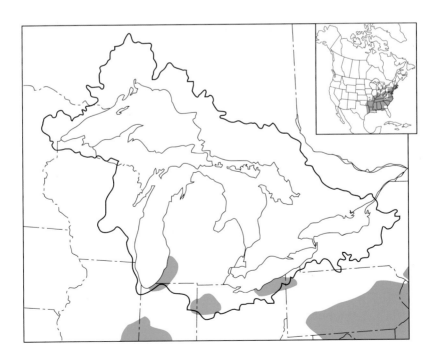

relict populations indicating a formerly wider northern distribution, perhaps during a warmer postglacial period.

This species is fairly common in many parts of its range but is generally uncommon or rare in the Great Lakes region. It is considered a threatened species in Michigan, where it is at the northern limit of its distribution.

Habitat and Ecology: Marbled Salamanders are most common in moist lowland forests but also occupy drier wooded ridges and rocky hillsides. They spend most of their time hidden beneath logs, rocks, and leaf litter, or below ground level in tunnels dug by small mammals, and are rarely seen outside of the fall breeding season. This species is quite tolerant of dry conditions but will move into deeper burrows to avoid the summer heat.

Adult Marbled Salamanders eat small invertebrates such as worms, slugs, snails, and various insects and their larvae. Their larvae feed on crustaceans, insects (immature and adult stages), and the eggs and larvae of other amphibians. By breeding in fall, this species gives its larvae a head start on spring-breeding salamanders that often share the same ponds. Thus, Marbled Salamander larvae have usually grown considerably by the time the larvae of other species, such as Spotted Salamanders and Eastern Newts, are just beginning to hatch, and can easily feed on them.

As in other *Ambystoma,* this species has granular ("poison") glands in its skin that are particularly concentrated on the upper surface of the tail. If threatened, a specimen will raise its tail and lash it at the potential enemy. This not only exposes the predator to the noxious skin secretions, but may attract its attention toward a less vital portion of the salamander's body. These defenses have been shown to work against shrews, which are potentially important predators in the forest floor environment.

Reproduction and Growth: Marbled Salamanders breed on land in the fall, unlike other eastern *Ambystoma* that breed in spring. From late September through October the adults migrate at night to the edges of woodland vernal ponds, which typically have receded or dried up during the summer. Here they hide beneath logs, leaves, fallen bark, or leaf litter. Courtship behavior is much like that described for the Spotted Salamander, except that it takes place on land. Marbled Salamanders reportedly will drown if submerged in water.

The males engage in much head butting and nudging of other salamanders, and a male may use his tail to block the retreat of another individual. If a female is encountered, the male tries to thrust his snout under
her vent, stimulating her to nudge the male's vent. This behavior often
results in the courting pair moving in circles and has been likened by
human observers to a waltz. Eventually the male moves forward and
deposits a spermatophore; the female can then move over the spermatophore and take up the sperm packet into her cloaca.

The female lays from 50 to over 200 eggs in a small cavity beneath leaf
mold, moss, fallen bark, a rotted log, or other cover. The location is generally at the edge or bottom of a dry pond bed that will refill with fall or
winter rains. The eggs may adhere together in a loose cluster but are not
surrounded by an enclosing gelatinous mass. They soon pick up soil par-
ticles and blend with their surroundings. The female often curls around
her eggs until the nest is flooded, probably helping to keep them moist
and offering protection from fungal invasion and small predators.

The time from egg laying to hatching is extremely variable, depending
on temperature and water levels, but is minimally about two weeks. The
developing eggs tolerate rather cool temperatures but are destroyed by
freezing. Normally the larvae emerge as the nest is inundated, but if rains
are delayed, they can survive in the egg for several weeks, or even
months. At hatching the larvae range from about 1.4 to 1.9 cm (0.5 to 0.7
in) in length. Larval growth rates depend on water temperatures and food
supply. Metamorphosis usually occurs in late spring or early summer,
when the larvae are from 4.5 to 7.5 cm (1.8 to 3 in) long. Losses of eggs,
larvae, and juvenile salamanders to predators and other hazards (such as
drying and freezing) are often extremely high; survivors can reproduce in
their third or fourth year and potentially live at least nine years.

Conservation: The unique fall breeding habits of Marbled Salamanders
can give them a competitive advantage over spring-breeding amphibians,
as noted above. However, this advantage may be lost over much of the
Great Lakes region, where small woodland ponds typically freeze completely during long, cold winters, leading to high losses of eggs and larvae. This factor may, at least in part, explain the general scarcity and
spotty distribution of the species in the Great Lakes basin. An effort should
be made to protect known Marbled Salamander localities, but it seems
unlikely that populations of this salamander will be able to expand in the

region without a general climatic warming. Scientists studying predictions about "global warming" might well focus some attention on the fate of this species in the Great Lakes basin!

Eastern Tiger Salamander *Ambystoma tigrinum tigrinum*

Description: Eastern Tiger Salamanders are robust animals with irregular yellow, olive brown, or tan blotches and spots on a black, gray, or brown background color. The head is large, with a broad, rounded snout. The eyes are small and often have gold irises. The belly is usually yellowish or olive yellow with invading dark pigment, but in some specimens it may appear gray with yellowish spots or streaks. This is the largest terrestrial salamander of the Great Lakes region. Costal grooves: 12–13. Adult length: 17 to 33 cm (6.7 to 13 in).

Males have proportionally longer, more compressed tails and longer, thicker hind legs than females. During the breeding season the male's vent area is greatly swollen.

Newly hatched larvae are usually yellowish green or olive with darker blotches along the back, a light stripe along each side, and whitish bellies. The older larvae often retain the light stripe on the sides and the light belly, but some develop numerous black dots on the upper surfaces, while others become darker, with light mottling on the tail and fins. All have pointed toes and broad, flattish rounded heads. In some populations a cannibalistic form of the Tiger Salamander larva may appear, possibly in response to crowded conditions. Compared to normal larvae, these individuals have larger heads, more flattened snouts, and longer teeth and feed largely on other salamander larvae, including their own species. In addition, neotenic populations of Tiger Salamanders occur in some places, mostly in the West, but also in the Upper and northern Lower peninsulas of Michigan.

Newly transformed specimens tend to be grayish or greenish brown in color, with a dull mottling of lighter pigment. Within a few weeks a scattering of widely separated yellow or tan spots appears, which gradually merge over time into the blotched pattern of the adult.

Confusing Species: Spotted Salamanders have rounded yellow spots in two irregular rows (not randomly distributed spots, streaks or blotches),

Eastern Tiger Salamander

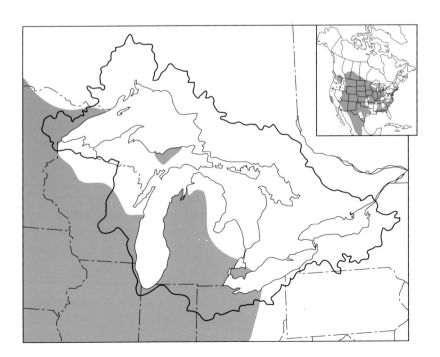

and grayish bellies. The large size of the Tiger Salamander will distinguish it from most other *Ambystoma.*

Distribution and Status: The Eastern Tiger Salamander is found from Long Island south along the coastal plain to the eastern Gulf of Mexico and east Texas, north through the western Ohio Valley and the southern Great Lakes basin and west to Minnesota and the eastern plains states. The species is absent from the Appalachian highlands and the lower Mississippi delta. A disjunct population occurs in Michigan's Upper Peninsula. Other subspecies of *Ambystoma tigrinum* are found from the Great Plains west to British Columbia and south to California and central Mexico. A number of introduced populations have become established outside the natural range of the species, probably due to the use of salamander larvae as fish bait.

This species varies greatly in abundance within its Great Lakes range. Large populations can occur where ideal breeding habitat is available, but elsewhere the species may be uncommon or rare, especially toward the northern periphery of the range.

Habitat and Ecology: Eastern Tiger Salamanders are less dependent on forested habitats than most other *Ambystoma.* They live in woodlands but also in more open habitats such as marshes, grasslands, farmlands, and suburbs. The primary requirement is access to permanent and semipermanent (preferably fishless) ponds for breeding, including farm ponds, gravel pits, floodings, and ornamental backyard ponds.

Adult Tiger Salamanders live underground for most of the year and are quite capable of digging their own burrows, in contrast to related species that usually use the burrows of other animals. They have been found over 60 cm (2 ft) below the surface. This burrowing habit allows them to escape the temperature extremes on the surface and may explain the wide habitat tolerances of the species. There are two major periods of surface activity—the late winter/early spring migration to breeding ponds, and a second, less directional movement in early fall. These nocturnal movements are often stimulated by rainfall and result in these creatures turning up in basements, window wells, garages, and swimming pools. Many are killed while trying to cross roads.

The food of this salamander includes worms, snails, insects, and slugs. Captive specimens will eat smaller salamanders, frogs, newborn mice, and baby snakes, and it is likely that similar items are also eaten in the wild when the opportunity presents itself. Tiger Salamander larvae begin feeding on small crustaceans (e.g., ostracods and copepods) and insect larvae but soon grow large enough to eat tadpoles and smaller salamander larvae, and even small fish.

Tiger Salamander eggs and smaller larvae are consumed by various aquatic insects and their larvae, including dragonfly nymphs, caddisfly larvae, and diving beetles, as well as by newts and larger salamander larvae. Older larvae are readily taken by wading birds, water snakes, and fish; this species may be eliminated from breeding ponds when game fish are introduced. Terrestrial adults and juveniles are eaten by snakes, larger birds, and mammalian predators. Their habit of remaining underground much of the time probably results in a fairly high adult survivorship.

Like other *Ambystoma*, Tiger Salamanders have granular ("poison") glands concentrated on the upper surface of the tail, and they can raise and lash their tails if prodded or otherwise threatened. This may discourage some predators. However, many specimens fail to display any defensive behavior when exposed, except for trying to walk away or wriggle out of a restraining hand.

Reproduction and Growth: Migration to the breeding ponds occurs in late winter or early spring, usually during a (relatively) warm night rain that results in a thawing of the ground surface. Males often arrive several days before the females, with the first to appear probably having overwintered nearer the breeding site. During the nocturnal courtship, a male uses his snout to nudge and butt other salamanders, which are sometimes lifted off the pond bottom in the process. Upon contacting a female, a male may literally shove her along with his snout, apparently to move her away from other males.

Eventually the male will walk under the female's chin, leading her forward, and she may follow, nudging his tail and vent area. This latter behavior stimulates the male to deposit a spermatophore. The female may wriggle the posterior part of her body until her vent contacts the spermatophore, allowing her to take sperm into her cloaca. The pair maintains contact as they move forward, with the female continuing to nudge the male's vent, and the latter producing additional spermatophores. There is much breeding competition in this species. Males will purposefully interfere with courting pairs and frequently cover the spermatophores of other males with their own.

Females lay their eggs at night, normally from 24 to 48 hours after courtship and insemination. The egg masses are attached to twigs, grass stems, or leaf litter, usually near the pond bottom. The masses can be globular or elongate in shape and contain from 1 to over 100 eggs. Larger masses may resemble those of the Spotted Salamander, but the jelly mass of the Tiger Salamander is less firm than the Spotted's and tends to fall apart if lifted from the water. Each female produces from 100 to over 1,000 eggs in a season.

Embryonic development may require from two to six weeks or more, depending on water temperature. Newly hatched larvae are 1.3 to 1.7 cm (0.5 to 0.7 in) long. The time from hatching to metamorphosis is quite variable and depends on the relative quality and permanence of the breeding site. In shallow ponds that dry out early in summer, larvae can transform in less than three months, at a length of about 7 cm (2.8 in). This is exceptional, however, and in more permanent ponds the larvae may not transform until they are four to six months old, at lengths of 8.5 to 15 cm (3.4 to 6 in). Some larvae may overwinter in the water and transform the following year, nearly reaching adult size in the meantime. Larger metamorphs are probably able to breed the spring following transformation. The many hazards of pond life can result in high mortality between egg deposition and metamorphosis, and often only a tiny fraction of eggs laid result in new salamanders entering the breeding population. Adults can potentially live long lives, however, and captives have survived over 20 years.

Conservation: Eastern Tiger Salamanders are generally harmless to human interests. They are efficient predators in their aquatic and subterranean habitats, and their prey undoubtedly includes some insect pests. The larvae are sometimes considered undesirable in fish hatcheries. Large larvae will feed on very small fish, but their main effect might be to act as competitors with the fish. As the fish grow larger they can turn the tables and feed on the salamander larvae. In some places larval *Ambystoma*, mostly *A. tigrinum,* are captured, usually with seine nets, and sold for fish bait.

Thousands of migrating Tiger Salamanders are killed on roads each year. The draining or polluting of ponds and other wetlands and the introduction of game fish into formerly fishless bodies of water are detrimental to this species. On the other hand, the construction of stock ponds and ornamental garden pools can provide new breeding sites, provided they are not stocked with predatory fish.

Lungless Salamanders
Family Plethodontidae

With over 230 species in 27 genera, this is the largest salamander family in the world. There are three centers of abundance for this family, in the eastern (Appalachian) and Pacific coastal regions in North America, and in Central America. Two species occur in southern Europe. It is likely that the ancestral Plethodontids evolved in stream habitats, probably in what is now the eastern United States. All members of this group lack lungs (hence the common family name); they "breathe" through their skins and membranes in the mouth and throat. Air-filled lungs might have been detrimental to aquatic, bottom-crawling animals, and their permeable skins were quite sufficient for oxygen absorption. Some lungless salamanders still live in or near streams and have aquatic gilled larvae, but others are fully adapted for a terrestrial life, laying their eggs on land and skipping the free-swimming larval stage.

Most lungless salamanders are rather small, narrow-bodied animals of moist woodlands. A defining characteristic of the group is a groove in the skin running between each nostril and the upper lip (see fig. 5). Called naso-labial grooves, they are thought to enhance the salamander's sense of smell by funneling odors to the nostrils and to play a part in finding prey and identifying potential mates. In some species the grooves extend downward below the upper lip in projections called cirri; these tend to be larger on males during the breeding season. In very small species or individuals a hand magnifying lens may be needed to see the naso-labial grooves. Many species will drop portions of their tails if attacked or roughly handled; though the tail will regrow, the new portion will usually be shorter and different in color than the original.

Northern Dusky Salamander   *Desmognathus fuscus fuscus*

Description: This relatively stout little salamander has hind legs that are larger than the front legs, and (usually) a light stripe that angles from the eye to the back of the jaw line. The dorsal coloration is highly variable, but many specimens have a broad yellowish gray, tan, or brown stripe running from head to tail, often spotted with darker color and bordered on each side with an irregular dark brown or black stripe. Juvenile specimens have a series of paired light (reddish or yellowish) spots along the

Northern Dusky Salamander

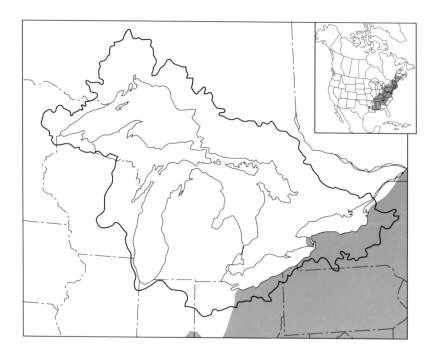

back, while older adults may darken and lose any trace of a dorsal pattern. The belly may be whitish or gray, often mottled with darker gray. The tail is flattened toward the tip and has a narrow ridge (keel) along the upper edge. Costal grooves: 13–15. Adult length: 7 to 14.2 cm (2.8 to 5.6 in).

Males tend to be longer than females, and their heads are broader and more swollen behind the eyes. During the breeding season the male's vent area becomes swollen, and there are tiny fingerlike projections (papillae) at the cloacal opening that are lacking in the female. The male also has a rounded lobe on the tip of the lower jaw (chin) called the mental gland.

The larvae, about 1.6 cm (0.6 in) long at hatching, have well-developed limbs and small, whitish gills. They are grayish or brownish above and usually have paired light spots running down the back and tail that are often separated by a light mid-dorsal stripe. The belly is white or gray.

Confusing Species: The Northern Dusky Salamander is very similar to the Mountain Dusky Salamander, but the Mountain Dusky has a rounded, unkeeled tail, and the stripe down the back (when visible) usually has straighter edges and is often well defined with black side stripes. All other small Great Lakes area salamanders lack the light line from the eye to the back of the jaw and have hind legs about the same size as the front legs.

Distribution and Status: The Northern Dusky Salamander is found from southern New Brunswick and Quebec south through New England to the western Carolinas and west to Ohio, southern Indiana, and Tennessee. In the Great Lakes region, they occur south of Lake Erie and Lake Ontario (including the Niagara River Gorge area in Ontario). A southern subspecies *(D. f. conanti)* extends the species' range to Louisiana and the Gulf coast.

This is a common-to-abundant species in many parts of its range, wherever there is suitable habitat. They are generally less common in formerly glaciated areas with low relief.

Habitat and Ecology: Northern Dusky Salamanders inhabit the edges of rocky streams, hillside springs, and seepage areas, usually in wooded or partly wooded terrain. They spend most of their time hidden beneath flat rocks, logs, and other objects, particularly those that are adjacent to or partially submerged in the water. If disturbed, they may enter the water and hide beneath rocks and other debris. They can remain active all winter in springs or seepages where moving water prevents freezing of the substrate.

These salamanders eat a variety of small invertebrates, including earthworms, slugs, snails, crustaceans, spiders, mites, and various insects. Feeding may take place on land or in water. The larvae eat aquatic crustaceans and insect larvae.

Numerous predators will eat Northern Dusky Salamanders, including raccoons, skunks, shrews, birds, snakes, and larger salamanders such as Northern Spring and Northern Red Salamanders. Dusky Salamanders appear to lack defensive skin secretions but are able to move quickly when disturbed and jump surprisingly well. They have slippery skins and are difficult to grasp, and may even try to bite an attacker. Like many lungless salamanders, this species can lose its tail when physically attacked; the wriggling tail may distract the predator's attention away from the escaping salamander. The tail is later regenerated.

Reproduction and Growth: Courtship and mating occur on land in both spring and fall. A courting male employs a tail-wagging display and nudges and prods the female with his snout, presumably to identify and stimulate his prospective mate. The male may forcefully press his chin (i.e., mental gland) on the female's back while arching the forward part of his body upward, then straighten his back with a sudden snap. Eventually he moves under the female's head until she can straddle his tail, with her chin contacting the base of his tail (which is supplied with secretory glands that presumably facilitate courtship). The pair may move about in this position for some time. The male then produces a spermatophore that the female can pick up with her vent, taking the sperm packet into her cloaca. The spermatophore may occasionally be deposited directly on the female's cloacal opening.

The female deposits her eggs in summer, in one or two compact clusters hidden in a cavity beneath a rock or log or under mats of rotting leaves. The nest site is normally adjacent to a stream or spring. The eggs, which number from 12 to around 40, are attended by the female until hatching, which occurs in about 50 to 80 days. The well-developed larvae may stay with the female for several days before moving to the water and can survive on land for considerable periods if required, as long as they remain moist. Larvae generally spend from 7 to 11 months in the water, usually transforming the following spring or summer at a length of about

2.8 to 4.4 cm (1.1 to 1.7 in). Young males reach maturity in two to three years, while females require three or four years before producing their first eggs.

Conservation: These salamanders are most common in shaded streamside habitats and can be harmed by forestry practices that remove tree cover and thus increase water temperature and decrease humidity. Pollution of streams by agricultural runoff or siltation would also threaten their survival.

Mountain Dusky Salamander *Desmognathus ochrophaeus*

Description: This slender little salamander has hind legs that are larger (stouter) than the front legs, and a slanting light line between each eye and the back of the jaw. Most specimens have a broad, straight-edged light stripe from head to tail tip that varies from yellow or orange to tan, olive, or gray. This stripe is often bordered by darker pigment that fades to mottled gray or brown on the lower sides; there may be a row of dark (sometimes V-shaped) spots within the stripe. The belly is usually an unpatterned brown or gray. Older males may darken and lose the characteristic color pattern. The tail is about half the animal's length and is rounded in cross section. Costal grooves: 13–15. Adult length: 7 to 11.2 cm (2.8 to 4.4 in).

Males differ from females in having a conspicuous mental gland, visible from below as a blunt lobe on the tip of the chin, and a more sinuous ("zig-zag") mouth line when viewed from the side. They also tend to be larger than females. As noted above, old males frequently lose the dorsal stripe and become dark brown or black on the back and tail.

The newly hatched larvae are usually yellowish, with two rows of small light spots on the rear of the back and a light spots on the snout and behind each eye. In older larvae the spotting becomes less conspicuous, and the dark-bordered dorsal stripe characteristic of the adult begins to appear.

Confusing Species: This species is most often confused with the Northern Dusky Salamander, which is a somewhat stouter animal with a tail that is keeled along the upper edge. The edge of the dorsal stripe in the Northern Dusky tends to be more irregular and often lacks a continuous dark bor-

Mountain Dusky Salamander

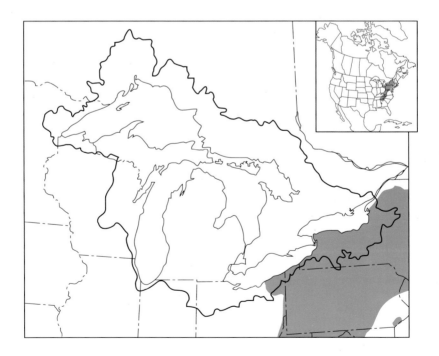

der. Hybridization between these two species is suspected in the area south of Lake Erie, possibly confounding the identification problem.

Northern Two-lined and Red-backed Salamanders may superficially resemble the Mountain Dusky Salamander, but both lack the slanting light line between the eye and back of the jaw, and have hind legs about the same size as the front legs.

Distribution and Status: Mountain Dusky Salamanders range from northern New York south through the Appalachian highlands to eastern Kentucky and Tennessee and northern Georgia. They occur in the eastern Great Lakes area south of Lake Ontario and Lake Erie to the northeastern corner of Ohio. These salamanders can be abundant in suitable habitats.

Habitat and Ecology: This species is usually found under logs, pieces of bark, leaf litter, flat rocks, and other shelter in cool, moist woodlands, usually close to springs, seepage areas, and small streams. They are more terrestrial than the Northern Dusky Salamander, however, and will move up the sides of ravines well away from water. Most activities occur within small, temporary home ranges of perhaps a square meter (10 square feet) or so in size. In winter they seek sites with flowing water, where they may remain active as long as the substrate remains unfrozen.

Mountain Dusky Salamanders are nocturnal foragers, with most feeding reportedly occurring soon after sunset when their invertebrate prey is most active. When food resources are limited, these salamanders may aggressively defend small feeding territories (such as the space beneath a rock or other cover object) against their own and other salamander species. Favored food items include small insects and insect larvae, earthworms, spiders, mites, and millipedes. The larval salamanders presumably eat small aquatic invertebrates.

These salamanders are eaten by small mammals (shrews, raccoons, possums, etc.), birds, snakes, and larger salamanders. They apparently lack defensive skin secretions but are quick moving and slippery, and their strong hind legs allow them to jump from danger (an unexpected maneuver for a salamander). Their tails break off easily, and the twitching of the lost tail may distract a predator, giving the salamander time to escape.

Reproduction and Growth: Mating may occur in both spring and fall. Courtship behavior closely resembles that of the Northern Dusky Salamander and other plethodontids and involves the male nudging and rubbing the female with his snout and chin, followed by the female straddling the male's tail as they move forward. Spermatophore deposition then follows; after the sperm packet is taken into the female's cloaca, sperm can be stored for several months until needed for fertilization of the eggs.

Females deposit from 11 to 16 eggs in a grapelike cluster attached to the underside of a rock, log cavity, or other shelter, usually in a seepage area or near a stream or spring. Most eggs are laid in late winter or spring, but some females lay their eggs in late summer. The females stay with their eggs, usually spending most of the incubation time coiled around the egg mass. The larvae hatch in about 7 to 10 weeks, at a length of 1.4 to 1.8 cm (0.5 to 0.7 in). They possess gills and a low tail fin, but have well-developed legs and soon move to the water. Growth rate is influenced by food availability and water temperature, and transformation to the terrestrial form can occur in as few as 4 months to as many as 10 months after hatching, at an average length of about 1.8 cm (0.7 in). Males become sexually mature by their third year, while females may not reproduce until their fourth year after hatching. This species has lived over 20 years in captivity.

Conservation: This species is dependent on the existence of shady woodlands with cool flowing waters such as small streams and springs. Clearcutting of trees, and thus removing the leaf canopy, can harm this species by raising ground and stream temperatures while lowering humidity.

Northern Slimy Salamander   *Plethodon glutinosus*

Description: This is a medium-sized black or blue-black salamander with a variable number of scattered white spots or flecks on the back, sides, legs, and tail. The head is widest behind the eyes, and the snout in front of the eyes is broadly rounded and quite short. The tail is round in cross section and makes up a half or more of the salamander's total length. The belly, throat, and underside of the tail are blackish or gray, usually slightly lighter than the back. True to their name, Slimy Salamanders secrete a whitish sticky slime from their skin glands when handled. This material adheres like glue and is hard to remove from the hands once it dries. Costal grooves: 15–17. Adult length: 10.5 to 20.6 cm (4.1 to 8.1 in).

Northern Slimy Salamander

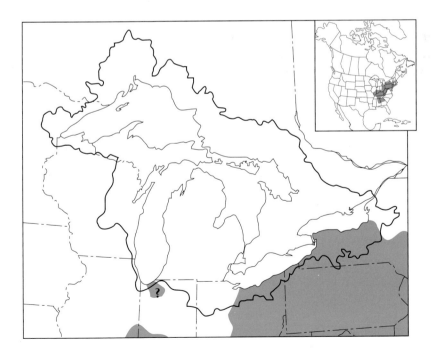

Males average slightly longer than females and have a conspicuous mental gland that looks like a circular swelling on the animal's chin.

There is no free-swimming larval stage. The young are colored like the adults but have proportionally shorter tails.

Confusing Species: The Blue-spotted, Jefferson, and other "mole" salamanders do not have a groove between the nostril and mouth (naso-labial groove). The Ravine Salamander and dark phase of the Red-backed Salamander are smaller and thinner, with more costal grooves, and their light markings are diffuse and less distinct.

Distribution and Status: The Northern Slimy Salamander ranges from southern New Hampshire and central New York west to southern Illinois and south to northern Georgia and Alabama. In the Great Lakes region it is found south of Lakes Ontario and Erie; an old (1948) record exists for the Indiana Dunes State Park, but there are apparently no recent sightings in that area. This salamander is one of a complex of species that are closely related and in some cases almost indistinguishable except by laboratory analysis of their genetic material or knowledge of geographical origin. These relatives extend the range of the "slimy salamander complex" south through the Atlantic coastal plain to central Florida and west to Missouri, Oklahoma, and Texas.

This species can be common in suitable habitat.

Habitat and Ecology: Moist forested hillsides and ravines are preferred habitat for Slimy Salamanders. They appear to avoid bottomland forests prone to flooding. Most specimens are found in rotting logs or stumps, or beneath rocks, bark, and leaf litter. They often forage on the surface on warm, rainy nights. In dry or cold weather they may descend deep underground, probably by following animal burrows, root systems, or crevices in rock outcrops.

These salamanders eat small invertebrates such as insects (ants, beetles, termites, etc.) and insect larvae, centipedes, millipedes, pill bugs, spiders, slugs, snails, and earthworms. The diet of any particular salamander is probably influenced largely by which prey species are most available.

The slimy skin secretions provide a defense against many potential predators. While the secretions reportedly are irritating if rubbed in the eyes, their adhesive properties may be the most effective predator deterrent. A snake attempting to grab a Slimy Salamander can find its mouth "gummed up" by these secretions and may forget the intended meal as it tries to wipe off the slime.

Reproduction and Growth: Mating occurs mostly in fall. During courtship, the male nudges and rubs the female with his snout and mental gland. Eventually he will move beneath the female's head while undulating his tail. The female then presses her chin on the base of his tail, and the two move forward with the female straddling the male's tail. At some point the male stops, moves his tail to one side, and deposits a spermatophore. They then move forward until the female can take the sperm packet into her cloaca.

Females appear to reproduce every other year in northern populations. From 10 to 38 eggs are laid in late spring or summer, in an underground burrow or in a cavity under a rock or within a rotting log. The eggs, which are suspended in a loose cluster from the side or upper surface of the nest cavity, are attended by the female. Hatching occurs in late summer or fall. The young, which range in length from about 2 to 3 cm (0.8 to 1.2 in), may have gills upon emergence from the egg, but these are absorbed in a few days. They can breed when 4 or 5 years old and may potentially live for 20 years or more.

Conservation: Northern Slimy Salamanders require moist wooded habitats with ample shelter in the form of rotting logs or rock outcrops. Forestry practices that remove the leaf canopy or eliminate natural ground debris could harm populations of this species.

Red-backed Salamander *Plethodon cinereus*

Description: These are small, thin-bodied salamanders with tiny legs and rounded tails. There are two common color phases. The "redback" phase has a red, orange-red, or brownish red stripe from the back of the head to the middle of the tail; this stripe is bordered on the sides by dark gray or black. The "leadback" phase lacks the red stripe and is entirely dark on the back and sides, sometimes with a faint speckling of lighter color. Some individuals appear to be intermediate between these two phases. In both the belly is mottled with gray and white in what is often described as a "salt and pepper" pattern. A rare erythristic color morph is almost

Red-backed Salamander. (Photo by R. W. Van Devender.)

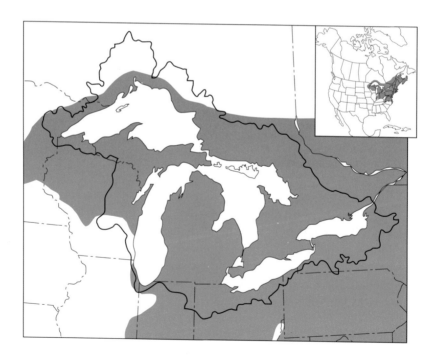

entirely reddish or reddish orange above, with black spots on the distal part of the tail and a light belly. (The relative distribution of these color phases is discussed under "Distribution and Status" below.) Costal grooves: 17–22 (usually 18 or 19). Adult length: 5.8 to 12.7 cm (2.3 to 5 in).

The male Red-backed Salamander is, on average, slightly smaller than the female and has a rounded mental gland under the chin, and a snout that looks slightly swollen around the naso-labial grooves. The cloacal area is often lighter in color in males than in females.

There is no aquatic larval stage; the young lose any remnant gill buds within a few days of hatching and are colored like the adults.

Confusing Species: All "mole" salamanders (*Ambystoma*) are heavier bodied than Red-backed Salamanders and lack naso-labial grooves. Among other plethodontids, the Ravine Salamander is similar to a "leadback" but has a more uniformly dark gray belly. The Northern Two-lined Salamander has a yellowish back stripe bordered by black side stripes and a yellow belly. The Four-toed Salamander has a white belly with bold black spots, a constriction at the base of the tail, and only four toes (instead of five) on the hind foot.

Distribution and Status: The Red-backed Salamander ranges from southern Quebec south to North Carolina, and north through Ohio and Indiana to Minnesota and the Lake Superior basin. They are generally more abundant north of the Wisconsinan glacial boundary and are the most common woodland salamander over most of the Great Lakes region.

The proportion of the two primary color phases in Great Lakes populations of the Red-backed Salamander is highly variable. Both phases occur together over most of the area. In general, the striped "redback" phase tends to be proportionally more common at higher altitudes and latitudes, while the unstriped "leadbacks" become more abundant in lowland habitats in the southern part of the basin. The "redback" phase does seem to constitute an increasingly higher proportion of the population as one goes from south to north in the Great Lakes region, with the "leadback" being uncommon or absent in Wisconsin and Minnesota.

The erythristic "red" phase of this salamander is rare or absent over most of the species' range but may make up from 15 percent to 25 percent of the population in northeastern Ohio (Lake Erie drainage), western New England, and southeastern New Brunswick.

Habitat and Ecology: Red-backed Salamanders occur in deciduous, coniferous, and mixed woodlands. Areas prone to frequent flooding or with dry, sandy soils are avoided, but otherwise a wide range of forest conditions are tolerated. They are most often encountered under logs, fallen bark, leaf litter, and rocks. Primarily nocturnal, they frequently forage on the surface on rainy nights and may even climb into shrubs and up tree trunks—a surprising feat considering their tiny, weak-looking legs. These salamanders prefer a humid environment, and retreat below the surface in hot, dry weather as well as in winter, following root systems, animal tunnels, and natural crevices. Numbers of overwintering individuals may congregate in preferred sites and can remain active and even feed if temperatures are suitable. Many may die during cold winters when snow cover is insufficient to insulate the ground and frost penetration is deep.

Individual Red-backed Salamanders tend to occupy fairly restricted temporary home ranges and may defend a territory against their own and other salamander species, using threat displays and a biting attack. Territories are marked with cloacal and mental gland secretions and fecal pellets. Territorial defense probably occurs most often when food resources are scarce, since at times numbers of individuals can be found sharing the same log or other cover.

This species will eat a variety of small invertebrate animals, including insects and their larvae (e.g., ants, beetles, springtails), spiders, mites, pill bugs, centipedes, snails, slugs, and earthworms. They are in turn eaten by various mammals, birds, snakes, and larger salamanders.

Red-backed Salamanders have several defenses against predators. When first uncovered they often remain still, but if touched they can use a combined "swimming-running" motion to move rapidly into the leaf litter. They are also able to jump, using the tail for propulsion. If seized by a predator, they writhe violently and can detach a portion of their tail, which continues to wriggle; this movement may distract the predator's attention long enough to allow the salamander to escape. A new tail is later regrown. This species has sticky skin secretions that may be distasteful or annoying to some mammalian predators such as shrews, though many birds and snakes appear to be undeterred. Some birds, such as robins and blue jays, reportedly avoid eating the erythristic (red) phase of the Red-backed Salamander, and it has been suggested that this morph is a mimic of the red eft (terrestrial form of the Eastern Newt), a species with toxic skin secretions.

Reproduction and Growth: Male Red-backed Salamanders seek females in the fall (October through December), but mating activity can continue through the winter to early spring in some places. Courtship is similar to other *Plethodon,* with the male rubbing his head and chin (with its mental gland secretions) on the female's snout. It is also thought that mating secretions may also be introduced directly into the female's bloodstream when the male scratches her skin with his teeth. Eventually the pair walk forward with the female straddling the male's tail, and with her head pressed against the base of the tail. Deposition of a spermatophore by the male and retrieval of the sperm packet by the female occur soon after.

Females probably breed only every other year, perhaps due to the great amount of energy required to produce and yolk the eggs. The nest may be underground or within a cavity in a rotting log or stump. From 3 to 17 eggs are laid in early summer, in a grapelike cluster that is usually suspended from the top of the cavity by a gelatinous stalk, though sometimes it simply rests on the cavity floor. The female stays with her eggs, probably using skin secretions to keep them moist and free of mold. She also aggressively defends her eggs against invertebrate predators and even larger foes such as other salamanders.

The young salamanders hatch in one to two months at a length of about 2 cm (0.8 in). They often remain with their mother for several days or weeks, at least until their remnant gill buds are absorbed. They may grow to maturity in two years, with females probably producing their first eggs at the beginning of their third year. Natural longevity is unknown, but adults in captivity have lived over five years.

Conservation: The Red-backed Salamander may be the most abundant vertebrate in many eastern North American woodlands. Population densities of about 500 to 9,000 salamanders per hectare (200 to 3,600 per acre) have been estimated for sites in Michigan, with variation between sites probably related to soil moisture and habitat structure. Estimates for sites in other states tend to fall between these extremes. Many studies have looked only at salamanders on the surface, though a portion of the population will be below ground during much of the year. Thus many published population studies may have underestimated the numbers of salamanders. In a study in a New Hampshire forest, salamanders (of which the Red-backed constituted 93.5 percent) outnumbered the birds and mammals combined, and their biomass (living weight) was more than 2.5 times the biomass of all breeding birds and equaled the biomass of small mammals in the woodland. (For further discussion and citations, see Burton and Likens 1975.)

This species plays an important ecological role in Great Lakes area forests. They "process and recycle" vast numbers of invertebrate prey and contribute to the food supply of numerous predators. It follows that the loss of these salamanders could have significant consequences for the forest environment. Red-backed Salamanders are a tolerant species that can persist in human-modified woodlands, as long as critical habitat components (e.g., fallen logs, leaf litter, humid underground retreats) are conserved. It is important to consider the welfare of this and related species in any forest management plan.

Ravine Salamander *Plethodon richmondi*

Description: The Ravine Salamander, like its relative the Red-backed Salamander, is often described as a "worm with legs." These are elongate, thin-bodied creatures with tiny legs. The upper parts are dark brown, gray, or black, with scattered whitish or bronzy speckles. The belly is dark gray, finely flecked with lighter gray; the chin may be more mottled and paler than the belly. Costal grooves: 19–22 (usually 20 or 21). Adult length: 7.5 to 14.4 cm (3 to 5.6 in).

Males are slightly smaller than females on average and have a conspicuous mental gland on the chin. As in other *Plethodon,* there is no aquatic larva in this species; larval development is completed within the egg, and hatchlings resemble their parents.

Confusing Species: The naso-labial grooves and elongate body shape will distinguish this salamander from small *Ambystoma* species. The Ravine Salamander is very similar to the unstriped "leadback" phase of the Red-backed Salamander. However, the Ravine usually has a more uniformly dark gray belly, while the Red-backed has a lighter, more mottled ("salt and pepper") belly.

Distribution and Status: This species occurs from western Pennsylvania and West Virginia west through central Ohio to southeastern Indiana, south to eastern Kentucky and extreme western Virginia and northwestern North Carolina. It enters the Great Lakes (southern Lake Erie) basin in north-central Ohio, particularly in Erie, Huron, and Lorain Counties.

Ravine Salamander

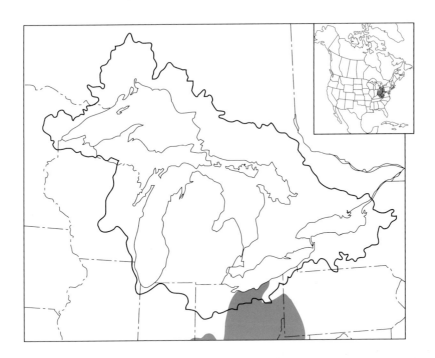

Ravine Salamanders can be common in proper habitat but rarely attain the population densities seen in the closely related Red-backed Salamander.

Habitat and Ecology: This salamander's common name comes from its preference for inhabiting the slopes of woodland ravines and valleys. It is usually found hiding beneath flat rocks rather than logs or bark. In the heat of summer they move well below the surface, sometimes to depths of over a meter (3.3 ft).

The diet of the Ravine Salamander consists of small insects, especially ants and beetles, as well as pill bugs, earthworms, spiders, and snails. Their enemies and defenses are probably similar to those described for the Red-backed Salamander.

Reproduction and Growth: Information on the reproductive habits of this species is limited, but its breeding cycle appears to be similar to that of the Red-backed Salamander, with courtship and mating occurring from fall through early spring. The females, which probably breed biennially, lay clutches of about 4 to 12 eggs in late spring or early summer, under rocks or in underground cavities. New hatchlings have been found in late August. They may grow to maturity in about two years.

Conservation: Ravine Salamanders seem to be somewhat more specialized than other Great Lakes area *Plethodon,* with a decided preference for rocky, wooded habitats with fairly steep gradients. Within these habitats they are undoubtedly important members of the woodland floor community.

Four-toed Salamander *Hemidactylium scutatum*

Description: This is a very small, slender reddish brown or grayish brown salamander with only four toes on each hind foot. The long tail is constricted (narrows) where it joins the body. The sides are often grayish, speckled with black and light bluish flecks (particularly in males). The belly is white or bluish white, with small black spots. Costal grooves: 13–14. Adult size: 5 to 10.2 cm (2 to 4 in).

Male Four-toed Salamanders are smaller, on average, than females and have relatively longer tails. When viewed from above, the male's snout is

Four-toed Salamander

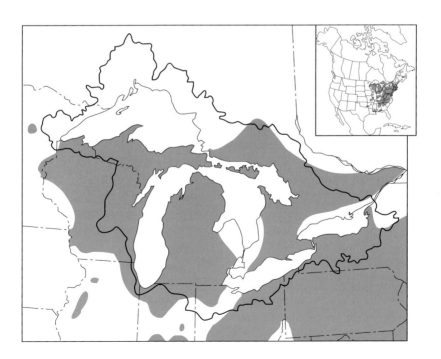

somewhat squared off (due to the swollen area around the naso-labial grooves); the female's snout looks more rounded. In addition, the male has an overhanging upper lip and an enlarged mental gland on the chin (the latter most prominent during the breeding season).

Soon after hatching, the aquatic larva is tinged with yellow, orange, and green on the head, and numerous black spots often merge to form a Y-shaped mark on the back of the head and a dark band behind each eye. (This dark eye band is often prominent in older larvae and newly trans-formed individuals as well.) The upper tail fin extends well up the back, nearly to the head. Hatchlings usually have all four legs, though the toes may not be fully developed.

Confusing Species: The combination of four-toed hind feet, pure white belly with black spots, and tail constriction will quickly separate this species from the several other small salamander species that might be in the same habitats.

Distribution and Status: Four-toed Salamanders are found from southern Maine west through New York and southeastern Ontario to Minnesota and south to northern Georgia and Alabama. A number of scattered, iso-lated populations occur from northern Illinois south to Louisiana and northern Florida and in Nova Scotia. It is likely that the species once had a more continuous range, but dramatic climatic fluctuations, particularly over the last two million years, may have led to range contraction and fragmentation.

This salamander is generally uncommon, and populations tend to be quite localized. It is considered a rare or threatened species in some states.

Habitat and Ecology: Adult Four-toed Salamanders inhabit moist decidu-ous, coniferous, or mixed woodlands, usually in the vicinity of spring-fed creeks, sphagnum seepages, bogs, or boggy ponds. Males and nonbreed-ing females are sometimes found with other salamander species under logs and other forest debris. In winter they hibernate in rotting logs, beneath leaf litter, or below ground in burrows or decaying root systems, and numbers may congregate in a suitable site.

The food of this salamander consists of small arthropods and other invertebrates, including various insects and their larvae (e.g., beetles, ants, springtails, flies), spiders, snails, and earthworms.

When disturbed by a potential predator, a Four-toed Salamander will often curl its body and tuck its head under its tail. The tail may be raised, exposing the bright white underside, perhaps to attract the predator's attention away from the head and body. If threatened, the salamander can voluntarily detach its tail, which separates readily at the constriction near its base. The lost tail continues to twitch, perhaps distracting the predator long enough to allow the salamander to escape. A new tail begins to regenerate soon after.

Reproduction and Growth: Courtship and mating reportedly take place in late summer and fall in this species. Mating behavior is reportedly very similar to that of the Red-backed Salamander and other plethodontids, with the male rubbing his snout, chin (mental gland), and sides on the female's snout, followed by a "tail-straddling walk" with the female pressing her chin on the base of the male's tail prior to spermatophore deposition.

Females migrate to breeding sites from late March through June, seeking woodland ponds, springs, or creeks where mosses, rotting logs, leaf litter, or clumps of grass or sedges are hanging over or at least adjacent to the water's edge. Sphagnum moss over shallow, permanent or semipermanent water appears to be a favored nest site when available. Within a small cavity the female turns upside down and deposits 15 to 64 eggs, which adhere to each other and the surrounding material. She may remain in her nest through much of the incubation period, eating spoiled eggs and perhaps using her skin secretions to retard fungus growth and predation. Attended eggs have been found to have a greater chance of hatching than those that are left unguarded. Frequently two or more females will lay their eggs in a communal nest, but only one female at a time will attend the eggs.

In one to two months the larvae hatch and wriggle or drop into the water. About 1.1 to 1.4 cm (0.4 to 0.6 in) long at hatching, the larvae metamorphose into the terrestrial form in three to eight weeks, at a length of 1.6 to 2.4 cm (0.6 to 1 in). They reach sexual maturity in their third year. The potential longevity of this species in unknown, but a captive specimen lived for nearly nine years.

Conservation: The spotty distribution of the Four-toed Salamander within the Great Lakes region and elsewhere is undoubtedly related to the scarcity of suitable breeding habitat. Populations are often restricted to

Nest of Four-toed Salamanders in moss

isolated colonies and opportunities for dispersal into new habitats may be limited or nonexistent. Such species are much more vulnerable to the effects of human activities than are those with wider habitat tolerances. Identifying and preserving known habitats of this salamander will have the added advantage of simultaneously preserving other rare and specialized species of animals and plants.

Northern Spring Salamander   *Gyrinophilus porphyriticus porphyriticus*

Description: This is a large and fairly robust salamander with a vertically flattened and keeled tail. The dorsal coloration varies from pinkish or

Northern Spring Salamander

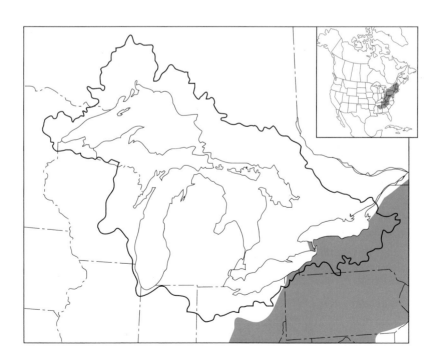

salmon to yellowish brown, mottled or clouded with darker pigment on the back. Young specimens are more brightly colored but tend to darken as they age. The lower sides and belly may be plain pinkish or yellowish, but scattered dark spots often appear on the belly, throat, and lower jaws of older adults. On the snout, a light line (often bordered with gray or black) runs between each eye and nostril, then down the naso-labial groove to the lip. Costal grooves: 17–19. Adult length: 12 to 23.2 cm (4.7 to 9.1 in).

Male and female Northern Spring Salamanders are very similar in external appearance. From fall through early spring, adult females may have yellowish white eggs visible through the belly skin. Adult males have glandular papillae on the inner surface of the cloaca, while the cloacal wall of the female is smooth.

Larval Spring Salamanders are yellow to yellowish white in color with a brownish, netlike mottling on the upper surfaces of the head and back. The tail may also be mottled, and the gills are reddish. The head is rather elongated and the eyes are small.

Confusing Species: All "mole" salamanders *(Ambystoma)* lack a naso-labial groove between nostril and lip. The eft stage of the Red-spotted Newt may be reddish, but efts have dull, nonslimy skins and lack costal grooves. Northern Red Salamanders have more rounded heads and do not have a light line between eye and nostril.

Distribution and Status: Northern Spring Salamanders range from southern Maine and Quebec west to Ohio and south to northern Georgia and Alabama. Within the Great Lakes basin they occur in Pennsylvania and New York in the region south of Lake Ontario and along the eastern shore of Lake Erie. There is an old record (1877) in the Niagara area of Ontario, but no recent records exist for the province.

This species can be common in suitable habitat but is generally uncommon and local in the Great Lakes drainage basin. This is probably due to the scarcity of habitats in formerly glaciated areas with low relief; in Ohio the species is largely absent from formerly glaciated terrain but is fairly common south of the glacial boundary on the Allegheny Plateau.

Habitat and Ecology: Spring Salamanders live in or near cool, well-oxygenated streams and springs, usually in wooded terrain or in caves. The adults can be found in the water or on land, in small stream bank cavities or beneath rocks or logs, though they may forage in the open on rainy nights. They sometimes move considerable distances away from breeding habitats by following underground springs. In winter these salamanders may remain beneath rocks and other debris in the streambed, or in seepage areas or burrows in unfrozen, saturated soil near the water's edge. Since their habitat rarely if ever freezes, they may feed actively all winter.

Feeding occurs both on land and in water. Insects, crustaceans, spiders, snails, worms, and various other terrestrial and aquatic invertebrates are included in the Spring Salamander's diet. In addition, they frequently eat other salamanders and their larvae, including Two-lined and Dusky Salamanders and smaller individuals of their own species.

These salamanders are undoubtedly eaten by a number of predators, but they are agile and have very slippery skins, making them difficult to grasp. When attacked, they will often coil their bodies and lash their tails. This species appears to have slightly noxious skin secretions but may gain additional protection from a resemblance (particularly when young) to the more toxic red eft stage of the Eastern Newt and the moderately toxic Northern Red Salamander.

Reproduction and Growth: Mating probably occurs from fall through spring. Courtship is similar to other plethodontid salamanders, with the male rubbing his head on the female's body, and a "tail-straddling" walk prior to spermatophore deposition. Females lay their eggs in summer (June–August) beneath stones or flat rocks in cool, flowing water. A female will turn upside down and attach from 16 to 160 eggs to the underside of the rock, with larger females laying larger clutches. Each egg, along with its gelatinous coverings, has a diameter of about 0.9 cm (0.4 in).

The eggs hatch in late summer or fall, into larvae that range from 1.8 to 2.6 cm (0.7 to 1.0 in) in length. The aquatic larval stage may last for three or four years. They metamorphose at a total length of about 8 to 12 cm (3.1 to 4.7 in), and become sexually mature a year or two later. A captive specimen lived over 18 years, but the potential longevity in the wild is unknown.

Conservation: Northern Spring Salamanders require clear, cool waters free of predatory fish. Their relatively large size compared to other lungless salamanders (with less oxygen-absorbing surfaces compared to body mass) suggests that they would be very sensitive to changes in dissolved oxygen levels. Forestry practices or other human activities that resulted in stream warming or siltation could adversely affect this species. In addition, being larger and feeding on other salamanders would place the Spring Salamander at a higher trophic level (i.e., higher on the "food chain") than many related species. Thus, they might be expected to be less abundant, to reproduce more slowly, and perhaps be more sensitive to environmental stresses than their smaller relatives.

Northern Red Salamander   *Pseudotriton ruber ruber*

Description: Red Salamanders, particularly when young, are among our most brightly colored amphibians. The head, back, and tail are coral red to reddish orange, grading to light salmon red on the lower sides and belly. Small black spots and dashes overlay the ground color from the nose to at least the first half of the tail; the lower jaw usually has some dark spotting, which may continue onto the belly. In older adults, the dark dorsal spots begin to spread and fuse, and the ground color darkens to dull orangish brown or purplish brown. The iris of the eye is yellow. This is a rather stout-bodied salamander with short, thick legs, and a short, rounded snout. The base of the tail is rounded in cross section, but the last third of the tail is vertically flattened. Costal grooves: 16–17. Adult length: 10 to 18.1 cm (3.9 to 7.4 in).

Male Northern Red Salamanders are slightly smaller, on average, than females, but the sexes are very similar in appearance. In gravid females, the yellowish yolks of the eggs may be visible through the belly skin.

Typical larvae are purplish brown on the upper surfaces grading to a lighter, yellowish color on the belly. The back, sides, and tail have evenly scattered black dots. Older larvae approaching metamorphosis often take on the brighter red or orange color that is normal for newly transformed juveniles. Compared to the larvae of the Northern Spring Salamander, larval Red Salamanders have more uniform and distinct dark spotting, shorter, more rounded snouts, and larger eyes.

Confusing Species: Young Red Salamanders are quite distinctive, but older adults can be confused with the Northern Spring Salamander. The latter species usually has a light line, bordered by black or gray, between eye and nostril and a longer, less rounded snout.

Northern Red Salamander

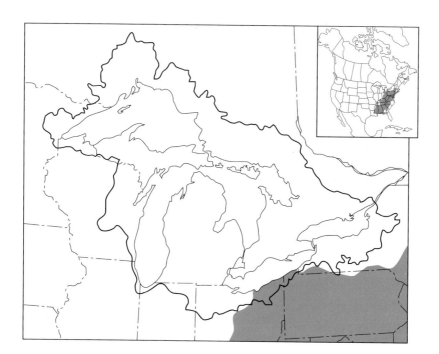

Distribution and Status: The range of the Northern Red Salamander extends from southern New York south through the western Carolinas and west to central Ohio and southern Indiana, then south to Alabama and northern Georgia. Other subspecies extend the species' range to Mississippi and the Florida panhandle. This salamander enters the Great Lakes region primarily in northeastern Ohio, where they are locally common at specific sites with suitable habitat.

Habitat and Ecology: Northern Red Salamanders live in or near cold, clear springs and small streams, usually in deciduous or mixed forest, but sometimes in open meadows and on hillsides. The adults are mostly aquatic in fall and winter, becoming more terrestrial in spring and summer. Largely nocturnal, they may move and forage on the surface on damp or rainy nights but otherwise remain hidden in burrows or beneath rocks, logs, or other shelter, sometimes in the company of other salamander species. In winter they appear to move into the deeper springs where temperatures can remain quite constant.

Adult Red Salamanders eat insects, worms, snails, slugs, centipedes, and various other invertebrates, as well as smaller salamanders. The larvae feed on crustaceans and aquatic insect larvae, and probably other salamander larvae.

Defensive behaviors in this species include curling the body, hiding the head beneath an upraised or undulating tail, and slapping the tail at the disturbing object. These maneuvers present the potential enemy with whitish skin secretions that are noxious and repellent. This salamander's bright reddish skin color may advertise their distastefulness to predators, as is true for the red eft stage of the Eastern Newt.

Reproduction and Growth: Pairing and spermatophore transfer probably can occur from late spring through fall. Courtship behavior (as observed in the laboratory) is similar to other plethodontids, with the male rubbing his snout on the female's head and chin, then moving beneath her chin. The female places her chin on the base of the male's undulating tail, and the two move forward. After arching his tail to one side, the male deposits a spermatophore and attempts to lead the female over it.

This species is unusual in that egg laying occurs in late fall and early winter. Females attach from 50 to 80 eggs to the underside of rocks in cold springs and streams. The incubation period lasts a minimum of 8 to 10 weeks, and newly hatched larvae are 1.3 to 2.3 cm (0.5 to 0.9 in) long.

They may spend between three and four years as aquatic larvae before transforming into terrestrial juveniles at lengths of 8 to 10 cm (3.1 to 3.9 in). They mature within the year following metamorphosis and potentially can live for 20 years or more.

Conservation: Northern Red Salamanders require clear, cold springs or spring-fed streams free of predatory fish, surrounded by terrestrial cover in the form of rocks, logs, or leaf litter. Comments on conservation of the related Northern Spring Salamander may be equally pertinent to this species.

Northern Two-lined Salamander   *Eurycea bislineata*

Description: This is a very small, slender salamander with tiny legs and a vertically compressed tail. There is a broad yellow, greenish yellow, or tan stripe running from head to tail, bordered on each side by a narrow black stripe that may break up into dashes toward the end of the tail. The light dorsal stripe often has a medial row of dark spots or flecks. The sides may be yellowish or mottled with dark pigment, and the belly is yellow. Costal grooves: 15–16. Adult length: 6.4 to 12.1 cm (2.5 to 4.8 in).

Males have a prominent mental gland on the chin, whitish glands on the lower eyelid, and cirri (downward projections of the naso-labial grooves), particularly during the breeding season (October–May). In spring, the eggs of gravid females may be visible through the belly skin.

Young larvae typically have a yellowish ground color with grayish or brownish spots and flecks on the head and back, and an irregular dark stripe down each upper side. Each of these stripes usually encloses a series of six to nine light spots. The short gills are light reddish brown (larvae of Dusky Salamanders usually have whitish gills). Older larvae often retain the hatchling color pattern but may develop a second row of light spots on each side.

Confusing Species: Both species of Dusky Salamanders have hind legs that are considerably larger than the front legs and a light line from the eye to the back of the mouth. Long-tailed Salamanders have vertical dark markings along the sides of the tail and 13 to 14 costal grooves. The Red-backed Salamander has a mottled "salt and pepper" belly and 17 to 22 costal grooves.

Northern Two-lined Salamander

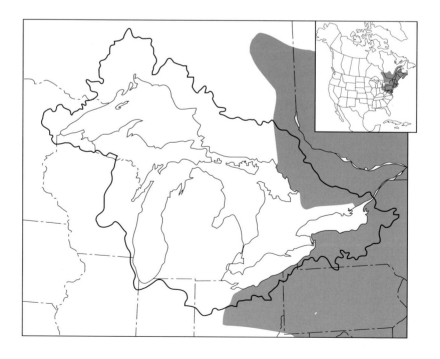

Distribution and Status: The Northern Two-lined Salamander is found from southern Quebec and New Brunswick south through New England to northern Virginia and west to northeastern Ohio. In the Great Lakes basin this salamander occurs in Ohio, Pennsylvania, and New York (south and east of Lake Erie and Lake Ontario) and in Ontario east of Georgian Bay. The Southern Two-lined Salamander, *Eurycea cirrigera,* until recently considered a subspecies of *E. bislineata,* occurs in eastern Illinois and central Indiana and south to Louisiana and west to coastal Georgia and the Carolinas. This species usually has only 14 costal grooves but is defined largely on the basis of genetic differences rather than external characters. Future research may better define the taxonomic relationships of Two-lined Salamander populations. A problematical record of the Two-lined Salamander from Berrien County, Michigan, has been rejected by recent authors, but an isolated population of Two-lined Salamanders (presumably *E. cirrigera*) is known from the Kankakee River drainage in northeastern Illinois.

This is one of the most common streamside salamanders throughout much of its range.

Habitat and Ecology: Two-lined Salamanders live in the vicinity of flowing water where there is sufficient cover in the form of rocks, logs, or mats of fallen leaves, both in woodlands and in more open habitats. Most often discovered by turning rocks along stream banks, they may also occur several meters from the nearest water. They often forage on the surface on rainy nights. In winter these salamanders may burrow deep under leaf litter, or remain active in saturated soil, seepage areas, or in springs and streams, where the temperatures remain above freezing.

Adults feed on small invertebrates, including insects (beetles, mayflies, springtails, etc.), spiders, pill bugs, centipedes, earthworms, and snails. The larvae eat aquatic insects such as the larvae of caddisflies, stoneflies, midges, mosquitoes, and beetles, as well as copepods and other crustaceans.

These little salamanders have numerous predators, including various birds, mammals, and snakes, as well as larger salamanders such as Northern Spring, Red, and Dusky Salamanders. However, Two-lined Salamanders are active animals that often escape using rapid undulations of the body and tail, and can jump by curving and then suddenly straightening their bodies. Like many related species, they can also drop a part of their tail when seized; the separated tail continues to wriggle, perhaps distracting the predator while the salamander escapes.

Reproduction and Growth: Courtship and spermatophore transfer take place from fall through early spring. Courtship behavior is reportedly very similar to that of the Red-backed Salamander and most other small plethodontids. A male will poke and nudge a prospective mate and often curls the front of his body around the female's head. It is thought that by scratching the female's skin with his teeth, stimulating secretions from his mental gland may enter her bloodstream. Eventually the two move forward together in a "tail-straddling" walk, with the female's chin pressed against the glandular area at the base of the male's tail. Spermatophore deposition soon follows.

Females lay their eggs in spring or summer, most often in April or May. By turning upside down, a female attaches from 15 to over 100 eggs to the underside of a rock beneath the flowing water of a spring or stream. She usually attends her nest for at least a portion of the incubation period. Two or more females may lay their eggs at the same site, but normally only one female is in attendance.

The larvae hatch out in about 30 to 60 days, at a length of 1.2 to 1.4 cm (0.5 to 0.6 in). They usually spend two (occasionally three) years as aquatic larvae before transforming into semiterrestrial juveniles. Sexual maturity may be attained the first fall after metamorphosis, or sometimes a year later.

Conservation: Two-lined Salamanders seem to tolerate a wider range of habitat situations than related streamside species. They reportedly suffer significant predation losses during their terrestrial movements, and presumably have a fairly high annual population turnover. Along with other small salamanders, Two-lined Salamanders are often collected by people for use as fish bait. Such exploitation, if sustained, could significantly reduce or eliminate an affected local population, particularly if collection methods disrupt the habitat.

Frogs and Toads
(Order Anura)

Frogs and toads, collectively called anurans, are short-bodied, tailless amphibians with enlarged hind limbs adapted for jumping or swimming. With over 3,500 anuran species in about 300 genera worldwide, this order must be considered one of the most successful vertebrate groups. In general, warty-skinned, short-legged, hopping anurans are called toads, while smoother-skinned, long-legged, leaping anurans are called frogs, although there are no widely accepted definitions for these terms. Two Great Lakes anurans are commonly called toads, both members of the family Bufonidae or "true toads." Important identifying characters of the order are shown in figure 6.

The reproductive habits of Great Lakes anurans follow a pattern typical for most north-temperate species. Males move to aquatic breeding sites in spring and use species-specific calls (the "advertisement" call) to attract females and (in some species) to warn other males away from their territories. Either the male or female may play the larger role in choosing a mate, depending on species. Using his front feet, the male clasps the female from above in an embrace called amplexus. In this position the male fertilizes the eggs externally as they are deposited by the female. Depending on species, the eggs may be laid singly, in submerged loose or globular masses, spreading surface masses, or (in toads) in long strings.

The aquatic larva, commonly called a tadpole or polliwog, has a short, oval body and a long compressed tail with an upper (dorsal) and lower (ventral) fin. The gills of new hatchlings are external but soon are enclosed by the opercular fold. During respiration, water taken in through the mouth passes over the gills and exits through an opening, called the spiracle, on the left side of the body. Tadpoles feed largely by filtering minute plants (algae), bacteria, and other organic material from the water or bottom debris. Their beaklike mouths, rimmed with keratinous denticles (toothlike structures), are used for scraping attached algae from rocks, plants, and substrate. A few species are at least partly carnivorous and may eat the eggs and larvae of other amphibians or even their own siblings.

113

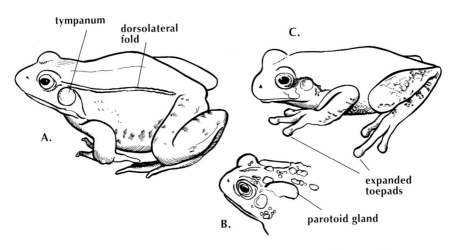

Fig. 6. Anuran characteristics. *A,* typical frog (*Rana*); *B,* toad (*Bufo*); *C,* treefrog (*Hyla*)

During metamorphosis, the hind legs become visible near the vent, while the front legs develop within the opercular (gill) chamber and are not visible until just before transformation. Numerous other internal and external changes must occur before the fishlike herbivorous larva becomes a semiterrestrial carnivorous tetrapod, including drastic modifications of the mouth parts and digestive tract.

Many anurans from subtropical and tropical regions display unique reproductive strategies that differ significantly from the "typical" life cycle summarized above. As with salamanders, there are some species that have direct development (i.e., lack a free-swimming larva and hatch directly into an immature "adult" form), but none are native to the Great Lakes area.

Unlike the largely silent salamanders, all native frogs and toads possess distinctive voices that facilitate field identification and population surveys. The spring "advertisement" calls of males are most familiar and are described in the species accounts. Other types of vocalizations include distress and warning calls, territorial announcements, and a "release" call that is given by a male or nonreceptive female frog or toad that is mistakenly grasped by another male.

Selected general references for anurans: Conant and Collins 1991, Duellman and Trueb 1986, Halliday and Adler 1986, Mattison 1987, Smith 1978, Stebbins and Cohen 1995, and Wright and Wright 1949.

True Toads
Family Bufonidae

True toads are terrestrial or burrowing anurans with relatively thick, warty skin and short legs. There are about 350 species in 33 genera distributed throughout most of the world's temperate and tropical regions. Only the genus *Bufo* is found in North America, characterized by toothless jaws and enlarged parotoid glands behind the eyes. Two species inhabit the Great Lakes region.

Eastern American Toad *Bufo americanus americanus*

Description: This is a typical "true toad," with a short, stocky body, warty skin, and relatively short hind legs. Unlike frogs, they walk or hop rather than making long leaps. This species is highly variable in color, ranging from tan, brown, or reddish brown to gray or olive. They have some color-changing ability, and the same animal may slowly darken or lighten, depending on its immediate environment. Most specimens display dark, rounded spots on the back, each of which encircles one or two warts. The large parotoid glands behind the eyes are oval or kidney shaped, and there are enlarged warts on the tibia (lower part of the hind leg, below the knee). A light line may run down the middle of the back. The throat and belly are whitish or yellowish with black or gray spotting, particularly on the "chest" area. Adult length: 5.1 to 11.1 cm (2 to 4.4 in).

Note: American Toads living on some islands in the Great Lakes reach considerably larger sizes than those on the mainland. Snout to vent lengths of up to 15.5 cm (6.1 in) have been reported. It is not yet known if the greater size of island toads is due to genetic differences, greater longevity, or other factors. Despite this uncertainty, some herpetologists have given the name *Bufo americanus "alani"* to the giant toads of northern Lake Michigan islands.

Male American Toads are generally smaller than females and have darkened, enlarged "thumbs" on the forefeet. The male's vocal sac is visible as a grayish flap of skin on the throat.

The tadpoles are blackish, with plump bodies and thin, rounded tails. The tiny black tadpoles often collected by children from suburban ponds are usually of this species.

Voice: A prolonged, high-pitched trill that may last over 30 seconds.

Eastern American Toad

Confusing Species: Fowler's Toads usually have three or more warts within each of the larger spots on their backs and lack enlarged warts on the tibia. In addition, Fowler's usually have unmarked whitish undersides, though some individuals may have one or a few dark spots on the chest. Their short, nasal breeding call is quite unlike the long, musical trill of the American Toad. These two toad species occasionally interbreed. The hybrid offspring may show a blending of traits, or they can resemble one of the parent species, but their advertisement calls are usually intermediate between the two.

Distribution and Status: The Eastern American Toad ranges from coastal Labrador and Quebec west to James Bay and southeastern Manitoba, south to Kansas and Mississippi, and east to Virginia and New England. It is found throughout the Great Lakes region. A smaller subspecies, the Dwarf American Toad *(Bufo a. charlesmithi)*, occurs from southern Indiana to Oklahoma and northeastern Texas.

This generally common species has experienced recent local population declines in portions of the Great Lakes basin.

Habitat and Ecology: American toads tolerate a wide variety of habitats, including open woodlands and woods edges, prairies, meadows, marshes, suburban yards and parks, and agricultural areas. Toads are most active on rainy or humid evenings. When not foraging, they usually remain buried in moist soil or leaf litter or beneath logs or rocks. When digging, they "back in" using their hind feet as shovels. During winter and prolonged dry periods they burrow deeply into the soil and remain dormant until conditions improve.

Long valued as a friend of the gardener and the farmer, American Toads eat many types of insects and insect larvae, as well as spiders, centipedes, millipedes, snails, slugs, and earthworms. The type of food chosen depends largely on which is most available. It is common for these amphibians to gather under yard lights and streetlights on warm nights to consume insects attracted there. Toads use a quick flick of their sticky tongues to capture prey and will use their front feet to push larger prey items into their toothless mouths.

American Toads have a number of behavioral and chemical defenses against predators. Encounters with predators are undoubtedly reduced by their cryptic coloration and burrowing habit. When approached by a potential enemy, a toad may lower its nose and hunch its body forward.

This makes the toad appear larger and also presents the attacker with the poison-producing parotoid glands. The whitish parotoid secretions contain steroidal chemicals that can affect heart function and blood pressure and can cause illness or death in small mammals that chew or consume a toad. A seized toad will expel urine and may puff up by inflating its lungs, perhaps making itself more difficult to swallow. Despite these defenses, certain predators regularly eat toads, including Common Garter and Eastern Hognose Snakes, hawks, herons, and some waterfowl. Raccoons feed on toads by eating them from the belly side and avoiding the glands on the head and back. Humans can handle toads safely, but avoid getting toad skin secretions into the eyes or mouth, as these can be irritating. Handling toads does not cause warts.

Reproduction and Growth: American Toads prefer to breed in shallow, temporary waters with sparse to moderate amounts of emergent and submergent vegetation. Typical sites include flooded fields, ditches, stock and ornamental ponds, open marshes, and backwaters of slow-moving streams. They will also use the shallows of larger lakes if other sites are lacking. First movement to breeding sites is often triggered by humid or rainy conditions combined with warm evening temperatures, typically in early to late April in the southern part of the basin to late May in the north. Males arrive a few days before the females, and most breeding occurs within a period of about 10 to 14 days. If interrupted by cold weather, breeding activity may be resumed after temperatures moderate and can (rarely) extend into June or July.

Male American Toads usually call while sitting upright in shallow water or on land at the water's edge. During the prolonged call, the large grayish vocal sac is fully inflated. A male will attempt to clasp any passing toad; if the intended mate is a male, it gives a special chirping "release" call while vibrating its body, to inform the first toad of its mistake. Once a receptive female is amplexed, the pair often moves to another part of the pond, perhaps to avoid attempts by other males to "cut in." Female toads sometimes drown when clasped by two or more competing males.

During amplexus, the female lays from 2,000 to over 20,000 eggs, which emerge in two gelatinous strings. The egg strings may be twined among submerged branches or vegetation or simply left in loops on the bottom. Hatching occurs in 2 to 14 days, depending on water temperature. The black tadpoles form schools during the day (often congregating preferentially with siblings) and move about together in the shallows, seeking warmth and food. They eat algae, diatoms, and other planktonic organisms, soft vegetation, and carrion. Although toad tadpoles appear to be repellent to some predators, they are readily eaten by many fish, diving beetles, and other aquatic insects.

The tadpoles grow quickly and transform in 6 to 10 weeks into tiny toadlets about 0.8 to 1.3 cm (0.3 to 0.5 in) long. At the time of metamorphosis young toads may swarm by the hundreds near breeding ponds, but few will survive the two to three years required to reach sexual maturity. These toads can survive over 10 years in the wild, and probably much longer; a captive specimen of a related species lived for 36 years.

Conservation: American Toads are adaptable animals, and populations often persist in urban parks, suburban gardens, and farming areas. Local declines in this species can result from the loss or degradation of breeding sites. Use of certain pesticides can also pose a threat, though more research is needed to determine levels of sensitivity to various chemical formulations. Another significant local threat is vandalistic destruction during the breeding season. Calling and amplexed toads in shallow waters are extremely vulnerable to wanton killing; sadly, such vandalism is often perpetrated by unsupervised children not sensitized to wildlife values.

Fowler's Toad *Bufo fowleri*

Description: This species resembles the American Toad in general appearance. Background color varies from tan or brown to olive green or gray, and there is usually a light stripe down the middle of the back. Most specimens have a number of dark spots or blotches on the back, with each large spot enclosing three or more warts. There are no enlarged warts on the tibia (lower leg). The throat and belly are white or dull yellow, sometimes with a dark spot or a few small spots on the chest. Adult length: 5 to 9.5 cm (2 to 3.7 in).

Male Fowler's Toads are smaller in average size than females and have thickened, dark thumbs and a grayish throat (vocal sac).

The blackish tadpoles are very similar to those of the American toad.

Voice: A rather mournful, low-pitched nasal bleat ("waaaaa") lasting from two to seven seconds. The call can be heard from a considerable distance away.

Fowler's Toad

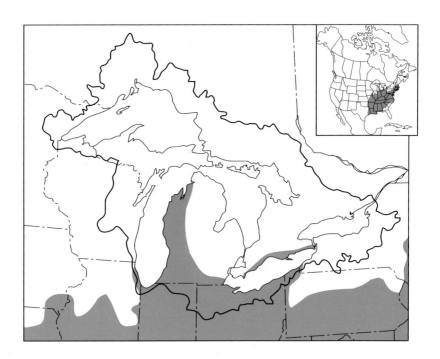

Confusing Species: American Toads typically have only one or two warts in each dark spot on the back and have enlarged warts on the tibia. They also have heavier dark spotting on the throat and chest. The breeding call of the American Toad is a prolonged trill, very unlike the nasal bleat of the Fowler's Toad. Populations of American and Fowler's Toads tend to be separated by differences in habitat preference and timing of breeding activity. There are many places where both species occur, however, and breeding periods occasionally overlap, leading to opportunities for interbreeding. The call and appearance of hybrid specimens may be intermediate between the two species, thus confounding attempts to identify them.

Distribution and Status: Fowler's Toad ranges from New England south to Virginia and the central Gulf coast, west to Arkansas, Missouri, and Illinois, and north to western Michigan. In the Great Lakes region it most often occurs along the southern and eastern shore of Lake Michigan and the Lake Erie shoreline. This toad was formerly considered an eastern subspecies of Woodhouse's Toad (*Bufo woodhousii*); Sullivan, Malmos, and Given (1996) offer reasons for considering Fowler's Toad a full species.

Though generally less abundant than the American Toad in the Great Lakes region, Fowler's Toads can be locally common in proper habitat. This species' distribution along the shores of Lake Michigan and Lake Erie suggests that it is less cold-hardy than the American Toad, since the lakes tend to moderate local temperatures compared to inland areas.

Habitat and Ecology: Open woodlands, sand prairies, meadows, and beaches are typical habitats for Fowler's Toads, though they also occur in suburban and agricultural areas. They are closely associated with sandy soils, particularly along lake shorelines and river valleys. This is a characteristic species of dune habitats in northwestern Indiana and western lower Michigan. Fowler's Toads seem to be more tolerant of warm temperatures than American Toads and are often active during the day, though in hot weather activity peaks during twilight and early evening. Conversely, they are less active under cold conditions, and enter dormancy earlier in fall and emerge later in spring than most other native anurans.

Fowler's Toads eat insects and other small terrestrial invertebrates. They are reportedly less likely to eat earthworms than the American Toad, though this may be related to their more diurnal feeding habits.

The potential predators and defensive behaviors of Fowler's Toads are much the same as those described for the American Toad. This species reportedly will "feign death" (i.e., become immobilized) if roughly handled; presumably this behavior has some defensive value.

Reproduction and Growth: Breeding sites for this species are usually warm, shallow waters that are fairly open, and include woodland and farm ponds, lake edges, stream backwaters, marshes, sloughs, and natural pools between dunes or along beaches. Migration to these sites and calling by males may begin as early as late April or early May, but the peak of breeding activity typically occurs in late May and June, well after the height of breeding activity in the American Toad.

From 7,000 to 10,000 eggs are laid in long gelatinous strings that closely resemble those of the American Toad. Close examination, especially with the aid of a magnifying lens, will allow eggs of the two species to be differentiated; the eggs of the American Toad are enclosed in a double-layered tube and are separated by partitions, whereas the eggs of Fowler's Toads are enclosed in a single tubular membrane and are not separated by partitions. The eggs hatch in two to seven days, and the tadpoles may metamorphose into tiny (1 to 1.4 cm; 0.4 to 0.6 in) toadlets 30 to 40 days later. Since incubation and growth is hastened by warmer temperatures, tadpoles of the late-breeding Fowler's Toad may transform at about the same time as those of the earlier breeding American Toad.

Fowler's Toads may grow to sexual maturity in one growing season, though slower-growing individuals may require 2 or even 3 years. A captive specimen lived for four years, but normal life expectancy is unknown.

Conservation: Preservation of known breeding sites is critical to the existence of Fowler's Toad in its limited range within the Great Lakes basin, but terrestrial habitats also need protection. Intensive recreational use of beach and dune habitats, particularly by off-road vehicles, is detrimental to this species. Agricultural chemicals have also been blamed for the decline or disappearance of this toad in some places.

Treefrogs and Relatives
Family Hylidae

The treefrogs and their kin form a large family (about 630 species in 37 genera) found throughout North and South America as well as parts of Europe, central Asia, and Australia. These are mostly small to medium-sized frogs, many of which have expanded sticky toe pads, giving them the ability to climb trees and shrubs, though some lack enlarged toe pads and are entirely terrestrial.

Blanchard's Cricket Frog   *Acris crepitans blanchardi*

Description: This is a very small, warty-skinned frog with long hind limbs and fully webbed hind toes. The toe tips are not obviously expanded. The snout is bluntly pointed, and there are usually two light bars extending from the corner and edge of the jaw to the eye. The upper surfaces can be brown, tan, olive, or gray, sometimes with scattered green, reddish, or black blotches or spots, and a broad light stripe down the back. A dark triangle, pointed backward, is usually visible between the eyes. Other markings often visible include a dark stripe from the shoulder to the groin, another dark stripe on the inner side of each thigh, and dark bars across the upper legs. Some Great Lakes specimens, particularly older individuals, can be dark gray or brown, without distinct markings. The belly is white or cream colored. Adult length: 1.6 to 3.8 cm (0.6 to 1.5 in).

Male Blanchard's Cricket Frogs have a slightly thickened pad on the inner part of the thumb and a yellowish, gray-mottled vocal sac; these features are most prominent during the breeding season.

The elongate tadpoles are usually olive to brownish, speckled with black. The upper and lower tail fins are rather narrow, and the tail has a conspicuous black tip.

Voice: A series of metallic clicks, similar to the sound made when two pebbles are tapped together. The call, which may last for over 30 seconds, usually starts slowly, then increases in tempo, sometimes ending in an irregular rattle.

Confusing Species: The Striped Chorus Frog has a whitish stripe along the upper lip and lengthwise brownish stripes on the sides and back; its toes are only slightly webbed. The Northern Spring Peeper has smoother skin and, usually, an X-shaped marking on the back.

Blanchard's Cricket Frog

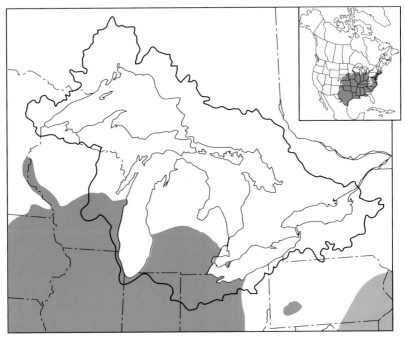

Note: Populations in Pennsylvania and eastward are the Northern Cricket Frog, *Acris c. crepitans.*

Distribution and Status: Blanchard's Cricket Frog ranges from southern Michigan (and Pelee Island, Ontario), Wisconsin, and southeastern South Dakota south through Texas and northern Mexico in the west to northern Tennessee in the east. Related subspecies extend the range of *Acris crepitans* to coastal Louisiana and the Florida panhandle northward to southeastern New York.

Within the Great Lakes basin this formerly common frog has experienced notable population declines since the early 1970s and is presently restricted to small localized colonies.

Habitat and Ecology: These frogs usually inhabit the more open edges of permanent ponds, bogs, lakes, and slow-moving streams or rivers. Where aquatic vegetation is abundant, the frogs are often seen on floating algae mats and water lily leaves; sparsely vegetated mud flats and muddy or sandy shorelines are also favored habitats. Cricket Frogs are generally diurnal during cool weather but are active throughout the day and night in the warmer months, particularly in the breeding season. Winter is spent beneath shoreline debris or burrowed into soil near water. Though they may emerge from hibernation as early as March or April, Cricket Frogs prefer warmer temperatures than most hylid species and do not breed until late in spring or early summer.

Blanchard's Cricket Frogs eat a wide variety of small terrestrial and aquatic insects and other invertebrates and appear to consume whatever food items of the proper size are most available in the habitat. They will feed on the shore, at the water's surface, or while submerged, both during the day and at night.

These little frogs are eaten by snakes, birds, and larger frogs. They attempt to evade enemies by leaping erratically on shore or by jumping into the water and hiding beneath vegetation or bottom debris. Vertical leaps of over 90 cm (35 in) and horizonal leaps of nearly 1.2 m (4 ft) have been reported.

Reproduction and Growth: In the Great Lakes area, Blanchard's Cricket Frogs usually breed from mid- to late May through early July. Warm, humid rainy weather seems to stimulate breeding activity. Males give their clicking call both night and day from the edges of ponds, streams, and sloughs; calling sometimes will continue into late summer. Amplexus and egg laying occur in warm shallows close to the calling sites.

From 200 to 400 eggs are laid singly or in small clusters; they may float at the surface or adhere to submerged twigs or plants and hatch within a few days. The tadpoles tend to be solitary bottom-dwellers. Metamorphosis occurs in 5 to 10 weeks, from late July through early September. The new froglets range from 1.0 to 1.5 cm (0.4 to 0.6 in) in length but grow quickly, and some may reach sexual maturity and breed the following year. Captive Cricket Frogs have lived over five years, but few wild individuals survive longer than one or two breeding seasons.

Conservation: Blanchard's Cricket Frog declined drastically in the northern portions of its range during the late 1970s and 1980s. Many formerly healthy populations in Michigan and Wisconsin are now greatly reduced or extirpated, and the species has reportedly disappeared from known sites in Ontario (Point Pelee and Pelee Island). Population declines are reported for northern Illinois and Indiana as well, though the species remains common in the southern and western parts of its range. Reasons for these declines are unclear, but suggestions for further study include contamination of wetlands and waterways by pesticides or other pollutants, vegetational succession, climatic fluctuations, drought, and competition from other frog species. It will be important to monitor existing populations of Cricket Frogs throughout their range, and to identify and preserve known habitats.

Striped Chorus Frog   *Pseudacris triseriata*

Description: This little frog has a distinctive white or cream-colored stripe along the upper lip, bordered above by a dark brown stripe running through the eye from nostril to the groin. There are usually three additional dark stripes running down the back, though these may be broken into rows of spots. The background color ranges from brown, reddish, or tan, to gray or olive, while the belly is cream or white, sometimes with dark spots on the throat and chest. The skin is moist and slightly bumpy, and the toes end in slightly expanded pads. Adult length: 1.9 to 3.9 cm (0.75 to 1.5 in).

The sexes are similar; males are slightly smaller on average and have a yellowish vocal sac, which (when the frog is not calling) can be seen as a loose, dark flap of skin on the chin and throat, particularly in the breeding season.

The tadpoles have plump, rounded bodies that are gray or brown

Western Chorus Frog

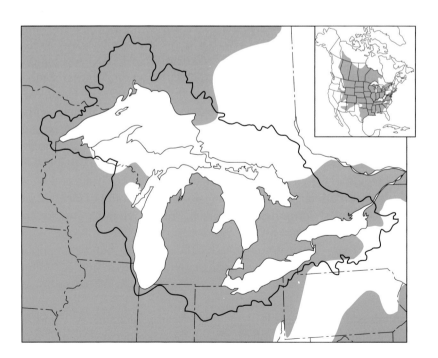

above, sometimes mottled with brassy color in older specimens. The tail fins are clear, with dark flecks. The intestinal coil shows through the bronzy belly skin. Maximum length prior to metamorphosis is about 3 cm (1.2 in).

Note: Two subspecies of *Pseudacris triseriata* occur in the Great Lakes basin. The description above applies to the Western Chorus Frog *(Pseudacris t. triseriata),* which has the widest range in the basin. The Boreal Chorus Frog *(Pseudacris t. maculata),* occurs in the extreme western portion of our area. It is very similar to the Western Chorus Frog but has shorter hind legs (tending to hop instead of leap) and often has greenish back stripes, frequently broken into spots.

Voice: A short, rising, scratchy "cree-ee-ee-ee-eek." The call has often been likened to the sound made by strumming the small teeth of a stiff pocket comb, from middle to end, with a fingernail. How close this simulation comes to approximating the actual call depends on both the quality of the comb and the extent of one's imagination.

Confusing Species: The Spring Peeper lacks a distinct white upper lip line and usually has an X-shaped marking instead of lengthwise striping on the back. Blanchard's Cricket Frog is wartier and also lacks the white lip stripe and dark back stripes. Small Wood Frogs have dorsolateral folds (a ridge of skin down each side of the back).

Distribution and Status: The Western Chorus Frog ranges from southern Quebec and northern New York west through the lower Great Lakes basin, Ohio, and Indiana to Minnesota and South Dakota, then south to Kansas and Oklahoma. Disjunct populations occur in New Mexico and Arizona. They appear to be absent from east-central Ontario and much of Michigan's Upper Peninsula. The Boreal Chorus Frog enters the Great Lakes region in the western and northern Lake Superior basin and on Isle Royale; its broad range extends from James Bay in northern Ontario west to the Northwest Territories and eastern British Columbia and south to northern New Mexico.

Chorus Frogs can be common to locally abundant, but recent population declines have been noted, particularly in suburban and agricultural areas.

Habitat and Ecology: This is generally a frog of marshes, meadows, swales, and other open habitats, though they also occur in damp woods and wooded swamps. They tend to remain near their breeding sites year-round, spending most of their time hidden beneath logs, rocks, and leaf litter, or in loose soil or animal burrows; they hibernate in these places as well. They occasionally move about on the surface on warm, rainy nights. Chorus Frogs are poor climbers but occasionally ascend clumps of grass or other small plants, perhaps in search of food.

These frogs consume a variety of small invertebrates, including beetles, ants, flies, moths, caterpillars, leaf hoppers, and spiders. The newly trans-formed froglets feed on tiny prey such as mites, midges, and springtails. The tadpoles are herbivorous and feed mostly on algae.

Garter and ribbon snakes are known to eat Chorus Frogs, and they are undoubtedly bite-size morsels for many birds, small mammals, and larger frogs. Their primary defense seems to be concealment, and they are rarely seen in the open except during the early spring breeding season. Even then these little frogs are difficult to see amid the dead grasses and reeds in their breeding sites; any disturbance will cause them to cease calling and dive to the pond bottom, where they hide in the mud or bottom debris.

Reproduction and Growth: Striped Chorus Frogs often begin calling when patches of snow still cover the ground and ice has barely receded from the edges of the shallow ponds, ditches, and flooded swales that are this species' favored breeding sites. Calling may extend from mid-March into late May, but most egg laying seems to occur in April, at least in the southern Great Lakes basin. Early breeding choruses are often heard on clear, sunny days, but as water and air temperatures warm, calling is mostly confined to evenings or cloudy, rainy days. Individual males some-times call in late summer and fall, perhaps in response to the shorter length of the day or hormonal changes, but the females are not ready to breed at that time.

During amplexus the female lays from 500 to 1,500 eggs in several loose, gelatinous clusters attached to submerged grasses or sticks. Each cluster contains from 20 to 300 eggs. The rate of development in both the eggs and larvae depends on water temperature. Hatching generally occurs in 3 to 14 days, and the tadpoles transform into tiny (0.8 to 1.2 cm; 0.3 to 0.5 in) froglets 40 to 90 days later. They can grow to maturity and breed in less than a year.

This species and others that breed in shallow, temporary bodies of water may avoid losing eggs and tadpoles to certain predators, such as fish, that require more permanent waters. There is a trade-off, however, since in drought years, most or all of these temporary ponds may dry up before metamorphosis can take place, leading to reproductive failure for the season.

Conservation: This frog appears to be quite tolerant of human activities, considering its presence in many agricultural and suburban areas. Local declines in Chorus Frog numbers have been reported but remain poorly studied; natural factors affecting populations (such as climatic variations) must be separated from those caused by humans. Many of the shallow breeding sites used by Striped Chorus Frogs are filled by surface run-off and are thus vulnerable to contamination by pesticides, herbicides, and other pollutants, some of which may affect this frog's eggs and larvae.

Northern Spring Peeper   *Pseudacris crucifer crucifer*

Description: A Spring Peeper is a small brown, tan, or gray frog with slightly expanded pads on its toe tips. Dark slanting stripes on the back usually merge to form an X-shaped marking, but the X may be incomplete or have spurs or side bars. A V-shaped line is usually visible between the eyes, and a dark stripe often runs from the nostril through the eye to the tympanum, sometimes extending down the side. The upper surfaces of the legs have crossbars, and the undersides of the hind legs and groin may be yellowish or pinkish. The belly is white, yellowish, or cream colored. This frog has some color-changing ability and can darken or lighten in response to its mood or surroundings. Adult length: 2 to 3.7 cm (0.8 to 1.5 in).

Male Spring Peepers are slightly smaller and darker, on average, than females. During the breeding season the male's vocal sac is visible as a mottled brownish or greenish area of loose skin on the throat.

Tadpoles, which grow to about 3 cm (1.2 in) long prior to transformation, are brown or green with metallic gold flecks on the upper surface. The belly is lighter and iridescent, and the tail fins may be clear or orange-tinted, with black or purplish blotches at the outer edges.

Voice: An emphatic, high-pitched rising "peep!" given about once per second, with the single large vocal sac fully inflated. A male Peeper may also give a lower-pitched trilled whistle, usually when another male has moved too close to its calling site.

Northern Spring Peeper, calling male

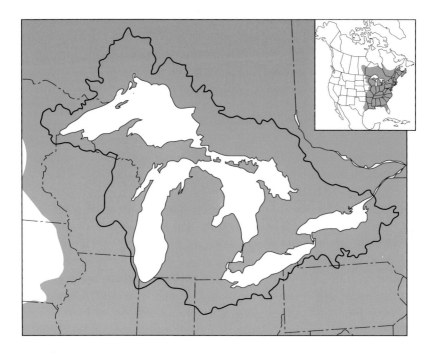

Confusing Species: Striped Chorus Frogs have a light upper lip line and lengthwise stripes (instead of an X-like marking) on the back. Cricket Frogs are wartier and have a dark stripe on the inner thigh.

Distribution and Status: Northern Spring Peepers are found throughout most of eastern North America, from Nova Scotia west to eastern Manitoba, and south to Texas and the Carolinas. The Southern Spring Peeper, *Pseudacris crucifer bartramiana,* is found in southern Georgia and northern Florida.

Spring Peepers are a generally common species throughout the Great Lakes basin and persist even in many suburban and agricultural areas.

Habitat and Ecology: Spring Peepers use temporary and permanent ponds, marshes, floodings, and ditches for breeding. After the breeding season they disperse into woodlands, old fields, and shrubby areas, where they are occasionally seen hopping through leaf litter or climbing on grass clumps, herbaceous plants, and shrubs, especially during rainy weather. Peepers overwinter beneath logs, bark, and fallen leaves and can survive subfreezing temperatures by producing a glucose-based "antifreeze" that causes ice to form in the extracellular spaces rather than in the body cells.

Peepers eat small arthropods such as spiders, mites, ticks, pill bugs, ants, beetles, springtails, and caterpillars. The tadpoles feed largely on algae and other soft or decaying plant material.

Water bugs, diving beetles, spiders, and dragonfly nymphs are known to capture tadpoles and adult Spring Peepers. Fish, larger frogs, snakes, and many birds will eat these frogs without hesitation. Spring Peepers are secretive and cryptically colored, and their habit of breeding in cool temporary waters in early spring undoubtedly reduces contact with many potential predators.

Reproduction: Northern Spring Peepers may begin calling from breeding ponds in late March or early April, and are the earliest calling frogs in some areas. (In other places Striped Chorus Frogs, which hibernate nearer the water, precede them by a few days.) Calling is particularly intense on warm, damp nights, though some individuals will call during the day, especially if stimulated by high humidity or rainfall. Males may call from the water's edge, while partially submerged, or from elevated perches such as emergent shrubs or grass clumps. (Some male Peepers—

called "satellite males"—do not call but instead remain near a calling male and attempt to intercept females attracted to the latter's call.) Although choruses can be heard well into May or even June, most actual breeding seems to occur in April, at least in the southern and central Great Lakes basin. Male Spring Peepers are often heard calling briefly in late summer or fall, usually some distance from the spring breeding sites.

Females may favor males with louder, faster calls; these are usually the older, larger males. The female approaches and contacts her chosen mate; amplexus soon follows. The eggs, which number from 750 to 1,300 per female, are laid singly or in small clusters, usually distributed in irregular rows attached to twigs or aquatic vegetation. The tadpoles hatch in 4 to 15 days and transform into tiny (about 1.3 cm; 0.5 in) froglets from 45 to 90 days later. Most Spring Peepers are able to breed the spring following their metamorphosis, at a length of about 2 cm (0.8 in). Their maximum life span is unknown, but a Peeper that reached its third breeding season would be fortunate indeed.

Conservation: Breeding choruses of Spring Peepers are still a welcome and familiar sign of winter's end throughout the Great Lakes region. While the species remains widespread and locally abundant, many populations of this frog have been reduced or eliminated by the draining of small wetlands and the conversion of its habitat to urban or agricultural use. Although many states and local governments have instituted regulations to protect wetlands, the need to conserve adjacent upland habitats and small temporary wetlands has received little attention by resource managers and politicians. If these critical areas are lost to development, even "common" species like the Spring Peeper will inevitably disappear along with their habitats.

Gray Treefrog   *Hyla versicolor* and *Hyla chrysoscelis*

Description: Gray Treefrogs have moist, warty skins and large adhesive pads on the tips of the toes. They have considerable color-changing ability, with the same frog varying from light gray to brown to pale green, or any color in between. (The change from one color to another may take an hour or more and is thought to be influenced by environmental factors such as temperature and humidity.) One or more irregular dark blotches,

Eastern gray treefrog

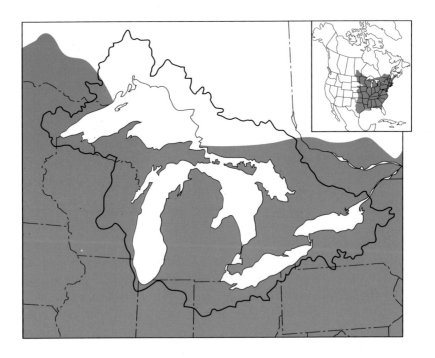

sometimes outlined in black, may be visible on the back. A dark stripe or band often slants from the back of the eye to the front leg, and most specimens have a squarish white spot beneath each eye. The belly is white, and the underside of the hind legs and groin is bright yellow or orange. Adult length: 3 to 6 cm (1.2 to 2.4 in).

Male Gray Treefrogs are, on average, slightly smaller than females and can be recognized by the loose, grayish skin covering the chin and throat area (vocal sac).

The tadpoles are greenish or yellowish above, with gold flecks or streaks, and whitish below. The rather high-arched tail fins are often blotched or tinged with reddish or orange, sometimes with black spots at the outer edges. Newly transformed juveniles are usually bright green, without extensive dark markings on the back.

Note: Two species of Gray Treefrogs occur in our area, the Eastern Gray Treefrog *(Hyla versicolor)*, a genetic tetraploid, and Cope's Gray Treefrog *(Hyla chrysoscelis)*, a genetic diploid. They are practically identical in habits and outward appearance, though Cope's Gray Treefrog tends to be slightly smaller and smoother skinned than its relative and is often entirely green when calling in spring. These differences are probably unreliable for field identification, due to character overlap. The two species are best distinguished by differences in the male advertisement calls (see below), and by laboratory tests that examine blood cells or chromosomes.

Voice: The Eastern Gray Treefrog gives a loud, musical trill lasting from one-half to three seconds. At the same air temperature, the call of Cope's Gray Treefrog is a faster, harsher, more nasal trill. When both species are calling at the same time, the calls are readily distinguished, but care must be taken when identifying treefrogs in a single species chorus, since temperature can affect the duration and pulse rate of the call. (For further details and a discussion of the possible origins of this species-complex, see "Effects of Glaciation on Amphibian and Reptile Distribution in the Great Lakes Region" in Part 1, pages 25–26.)

Confusing Species: Gray Treefrogs are unlikely to be confused with other Great Lakes frogs. The much smaller Northern Spring Peeper has smaller toe pads and lacks yellow color under the hind legs. When listening to spring choruses of unseen anurans, note that the trill of the American Toad is considerably longer in duration (6 to 30 seconds) than that of the treefrog, while the trilled "warning call" of the Spring Peeper is almost always preceded or followed by a series of the typical short "peep" calls.

Distribution and Status: Gray Treefrogs range from New Brunswick and Maine west to southern Manitoba and south across most of the eastern United States to Texas, the Gulf of Mexico, and the south Atlantic states, excluding most of peninsular Florida. Within this range, the Eastern Gray Treefrog is generally most common in the north and northeast, while Cope's Gray Treefrog is widespread in the western and southern portions, but there are numerous areas of overlap, including the western Great Lakes region. Additional studies are needed to better define the comparative distribution of these frogs. *Hyla versicolor* is the common treefrog from the eastern Great Lakes through lower Michigan, while both species may share the same breeding ponds in Wisconsin and northern Michigan.

Gray Treefrogs are common throughout most of the Great Lakes area.

Habitat and Ecology: Gray Treefrogs are found in deciduous or mixed forests, farm woodlots, swamps, old fields, and well-planted suburban yards—almost anywhere that suitable breeding ponds are adjacent to trees or shrubs. Largely nocturnal, they may forage in low shrubbery or climb to heights of 9 meters (30 ft) or more above the ground. Mucus produced on the large toe pads enhances surface tension, allowing the frogs to adhere to smooth surfaces. On warm nights these frogs are often seen on windows or near yard lights or streetlights, feeding on moths and other insects attracted to the light. In winter treefrogs hibernate on land, under logs, leaf litter, or loose house siding, or in hollow trees. They tolerate subfreezing temperatures by producing large amounts of glycerol in blood and body tissues, which acts as a natural "antifreeze" to prevent ice from forming in the body cells. Experiments have shown that Gray Treefrogs can survive temperatures as low as –6°C (21°F) for several days, when over 40 percent of their body fluids may be frozen.

Insects and their larvae form the bulk of the adult Gray Treefrog's diet, along with spiders, mites, harvestmen, and snails. The tadpoles consume algae and other vegetable matter, either by filter-feeding at the surface or by rasping food off plants or the bottom substrate.

Gray Treefrogs are readily eaten by many snakes, birds, and small mammals, but their arboreal habits, cryptic coloration, and inactivity during daylight hours undoubtedly reduce their visibility to potential predators. They are most vulnerable at or near breeding ponds in spring. Giant water bugs have been seen attacking these frogs in the water. Green Frogs and Bullfrogs sometimes locate and eat breeding male treefrogs by orienting to their calls.

Reproduction and Growth: Temporary ponds, swamps, floodings, and the shallower edges of permanent lakes and sloughs are used by breeding Gray Treefrogs, and these sites may be surrounded by forest or in unshaded, open situations. Although the frogs may emerge from winter dormancy quite early in spring, breeding choruses are rarely heard before late April or early May, usually after evening air temperatures remain at 15°C (60°F) or higher. Breeding may extend into late June or early July, particularly if interrupted by periods of cool weather. Calling is generally most intense between dusk and midnight, though loud choruses can sometimes be heard at midday on warm, overcast days.

Male Gray Treefrogs call from the water's edge, from clumps of emergent vegetation, or from overhanging branches, though it appears that unobscured horizontal perches over the water are preferred. A special prolonged call is used to warn away rivals, and calling territories may be aggressively defended. Noncalling "satellite" males often hide near a calling male, waiting for an opportunity to take over the latter's perch when he leaves. Males will remain at the ponds for several weeks, while females visit the site only briefly, to mate and deposit eggs. At the end of the breeding season, males often continue to call for some time as they gradually retreat from the pond and move into nearby trees and shrubs. Individual males may call briefly during late summer or fall, especially on rainy days, but this generally occurs well away from breeding ponds and is not associated with reproduction.

Females reportedly choose males with the longest and most frequently repeated calls. A male being approached by a female often gives a distinctive "courtship call" that is longer and more emphatic than the advertisement call. During a sometimes prolonged period of amplexus, the female deposits from 1,000 to 2,000 eggs, divided into small loose clusters of 10 to 40 eggs that are usually attached to plants or other objects near the water's surface. The tadpoles hatch in three to seven days, depending on water temperature, and metamorphose into tiny (1.5 cm; 0.6 in) green treefroglets in about six to eight weeks. They reach maturity after their second winter. Their potential life span is unknown, but captive specimens have survived over seven years.

Conservation: Gray Treefrogs remain common over much of the Great Lakes basin and often persist in the presence of agricultural activity and low-density residential development provided suitable breeding ponds are available. Most people seem to enjoy having these frogs around their homes. The drainage or degradation of small ponds, marshes, and other wetlands can eliminate treefrog populations in a short time. The introduction of game fish into formerly fishless ponds can also be detrimental to treefrog reproduction. Pesticide applications on trees and shrubs or near wetlands inhabited by treefrogs could be harmful to these animals, but research is needed to assess the direct and indirect effects of different chemicals and formulations, including the presumed reduction in insect prey.

Typical Frogs
Family Ranidae

Anurans in the family Ranidae are called typical or "true" frogs, largely because the 250-plus species in the genus *Rana* (the only ranid genus in the United States and Canada) are what many people would consider "normal" frogs—mostly medium- to large-sized frogs with long legs, generally smooth, moist skin, and rather low-pitched "croaking" calls. The family contains about 670 species in 47 genera and is found on every major continent in the world with the exception of Australia and Antarctica. An important identifying characteristic is the presence or absence of a ridge of skin along both sides of the back, starting above the tympanum (eardrum). Called the dorsolateral fold, this feature is found on all Great Lakes ranids except the Bullfrog and some Mink Frogs.

Bullfrog   *Rana catesbeiana*

Description: The largest frog species in North America may be green, yellow green, olive, or brown, sometimes with brownish spots or blotches on the back and dark bands on the upper legs. Dorsolateral folds are lacking, but there is a ridge of skin beginning at the eye and curving behind the tympanum to the shoulder. The dorsal skin of young Bullfrogs is smooth but becomes bumpier as they get larger. The belly is white or cream colored, often mottled with gray. The toes of the hind feet are fully webbed except for the tip of the fourth (longest) toe. Adult body length: 9.5 to 20.3 cm (3.7 to 8 in).

In male Bullfrogs the tympanum is much larger than the diameter of the eye, and their throats are yellow. The female's tympanum is roughly the same size as the eye, and its throat is usually whitish. Males are, on average, more uniformly colored and smaller than females.

Bullfrog tadpoles are green, olive, or brownish above, often with dark spotting that extends onto the upper tail fin. (Green Frog tadpoles are similar, but usually have dark spotting on both the upper and lower tail fins.) The belly is white to yellowish white. They may reach a length of over 15 cm (6 in) during an extended larval period that may last two years or more.

Voice: The advertisement call is a low-pitched, resonating "brr-rr-rr-um." The challenge call, given when a male detects an intruding male, is a one- or two-noted call, described as a "squawk" or "hiccup." Other, nonreproductive, calls are described below.

Bullfrog

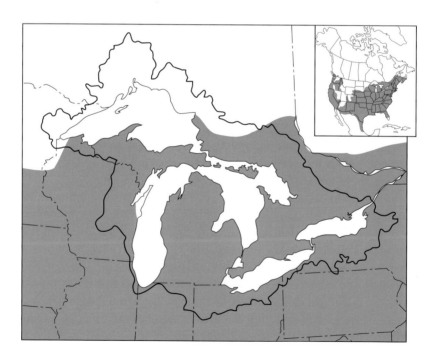

Confusing Species: Green Frogs have distinct dorsolateral folds extending at least part way down the back, and their adult size is smaller. The smaller, darker Mink Frog of the far north may lack dorsolateral folds but has rounded spots or lengthwise blotches on the upper surface of the hind legs and a musky, minklike odor when handled.

Distribution and Status: The natural range of the Bullfrog extends from Nova Scotia to central Florida, east to Wisconsin and southern South Dakota, and south through Oklahoma and eastern Texas to the western Gulf of Mexico. Due to numerous accidental and purposeful introductions, this species is now well established over much of the western United States, southwestern British Columbia, and elsewhere.

Bullfrogs occur throughout most of the Great Lakes region, though they are less common to the north and are absent from the northern Lake Superior basin. This species can be locally common, although it has recently declined or even disappeared from some areas of former abundance.

Habitat and Ecology: Almost any still, permanent body of water may be home to this species, including river backwaters, sloughs, lakes, farm ponds, impoundments, marshes, and shallow Great Lakes bays. Places with abundant submerged and emergent vegetation are preferred. Temporary waters are rarely used, except as resting places for dispersing juvenile frogs. Both tadpoles and adult frogs usually bury themselves in the bottom mud during hibernation, which may last from mid-October until April or May. Adult frogs often cease activity earlier in fall and emerge later in spring than the tadpoles or juvenile frogs. These warmth-loving frogs remain generally inactive until water temperatures approach about 15°C (60°F).

Bullfrogs will eat nearly any animal they can capture and swallow, including vertebrates such as fish, amphibians (including juvenile and larval Bullfrogs), snakes, turtles, young waterfowl and other birds, and small mammals. They are known to locate (and eat) smaller frogs by orienting to their breeding calls. However, much of the Bullfrog's diet is made up of aquatic and terrestrial invertebrates such as dragonflies, beetles, and other insects, spiders, snails, and crayfish. Food may be captured either above or below the water's surface. The tadpoles feed mostly on algae and other aquatic plants, though they will scavenge in the bottom debris and consume decaying animal matter.

Despite being formidable predators, Bullfrogs (and their larvae) are eaten by a host of fellow carnivores, including fish, larger frogs, snakes, turtles, herons, raccoons, otters, and mink. Due to their large size, Bull-frogs are hunted by humans for their legs. Most hunting takes place at night, since these frogs tend to "freeze" in a bright flashlight beam. They are wary during the day, leaping into the water at any disturbance, often giving a single "yelp" (which can actually sound more like a "burp"!) as they jump. When seized by a predator, they can emit a piercing scream or wail that presumably might startle an attacker long enough to allow the frog to escape. Bullfrog tadpoles are reportedly distasteful to some fish.

Reproduction and Growth: Breeding activity rarely begins before mid-May, usually peaks in June, and often continues well into July. Males call most vigorously on warm nights, but some continue calling during the day. A male may call while partly submerged or perched on a log or float-ing vegetation. The larger males defend roughly circular calling territories about 2 to 5 m (6 to 18 ft) in diameter, with the largest males taking the most desirable breeding sites. A territorial male uses a one- or two-note challenge call to warn an intruding male; if the warning is not heeded, a direct conflict that resembles a shoving or wrestling match may result. More often than not, the resident male succeeds in driving the intruder from his territory.

A female Bullfrog appears to choose a mate according to the suitabil-ity of its territory as an egg-laying site, although some pairs will move away from the calling area before eggs are laid. During amplexus the female deposits from 5,000 to over 20,000 eggs in a very thin floating mass that may be up to a meter (3.3 ft) in diameter. Individual eggs are tiny, only 0.12 to 0.17 cm (0.05 to 0.07 in) in diameter. Hatching occurs in three to six days. Some of the tadpoles will transform into froglets dur-ing their second summer, but many others will overwinter a second time and metamorphose in July or August of their third summer. Young Bull-frogs generally reach breeding size in two to four years, when they are 10 to 12 cm (4–4.7 in) in body length. One Bullfrog lived over 15 years in a zoological park.

Conservation: Local declines in Bullfrog populations have been attrib-uted to habitat degradation and loss, water pollution, pesticide contami-nation, and overharvesting. Lakeside residential developments often lead to removal of shoreline and submerged vegetation, and heavy recre-ational use of these waters undoubtedly disrupts Bullfrog reproductive activities. More information is needed on the sensitivity of this species to the various pesticides that are used in or near lakes and wetlands. Bullfrogs have been heavily collected for the restaurant and biological sup- ply trades. It is unlikely that this species can tolerate intensive exploita- tion for commercial or even personal use, due to the extended time period needed for its development and maturation and comparatively slow population replacement rates. Bullfrogs are considered game ani- mals by most state and provincial resource agencies, and their harvest is controlled by closed seasons and "bag" limits throughout the Great Lakes area.

Green Frog *Rana clamitans melanota*

Description: A Green Frog may be green, yellowish green, olive, or brown, or any combination of these colors; occasional aberrant individu- als are blue. The upper lip area is green or yellow. Many have dark spot- ting on the back and sides, and the hind legs have dark crossbands. A ridge of skin (the dorsolateral fold) extends from each eye to about one- half to two-thirds of the way down the back; a spur of this ridge curves behind the tympanum. The belly is white, sometimes mottled with gray. Adult length: 6 to 10.8 cm (2.4 to 4.2 in).

In mature males the throat is bright yellow, and the tympanum is much larger than the eye. The female has a white, light yellow, or cream-colored throat, often mottled with gray or black, and a tympanum about the same size as the eye.

The plump, long-tailed tadpoles are olive to brownish green above, with varying amounts of dark flecking extending over the back and upper and lower tail fins. (In the very similar Bullfrog tadpole, dark spots are usually restricted to the upper half of the tail fin.) The belly is iridescent white or cream, often mottled with gray, and the intestinal coil is not vis- ible through the skin.

Voice: The male's advertisement call is a brief "clung!" (often com- pared to plucking a loose banjo string) that may be given singly or several times in succession. A low growl is sometimes heard just prior to or dur- ing territorial battles.

Confusing Species: Bullfrogs are similar but larger, and lack dorsolateral folds on the back. Green Frogs are often heavily marked with dark pigment like Mink Frogs where the two species' ranges overlap and may (rarely) lack dorsolateral folds. A form of mimicry may be occurring; Mink Frogs have protective musky skin secretions and a strong odor, which Green

Green Frog, male

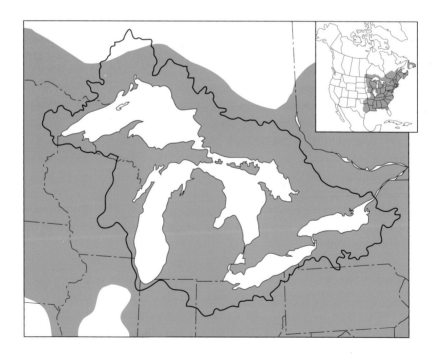

Frogs lack. The possibility of hybridization between these species is also being investigated. Green Frogs have dark crossbands on the hind legs, while Mink Frogs generally have rounded spots or lengthwise stripes.

Distribution and Status: Green Frogs range from Maine and the Canadian Maritime provinces west through the Great Lakes region to western Ontario, south to Oklahoma and northern Arkansas, and east through Tennessee and northern Georgia to coastal North Carolina and northward. Another subspecies, the Bronze Frog (*Rana clamitans clamitans*), extends the range to east Texas and the Gulf Coast to northern Florida.

This is one of the most abundant frogs in the Great Lakes region; it is certainly the most conspicuous species around many permanent water habitats.

Habitat and Ecology: Ponds, lakes, swamps, sloughs, impoundments, and slow streams are all inhabited by Green Frogs. They seem to be more tolerant of open, sparsely vegetated sites than the larger Bullfrog. Shallow, temporary waters are generally avoided, at least by the adults. Green Frogs spend most of their time around the water's edge, but may take advantage of warm, rainy nights to disperse overland to new habitats. At these times, large numbers of mostly juvenile frogs can be seen crossing roads and yards, often taking up a brief residence in small ponds, ditches, and puddles. Green Frogs overwinter in the water, shallowly buried beneath bottom mud or debris. Dormancy typically lasts from early November to early April, but frogs inhabiting ice-free waters (such as creeks or spring-fed ponds) may be active and bask on sunny days even in midwinter.

Green Frogs are largely "sit and wait" predators, taking any prey of appropriate size that comes within reach. They consume a variety of aquatic and terrestrial insects and other invertebrates, including beetles, flies, butterflies, caterpillars, grasshoppers, spiders, millipedes, slugs, snails, and crayfish. Large individuals also eat smaller frogs, snakes, and hatchling turtles. The tadpoles feed on whatever ingestible material is most available, largely algae (e.g., diatoms), along with other planktonic organisms and decaying animal and plant debris.

These common frogs contribute to the food supply of many other animals. Their eggs are eaten by leeches, aquatic insects, and Painted Turtles. The tadpoles also fall prey to predaceous insects, as well as fishes, turtles, and herons. After metamorphosis, Green Frogs are eaten by larger frogs, turtles, snakes, wading birds, raccoons, otters, mink, and occasionally humans. This species appears to lack repellent skin secretions and is generally palatable to predators. However, they are wary and agile; when disturbed they leap into the water, often simultaneously giving a loud squeaking cry, and then bury themselves in the bottom mud or hide under submerged objects.

Reproduction and Growth: Males usually begin calling in early to mid-May and may continue to call throughout the prolonged breeding season, sometimes into August. The area around a calling site is defended against other males. When an intruder is detected, the normally single-noted advertisement call may be repeated rapidly several times. If the challenger does not retreat, an emphatic squawklike version of the advertisement call may be given as the defender advances. Usually the intruder retreats; if not, a "wrestling match" may occur, accompanied by low growl-like sounds.

Unlike the persistent males, a female will spend only a brief time at the breeding site, apparently seeking a mate with a desirable territory for egg laying. She approaches and turns her back toward the chosen male; he will initiate amplexus when contacted by the female. Egg laying normally occurs at night, often during rainy weather. The thin, floating egg mass is usually attached to emergent or surface vegetation and contains from 1,000 to 5,000 eggs. Hatching occurs in three to five days. Tadpoles that hatch early in the season may transform into froglets late in their first summer, but those hatching later will overwinter as larvae and transform during the following summer. The newly metamorphosed froglets average about 3 cm (1.2 in) long, but can double their length the first year, reaching maturity the following summer. Maximum size is reached in 4 to 5 years. The potential life span is unknown, but zoo specimens have lived at least 10 years.

Conservation: Green Frogs are occasionally harvested by people seeking "frog legs," though relatively few specimens reach a size worthy of such attention. This species remains widespread and abundant over most of the Great Lakes region, but their populations should be monitored and studied nevertheless. It is as important to understand the success of common species as it is to study species that are rare and declining. Should Green Frogs ever suffer a sustained decline, we would certainly have cause for concern.

Mink Frog   *Rana septentrionalis*

Description: Mink Frogs are named for the musky odor produced by the skin when handled, which is said to resemble the smell of a mink—or rotting onions. The back and sides are green, olive, or brown, moderately to heavily marked with darker spots and/or irregular blotches and reticulations. The upper surfaces of the hind legs have rounded spots or lengthwise bars or stripes, and the upper "lip" area is green. Dorsolateral folds tend to be poorly developed or even absent, but are occasionally prominent. Undersides are whitish, often grading to pale yellow on the sides and chin, or sometimes entirely yellow. Adult length: 4.8 to 7.6 cm (1.8 to 3 in).

In male Mink Frogs the tympanum is larger than the eye, and the throat is often bright yellow. Females have a tympanum that is smaller or the same size as the eye, and their throats are white or pale yellow.

The tadpoles may reach 10 cm (nearly 4 in) in length prior to metamorphosis. The dorsal coloration is green, olive, or brown, often with a scattering of small, dark spots or heavy mottling that may extend onto the tail. The tail is long, with a pointed tip, and the fins may be edged with pinkish-buff spots. The belly is yellowish and opaque.

Voice: The advertisement call of the male Mink Frog is a series of rather soft, low-pitched croaks ("tok . . . tok, tok, tok, tok . . .") that has been likened to the sound of distant hammering.

Confusing Species: Young Bullfrogs tend to be green with only a scattering of small spots. Green Frogs are often heavily marked with dark pigment where their range overlaps that of the Mink Frog, and confusion between the two is common. Only Mink Frogs have a musky odor when handled, and they have dark spots or lengthwise stripes on the hind legs, while Green Frogs have dark crossbands. Additionally, the hind-foot webbing of the Mink Frog reaches the tip of the fifth (outer) toe and the last joint of the fourth toe, while the webbing in the Green Frog fails to reach the tip of the fifth toe and rarely passes the second joint of the fourth toe. Possible mimicry and/or hybridization between these two species is being studied.

Distribution and Status: This northern species ranges from central Quebec and Labrador south to Maine and northern New York, west to southeastern Manitoba and northern Minnesota. In the Great Lakes basin they occur from eastern Lake Ontario to Georgian Bay and the northeastern

Mink Frog

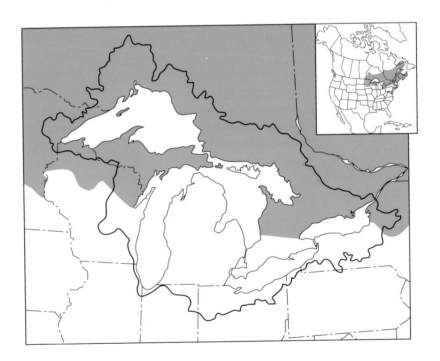

shore of Lake Huron, then west through the Lake Superior basin and south through Michigan's Upper Peninsula to the northern shore of Lake Michigan. They are absent from Michigan's Lower Peninsula and the southern two-thirds of Wisconsin.

Mink Frogs are locally common in suitable habitat.

Habitat and Ecology: Cool, permanent waters with ample emergent and floating vegetation are the preferred habitat for these frogs. Favored sites include sluggish streams, boggy lake inlets, and spring-fed ponds, particularly where lily pads, spatterdocks, or clumps of pickerel weed are abundant. They rarely leave the immediate vicinity of water, although juveniles may disperse to new habitats during periods of heavy rainfall. Mink Frogs hibernate under water in the bottom mud, often entering dormancy by late September and remaining inactive until well into May.

The Mink Frog's diet reflects its preferred habitat, being made up largely of aquatic insects and other invertebrates. Most feeding occurs at the water's surface or on lily pads, and includes whirligig and diving beetles, water boatmen, water striders, stoneflies, mayflies, blackflies, dragonflies, damselflies, spiders, and snails. Terrestrial insects that fall in or fly over the water are readily taken. The tadpoles eat algae.

This frog's musky skin secretions are presumably distasteful to some predators, but giant water bugs, herons, raccoons, and large Green Frogs will eat both adults and tadpoles. Leeches often parasitize them as well. Mink Frogs are wary, and any disturbance will send them skimming over the lily pads and the water's surface before diving to the bottom, where they conceal themselves in the mud and may remain for some time.

Reproduction and Growth: The breeding season of this "north woods" frog may extend from late May into early August, depending on local climate; in the Great Lakes area most egg deposition occurs in June and July. The males may call day or night, either singly or in a group chorus.

During amplexus, from 500 to 4,000 eggs are laid in brownish, globular clusters from 7.5 to 15 cm (3 to 6 in) in diameter, attached to water lily stems or other submerged vegetation. The egg mass may be over a meter (3.3 ft) below the surface and often sinks to the bottom prior to hatching. Cold, well-oxygenated water is needed for proper development of the embryos. The tadpoles spend about a year (sometimes two) as larvae before transforming into froglets measuring between 3 to 4 cm (1.2 to 1.6 in) in length. Male Mink Frogs become sexually mature in a year or less, but the slightly larger females may need a second year to reach breeding size. The average and maximum life span is unknown.

Conservation: These cold-adapted frogs would seem to have ample available habitat within their restricted northern range. It is possible that Mink Frogs were more abundant and widespread during cooler glacial and postglacial periods, and that their range has contracted as the climate warmed. Anecdotal reports suggest that some Mink Frog populations may be declining, while Green Frogs appear to be maintaining their numbers or even increasing at the same sites. Mink Frogs are somewhat more specialized than the larger and more ubiquitous Green Frog, and studies that focus on interactions between these species could provide useful information for evolutionary biologists and conservation planners.

Wood Frog *Rana sylvatica*

Description: This is a brown frog with a dark "mask" extending from the eye through the tympanum to the shoulder, a dark stripe from eye to snout, and a white line along the upper lip. The dorsal color actually varies from grayish brown to bronze, reddish brown, or tan. (Males in cold breeding ponds are often very dark, with an inconspicuous mask.) There may be black spots along the prominent dorsolateral folds and on the sides, and dark bands across the hind legs. The belly is white, sometimes mottled with gray; some specimens have a yellowish tinge on the sides or in the groin area. Wood Frogs from the northern parts of the region often have a light stripe down the middle of the back and, occasionally, light lengthwise stripes on the hind legs as well. Adult length: 3.5 to 8.3 cm (1.4 to 3.3 in).

In male Wood Frogs the edges of the webbing between the hind toes is straight or curved outward. During the breeding season, males are usually darker than females, their thumbs are thickened with an inner pad, and the paired vocal sacs may be visible as skin folds between the end of the jaw and the shoulder. Females have the edge of the webbing between the hind toes curved inward, and they tend to be larger and lighter in color than their mates.

The tadpole, which can reach a length of up to 4.8 cm (1.8 in), is plump bodied, with a short, high tail fin. The body is brown or olive, often speckled with black and gold; the tail is lighter, sometimes with black spotting. The belly is iridescent whitish to bronze, with the intestinal coil usually visible through the skin.

Wood Frog

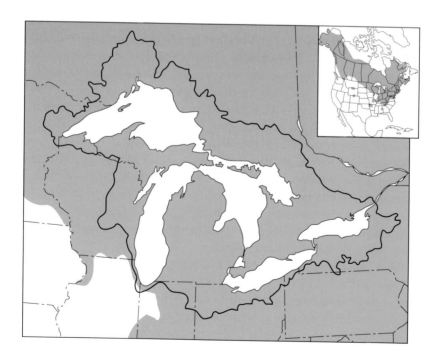

Voice: The male's advertisement call is a series of clucklike croaks, and a chorus may sound like quacking ducks when heard from a short distance. A chirplike "release" call is given by the male when accidently clasped by another male Wood Frog in the breeding pond.

Confusing Species: The Striped Chorus Frog also has a brown masklike facial stripe and light upper lip, but is smaller, lacks dorsolateral folds, and has slightly expanded toe pads.

Distribution and Status: Wood Frogs range farther north than any other North American amphibian, occurring from Labrador and northern Quebec south to Georgia, then north through the entire Great Lakes region, Minnesota, northeastern North Dakota, and across Canada to the edge of the permafrost in northern Alaska. Isolated populations are found in Alabama, Arkansas, Missouri, Wyoming, and Colorado. These relict populations are evidence that Wood Frogs occupied a more southerly range during the Pleistocene.

This is a common species in suitable habitat.

Habitat and Ecology: Wood Frogs prefer moist wooded habitats (including deciduous, coniferous, and mixed forests), and the adults are rarely found in water except during the short breeding season. They will cross open areas to reach a suitable breeding pond, but otherwise normally remain under the tree canopy. These frogs usually hibernate on land beneath loose soil, leaf litter, or decaying logs. They survive periods of subfreezing temperatures in winter by producing large amounts of glucose, which acts like a natural "antifreeze," causing ice to form in the extracellular spaces rather than within the body cells.

Wood Frogs eat mostly terrestrial invertebrates such as beetles, crickets, caterpillars, spiders, earthworms, slugs, and snails. Juveniles include a somewhat higher percentage of aquatic invertebrates in their diets. The tadpoles typically consume algae, diatoms, and decaying plant and animal matter, but at times they can become quite carnivorous, feeding on eggs and larvae of other amphibians.

Wood Frog eggs are consumed by leeches, aquatic insects and their larvae, and Eastern Newts, while the tadpoles fall prey to predaceous diving beetles, water bugs, and the larvae of *Ambystoma* salamanders. Tadpoles approaching metamorphosis develop poison glands that repel some insect predators. In most years the worst danger to tadpoles is the threat of their ponds drying up before they can transform. Numerous predators will eat Wood Frogs, including larger frogs, garter, ribbon, and water snakes, herons, raccoons, skunks, and mink. Their skin secretions are reportedly repellent to shrews. Wood Frogs are most vulnerable when gathered in their early spring breeding choruses, but cool temperatures at that time would limit the activity of reptilian predators. When disturbed on land, they will often make a series of erratic leaps and then freeze, sometimes seeming to disappear amidst the vegetation and leaf litter. When seized, a Wood Frog can give a piercing cry that might temporarily startle its attacker, allowing it to escape.

Reproduction and Growth: Vernal ponds, floodings, wooded swamps, and quiet stream backwaters are all used by Wood Frogs during their rather short 6- to 14-day breeding season. Males move rapidly to these sites during the first warm days of early spring (late March to early April), often while patches of snow still persist in the woods and ice remains on the shady edges of the ponds and swamps. Their frantic clucking, along with the white flashes of their paired vocal sacs, soon attracts the females. The males outnumber the females at any one time and will attempt to clasp anything that remotely resembles another Wood Frog; other males give a chirplike release call when grabbed, while egg-laden females remain silent.

Once in amplexus, a pair usually moves to a deeper part of the pond before the female deposits from 500 to over 3,000 eggs in one to several rounded gelatinous masses, usually attached to plant stems or twigs near the surface. The gelatinous egg cluster is clear to grayish when first laid, but later may turn green from algae growth. Often many pairs of frogs will lay their eggs in one place in the pond, and several advantages to this communal nesting have been suggested. Large numbers of dark egg masses absorb heat more efficiently than a lone mass, and temperatures within the center of communal egg aggregations can be warmer than the surrounding water. In addition, the great bounty of eggs could glut predators, assuring that some will survive to hatch. It is also possible that moisture retention is enhanced in communal masses, giving some protection to the embryos if water levels fall during rainless periods.

The incubation period is temperature dependent, ranging from as little as 4 days to as long as 4 weeks. The tadpoles grow quickly, and are normally ready to transform in 6 to 15 weeks. The juvenile froglets, which range from 1 to 2 cm (0.4 to 0.8 in) in length, can often be seen in large numbers around the edges of the ponds from late May through early July, but soon disperse into the surrounding woods. Males can reaching breeding size in one to two years, females in two to three years.

Conservation: Wood Frogs appear to be holding their own wherever woodlands enclosing or adjacent to suitable breeding ponds persist. They disappear when forest cover is removed or breeding sites are drained or filled. Large numbers of migrating adults can be killed by automobiles when roads are built between terrestrial habitats and breeding sites, and their eggs are reportedly sensitive to runoff of road salt. Studies on the sensitivity of this frog's eggs and larvae to the effects of acid precipitation show that their shallow breeding ponds can experience rapid changes in acidity due to melting snows and rainfall. Tolerance appears to vary regionally, with acid-exposed populations showing better tolerance to acidity than unexposed populations.

Northern Leopard Frog   *Rana pipiens*

Description: Northern Leopard Frogs are green, greenish brown, or brown above, with a variable number of rounded dark spots scattered over the back and sides. The spots may have whitish or yellowish borders. There is usually a dark spot over each eye and on the snout; the legs are also spotted or barred. A white line extends from the nose to the shoulder above the upper lip, and the dorsolateral folds are light-colored and conspicuous. The belly is white to a pale greenish white, sometimes faintly yellowish in the groin area. Adult length: 5 to 11.1 cm (2 to 4.4 in).

Male Leopard Frogs have thickened pads on the thumbs and are usually smaller than the females, which also appear fatter when swollen with eggs in spring. There is no difference in the size of the tympanum between sexes. During calling, the male's paired vocal sacs inflate over his shoulders.

The tadpole, which reaches a maximum length of 8.4 cm (3.3 in), is green, olive, or brown above, often with a light speckling of yellow and/or black. The otherwise light-colored tail may also be weakly spotted with black. The belly is an iridescent white or cream color, with the intestinal coil visible.

Voice: The male's advertisement call sounds much like a low, rumbling snore, punctuated with hoarse clucks and croaks. Both males and nonreceptive females may give a vibrating chuckle (the "release" call) if accidently clasped by a male. When seized by a predator, a Leopard Frog can give a loud, pitiful scream.

Confusing Species: The Pickerel Frog has spots that are more angular and arranged in two rows between the dorsolateral folds, and has bright yellow or orange on the groin and undersurfaces of the hind legs.

Northern Leopard Frog

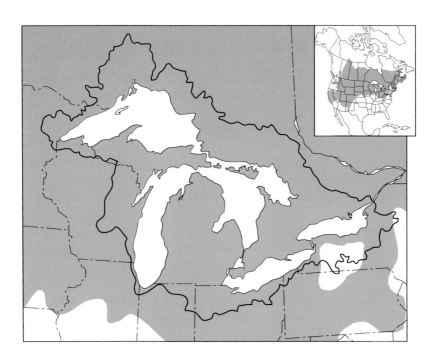

Note: The range of the Plains Leopard Frog *(Rana blairi)* approaches the lower Lake Michigan basin in Cook and Will Counties in northeastern Illinois. This species differs from the Northern Leopard Frog in having dorsolateral folds that are "broken" over the hind legs, with the distal pieces displaced towards the middle of the back. It is a brown frog with a light spot on the tympanum, and dark dorsal spots that often lack distinct light borders (see p. 347).

Distribution and Status: Northern Leopard Frogs are found from Labrador and Quebec west to southern British Columbia, then south through the Rocky Mountain region to Nevada and Arizona, with numerus disjunct populations in Washington and California. In the eastern United States it occurs in much of New England, west through the entire Great Lakes basin and the northern Great Plains, and south to northern Kentucky, West Virginia, and Pennsylvania. Related species in the "leopard frog complex" occur throughout the southeastern United States and the prairie and desert regions of the central and southwestern States and northern Mexico.

Northern Leopard Frogs were generally abundant over most of the Great Lakes basin until the late 1960s and 1970s, when they suffered a notable population decline. They remain uncommon or rare in many places, but can be locally abundant when conditions are favorable.

Habitat and Ecology: Northern Leopard Frogs are typically found in open habitats, including marshes, bogs, lake and stream edges, sedge meadows, hay fields, and suburban lawns. They usually overwinter in permanent waters (larger ponds, lakes, and streams), where they may sit on the bottom or under the edges of rocks or logs, or conceal themselves beneath a light layer of silt. In early spring these frogs seek shallower water for breeding, sometimes migrating to temporary ponds, stream backwaters, or marsh pools over a kilometer (0.6 mi) from the hibernation site. In summer they often disperse well away from the water into meadows and other grassy places, more rarely into open woodlands. They tolerate dry conditions by absorbing moisture from dew or damp soil through their skin. In fall they migrate back to their "home" waters prior to hibernation.

Leopard Frogs feed on terrestrial invertebrates such as insects and insect larvae, spiders, slugs, snails, and earthworms. Larger adults will also eat small vertebrates, such as Spring Peepers and Chorus Frogs. Considering the frequent movement of this frog into gardens and agricultural fields, its feeding habits are undoubtedly beneficial to human interests. The tadpoles consume algae, diatoms, and minute animal life, either filtered from the water and bottom debris or gleaned from plants and other surfaces.

A host of predators eat Leopard Frogs; a partial list would include giant water bugs, fish (e.g., bass and pike), Green Frogs and Bullfrogs, garter and water snakes, hawks, waterfowl, herons, raccoons, foxes, mink, and otters. Humans capture large numbers of this species for research and classroom study and even for food (i.e., "frog legs"). Leeches, newts, and turtles consume Leopard Frog eggs, while the tadpoles are eaten by diving beetles, water bugs, and most of the vertebrates mentioned above. Newly metamorphosed froglets are especially vulnerable; mortality may exceed 95 percent in the first months after transformation.

These frogs escape enemies by leaping into the water and burying themselves in the bottom mud, or (when on land) by taking several erratic jumps and then obscuring themselves beneath the vegetation; their green or brown coloration often blends with their surroundings. They do not appear to have skin secretions effective in deterring predators. Some Leopard Frogs (especially certain populations in Wisconsin and northern Michigan) display the more squarish dorsal spots that are a characteristic of Pickerel Frogs, which may share the same habitats. Because Pickerel Frogs have skin secretions repellent to some predators, this may represent a case of evolving mimicry. Leopard Frogs that more closely resembled their noxious relatives could presumably have a survival advantage over normally patterned frogs. However, hybridization between Leopard and Pickerel Frogs has also been reported and offers an alternative explanation for this phenomenon.

Reproduction and Growth: Males move to breeding sites in early spring and begin giving their snorelike calls, either while sprawled on or just below the surface in shallow water. The peak of breeding is usually in April, though the season may extend into May in northern parts of the region. Calling and amplexus occur most often in the evening, occasionally during the day.

An amplexed pair will often move to an area where other pairs have already deposited eggs before leaving their own complement. A female lays from 300 to 6,000 eggs in one or more globular or flattened oval masses, usually attached to submerged twigs or stems. Each egg is black above and white below. As with Wood Frogs, communal egg laying in this species may aid in heat absorption or as a defense against excessive losses to egg predators. Hatching occurs in one to three weeks, depending on water temperature, and the tadpoles are ready to transform in two to three months. The 2 to 3 cm (0.8 to 1.2 in) froglets will grow to maturity in one to three years (depending on individual growth rate) and may live up to nine years, though few will be lucky enough to attain such longevity.

Conservation: The Northern Leopard Frog was probably the most abundant (and certainly the most conspicuous) anuran in the Great Lakes region prior to the late 1960s, but since that time naturalists and biologists have reported population declines over much of the species' range. Many explanations have been offered for this phenomenon. The intensive and often unregulated harvest of *Rana pipiens* for the biological supply and fish bait trades is known to have reduced local populations. Fragmentation and loss of wetland and adjacent upland habitats are undoubtedly important factors that affect the species rangewide.

The increased use of persistent pesticides in the mid–twentieth century is also a suspected cause of Leopard Frog decline. Experimental evidence indicates that this species may be more sensitive to the effects of certain pesticides (e.g., DDT) than certain other native ranid species, but additional research is needed to clarify this problem. They are also intolerant of acidification of breeding waters; a pH of 4.8 suppresses egg development. Massive seasonal die-offs of these frogs have been attributed to disease or winter freezing and oxygen deprivation. Dead Leopard Frogs often have a reddish flushing of the underparts ("red-leg"), a symptom caused by various bacteria, particularly *Aeromonas hydrophila*. Such infections are thought to be related to physiological stress (see photo on p. 159).

Where habitat is available, Northern Leopard Frogs have the reproductive potential to recover from population declines, and in some places the species has rebounded from earlier lows. It seems probable that numbers of these frogs have naturally varied from year to year, depending on environmental (especially climatic) factors. However, Leopard Frogs remain scarce or absent in many locations where they were formerly common, and continued monitoring of their populations and habitats is important.

Pickerel Frog *Rana palustris*

Description: The Pickerel Frog is a medium-sized spotted frog with a light line along the upper lip. Although similar in appearance to the Northern

Leopard Frog, it has more angular (squarish) brown spots, often outlined in black and arranged in two irregular rows between the light-colored dorsolateral folds. In a rare variation, these dorsal spots may merge into lengthwise stripes. The background color is light brown, tan, gray, or olive, sometimes with a bronze or yellowish green cast. Bright yellow, orange, or gold color is present on the groin and undersides of the hind legs, contrasting with a whitish belly and throat. Adult length: 4.4 to 8.7 cm (1.7 to 3.4 in)

Males tend to be slightly smaller than females and have enlarged thumbs (with inner pads) during the breeding season.

Pickerel Frog tadpoles reach a total length of 5 to 7.6 cm (2 to 3 in) prior to metamorphosis. They are green, grayish brown, or brown above, often with scattered black and yellow spots, and iridescent white or cream bellies. Their tail fins are heavily pigmented with dark spots or blotches (in contrast to the lighter, more faintly spotted tail fins of larval Northern Leopard Frogs).

Voice: The male's advertisement call is a low-pitched, snorelike croak, similar to the Leopard Frog's call but shorter and with less carrying power.

Dead Northern Leopard Frog, showing "red-leg" disease

Confusing Species: Northern Leopard Frogs have light-bordered, rounded or oval spots on the back and lack bright orange or yellow color on the groin and undersides of the hind legs. Occasional Leopard Frogs appear to "mimic" the Pickerel Frog spot pattern and may have a faint yellowish color in the groin area, making identification difficult. In the Plains Leopard Frog, the dorsolateral folds are broken and offset above the hind legs.

Distribution and Status: Pickerel Frogs range from Nova Scotia and southern Quebec south to the Carolinas and northern Georgia and west to Minnesota and the northern Mississippi valley to eastern Oklahoma and Texas. The species is largely absent from parts of Ohio, Indiana, and Illinois formerly dominated by prairie habitat. This frog has been recorded throughout most of the eastern and central Great Lakes basin.

Pickerel Frogs are generally uncommon to rare over the region but can be locally common in suitable habitat.

Habitat and Ecology: This frog can be found in or near bogs, fens, ponds, streams, springs, sloughs, and lake coves. Cool, clear waters are preferred; conversely, polluted or stagnant water is avoided. Favored habitats include grassy stream banks and places where streams or cold springs flow into bogs, marshes, or weedy ponds. They are active both day and night in spring, though they become more nocturnal in the heat of summer. In winter Pickerel Frogs hibernate in soft mud or beneath submerged logs or rocks on stream bottoms or in the deeper parts of ponds and bogs. Those occupying streams, springs, or spring-fed ponds may remain active all winter, though they probably do not feed during the coldest months. Most emerge from hibernation in April and move to shallow, quiet water for breeding. Afterward these frogs may move into nearby meadows and open woods for the summer but seem less inclined than Northern Leopard Frogs to wander far from water.

Pickerel Frogs eat insects, spiders, and other invertebrates and will take either terrestrial or aquatic prey species, depending on availability. Tadpoles are largely herbivorous, consuming mostly algae and other soft plant material, but also scavenging dead animal matter in the bottom mud.

This species produces skin secretions that are at least distasteful, and possibly toxic, to many potential predators. However, literature accounts describing the reactions of various predators to Pickerel Frogs are largely anecdotal and sometimes conflicting. Most garter, ribbon, and water

Pickerel Frog

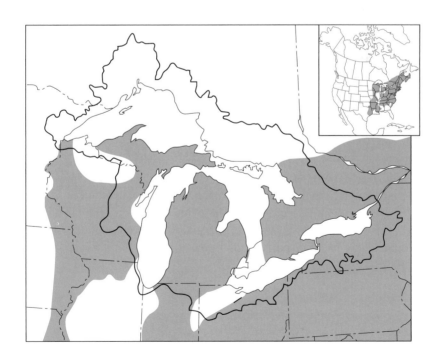

snakes appear to avoid eating them, though several instances of snake predation are known. Other frog species kept in close confinement with Pickerel Frogs may die, but Bullfrogs and Green Frogs apparently eat them without consequence. Dogs are said to be repelled by these frogs, while mink are known to eat them. The name *Pickerel Frog* has been attributed to the popularity of this species as a bait for pickerel, which suggests that its skin toxins are ineffective in repelling at least some predatory fish.

Reproduction and Growth: The majority of breeding takes place in April, though the season can be delayed by cold weather until well into May, particularly in the north. Most breeding takes place when water temperatures are between 10° and 20°C (50° to 68°F). Males may congregate in large choruses at preferred sites, and their low snorelike calls may seem to merge into a continuous drone. A male can call while floating at the surface or while submerged.

During a period of amplexus that may extend over several days, a female will deposit from 800 to 3,000 eggs in one to several globular clusters attached to submerged twigs or grasses. Freshly laid eggs are brown above and yellow below, with the egg mass having a light brownish appearance. The tadpoles hatch in 10 to 21 days, with higher temperatures shortening the incubation period. Metamorphosis generally occurs in 60 to 90 days, with the newly transformed froglets measuring from 2 to 3 cm (0.8 to 1.2 in) in length. They reach sexual maturity during the second spring after hatching.

Conservation: Pickerel Frogs are somewhat specialized in their preference for cool, clear waters, and are intolerant of pollution. Human activities have certainly reduced or degraded many formerly occupied habitats.

It is unclear whether the Pickerel Frog has suffered a population decline similar to that noted for its look-alike relative, the Northern Leopard Frog. Although generally rare and local over most of the Great Lakes area, this species persists in numbers equal to or greater than those of the Leopard Frog in other parts of its range (e.g., the northeastern United States and New England).

Reptiles
(Class Reptilia)

Turtles (Order Testudines)

About 260 species of turtles and tortoises exist worldwide, arranged within 75 genera and 13 families. While greatly outnumbered by lizards and snakes in numbers of species, turtles have a comparable diversity at the family level and have been an ecologically successful group of reptiles since the early Mesozoic era. The probable reason for this long success, and the defining character of the group, is the shell, which has retained its basic form since the late Triassic period, about 225 million years ago.

The top part of the shell, the carapace, is formed from dermal bones fused to the ribs and vertebrae. The lower shell, or plastron, is derived from bones of the shoulder girdle and abdominal ribs. The plastron and carapace are connected at each side by a bridge of bone or cartilage. Overlying the bony layer of the shell are broad, flat horny scales, called scutes (fig. 7). These shell elements are reduced in some species, apparently an adaptation to increase mobility at the expense of protective armor. In the fast-swimming softshelled turtles much of the bony portion of the shell has been lost, and leathery skin covers the shell's surface. In snapping and musk turtles, the plastron is reduced to a cross-shaped structure, perhaps facilitating their bottom-walking habits. The well-armored Box and Blanding's Turtles have evolved a flexible hinge across the plastron, allowing the two plastral lobes to move upward to better protect the withdrawn head, limbs, and tail.

All living turtles are toothless, but their sharp-edged horny jaws are quite capable of grabbing and slicing food items—and sometimes their enemies. Some native species, such as Common Musk, Blanding's, Common Map, and Spiny Softshell Turtles, are largely carnivorous, while others, including Wood, Box, and Painted Turtles are omnivorous, with plant products forming a considerable part of their diet. Some turtle species are totally herbivorous (e.g., most true tortoises and certain marine species), but none of these occur naturally in the Great Lakes region.

Turtles reproduce with internal fertilization and shelled eggs. After

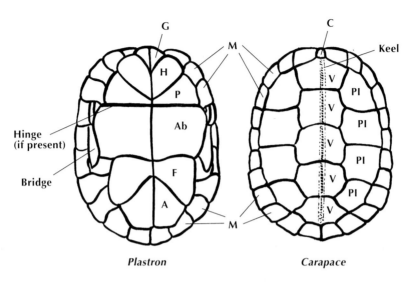

Plastron   *Carapace*

Fig. 7. Names given to the scutes of the turtle shell. Plastron: A = anal, Ab = abdominal, F = femoral, G = gular, H = humeral, P = pectoral. Carapace: C = cervical (*nuchal* of some authors), M = marginals, Pl = pleural (*costal* of some authors), V = vertebral

engaging in courtship behavior that varies in complexity from species to species, the male will mount the female's carapace and attempt to bring his vent into contact with that of his mate; the penis is then inserted into the cloacal opening to effect fertilization. Females of some species, including Spotted, Eastern Box, Blanding's, and Common Snapping Turtles, may store sperm and produce fertile eggs for two to four years after a mating. Again depending on species, turtle eggs are either round or elliptical in shape and have shells that are either rigid and rather brittle or flexible and easily dented. Eggs of Common Snapping and Blanding's Turtles often have rigid shells when first laid, but they soon become flexible as water is absorbed and incubation progresses.

Females of most turtle species deposit their eggs in an underground nest excavated with their hind feet. Some species will moisten the nest site with water stored in accessory bladders located around the cloaca. After the eggs are laid, the nest cavity is refilled and then abandoned. A female turtle never sees her eggs and offers no protection or care to her nest or offspring. Predation on turtle nests is typically quite high; losses routinely exceed 70 percent and can approach 100 percent of all nests in some places, depending on predator numbers and the availability of nesting sites. Raccoons are the major nest raiders in the region, although shrews, skunks, mink, foxes, coyotes, and bears also relish turtle eggs.

In the Great Lakes area, most nesting occurs from late May through early July. Incubation generally requires from two to three months, with hatchlings emerging in August or September. Hatching turtles have a pointed caruncle ("egg tooth") on the snout to assist in breaking or slicing the egg shell. Hatchlings of some species, such as Painted Turtles, can overwinter in the nest and delay emergence from the ground until spring.

In many turtle species the sex of the hatchling is determined by the temperature of the egg at a critical period during incubation. The most common pattern is for males to result from cooler egg temperatures and females from warmer temperatures. A precise "pivotal" temperature, which varies between species and even populations within species, results in a roughly equal sex ratio. For example, in Painted, Map, Blanding's, Box, and Spotted Turtles, eggs incubated at 25°C (77°F) will produce nearly all male hatchlings, whereas those kept at 30°C (86°F) will produce only females. Pivotal temperatures in the Painted Turtle were found to vary from 27.5 to 29°C (81.5 to 84.2°F) across its range. Snapping and Common Musk Turtles follow a similar pattern, but in these species females are also produced at still lower temperatures, close to the coolest temperature at which the egg can successfully develop (about 21.5°C or 71°F). In a few species, including the Spiny Softshell and Wood Turtle, sex is not affected by incubation temperatures but is genetically determined as in birds and mammals. The ecological consequences of temperature-dependent sex determination are still under study. The variability of temperatures within nests and between sunny and shaded nest sites presumably allows for sufficient numbers of each sex to be produced, particularly over a number of years (Ewert, Jackson, and Nelson 1994).

Note: Any shelled reptile can be properly called a turtle. In North America, the word *turtle* is used for all marine, freshwater, and semiterrestrial members of the order, while the word *tortoise* is applied only to members of the exclusively terrestrial family Testudinidae, none of which is native to the Great Lakes region. The word *terrapin* (of American Indian origin) is restricted to the species *Malaclemys terrapin,* of the brackish coastal marshes of the Atlantic and Gulf states, while outside North America it is sometimes applied more broadly to semiaquatic turtles. In Great Britain and Australia, marine species are called "turtles," while "tortoise" is often used for both freshwater and terrestrial species.

Selected general references: Carr 1952, Conant and Collins 1991, Ernst, Lovich, and Barbour 1994, Halliday and Adler 1986, and Harless and Morlock 1979.

Snapping Turtles
Family Chelydridae

These are large aquatic turtles with long tails, reduced plastra, and quick, sharp jaws used for defense. There are two species in two genera. The Alligator Snapping Turtle *(Macroclemys temminckii),* the largest freshwater turtle in North America, reaches a length of 80 cm (31.5 in). Its range centers on the lower Mississippi drainage system, extending from Iowa in the north to east Texas and the Florida panhandle in the south. It is threatened by overharvest in many areas. The smaller and more widespread Snapping Turtle *(Chelydra serpentina)* is described below.

Common Snapping Turtle   *Chelydra serpentina serpentina*

Description: The "snapper" has a broad brown, black, or olive carapace that is often obscured with mud or algae. The scutes at the rear edge of the carapace are pointed. Young specimens have three lengthwise keels (ridges) on the carapace, but shells of older adults may be nearly smooth. The yellow, tan, or gray plastron is small and cross-shaped, leaving much skin exposed around the muscular legs. The feet are webbed and bear heavy, curved claws. The head is large, with a short, pointed snout and sharp jaws with a hooked upper beak. The jaws are sometimes marked with dark streaks. There are two barbels on the chin, and the skin on the long neck is warty and often covered with blunt tubercles. Skin color on the upper surfaces of the head, neck, and legs is usually dark brown, gray, or olive, grading to lighter shades or dull yellow below. There may be one or two light yellowish stripes slanting back from the eye, and a few yellow spots elsewhere on the neck and legs. Three rows of upright triangular scales run down the long, thick tail, with the middle row being larger and more conspicuous. This is the largest Great Lakes turtle. Adult carapace length: 20.3 to 50.3 cm (8 to 19.8 in).

Note: Common Snapping Turtle size is often expressed as total mass (i.e., weight). An average female snapper nearing sexual maturity will have a 20.3 cm (8 in) carapace and weigh about 2 to 2.5 kg (4.4 to 5.5 lbs). By the time its carapace is 30 cm (12 in) long, it may weigh around 6.4 kg (14 lbs), and if it survives to a shell length of 35 cm (13.7 in), it might tip the scales at around 10 kg (22 lbs). One Minnesota snapper had a carapace 49.5 cm (19.5 in) long and weighed 30.4 kg (67 lbs); the

Common Snapping Turtle

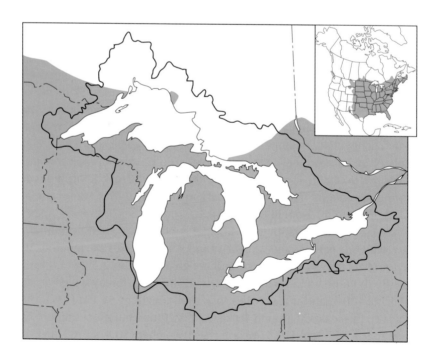

record weight for a wild-caught specimen was 34 kg (75 lbs), while the record for a fattened captive was 39 kg (86 lbs). Of course, the weight of any individual turtle can vary according to the season and its nutritional state.

The sexes are similar and sometimes difficult to distinguish based on external characters. In males the precloacal tail length (measured from the end of the plastron to the vent) is proportionally longer than in females. When the tail is extended, the male's vent is usually beyond the rear edge of the carapace, while the female's vent is usually beneath the edge of the carapace. Male snappers grow larger than females; most specimens weighing over 10 kg (22 lbs) will be males.

Hatchlings are black or dark brown, often with white spots below the edge of the carapace and on the plastron, with a carapace length of 2.5 to 3.8 cm (1 to 1.5 in). Their tails are usually longer than their shells.

Confusing Species: The combination of large head, muscular legs, long spike-topped tail, tiny plastron, and belligerent attitude should distinguish the Common Snapping Turtle from all other Great Lakes turtles. The much smaller Common Musk Turtle also has a relatively small plastron and a feisty disposition, but its tail is short and its carapace is highly domed.

Distribution and Status: Common Snapping Turtles range from Nova Scotia west to southern Alberta, south to New Mexico and east to the Atlantic and Gulf coasts. This encompasses nearly all of the United States east of the Rocky Mountains and includes the entire Great Lakes region, except the area north of Lake Superior. Other subspecies occur in peninsular Florida and portions of Mexico, Central America, and northwestern South America.

This species is generally common throughout most of the Great lakes basin, except where local populations have been depleted by overharvesting.

Habitat and Ecology: Common Snapping Turtles inhabit most permanent bodies of water in the region, including shallow, weedy inlets and bays in the Great Lakes themselves. Quiet, mud-bottomed ponds, lakes, sloughs, and slow streams with dense aquatic vegetation support the largest populations. This species appears to be quite tolerant of polluted waters. Daylight hours are usually spent in shallow water, buried in mud, in weed beds, or hidden under logs or other cover. Although capable of swimming, they more often walk along the bottom. They are less inclined to bask in the open than other turtles but occasionally haul out on logs, stumps, or sloping banks on cool sunny days; more often they warm themselves by floating near the surface.

In the warmer months Common Snapping Turtles often restrict their activities to the morning and early evening or may even become nocturnal. Despite strong aquatic tendencies, they will travel overland when necessary and are sometimes found considerable distances from water. The colder months are spent hibernating in shallow water, where they may simply sit on the bottom, or dig into bottom mud or under submerged debris or overhanging banks. They may congregate in numbers in preferred sites. Snapping Turtles are generally dormant from mid-October until early April in the Great Lakes region, but they are sometimes seen moving about under the ice in winter.

Common Snapping Turtles often remain within a certain home range for a number of years. Reported home ranges of adults range from about 0.25 hectares (0.6 acres) to nearly 9 hectares (22 acres), but the turtles may regularly use only a small portion of the calculated home range. There are many published accounts of vicious fights between male Snapping Turtles, and it is possible that some males will aggressively defend portions of their home range against other males, at least during the breeding season.

These turtles eat both plant and animal food and also scavenge dead animals that are not too decayed. A complete dietary list would undoubtedly include many of the invertebrate and smaller vertebrate animals that share the turtle's habitat, along with a variety of aquatic plants. Snappers will stalk potential prey by creeping slowly forward with head lowered and partly withdrawn. When in range, the prey is seized with a rapid extension of the head and neck; smaller prey items may literally be sucked in, since the turtle strikes open-mouthed, causing a rush of water (and often much debris and vegetation) into its throat. Small Snapping Turtles will actively pursue prey, but large adults tend to employ a sit-and-wait strategy. The forefeet and claws are used to tear larger prey into bite-size pieces, and all food is swallowed underwater.

Snapping Turtle eggs and young suffer very high losses to predators. Nest losses typically range from 60 percent to 100 percent, depending on local conditions, with raccoons being the primary egg predators in the Great Lakes area, followed in frequency by skunks, foxes, and mink. Hatchlings and juveniles are eaten by these mammals, as well as by large fish (e.g., bass and pike), Bullfrogs and Green Frogs, Northern Water Snakes, crows, ravens, gulls, and herons. Adult snappers have few enemies except for humans and their automobiles. A number of adult specimens in Ontario were reportedly killed by otters during winter dormancy. Many Snapping Turtles are parasitized by leeches (*Placobdella* sp.).

When on land, a Snapping Turtle normally turns to face a potential enemy and, if closely approached, strikes quickly with its sharp jaws. The long neck allows a striking distance about as great as its shell length and the jaws can cause severe lacerations to unprotected skin. The safest way to handle a large snapper is by grabbing the base of its tail, keeping the head pointed away from your body. However, lifting a large turtle off the ground with this method may injure its tail vertebrae (and perhaps lead to spinal cord injury) and it is best to avoid handling them whenever possible. When disturbed underwater, snappers prefer to flee or conceal themselves in the mud and rarely bite unless restrained. Biting is a less effective defense for hatchlings and small juveniles, but they can secrete a foul-smelling musky fluid from glands along the lower edge of the carapace and bridge, which may repel some predators.

Reproduction and Growth: Mating can occur at anytime during the active season but is most frequent in spring and fall. A courting pair will sometimes face each other and sway their heads back and forth in a horizontal arc. Often the male simply mounts the female's carapace after a brief chase and grasps the edge of her shell with his claws. While mounted the male will extend his neck and press the female's snout with his own, or grip her neck skin with his jaws, usually without causing serious injury. His tail is eventually extended beneath the female's, bringing the cloacal openings into contact and allowing copulation.

Nesting generally occurs from late May through early July; in most years nesting activity peaks in mid-June. Females may travel a kilometer (0.62 mi) or more from the water to find a suitable nest location, often starting and abandoning several holes before completing a nest. Open, sunny locations with moist but well-drained sand or soil are preferred, but they will nest in gravel beds, road edges, and lawns if better sites are not available. Using her hind feet, the female snapper scoops out a narrow-necked, flask-shaped cavity and deposits from 10 to over 100 (usually 25 to 50) eggs. She then refills the cavity and returns to the water. Larger females tend to lay more and larger eggs. The eggs are spherical and range from 2.5 to 3.5 cm (1 to 1.4 in) in diameter. Freshly laid eggs usually have rigid shells, but after a few days they absorb water and the shells become flexible. Females probably produce only one clutch in a season in the Great Lakes area and may not nest every year.

Under normal conditions Common Snapping Turtle eggs hatch in 65 to 95 days. While cooler, damper conditions tend to lengthen the incubation period, warmer, drier conditions will shorten it. Incubation temperature also influences the sex of the hatchlings in this species (see page 165). The newly hatched turtles remain in the nest for several days while they absorb their sacs of leftover yolk, and then may dig to the surface and emerge almost simultaneously or over a period of hours or days. Hatchlings from later nests sometimes attempt to overwinter in the nest, but, in colder winters and in northern parts of the range, many of these young freeze to death. Newly emerged hatchlings are vulnerable not only to predation, but also to desiccation (if they cannot find water) and to drowning (if the water is too deep or lacks supportive vegetation).

Growth is rapid in young snappers but slows as they mature and may practically cease in older adults. In the southern Great Lakes basin a female Common Snapping Turtle will reach sexual maturity in 11 to 16 years, at a carapace length of about 20.3 cm (8 in). Farther north they mature in about 17 to 20 years, at a slightly larger size. A female's first nesting is more related to reaching a minimum size than to a minimum age. The maximum age attained in the wild is unknown, but a zoo captive lived over 38 years.

Conservation: Snappers are often blamed for reducing populations of game fish and waterfowl. Studies in natural lakes, marshes, and streams show that the quantities of game fish eaten by Common Snapping Turtles are generally insignificant and of no concern to sport fish management. Mammalian nest predators and large game fish take a far greater toll on waterfowl reproduction than do turtles. Being opportunistic feeders, Snapping Turtles can be a problem in fish hatcheries and in enclosed, intensively managed waterfowl-breeding areas; their removal might be justified in these situations.

Common Snapping Turtles are important members of lake and stream communities in the region. Their eggs and young provide a considerable food resource for an assortment of predators, while the adults play an important role as both predator and scavenger. Snappers are large enough to be harvested as human food, although they are of minor economic importance. Commercial trapping can lead to severe local declines in turtle numbers if not carefully managed. Serious doubts have been raised as to whether Common Snapping Turtles can be commercially harvested on a truly sustainable basis, since their population stability is dependent on the relative longevity of breeding adults. Research on a stable population in southern Michigan revealed that annual survivorship of adult females ranged from 88 percent to 97 percent, while juvenile survivorship averaged about 77 percent. Almost any increase in the loss of mature turtles (such as by trapping) would predictably cause the population to decline. Additionally, there is no evidence that removing mature turtles from a population results in increased reproductive success for those remaining. Recovery of a depleted population could take many years, even if further exploitation was halted (Congdon, Dunham, and van Loben Sels 1994).

Common Snapping Turtles can store environmental contaminants in their body fat, liver, muscle tissue, and eggs. Specimens taken from polluted waters were shown to carry high concentrations of organochlorine pollutants such as polychlorinated biphenyls (PCBs). Thus, the harvest and consumption of turtles from certain Great Lakes waters might be inadvisable from a human health as well as a conservation standpoint.

Plastron of Common Snapping Turtle, showing musk glands

Musk and Mud Turtles
Family Kinosternidae

These are mostly small, bottom-walking turtles of shallow waters. Twenty species range from southern Canada to Argentina, with the greatest diversity in Mexico and Central America. The musk turtles *(Sternotherus)* have very small plastra with a single hinge and varying amounts of skin showing between the plastral scutes. Mud turtles *(Kinosternon)* have larger, more solid plastra with two transverse hinges. All members of the family can secrete a musky-smelling substance from glands at the edge of the carapace and bridge, presumably to repel predators. Only one species occurs in the Great Lakes basin.

Common Musk Turtle   *Sternotherus odoratus*

Description: This is a small turtle with a rather narrow, domed carapace, and a large head with a pointed snout. The brown, gray, or black carapace is sometimes streaked or spotted with dark pigment and is smooth (but often algae-covered) in adults and keeled in juveniles. The yellowish or brownish plastron is small, somewhat cross-shaped, and usually has areas of smooth skin between the scutes, especially toward the center. The front part of the plastron is flexible and can move upward, but this flexure offers little additional protection to the turtle's soft parts. Two yellow stripes extend from the nose, above and below the eye, and along the side of the head and neck; these stripes often fade in older specimens. There are two or more pointed barbels on the chin and throat. Adult carapace length: 7.5 to 13.7 cm (3 to 5.4 in).

The sexes are similar in size. The male has wide areas of skin between the plastral scutes, a longer, thicker tail with a stiff blunt spine at its tip, and two patches of rough scales on the inner side of each hind leg. The female has less skin between the plastral scutes and a very short tail.

The tiny hatchling Common Musk Turtle has a carapace length of 1.9 to 2.5 cm (0.7 to 1 in). The rough black carapace has white spots on the outer edge of the marginal scutes. The central keel is prominent, and two lateral keels may also be evident. The yellow head stripes are usually well defined.

Confusing Species: The Common Musk Turtle's small plastron and willingness to bite in self-defense sometimes leads to its being mistaken for a

Common Musk Turtle

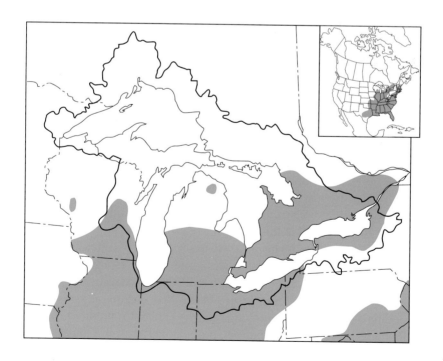

young Snapping Turtle; the snapper, however, has a very long, thick tail topped with a row of large, upright scales. Mud turtles *(Kinosternon)*, which are probably absent from the Great Lakes basin, have a relatively larger plastron with two hinges.

Distribution and Status: This species occurs from southern Maine and southeastern Ontario south through peninsular Florida, west to central Texas and north to southern Wisconsin. They are generally absent from higher elevations. In the Great Lakes region they range from the Lake Ontario and Lake Erie drainages north to Georgian Bay and west across the lower half of Michigan's Lower Peninsula to the southern drainages of Lake Michigan.

Common Musk Turtles are locally common in the lower Great Lakes area. Some populations have declined or disappeared in recent years, particularly where lake edges have been altered by residential development.

Habitat and Ecology: These little turtles inhabit a wide variety of permanent waters, including ponds, lakes, marshes, sloughs, and rivers. In the Great Lakes area they seem to be most common in clear lakes or ponds with marl, sand, or gravel bottoms and a moderate growth of aquatic plants. Common Musk Turtles are highly aquatic and rarely wander far from water. If kept dry they lose body water faster than other native turtles. Though they occasionally climb out on rocks, branches, or logs to sun themselves, most basking is done while partially submerged in shallow water. During the warmer months these turtles are most active in early morning and evening; in hot weather they may be largely nocturnal. They are often seen walking along the bottom in weedy shallows, but will use deeper waters to escape summer heat or predators. Common Musk Turtles usually enter hibernation when water temperatures drop below 10°C (50°F). They burrow into bottom mud or beneath logs, overhanging banks, or muskrat houses. This dormant period generally lasts from mid-October to early April in the region.

Common Musk Turtles eat a variety of small animals, including worms, leeches, aquatic insects, snails, crayfish, small fish, and tadpoles. Carrion, such as dead fish, is also eaten if it is not overly decayed. Live, healthy game fish are rarely, if ever, taken. They also consume aquatic plants, including algae, rooted plants, and seeds. A hungry Common Musk Turtle will creep slowly along the bottom, probing with its snout into the mud, clumps of algae or other plants, and under the edges of submerged branches and other debris. Large food items are held in the jaws and torn into smaller pieces with the front claws.

Musk turtle eggs are eaten by many predators, including crows, rodents, raccoons, and skunks, and nest mortality in a given area often exceeds 80 percent. The hatchlings and juveniles are prey for predatory fish such as bass and pickerel, large frogs, water snakes, and herons. Raccoons, otters, mink, and Bald Eagles will eat both juveniles and adults. Muskrats will attack dormant turtles in winter. Older turtles often show signs of injury from previous encounters with predators. When disturbed or handled, Common Musk Turtles may attempt to bite or at least threaten with mouth open. They can secrete a musky smelling substance from glands located at the edge of the bridge and carapace, which may repel some predators. For this reason the species is sometimes called "stinkpot."

Reproduction and Growth: Mating occurs underwater, usually in April or May, though breeding activity may resume in fall. A courting male will chase the female while nudging or biting her head and carapace edges. A receptive female will eventually slow down enough to be caught, allowing the male to crawl over her and cling to her carapace with the claws of all four feet. The scaly patches on the inner side of the male's hind legs may be employed to hold the female's tail, while his tail is curled around the female's, with the stiff, spinelike tip contacting her cloaca, thus bringing the vents together and facilitating copulation.

Nesting usually occurs between late May and early July. Female Common Musk Turtles may dig a typical nest cavity in sand or soil with the hind feet, but as often the eggs are deposited in shallow excavations beneath logs, clumps of vegetation, or shoreline debris, or in the tops of rotting stumps or muskrat houses. Sometimes the eggs are not even completely covered. Common Musk Turtles farther south may lay two or more clutches per year, but a single clutch appears to be the norm in the Great Lakes area. From one to nine eggs (usually three to five) are laid at one time. The eggs are elliptical, range from 2.3 to 3.1 cm (0.9 to 1.2 in) in length, and have rigid, brittle shells that give the embryos added protection against drying out—a useful adaptation considering this turtle's rather casual approach to nest construction.

Incubation can require between 60 and 90 days, depending on incubation temperature. Incubation temperatures also determine the sex of the hatchlings (see discussion, p. 165). Young Common Musk Turtles grow rapidly, but growth slows as they approach sexual maturity; older adults may practically stop growing. Males are able to reproduce in their third or fourth year, but females may require 7 to 11 years to mature, depending on growth rate. Counting growth rings (annuli) visible on the scutes of the carapace or plastron may give a reasonable estimate of age up to about 10 years, after which wear and a slowing growth rate make the method unreliable. Common Musk Turtles have reached a known age of at least 28 years in the wild and over 54 years in a zoo.

Conservation: Dietary studies confirm that these inconspicuous little turtles do no harm to game fish populations and are generally harmless to human interests. Common Musk Turtles are frequently caught by people fishing with live bait and are sometimes killed for being a nuisance or in the mistaken belief that they consume game fish. This practice is unfortunate and can deplete local populations. Probably the most serious threat to the Common Musk Turtle is residential shoreline development, which often results in removal of aquatic vegetation from shallow waters (to improve swimming and boating) and the loss of suitable terrestrial nesting sites.

Pond and Box Turtles
Family Emydidae

This is the largest and most diverse of turtle families, with over 90 species in 31 genera distributed over most temperate to tropical parts of the Americas, Europe, Asia, and northern Africa. Emydids range in size from the little 10 cm (4 in) Bog Turtle (described below) to the Painted Terrapin *(Callagur borneoensis)* of Southeast Asia, which may reach a carapace length of 76 cm (30 in). Most are aquatic to semiaquatic pond, lake, or river dwellers with fairly strong shells and at least partially webbed feet; a few, like the American Box Turtles (genus *Terrapene*), are largely terrestrial.

Spotted Turtle   *Clemmys guttata*

Description: This very small turtle is named for the rounded yellow spots scattered over the smooth, unkeeled black or brownish black carapace. These spots are highly variable in number; an occasional specimen will have no carapace spots, while in others the original spots may fade or darken with age. There are nearly always at least a few spots on top of the mostly black head and one or more irregular orange or yellow blotches on each side of the head. The outer surfaces of the legs are black, usually with a few yellow spots, while the lower surfaces of the legs, neck, and other "soft parts" are often orangish or pinkish, mottled with black. The hingeless plastron is usually yellow or orange with a black blotch covering the outer portion of each scute; sometimes the black color may cover most or all of the plastron, particularly in males. Adult carapace length: 9 to 13.6 cm (3.5 to 5.4 in).

The sexes are quite distinct in form and coloration. Males typically have a slightly compressed and elongate carapace and a concave (centrally depressed) plastron. The vent is beyond the edge of the carapace when the tail is fully extended. The male's eyes are brown, and the chin (lower jaw) is tan, brown, or black. The female's carapace is comparatively broader and higher, the plastron is flat or slightly convex, and the tail is thinner, with the vent beneath the carapace edge with the tail extended. The female has orange eyes and a yellowish or orange chin.

The hatchlings average about 2.9 cm (1.14 in) carapace length and are nearly circular in outline. They are colored above like the adults, but usually with just one spot per carapace scute. The plastron is yellowish

Spotted Turtle

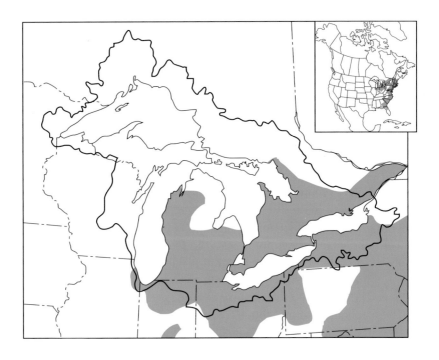

orange, with a central dark blotch. Carapace scute annuli (growth rings) are more conspicuous in juvenile Spotted Turtles than in adults.

Confusing Species: The Bog Turtle lacks round yellow spots on the carapace and head. (Even Spotted Turtles lacking carapace spots will have a few spots on the head.) Some Blanding's Turtles may have yellow spotting on a dark head and carapace, but the spots are smaller and more numerous, and the entire chin, throat, and lower neck are solid yellow. Most Blanding's Turtles have a functional plastral hinge (allowing at least partial closure of the shell) that is lacking in the Spotted Turtle.

Distribution and Status: Spotted Turtles range from extreme northeastern Illinois east to southern Maine and south along the Atlantic coastal plain to northern Florida. There are isolated records for southeastern Quebec, northern Vermont, the western Carolinas, and central Illinois. In the Great Lakes region they occur south of Lake Ontario, west through the Lake Erie and Lake St. Clair basins, north to Georgian Bay, and across the southern and western portions of Michigan's Lower Peninsula to the eastern and southern shore of Lake Michigan.

Spotted Turtles are uncommon to rare throughout their Great Lakes range and tend to occur in isolated colonies surrounded by unoccupied or unsuitable habitats.

Habitat and Ecology: These turtles are found in shallow ponds, wet meadows, tamarack swamps, bogs, fens, marsh channels, sphagnum seepages, and slow streams. Common qualities of occupied habitats include clear, shallow water with a mud or muck bottom and ample aquatic and emergent vegetation. Spotted Turtles tolerate cool water temperatures and resume activity earlier in the year than most other turtle species. On cool, sunny spring days they may bask on logs, muskrat houses, and grass or sedge hummocks. They are inactive at night.

Spotted Turtles often wander on land and may turn up in temporary ponds; males appear to travel longer distances, particularly in spring, perhaps to increase mating opportunities. Spotted turtles are difficult to find in summer, due to reduced movement and lack of basking activity, along with the seasonal proliferation of wetland vegetation. Some individuals become dormant (aestivate) during hot weather, especially if their habitat begins to dry out; at this time they may enter muskrat burrows or dig into the mud or under submerged root systems. Others will leave the water and burrow into soil or leaf litter. They typically hibernate in shallow water from mid-October to late March. Spotted Turtles tend to remain within small home ranges of about 0.5 to 3.5 hectares (1.2 to 8.6 acres), however the total area of suitable habitat available for many local populations often falls within this range.

Spotted Turtles are omnivorous, but with a decided preference for animal food. They will also eat carrion. Favored prey include worms, mollusks, small crayfish, spiders, adult and larval insects, and tadpoles. Vegetable foods include algae, tender plant leaves, and water lily seeds. Feeding occurs almost entirely underwater, although food may be captured on land and taken to the water for swallowing.

Spotted Turtle eggs are often eaten by mammals such as raccoons and skunks, and the juvenile and adult turtles are also vulnerable to these and other predators. Spotted Turtles that become dormant in active muskrat burrows risk attack by the opportunistic rodents. Many living turtles bear the scars of past predatory encounters, and it is common to find specimens that are missing parts of limbs or the tail. When frightened while in or adjacent to water, they dive to the bottom and bury themselves in the mud or beneath vegetation. They are most at risk during their terrestrial wanderings. These shy turtles rarely bite when threatened, and their only direct defense is to withdraw into their shells—a largely ineffective tactic when confronted with a persistent raccoon or other narrow-snouted predator.

Reproduction and Growth: Spotted Turtles begin breeding practically as soon as they emerge from winter dormancy in March or April; mating may also occur in fall prior to hibernation. Mating activity has been recorded at a body (cloacal) temperature as low as 8°C (46°F). Male Spotted Turtles often fight with each other at this time, presumably due to sexual rivalry, though battles are not always in the immediate vicinity of a female. Combatants will bite aggressively and often attempt to mount or to overturn their competitors; eventually the victor will drive its rival from the immediate area. Courtship typically involves the male chasing the female while biting at her legs, tail, and carapace edges. A successful male will climb over the female's shell and bite at her head and neck while clasping the edges of her carapace with his claws. He then slides backward or to one side of her carapace and curls his tail under hers, allowing the vents to come into contact. Copulation usually occurs in shallow water, and may last from 15 minutes to over an hour.

Nesting usually occurs in early to mid-June in the Great Lakes area. The female will leave the water in the early evening and seek a sunny, open spot with sandy or loamy soil that is moist but well drained. If such places are scarce, they may also nest in grassy sites or in the tops of grass or sedge hummocks. The female digs a flask-shaped nest cavity with her hind feet and deposits from two to seven elliptical, flexible-shelled eggs; the cavity is then refilled, and the nest site is abandoned. Each egg is from 3 to 3.4 cm (1.2 to 1.3 in) long. Occasionally a female will lay a second, smaller clutch a few days or weeks after the first, with a reported maximum total production of nine eggs per year.

The incubation period ranges from 45 to 83 days, with warmer temperatures increasing the development rate. Nest temperatures also influence the sex of the offspring. Eggs experimentally incubated between 22.5° and 27°C (72.5° to 80.6°F) produced from 70 percent to 92 percent male hatchlings, while those kept at 30°C (86°F) produced only females. Most young Spotted Turtles emerge from the nest in August or September. Overwintering in the nest has been reported, but its frequency in the Great Lakes area is unknown. A young Spotted Turtle can grow rapidly, and a hatchling may nearly double its size in the first year. Growth slows considerably after the young turtle reaches sexual maturity at an age of 7 to 14 years. Northern turtles generally grow more slowly and mature later than those in the southern parts of the range. A wild individual had a known age of 26 years, and a captive specimen survived for 42 years.

Conservation: The boggy habitats preferred by Spotted Turtles were probably quite widespread over the southern Great Lakes basin up until the last few decades, but most have now been drained and converted to agricultural and other human uses. In this region Spotted Turtles survive mostly in small isolated colonies in remnant wetlands, many of which are threatened by development and pollution. Preserving viable populations of the species will require identifying and then protecting the core wetland habitats, along with adjacent upland nesting sites and dispersal routes between colonies.

Unfortunately, Spotted Turtles are not secure even where their habitat is protected. These turtles are highly valued by reptile hobbyists due to their small size and bright coloration, and collectors have reduced or eliminated many populations throughout the species' range. This turtle has been given varying degrees of legal protection in most states and provinces of the Great Lakes region; rangewide protection is fully warranted and will be necessary to eliminate the commercial trade. Other threats to this species include road mortality, large predator populations (particularly raccoons), and vandalistic shooting.

Wood Turtle *Clemmys insculpta*

Description: The Wood Turtle's scientific name means "sculptured turtle," and its rough brown or grayish brown carapace does look as though it was carved from wood. There is usually a low central keel, and the carapace scutes have well-defined growth lines (annuli) crossed by raylike ridges (fig. 8). Many specimens also have a pattern of radiating yellow and black lines on the vertebral and pleural scutes. The plastron is yellow with a black blotch at the rear outer corner of each scute, and has a V-shaped notch at the tail. The head and upper surfaces of the neck, legs, and tail are black; the large outer scales of the front legs are black or brown, often edged or speckled with yellow. The lower surfaces of the neck, legs, tail, and other "soft parts" vary in color from yellow or yellowish orange (in the Great Lakes area) to bright orange (mostly in the central and eastern part of the range), or even reddish (in specimens from the eastern edge of the range). Adult carapace length: 16 to 25 cm (6.3 to 9.8 in).

Mature males and females are easily distinguished. Males have comparatively higher, often narrower shells, larger, wider heads, and more robust limbs and feet, with thicker claws. The male's tail is longer and thicker than the female's; with the tail extended, the vent is well beyond the rear edge of the carapace. The male's plastron is concave (depressed

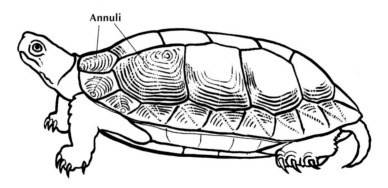

Annuli

Fig. 8. Wood Turtles have prominent growth rings (annuli) that can be used to estimate a turtle's minimum age. This specimen would probably be at least 12 to 13 years old.

Wood Turtle

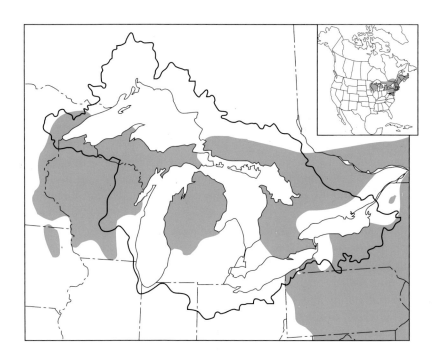

in the center). In comparison, the female's carapace is broader and less domed, and the rear marginals are more outwardly flaring. The tail is narrower and (with tail extended) the vent is at or beneath the rear edge of the carapace. The female's head and limbs are less massive, the claws are thinner, and the plastron is flat or slightly convex. Immature males may be mistaken for females when the above criteria are applied to specimens with carapace lengths of less than about 16 cm (6.3 in), since female characters are essentially juvenile characters.

Hatchlings are a uniform gray, tan, or brown color, and have nearly circular carapaces and long, thin tails. They range from 2.8 to 3.8 cm (1.1 to 1.5 in) in carapace length. The typical color pattern (described above) is usually acquired during the first full year of growth.

Confusing Species: Blanding's Turtles are also yellow under the neck and legs and have a similar plastral pattern, but they have a hinged plastron and an unkeeled, domelike carapace. The Bog Turtle does not exceed a carapace length of 11.5 cm (4.5 in) and usually has a large orange or yellowish orange blotch on each side of its head.

Distribution and Status: Wood Turtles are found from Nova Scotia west through southern Quebec and Ontario to eastern Minnesota and northern Iowa, and south through New England, New York, and Pennsylvania to northern Virginia. Within the Great Lakes basin the species occurs from the western end of Lake Superior through northern Wisconsin and the western and central Upper and northern Lower Peninsulas of Michigan. It is also recorded from a small area east of Whitefish Bay and from Georgian Bay to the western end of Lake Ontario and portions of northwestern New York.

Within its Great Lakes range the Wood Turtle is generally uncommon to rare, and in recent years many local populations have been greatly reduced or extirpated by human activities. The species can be locally common where the habitat is intact and human disturbance is minimal.

Habitat and Ecology: Wood Turtles are most common in or near sandy-bottomed streams or rivers, although they also occur in streams with partially rocky or silty beds. They are largely aquatic and sometimes gregarious from fall through late spring but are generally more solitary and terrestrial during the summer months, wandering through woodlands, alder thickets, swamps, wet meadows, and fields within or near the floodplain. Some Wood Turtles stay in or near the water throughout the year, and those found on land are usually within 150 m (500 ft) of moving water. Juveniles tend not to wander as far from water as the adults. Wood Turtles generally remain within rather restricted home ranges of about 1 to 5 hectares (2.5 to 12.4 acres), though some individuals will move considerably greater distances using a stream or river as a dispersal route. These animals have modest homing ability, and can return to a home range if displaced up to 2 km (1.24 mi).

Wood Turtles are diurnal and fond of basking, whether on logs over water or in sunny places on land; in hot weather they return to water or bury themselves in soil or plant debris. Hibernation (typically mid-October through mid-April) nearly always occurs under water. A dormant Wood Turtle may rest unburied on the stream bottom or wedge itself under a submerged log, rock, or an overhanging bank. They sometimes congregate during winter dormancy, a habit not clearly related to a lack of suitable hibernation sites.

Wood Turtles are able to feed both under water and on land. They are opportunistic omnivores, consuming various leaves (including violet, strawberry, dandelion, and willow), berries (strawberry, raspberry, blackberry), algae, fungi, insects (both aquatic and terrestrial), slugs, snails, and earthworms. They will also scavenge recently dead animals. Wood Turtles sometimes use an unusual method of procuring earthworms—the worm-hunting turtle will "thump" the ground with alternating movements of its front feet, or by pushing down with the feet to lift and then drop the front of the plastron. It is thought that the resulting vibrations cause the worms to surface, where they are seized by the turtle. Wood Turtles use a similar "thumping" behavior during courtship and during aggressive encounters with other Wood Turtles, but it is unknown whether the use of the behavior for feeding is instinctive or fortuitously learned by a few individuals.

Nest mortality typically exceeds 80 percent; the raccoon is usually the most abundant and efficient nest predator, but in some areas skunks, mink, otters, foxes, coyotes, and ravens destroy many eggs. Hatchling and small juvenile turtles are eaten by these same enemies as well as by feral cats and dogs, large fish, and frogs. Adult Wood Turtles are better protected against attacks, but raccoons are sometimes able to kill them, and the turtles often sustain serious injuries during nonfatal encounters. Wood Turtles rarely bite in self-defense, and withdrawal into the shell is their only recourse when attacked. The lack of a plastral hinge leaves them especially vulnerable to narrow-snouted predators during their terrestrial wanderings. In many populations, a high percentage of adult turtles examined will be missing one or more limbs or the tail, and often have healed cracks and puncture wounds in the shell. Porcupines sometimes gnaw on the shells of living and dead turtles, presumably for the mineral content. Wood Turtles are often host to leeches (*Placobdella* sp.) during their aquatic periods.

Reproduction and Growth: Although they do not specifically defend territories, Wood Turtles will chase and attack other individuals of the same or the opposite sex and are known to form dominance hierarchies in the wild. Dominant males (most often the larger, older animals) appear to have better success at mating and fertilizing eggs than do subordinate males. Mating nearly always occurs in shallow water and is more frequent in spring and fall when these turtles are most aquatic. A courting pair of Wood Turtles may perform a mating "dance" in which the two face each other and swing their heads back and forth. Perhaps more frequently the male simply pursues and mounts the female by clinging to the edges of her carapace with his claws. He often bites at her head and legs and may rock from side to side or bang his plastron against the female's carapace by extending and then relaxing his forelegs (presumably to discourage her from trying to escape his attentions). Copulation may last for several hours. Successful fertilization reportedly occurs in only a small fraction of mating attempts.

Female Wood Turtles lay one clutch of 3 to 18 (usually 5 to 13) eggs in late May or June, though not all will reproduce annually. Most females nest in the evening; preferred nest sites are open and unshaded (having little or no vegetation cover), with moist sand or sandy soil, and sufficiently elevated above the water that flooding is unlikely. She may make several exploratory attempts at digging with her front and/or hind feet before settling on one spot, but the nest cavity itself is dug only with the hind feet. The elliptical, flexible-shelled eggs range in length from 2.7 to 4.2 cm (1.1 to 1.7 in). Incubation requires from 47 to 69 days, with most hatchlings emerging in late August or early September. Nest temperature will affect the rate of embryonic development, but does not determine the sex of the hatchling in this species.

Young Wood Turtles attain sexual maturity in 12 to 20 years in the wild. Attainment of maturity generally takes longer in northern populations, due to the shorter season of activity and resultant slower growth. A count of scute annuli will give a reasonable estimate of age in juvenile and subadult specimens; annuli counts will tend to underestimate true age in mature specimens. In a Michigan study, most reproductive adults were in their third and fourth decade of life. A captive specimen lived 58 years, and it is likely that wild individuals occasionally survive as long.

Conservation: Wood Turtle numbers have declined significantly over much of their Great Lakes range, including areas where suitable habitats remain. There is no doubt that in some places they have suffered from habitat fragmentation and surface water pollution. The building of roads close to rivers and streams has lead to the untimely deaths of many turtles. Certain fisheries management practices, such as sand bank stabilization and the digging of sand traps in streams, can eliminate nesting sites and reduce preferred turtle habitat. On the other hand, human activities that open up dense, unbroken floodplain forest can potentially create new feeding, basking, and nesting areas. Wood Turtle populations can persist despite modest levels of riparian development and use, such as timber harvest, light grazing, low-intensity agriculture, and recreational activities such as fishing and canoeing, provided the turtles themselves (along with critical nesting sites) are left undisturbed. Unfortunately, this last provision is rarely assured.

In the past Wood Turtles have been exploited for human food and by biological supply companies for use in teaching and experimentation. More recently the species has been in great demand in the pet trade. The tendency for Wood Turtles to congregate in shallow streams in winter and their linear habitats in general make them extremely vulnerable to mass

Wood Turtle, hatching

collecting, and commercial collectors have seriously depleted, or even eliminated, local populations. The species is legally protected over the entire Great Lakes region (and over practically all of its range elsewhere), but poaching will likely continue as a threat as long as demand remains high. Incidental collecting by canoeists and hikers and the shooting of basking turtles by vandals are additional drains on their numbers.

Wood Turtle populations are characterized by high nest mortality, delayed sexual maturity, and long adult life. Turtle species with these characteristics depend on a very high annual survivorship of adults, and a surprisingly high survival rate for immature animals, to maintain a stable or growing population. Any factor that increases mortality beyond normal low levels will inevitably lead to a population decline and, over the long term, possible local extinction.

Bog Turtle   *Clemmys muhlenbergii*

Description: This very small turtle has a brown or black, somewhat domed carapace with a low central keel. A light central blotch or a radiating pattern of light lines may occur on each of the large carapace scutes. The plastron is also brown or black, often with contrasting yellowish blotches, particularly toward the center or the front edge. Scutes on both the carapace and plastron are usually sculptured with circular ridges (annuli), but in older specimens the shell may be worn nearly smooth. A conspicuous, irregularly shaped orange, yellowish, or reddish blotch is usually present on each side of the head and neck. In some specimens the blotches may meet on top of the neck to form a continuous band, while in old adults the blotches may fade or darken. Otherwise the head, neck, limbs, and tail, are mostly dark brown, frequently mottled with red, orange, or yellow. Adult carapace length: 7.9 to 11.4 cm (3.1 to 4.5 in).

An adult male Bog Turtle has a concave plastron and a long, thick tail. With tail extended, the male's vent is beyond the rear edge of the carapace. The female has a flat plastron and a thinner tail. With tail extended, the female's vent is at or beneath the rear edge of the carapace. The male's carapace is usually flatter and less domed than the female's.

Hatchling Bog Turtles are colored like the adults but have rounder carapaces and proportionally longer tails, and measure from 2.3 to 3.4 cm (0.9 to 1.3 in) in carapace length.

Confusing Species: The Spotted Turtle has rounded yellow or orange spots on the head and neck, and usually on the smooth, black carapace as well.

Bog Turtle

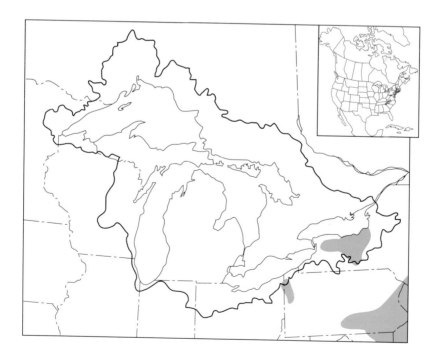

Wood Turtles lack the bright orange blotches on the sides of the head and quickly grow to exceed the size of the largest Bog Turtle.

Distribution and Status: The Bog Turtle exists in small, isolated colonies within a highly fragmented range, the largest portion of which extends from eastern New York and western Massachusetts south through New Jersey and southeastern Pennsylvania to Maryland. Another portion, at generally higher elevations, extends from southern Virginia through western North Carolina and eastern Tennessee to northeastern Georgia. Bog Turtles also occur (or recently occurred) in northwestern Pennsylvania and enter the Great Lakes drainage basin in north-central New York, south of Lake Ontario. They have recently disappeared from several known sites in the basin, where their continued existence is precarious at best.

This species is uncommon to rare and extremely localized in distribution throughout its range.

Habitat and Ecology: Bog Turtles occur in saturated wetlands such as sphagnum bogs, fens, wet meadows, alder swamps, and sedge marshes. Open habitats with slowly flowing, mud or silt-bottomed streams, springs, rivulets, or surface seepages are preferred, while densely shaded sites are avoided. Bog Turtles spend much time basking in the sun in spring and on cooler summer days, but may aestivate in burrows or under vegetation during periods of hot weather or drought. They often move about by following rivulets or by tunneling through sphagnum moss or other vegetation; they also utilize the tunnel systems of muskrats, voles, and bog lemmings. When not basking, active Bog Turtles are usually in shallow water. Home ranges reported for these turtles are quite small, ranging from about 0.1 to 2 hectares (0.2 to 5 acres); however, the total area of suitable habitat in many Bog Turtle colonies often does not exceed this range. Males appear to range slightly farther, on average, than females. In winter Bog Turtles generally burrow into the mud beneath moving water, such as in marsh rivulets, rodent burrows or runways, or under sedge clumps, moss, or roots. Dormancy typically lasts from early October through early April.

Bog Turtles can eat on land or under water. They feed mostly on invertebrates such as insects, snails, slugs, crayfish, and earthworms but will opportunistically scavenge carrion and capture small vertebrates such as tadpoles and frogs. Some plant material is also eaten, including berries, pondweed (*Potamogeton* sp.), watercress, and the seeds of pondweed and sedge (*Carex* sp.).

These little turtles are attacked and sometimes eaten by raccoons, skunks, foxes, dogs, mink, and even shrews. These same predators will also consume Bog Turtle eggs. In some populations, a significant percentage of adults will have injuries from past predatory attempts, including shell fractures or missing limbs or tails. The use of muskrat tunnels by these turtles may lead to occasional attacks from the opportunistic rodents. Bog Turtles blend well into their surroundings and spend much of their time in concealed situations. When surprised while basking, a Bog Turtle will usually dive into the water and quickly burrow into the mud or vegetation, but some individuals remain motionless, perhaps to avoid attracting attention.

Reproduction and Growth: Male Bog Turtles often show aggression toward one another, including open-mouthed threats and actual shoving and biting. It is unclear whether these encounters involve the formation of dominance hierarchies, or if they represent defense of territory or competition for mates. Mating occurs from late April through early June and can take place either in water or on dry land. Courtship begins with the male approaching and sometimes circling the female while nudging or "smelling" her tail region, perhaps seeking cues for sexual recognition. He then bites at her head and legs in an attempt to keep her from escaping, and eventually mounts her carapace and holds on with his claws. In some cases the male will thump the female's carapace with his plastron, a behavior also seen in the related Wood Turtle. The male may continue to nip at the female's head during copulation, which normally lasts about 20 minutes.

Nesting is in late May, June, and early July. When seeking a place to nest, the female moves from the wetter parts of the habitat to a higher, drier area. Typical nest sites include the tops of sedge or grass tussocks, mounds of decaying moss or other vegetation, muskrat houses, or elevated road or railroad beds. The nest cavity is dug with the hind feet, and one to six eggs are deposited, arranged in the nest, and then covered. A female may tamp the top of the nest with her plastron before leaving the site.

The eggs are white and elliptical and average about 3 cm (1.2 in) in length. Incubation requires from 45 to 65 days, with most hatchlings emerging in August and September. As with most turtle species, growth is quite rapid in the early years but slows after maturity is attained. Most Bog Turtles reach breeding size in 6 to 10 years and can probably live for 30 years or more; a zoo specimen attained a minimum age of 40 years.

Conservation: The boggy wetlands preferred by Bog Turtles were probably quite widespread after the retreat of continental glaciers and were not an uncommon habitat type even up to historical times. Range fragmentation in this species may have begun long before the arrival of European settlers in eastern North America, due to natural changes in climate and vegetation. Human activities have greatly accelerated the loss of suitable habitat over the last century, since bogs and sedge meadows are prime targets for drainage and filling; these turtles quickly disappear along with their habitats.

Natural wetland succession resulting in the invasion of open areas by trees and shrubs is also detrimental to the sun-loving Bog Turtles. At one time they were usually able to shift their home ranges into new habitat as required, but now, with wetlands hemmed in by human development, such succession can result in local extinction of the turtles. The trapping of beavers and the suppression of fire in the northeast have also hastened the succession of open wetlands into shaded swamps and woodlands. Light grazing by domestic livestock, especially horses, may benefit Bog Turtles by suppressing the spread of shade-producing plants. Another potential threat is the invasion of wetlands by introduced plants such as purple loosestrife (Lythrum salicaria), which may displace native plant communities favored by the turtles.

Identifying, protecting, and managing critical habitats are key elements in conserving Bog Turtle populations. Unfortunately, even setting aside dedicated reserves is not enough. Bog Turtles bring high prices in the commercial pet trade, due to their rarity and small size. Unscrupulous collectors have been known to remove whole populations, sometimes invading protected wildlife reserves and sifting through entire bogs to do so. This species is afforded legal protection throughout its range and is given the highest level of protection from international trade; it is listed on Appendix I of the CITES Treaty (Convention on International Trade in Endangered Species of Wild Fauna and Flora). Unfortunately, enforcement is difficult and poaching is likely to continue as long as the potential profits from illegal collecting remain high.

Eastern Box Turtle   *Terrapene carolina carolina*

Description: This is a small land turtle with a domed ("helmet-shaped") carapace and a hinged plastron. The carapace has a slight keel along the midline, and the scutes usually have prominent annuli, though shells of older individuals may be worn quite smooth. The carapace coloration is

Eastern Box Turtle, male

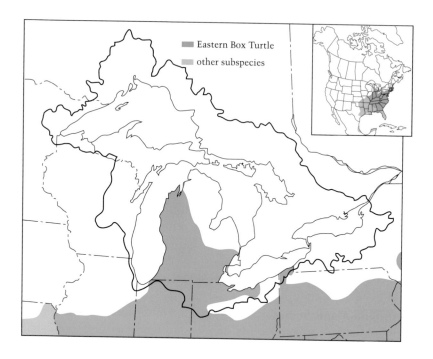

variable but is usually brown or black with a radiating pattern of yellowish or orange spots, blotches, or lines in each scute. In some specimens the lighter color may cover much of the shell, so that they appear as yellow animals with dark markings. The plastron, which nearly fills the opening of the carapace, has a distinct flexible hinge between the pectoral and abdominal scutes, allowing total closure of the two plastral lobes. Plastron coloration can be a solid black, brown, tan, or yellow, or any combination of these colors arrayed in blotches or streaks. The upper jaw forms a short, hooklike beak. Skin color on head, neck, and legs is as variable as the shell color, being typically brown with some yellow, orange, or white spots or streaks. In some turtles (usually males) the lighter colors may predominate. The tail is very short. Adult carapace length: 11.8 to 19.8 cm (4.6 to 7.8 in); few adults ever exceed a carapace length of 16 cm (6.3 in).

Males usually have red eyes (irises), and their carapace margins are more flared at the rear. The rear lobe of the males's plastron is concave, the hind claws are thick and quite curved, and the tail is slightly longer and thicker than the female's, with the vent at or beyond the end of the carapace with tail fully extended. Females usually have brown or yellowish brown eyes and have less flared rear marginal scutes. The female's plastron is flat to slightly convex (occasionally very slightly concave), the hind claws are comparatively thin and less curved, and the tail is short, with the vent beneath the rear edge of the carapace.

Hatchling Eastern Box Turtles have flatter, more circular carapaces that are brown or grayish brown with a light spot in the center of each scute. The plastral hinge is nonfunctional. Carapace length at hatching ranges from 2.6 to 3.1 cm (1 to 1.2 in).

Confusing Species: Blanding's Turtle also has a plastral hinge, but its elongated carapace is smooth and unkeeled, its upper jaw is notched (rather than hooked) at the front, and its throat and lower neck are usually bright yellow. The sometimes terrestrial Wood Turtle has a broader, less domed carapace, and its plastron lacks a hinge. The Ornate Box Turtle (p. 350) has a dorsally flattened, usually unkeeled carapace, and a less variable color pattern on the carapace consisting of radiating yellow lines on a dark background; the plastron is similarly patterned.

Distribution and Status: The Eastern Box Turtle ranges from southern Maine south to northern Florida, and west to Tennessee and southern Illinois, and north through Indiana, southern Michigan, and southern and western Pennsylvania. In the Great Lakes area it has been found from Grand Traverse County, Michigan, south along the Lake Michigan shore to northern Indiana and east through southern Michigan and northwestern Ohio; it also occurs in Erie County, Pennsylvania. Other subspecies extend the range of *Terrapene carolina* to eastern Oklahoma and Texas and east through the Gulf Coast region and peninsular Florida.

The apparent scarcity or absence of Box Turtles in a band from east-central Indiana to northeastern Ohio has been attributed to forest regression during the postglacial xerothermic period; subsequent deforestation due to intensive cultivation undoubtedly eliminated remaining habitat, perhaps discouraging the turtle's spread into the area. Archaeological records indicate that Box Turtles were probably present in the Lake Ontario drainage basin of western New York, and in adjacent southern Ontario, within the last 1,000 years but had practically disappeared by about 1700. Their extinction in this area has been linked to overexploitation and habitat modification by American Indians, who collected the turtles for food and for ceremonial purposes (for discussion, see Adler 1970). Box Turtles are sometimes found in places outside of their recognized range, or where they were thought to be extirpated. Recent examples include a possibly viable population reported near Cleveland, Ohio, and several records in southern Ontario (including Point Pelee National Park). These and other out-of-range records are often attributed to the intentional or accidental release of pet turtles. However, given this animal's potential longevity, the possibility that some of these occurrences represent the last vestiges of former natural populations should not be discounted without evidence to the contrary.

Eastern Box Turtles are now an uncommon to rare and steadily declining species in the region but were historically quite common and widespread in the woodlands of the eastern Lake Michigan and western Lake Erie basins; they can remain locally common in intact habitats that are not bisected by busy roads.

Habitat and Ecology: Eastern Box Turtles favor deciduous or mixed woodlands, especially those with sandy soils, but also utilize adjacent thickets, old fields, pastures, vegetated dunes, marshes, and bog edges. Access to water (e.g., small ponds, seepages, springs, bogs, or slow streams) is an important factor, as is the availability of unshaded nesting sites. Moist, open hardwood forest and forest/old field edges with some relief, such as ravines or modest slopes tend to support higher turtle densities than drier forests in flat terrain, or often-inundated floodplain woods. These turtles are diurnal and most active in spring and fall; during the summer they may have a brief activity period in the morning, or following moderate to heavy rain showers, but otherwise spend much time buried in leaf litter, shallow burrows, or under the edges of brush piles or rotting logs. During hot weather Box Turtles are often found soaking around the edges of ponds or small streams, or even paddling in open water. They are rather inefficient swimmers, tending to float on the surface with poor directional control, but individual turtles may temporarily adopt aquatic habits and can become fairly proficient at swimming and bottom walking.

At the onset of cool weather in the fall these turtles dig into the soil, typically going deeper as temperatures decline. While some eventually burrow as far as 60 cm (24 in) into the ground, other hibernating Box Turtles successfully overwinter in far shallower burrows, sometimes with the tops of their carapaces still visible below the leaf litter. They are able to tolerate subfreezing body temperatures, with over half of their body water frozen, for periods of several days. Some Box Turtles die, however, when early spring thaws stimulate early emergence, only to be followed by a return to severe cold. Most emerge from dormancy in mid- to late April, when warmer weather is more reliable. Occasionally, a Box Turtle will overwinter completely submerged in a pond or stream.

Box Turtles frequently spend many years, or even their entire lives, within small home ranges of about 1.5 to 16 hectares (3.7 to 40 acres). Home ranges of several turtles may overlap. Although "nip and tuck" battles between males may take place on occasion, there is no clear evidence of territorial defense. Brief trips beyond the normal home range for nesting or mating may occur, and these turtles have modest homing abilities. Adult specimens have successfully returned to their home range when displaced a kilometer (0.6 mi) or so away, probably using the sun for orientation. Homing success falls as displacement distances increase. Some Box Turtles, mostly males, appear to be habitual transients, and their movements through the home ranges of other turtles may be important in maintaining genetic diversity within and between populations.

These turtles consume a wide variety of plant and animal foods, including earthworms, snails, slugs, insects, mushrooms, various leafy greens, and fruits. They often remain within patches of ripening raspberries or blackberries until every reachable berry is consumed. Box Turtles act as seed dispersal agents for many forest plants and may be particularly important to reproduction and dispersal of the may-apple (*Podophyllum peltatum*); seed germination for this species was found to be much enhanced after passing through a turtle's digestive tract. Hatchling and small juvenile Box Turtles appear to be more carnivorous than adults, gradually adding more plant foods to their diet as they grow.

Skunks, raccoons, and foxes seek out Box Turtle eggs, and the smaller juveniles are prey to these mammals as well as to shrews, birds, and snakes. Shrews are a particularly serious threat, since they move through leaf litter and along rotting logs where very young Box Turtles often hide. Hatchlings and small juveniles do not have functional plastral hinges, but they can produce a musky-smelling secretion that may deter some predators. Adult turtles can use the plastral hinge to completely close up their shells and are usually safe from most predators. Many specimens are found with shell injuries or scarring from past predatory attempts or ground fires. While most Box Turtles quickly retire into their shells when threatened, some individual turtles are reluctant (or sometimes too fat!) to fully withdraw and are more vulnerable to attack. In many places automobiles probably kill more Box Turtles than all natural hazards combined.

Reproduction and Growth: Eastern Box Turtles may mate at any time during the active season, but breeding activity is most frequent in spring and fall. Males sometimes fight each other, but territorial defense and hierarchy formation has not been demonstrated in the wild. (In captive groups of Box Turtles kept outdoors, one or two males will often be more active and do most of the mating.) During courtship, the male typically circles the female while biting the edges of her shell and shoving her with his front feet. The female usually withdraws into her shell, and the male soon climbs on top of her carapace and continues biting at her head. Eventually he slips back until his hind claws can grip under the edge of her carapace; the female may then close her plastron on his hind feet, holding him securely. Copulation can occur only when the female opens her rear plastral lobe and the male assumes a vertical position, allowing the vents on their short tails to come into contact. During intromission, he will fall backward until his carapace is resting on the ground. After mating is complete, the male is usually left upside down and must right himself quickly or face possible death by overheating or suffocation.

Most nesting occurs on warm evenings in June or early July. The female seeks a sunny, often elevated spot, preferably with moist sandy soil and sparse vegetation, and digs a nest cavity with alternating movements of her hind feet. From 3 to 11 eggs are laid, then covered and left to their fate. The eggs are oval, flexible-shelled, and from 3 to 4 cm (1.2 to 1.6 in) in length. Some female Eastern Box Turtles may produce more than one clutch per year, though a single clutch is probably the norm in the region.

Females can store sperm and produce fertile eggs up to four years after mating. Incubation requires from 50 to 90 days, with warmer nest temperatures resulting in earlier hatching. Hatchlings typically emerge in September or October, but those from later nests may overwinter in the nest. Sex in this species is determined by nest temperatures about midway through embryonic development. Under laboratory conditions, mostly males were produced at 27°C (80.6°F) or lower, while only females developed at 30°C (86°F) or higher.

For the first few years of life Eastern Box Turtles can grow about 1 to 2 cm (0.4 to 0.8 in) per year, but growth slows after maturity. Sexual maturity may occasionally be reached in 5 or 6 years, but can require 10 years or more in northern parts of the range. In most populations a majority of breeding adults will be greater than 15 years of age. Counting the annuli on a shell scute will give a reasonable estimate of age in a juvenile specimen, but annuli counts will tend to underestimate the age of adult turtles. This species is known for its longevity. Box Turtles routinely live to ages of 40 to 50 years, and a few individuals will surpass the century mark. The known longevity record is 138 years.

Eastern Box Turtle, closed plastron

Conservation: Eastern Box Turtles are generally harmless to human interests. They occasionally wander into gardens and sample the produce, but this minor problem can be solved by installing a low fence or simply moving the offender a short distance away. Box Turtles may aid horticultural efforts by consuming slugs and insect pests. As noted above, these turtles act as seed dispersers and fill numerous other ecological roles in the woodland/woods edge community.

The rapid conversion of woodlands and wetlands into agricultural land over the last century has eliminated Box Turtles from much of their former range in the region, and the present spread of suburban development continues to fragment habitat and isolate the remaining populations. Due to their sedentary habits and longevity, these turtles often survive in small pockets of habitat such as farm woodlots, abandoned cropland, and parks. Unfortunately, these remnant populations may not be viable over the long term, especially if road mortality or collecting continuously whittles down their numbers. Demand for Box Turtles in the domestic and international pet trade has encouraged poaching and caused an additional drain on their numbers. Box Turtles are afforded varying degrees of legal protection throughout the region, but these laws fail to protect them from their worst enemies, bulldozers and automobiles.

Blanding's Turtle   *Emydoidea blandingii*

Description: The moderately high, domed carapace of an adult Blanding's Turtle is elongate and quite smooth, without keels or sculpturing. It is black or brown, often marked with a highly variable pattern of tan or yellowish spots or streaks. The plastron is yellowish, with a dark blotch at the outer rear edge of each scute, and usually has well-defined annuli and a shallow V-shaped notch at the tail. Rarely, dark color may cover most or all of the plastron. Most adult specimens have a hinge between the pectoral and abdominal scutes, but hinge flexibility varies greatly between individuals. The head is rather flat, with a short, rounded snout; the upper jaw is notched at the front, giving this turtle a permanent "smile." The top and sides of the head may be black, brown, or olive, with yellowish or brownish spots or mottling, while the chin, throat, and lower surface of the very long neck are bright yellow. Adult carapace length: 15.2 to 27.4 cm (6 to 10.8 in).

A male Blanding's Turtle's plastron is moderately concave, and the vent is beyond the rear edge of the carapace when the tail is fully extended.

Blanding's Turtle

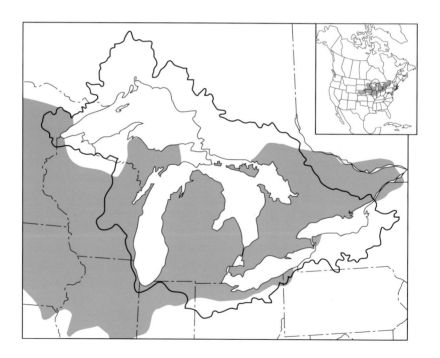

Females have a flatter plastron and a narrower tail, with the vent at or beneath the rear edge of the carapace when the tail is extended.

The hatchling has a gray, brown, or black carapace, 3 to 3.5 cm (1.2 to 1.4 in) long, with a low keel and sometimes a light spot in the center of each scute. The plastron usually has a black central blotch rimmed by yellow or cream color; the hinge is not functional. The tail is proportionally longer and thinner than that of the adult. Immature Blanding's Turtles are often more brightly marked than the adults and their carapace scutes may show distinct growth rings.

Confusing Species: Wood Turtles have a lower, more sculptured carapace and an unhinged plastron. Spotted Turtles have larger, more rounded spots on the head and carapace and also lack a plastral hinge. The Eastern Box Turtle has a hooked (not notched) upper beak and generally does not have a plain yellow throat and lower neck.

Distribution and Status: The primary range of the Blanding's Turtle extends from extreme southwestern Quebec and southern Ontario west to Minnesota and Nebraska and south to central Illinois. There are disjunct populations in parts of New England (southern Maine, southeastern New Hampshire, and eastern Massachusetts), and in eastern New York and southern Nova Scotia. This range fragmentation suggests that the species enjoyed a much wider distribution at some point since the end of the Pleistocene. In the Great Lakes basin Blanding's Turtles are found throughout southern Ontario (Point Pelee to Georgian Bay), along both shores of Lake Erie (though they may be nearly extirpated in Pennsylvania), in Michigan (Lower and central Upper Peninsula), northern Ohio, Indiana, eastern Illinois, and Wisconsin (Lake Michigan drainage). They are also reported from New York at sites near the St. Lawrence River (Jefferson County) and the Niagara River (Niagara County).

Destruction and degradation of wetlands and adjacent uplands has eliminated the Blanding's Turtle in many places, though they can be fairly common where suitable habitat exists. The Great Lakes area is presently a stronghold for this turtle, which is vulnerable and generally in decline at the periphery of its range.

Habitat and Ecology: For most of the year Blanding's Turtles live in and around shallow, weedy waters such as ponds, marshes, swamps, and lake inlets and coves. They are sometimes found in rivers but concentrate their activities in backwaters, embayments, and sloughs, and are only transient in portions of streams with more than a sluggish current. Terrestrial movement by adult males and females is common in spring and, to a lesser extent, in fall. Males may travel overland to increase their mating opportunities, while females are most likely concerned with finding suitable nesting sites.

On cool sunny days, Blanding's Turtles will emerge to bask on logs, grass clumps, sloping banks, or other high perches near water. In the heat of summer, they may restrict their activities to early morning and evening, or even adopt nocturnal habits. The drying of their shallow water habitats spurs some individuals to migrate overland to new bodies of water, while others will burrow under roots, mud, or plant debris and aestivate until conditions improve. They hibernate underwater (more rarely under debris close to water) from late October or early November until early April. They are quite cold tolerant, however, and are frequently seen moving sluggishly under the ice.

Crustaceans, particularly crayfish, are favored food items, with insects, worms, leeches, snails, small fish, tadpoles, frogs, and some plants rounding out the diet. Most feeding occurs under water, though prey is sometimes seized on shore and carried to the water for swallowing. These turtles are capable of eating on land but appear to do so infrequently. They often forage by creeping along the bottom in shallow water, sweeping their lowered heads back and forth over the substrate. A Blanding's Turtle will stalk a crayfish or other prey by slowly creeping forward with its head partly retracted. When within range, the long neck darts out and the mouth and throat gape, causing water and prey to be sucked in. Small animals are swallowed whole, but larger prey are held in the jaws and torn into pieces with the front claws. In summer they often forage and feed after dark.

Raccoons, skunks, and foxes are the principal predators on Blanding's Turtle eggs, and these mammals along with fish, frogs, snakes, wading birds, crows, and other animals will eat hatchling and juvenile turtles. Adult Blanding's Turtles have far fewer natural predators. When on land they depend on their shells for protection and rarely, if ever, bite defensively. As noted above, the plastral hinge varies in its utility. Many individuals can close up almost as tightly as a Box Turtle, while some have little or no hinge flexibility. Blanding's Turtles are strong swimmers. When surprised in or near water, these turtles usually dive in and either swim to deeper water or conceal themselves in bottom mud or vegetation.

Reproduction and Growth: Mating can occur from April to November but is most frequent in spring. A courting male typically approaches the female in shallow to fairly deep water and mounts her carapace in a quick rush. Clasping her carapace edges with his claws, he may bite at her head and forelimbs or extend his neck and press his chin on her snout, forcing her to remain withdrawn. He may also swing his head back and forth over the female's head or bob his head vertically and blow a stream of water or bubbles over her head. A copulating pair may sink to the bottom, float near the surface, or hang on to emergent branches or vegetation.

Fewer than half of the adult females in a population may reproduce in a given year. Most nesting is in June. Gravid females may travel over a kilometer (0.6 mi) from the water to find suitable nest sites, which ideally are open, sunny spots with moist but well-drained sandy or loamy soil. Lawns, gardens, plowed fields, or even gravel road edges are used if better sites are lacking. The nest cavity is dug with alternating movements of the hind feet. Clutch size varies from 6 to 21 eggs, which are elliptical and average about 3.6 cm (1.4 in) in length. The egg shells may initially be quite rigid, but they absorb water and become more flexible as incubation progresses.

Eggs not destroyed by predators or other hazards will hatch in 50 to 75 days, with most hatchlings emerging in August or early September. Blanding's Turtles have temperature-dependent sex determination; eggs incubated at 25°C (77°F) or lower will produce nearly all males, while those incubated at 30°C (86°F) or above will produce females. A Blanding's Turtle will grow to sexual maturity in 14 to 20 years. Counting plastral scute annuli will usually give a reasonable age estimate in juvenile and young adult specimens; after maturity, annuli counts will tend to underestimate actual age. Adults are potentially long-lived, and individuals 50 to 70 years old were still reproductive. A Minnesota female was known to be at least 77 years old, and it seems possible that a few individuals may reach the century mark.

Conservation: The lower Great Lakes basin is probably the center of abundance for the Blanding's Turtle, but even here the loss and degradation of wetland habitats has greatly reduced or even eliminated local populations. Efforts by government agencies and private citizen's groups to conserve the larger remaining wetlands will not ensure the future of these turtles unless attention is paid to protecting smaller ponds and marshes as well as adjacent upland corridors and nesting sites. Road mortality constitutes a major drain on turtle numbers, and the construction of a road between an aquatic habitat and the only available upland nesting sites may result in a long-term death sentence for a local Blanding's Turtle population.

Blanding's Turtles rarely feed on game fish and are of no concern to fish management or other economic interests. They have, to date, attracted minimal attention from the pet trade, though they have been exploited in the recent past by biological supply companies and for human food in Ohio and Wisconsin and perhaps elsewhere. It is extremely doubtful whether the concept of "sustained harvest" can be applied to these long-lived, slow-maturing turtles. A long-term study of a Blanding's Turtle population in southern Michigan (Congdon, Dunham, and van Loben Sels 1993) revealed that to maintain population stability, annual survivorship for adults had to exceed 93 percent, while at least 72 percent of juveniles (age 1–13) had to survive each year. Any factor that increases losses beyond these normal low levels will inevitably cause the population to decline.

Common Map Turtle *Graptemys geographica*

Description: The Common Map Turtle is named for the network of dark-bordered, yellowish to orange lines on the otherwise olive or grayish-brown carapace that, with some imagination, may resemble waterways or contour lines on a map. In older individuals this pattern may be obscured by dark pigment. The carapace is fairly broad, with a low to moderate keel along the midline, and a flared hind margin that is serrated (due to the projecting rear edges of the marginal scutes). The broad, flat plastron is usually plain yellow, but juveniles and males may have dark markings along the scute borders. The head, neck, and limbs are dark olive, brown, or black, with numerous thin yellow, green, or orangish stripes. Most specimens will have a small oval or triangular light spot behind each eye. Adult female carapace length: 17 to 27.3 cm (6.7 to 10.7 in); adult male carapace length: 10 to 16 cm (3.9 to 6.3 in).

An adult male Common Map Turtle is smaller than the adult female and has a narrower, more oval carapace with a distinct vertebral keel. It also has a comparatively narrower head, longer front claws, and a longer, thicker tail, with the vent opening beyond the edge of the carapace when the tail is extended. The adult female is larger than the male, with a broader carapace and a lower keel. Females have wider heads, shorter

Common Map Turtle

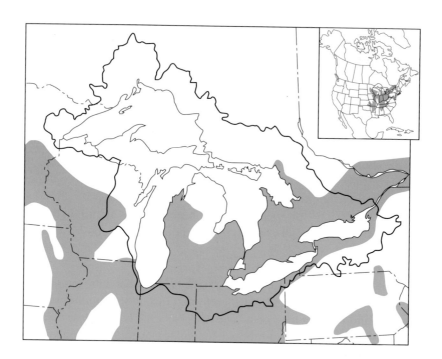

front claws, and short tails, with the vent beneath the edge of the carapace with the tail extended.

A typical hatchling Common Map Turtle has a rounded gray or grayish-
brown carapace about 2.8 cm (1.1 in) long, with light circular markings
and a distinct central keel. The plastron is light yellow or off-white, with
dark borders on the scutes. The striped pattern on the head and limbs is
like that of the adult.

Confusing Species: The Wood Turtle lacks yellow striping on head, neck,
and limbs and has a sculptured-looking carapace with prominent scute
annuli. A Painted Turtle has a smooth, unserrated and unkeeled carapace
with red markings under the marginal scutes, and (in the Midland subspecies) red striping on the legs and neck. Red-eared Sliders have a reddish or orange stripe behind the eye and large black spots on the plastron
(except for some old male Sliders, in which black pigment suffuses the
shell and may obliterate skin striping). The False Map Turtle, which is
probably not native to the Great Lakes basin (see p. 351), has a narrow
head (in both sexes) marked with a yellow bar or crescent behind each
eye, a more prominent vertebral keel, and usually retains dark markings
on the plastron into adulthood.

Distribution and Status: This species has been found from southern Quebec and northwestern Vermont (Lake Champlain) west to the Mississippi
drainage of Minnesota and south to Arkansas and northern Alabama. Disjunct populations occur in eastern New York (Hudson River drainage),
western New Jersey (Delaware River), and eastern Pennsylvania (Susque-
hanna River drainage). Its Great Lakes range includes Ontario from the St.
Lawrence River west to Georgian Bay and south to Lake Erie, New York
(south shore of Lake Ontario), all of northern Ohio and Indiana, the
southern and western Lower Peninsula of Michigan, northeastern Illinois,
and central Wisconsin.

Map Turtles have disappeared from the more heavily polluted urban
rivers but remain locally common throughout much of the lower Great
Lakes basin.

Habitat and Ecology: These highly aquatic turtles inhabit the larger lakes,
rivers, reservoirs, oxbow sloughs, and open marshes, including some of
the bays and inlets of the Great Lakes themselves. They are less common
in smaller lakes and streams, though juveniles may reside in small ponds,
then move into larger bodies of water prior to maturity. Acceptable bot-

tom substrates range from soft mud to sand, gravel, or marl, and the habitat may be weedy or fairly open.

Map Turtles are often seen basking in groups on emergent logs, brush, rocks, and sloping banks or sandbars; at the slightest disturbance they dive into the water and hide in mud or vegetation or head for deep water. They are mostly diurnal but may feed in the evening or after dark during the warm summer months. Map Turtles cease feeding and are generally dormant from early November through early April, spending most of this time under water, wedged beneath submerged logs, partially buried in shallow depressions in the bottom mud, or in muskrat burrows. However, they often change locations during the winter, at which times they may be seen moving slowly about under the ice.

Feeding always takes place in the water. Adult females, with their massive heads and powerful jaws with flat bony crushing surfaces, are well equipped to process and consume the snails, clams, and crayfish that make up the bulk of their diet. The narrower-headed males depend more on aquatic insects and smaller crustaceans and snails. Both sexes also take carrion, such as dead fish, and small amounts of plant material.

The nests of this species are frequently plundered by raccoons and other predatory mammals, and hatchlings and small juveniles are vulnerable to large fish, frogs, and herons. Older juveniles and adults probably have few natural predators, as they are powerful swimmers and extremely wary. Only nesting females are likely to be encountered away from water, and these tend to be shy, withdrawing into their shells at the slightest disturbance. Most specimens are reluctant to bite, but a large female that opportunistically seizes a predator's nose—or a human finger—with her oversized jaws can inflict a painful pinch.

Reproduction and Growth: Mating probably occurs in spring and fall, but detailed accounts of courtship behavior or copulation are lacking. Most mating may take place in deeper waters where observation by curious humans is less likely.

The nesting period lasts from late May through early July, with mid-June being the peak nesting time in the Great Lakes area. Females typically emerge from the water to seek a nest site in the early morning or late evening. Warm rains, especially thundershowers on warm, humid days, may stimulate nesting even at midday. Unshaded sites with sandy or loamy soils are preferred, and a female may move distances of up to several hundred meters from the water to find suitable conditions. The flask-shaped nest cavity is dug with the hind feet. A clutch contains from 6 to 20 oval, flexible-shelled eggs that range in length from 3.2 to 3.5 cm (1.2 to 1.4 in). After laying the last egg, the female fills the cavity and may then flatten the nest site with her plastron. Some females will lay two clutches of eggs during a season.

Hatching occurs 50 to 70 days after laying, with most hatchlings emerging in August or September. Hatchlings from late nests may over-winter in the nest and emerge from the ground in spring. This species has temperature-dependent sex determination. Eggs incubated in the labora-tory at temperatures between 22.5° and 27°C (72.5 to 80.6°F) produced only males, while those kept at 30°C (86°F) resulted in females. The size difference between the sexes becomes apparent by the third year after hatching; females reportedly begin to grow faster than males after the sec-ond year of growth. Males reach sexual maturity in 3 to 5 years, while females require 10 to 14 years to mature. A specimen captured as an adult lived in a zoo for 18 years.

Conservation: Common Map Turtles do not feed on game fish and do no harm to human interests. Their mollusk-eating habits may be beneficial, since snails are the intermediate hosts for many species of trematode worms that parasitize game and domestic animals and humans (including the blood fluke that causes "swimmer's itch"). These turtles are only rarely harvested as food and fortunately attract little interest from the pet trade. This species has a well-deserved reputation for being difficult to maintain in captivity, perhaps due to its shyness and specialized diet.

Populations of the Common Map Turtle have been reduced or elimi-nated in some areas, due largely or in part to pollution and destruction of suitable nesting sites. However, these turtles frequently persist in rivers running through suburban and agricultural areas, including those affected by modest levels of organic pollution. Map Turtles living in lakes are often injured or killed by boat propellers and are accidentally caught on fish-hooks baited with live bait. The use of basking turtles as targets by vandals with firearms can be a serious drain on turtle numbers, and Map Turtles are particularly vulnerable to this deplorable practice.

Painted Turtle   *Chrysemys picta*

Description: This well-named little turtle has a smooth, unkeeled black or olive carapace with red bars or blotches on the marginal scutes; some

Midland Painted Turtle, female

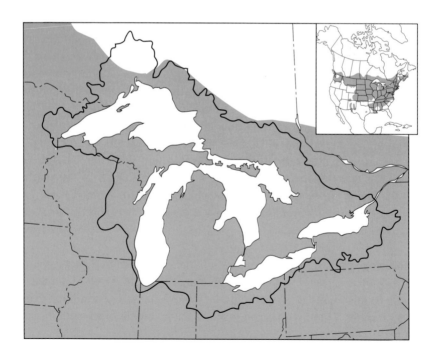

specimens have light borders on the larger carapace scutes, and there may be a thin red stripe down the midline. Rear marginals are unserrated. The flat, hingeless plastron is yellow, often tinged with red, pink, or orange, and usually has a dark central blotch or figure that varies according to subspecies (described below). Occasionally the entire shell is stained a dark reddish brown from minerals absorbed from the water or substrate. The skin is black or olive. Both head and throat have yellow stripes, sometimes with a yellow bar or streak behind the eye; the eye itself is yellow with a dark horizontal bar through the pupil. The upper jaw has two toothlike cusps on either side of a terminal notch. The upper neck, legs, and tail are striped with red and/or yellow. Adult carapace length: 9 to 25 cm (3.5 to 9.8 in).

Male Painted Turtles are generally smaller and flatter than females and have greatly elongated front claws; with the tail extended, the male's vent is beyond the back edge of the carapace. Females have shorter front claws and shorter tails; with tail extended, the vent is at or beneath the rear edge of the carapace.

The hatchling has a rounded, slightly keeled carapace that averages about 2.5 cm (1 in) in length. Hatchling coloration is like the adult's but is brighter and more contrasting.

Note: Four distinct subspecies of this turtle are recognized, two of which are found in the Great Lakes basin. The Midland Painted Turtle *(Chrysemys picta marginata)* tends to have prominent red stripes on the forelegs and neck, and its plastron is usually yellow or orangish yellow with an elongate dark central blotch that does not cover more than half the plastral width. The Western Painted Turtle *(Chrysemys picta belli)* typically has narrow yellow stripes on the forelegs and neck, and a pattern of light lines on the carapace. Its plastron may be quite reddish or orangish, with a complex central pattern of dark and light lines that extends out along the scute seams and often covers more than half of the plastral width. These two subspecies overlap in the western Great Lakes area, with intergrade individuals displaying a variable blending of the above characteristics.

Confusing Species: Map Turtles lack red markings and have a keeled carapace with a serrated (notched) rear margin. A Red-eared Slider has a single reddish band or stripe behind each eye, lacks red carapace markings, and has a yellow plastron, usually with a single black spot in each scute.

Distribution and Status: The range of the Painted Turtle encompasses most of the United States and adjacent southern Canada east and immediately west of the Mississippi River (excepting southern Georgia and Florida), along with the northern plains region from Kansas and Colorado north to southern Saskatchewan and Alberta, and the Pacific Northwest from northern Oregon to southern British Columbia. There are isolated populations in New Mexico and elsewhere in the southwest. This species is found throughout the Great Lakes region, with the Midland Painted Turtle being the dominant subspecies from the Lake Ontario drainage to Georgian Bay and west through lower Michigan, Ohio, and most of Indiana. The Western Painted Turtle occurs in the western and northern Lake Superior basin and intergrades with the Midland race from the Upper Peninsula of Michigan south through Wisconsin to the Indiana Dunes.

This is a common-to-abundant turtle throughout most of the region, though population densities tend to be lower in the far north.

Habitat and Ecology: Painted Turtles prefer quiet or slow-moving permanent waters with a soft bottom substrate, abundant aquatic plant life, and basking sites such as emergent logs, rocks, or mats of floating vegetation. However, they will at least temporarily occupy vernal ponds, sterile impoundments, ditches, and the faster-moving streams and rivers, and are able to tolerate fairly high levels of organic pollution. These turtles do not hesitate to move overland if necessary, and individuals of both sexes may commute between several bodies of water. Deeper or spring-fed waters are often favored during the fall and winter, followed by a spring movement to shallower, more productive ponds, marshes, and lake edges. Hibernation occurs underwater, with most Painted Turtles burrowing into the bottom mud and remaining dormant from October or November until late March or early April. These are cold-tolerant turtles, however, and it is not uncommon to see one swimming under the ice on a sunny winter day or attempting to bask in early spring when parts of the habitat are still ice-covered. Active foraging and feeding begin when the water temperature reaches about 20°C (68°F).

Basking is an important activity for this turtle, and numbers may congregate or even pile up at favored spots. During cooler weather, especially in spring, they may bask intermittently throughout the day, but in summer basking may be restricted to the morning or late afternoon. These turtles are generally inactive at night but sometimes forage after dark during the summer months.

Painted Turtles are omnivorous, with aquatic insects, crustaceans, algae, duckweed, and rooted plants forming the bulk of their diet. Additional foods include snails, leeches, worms, tadpoles, small fish, and carrion. Foraging strategies include active searching and probing, quiet ambush, and surface skimming—the latter accomplished by opening the mouth at the surface and expanding the throat, causing floating plants and animals to flow into the throat cavity. These turtles are unable to swallow unless their heads are submerged. Hatchlings and juveniles are more carnivorous than adults. Painted Turtles living in nutrient-rich (e.g., organically polluted) habitats with greater availability of animal foods have been found to grow faster and reach a greater size than those living in less enriched habitats and eating a higher percentage of plant foods.

Mammalian predators such as raccoons and skunks destroy many Painted Turtle nests. Hatchlings and juveniles are eaten by frogs, snakes, herons, mink, and raccoons. Adults are wary and have few enemies in the water, but many are killed by predators or automobiles during terrestrial wandering. When handled, these turtles may retire into their shells or attempt to scratch and bite, although their weak jaws can cause little damage.

Reproduction and Growth: Courtship and mating can occur at any time during the active season but is most common in spring. A courting male will swim backward in front of his intended mate and vibrate his long foreclaws on the sides of her head and chin. If receptive, the female may touch his forelegs with her own claws. Eventually she will sink to the bottom, allowing the male to mount and clasp her shell from above. Copulation occurs when the male slips backward, bringing their vents into contact.

Painted Turtles nest between mid-May and mid-July, most often in the late afternoon or early evening. The females seek open, sunny sites with moist, workable sand or soil; they prefer to nest near the water but will travel distances of several hundred meters from water if necessary. In loose sand the female may dig a preliminary depression with her front feet, but the nest cavity itself is dug with alternating movements of the hind feet only. She frequently moistens the site with liquid from her cloacal bladders. A clutch contains from 3 to 20 elliptical, flexible-shelled eggs that average about 3 cm (1.2 in) in length. The largest clutches are produced by female Western Painted Turtles and intergrades in the northern and western portions of the region; Midland females rarely lay more than 10 eggs at one time. Some females produce two clutches per season, but they may not reproduce every year.

The incubation period depends on temperatures and humidity within the nest, but generally ranges from 50 to 80 days. Many (probably most) hatchlings overwinter in the nest and postpone emergence until spring. The baby turtles are quite resistant to freezing, but prolonged cold temperatures with little insulating snow cover may result in high hatchling mortality. Painted Turtles have temperature-dependent sex determination; eggs incubated at temperatures of 25° to 27°C (77° to 80°F) produced only males; females result if temperatures range between 30° and 32°C (86° to 90°F).

In good habitat, young Painted Turtles can grow rapidly; hatchlings may double their length during their first growing season. Fast growth is advantageous, since survival chances improve as size increases. Growth rates slow once sexual maturity is attained, and older adults may not grow at all. Males reach maturity in 3 to 7 years, females in 6 to 10 years. Potential life span for this species is thought to be about 35 to 40 years, though relatively few individuals will survive this long.

Conservation: Painted Turtles are harmless to human interests. Their consumption of aquatic insects, including mosquito larvae, may be useful, and they have considerable aesthetic value for many boaters and canoeists (though their attraction to live bait can be a minor annoyance to fishermen). These turtles are occasionally eaten by people, but they are too small to have commercial food value. In some places they have been exploited for laboratory use and for the pet trade.

Painted Turtles remain common in many urban and suburban waters and have benefited from the construction of farm and ornamental ponds. On the other hand, great numbers are killed annually on roads, and human activities often lead to increased populations of nest predators, particularly raccoons. Basking Painted Turtles are sometimes shot by vandals with firearms. Local die-offs of Painted Turtles are occasionally reported, and it is important to determine whether the cause for such mortality is natural or human-induced, since any pollutant that can kill these hardy reptiles could conceivably pose a threat to game species and to people as well.

Red-eared Slider   *Trachemys scripta elegans*

Description: This medium-sized aquatic turtle has a smooth brownish or olive carapace decorated with a variable pattern of yellow and black bands and stripes. The carapace may be unkeeled or have a low central keel, and the flaring rear edge is weakly serrated. The plastron is yellow, usually with a dark spot or smudge in the center of each scute. Head and legs are green, olive, or brown, with numerous narrow black and yellow stripes; a few broader yellow stripes slant downward from the snout, mouth, and lower corner of the eye. This turtle is named for the broad red or orange stripe that extends backward from each eye. In some individuals this band may be poorly developed or obscured. Large males often become quite dark (melanistic), with black pigment obscuring the normal color and pattern on the shell and skin. Adult carapace length: 12.5 to 28.9 cm (5 to 11.4 in).

The male Red-eared Slider is smaller than the female and has greatly elongated claws on the front feet and a comparatively longer tail. With tail extended, the male's vent is usually positioned beyond the carapace edge. The female has shorter front claws and a short tail, with the vent beneath the rear edge of the carapace.

Hatchlings typically range from 2.8 to 3.3 cm (1.1 to 1.3 in) in length. The hatchling's carapace has a low keel and both carapace and skin are bright green; yellow stripes and other markings may be less defined by dark pigment than those of older turtles, but the black spots on the plastral scutes are usually prominent.

Confusing Species: Painted Turtles have reddish markings on the marginal scutes and limbs, and a centralized blotch or pattern on the plastron. Common Map Turtles lack the red stripe behind the eye and have a mostly unmarked plastron.

Distribution and Status: The Red-eared Slider is found from West Virginia west to northern Indiana and Illinois, south to the Gulf coastal states from western Georgia through Texas to northern Mexico and eastern New Mexico. Disjunct populations in California, Maryland, southern Ohio, southern Michigan, southern Ontario, and elsewhere are usually attributed to human introduction. The natural range of this subspecies reaches the Great Lakes basin at the southern end of Lake Michigan. Whether any of the Michigan populations are natural remains problematical; shell fragments from archaeological sites (American Indian middens) in Michigan

Red-eared Slider

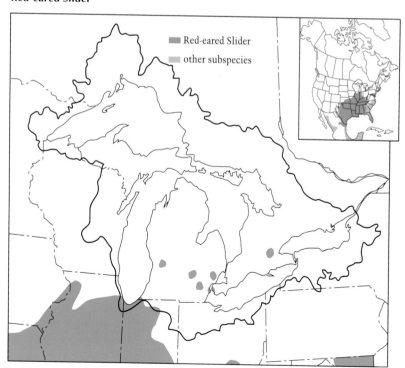

and Wisconsin indicate that the species once ranged farther north than at present. Red-eared Sliders have been introduced into parts of Europe, Africa, and Asia. (See discussion under "Conservation" below.) Additional subspecies extend the range of *Trachemys scripta* to eastern Tennessee, the Atlantic coastal plain (southern Virginia to northern Florida), and through parts of Mexico and Central America to Venezuela.

Though generally common throughout most of its range, the Red-eared Slider is restricted to widely scattered and very localized populations in the Great Lakes region.

Habitat and Ecology: Sliders inhabit ponds, lakes, reservoirs, ditches, sloughs, swamps, and the backwaters and slower sections of streams and rivers—almost any permanent body of water with ample aquatic vegetation and suitable basking sites. They will travel overland in search of new habitat or to nest but are rarely far from water. Adult Sliders seem to prefer somewhat deeper water than do Painted Turtles in the same habitats, although juveniles of both species tend to remain in weedy shallows. Sliders spend much time basking on logs and other emergent debris or floating in mats of vegetation. The common name *Slider* refers to their habit of quickly sliding from basking sites into the water upon the slightest disturbance. They are inactive at night, generally forage underwater in the early morning and late afternoon, and often bask for much of the midday period.

These turtles are inactive at water temperatures below 10°C (50°F) and are usually dormant from mid-October to early April in the northern part of their range. Most Sliders hibernate underwater, digging into the bottom substrate, under overhanging banks, or in muskrat tunnels.

Red-eared Sliders are omnivorous, eating a variety of small aquatic animals and vegetation. The former include insects, snails, crayfish and other crustaceans, and occasionally small vertebrates (tadpoles, fish) and carrion. Plant foods include algae, duckweed, rooted plants, and seeds. Juvenile Sliders take a higher percentage of animal foods than adults, perhaps due to their higher requirements for protein and calcium, and/or the greater availability of small animal prey in the shallow waters frequented by the younger turtles.

Red-eared Slider eggs and hatchlings are readily consumed by raccoons, skunks, and other predators; typical mortality rates for eggs and new hatchlings range from about 70 percent to nearly 100 percent in any one year or place. Juveniles have fewer enemies as they grow, and the wary adults are fairly safe from most natural predators while in the water.

Sliders are most vulnerable to predators when they leave the water. (Human-induced mortality is discussed under "Conservation" below.) When handled, some feisty individuals will bite, but most retire into their shells or flail their legs in an attempt to escape. Hatchling Sliders may be distasteful to some predatory fish; Largemouth Bass have been found to reject hatchlings as prey, perhaps because the little turtles scratch and bite when ingested.

Reproduction and Growth: Most courtship and mating occurs in spring and fall. Courtship behavior is similar to that of the Painted Turtle. The male swims backward in front of the female and, with "palms" turned outward, vibrates his long foreclaws on her head and chin. If receptive, the female eventually sinks to the bottom and allows the male to clasp her carapace from above. The male then curls his tail beneath that of the female to bring their vents into contact and usually assumes a nearly vertical position during copulation.

Sliders nest from late May through early July. The female leaves the water in the early morning or late afternoon and seeks a sunny, elevated location with moist soil or sand; the site is often moistened with water from the turtle's cloacal bladders. The globular nest cavity is dug entirely with the hind feet. After the eggs are laid, the nest opening is refilled with the premoistened soil and tamped with the hind feet and plastron, leaving a mud plug that can initially be fairly conspicuous. Most female Sliders lay one clutch per year, but a few may produce a second clutch about two to four weeks after the first. A clutch can contain from 2 to 30 whitish, oval, flexible-shelled eggs ranging from 3.1 to 4.3 cm (1.2 to 1.7 in) in length; larger females generally produce more eggs—but not necessarily larger eggs—than smaller females.

Incubation requires from 65 to 80 days under normal conditions. Hatchlings can either emerge and enter the water in late summer or fall, or overwinter in the nest and emerge in spring. Nest temperatures about midway through incubation determine the sex of the hatchlings; eggs incubated at temperatures between 22.5° and 27°C (72.5°–80.6°F) produce only males, while eggs kept at 30°C (86°F) produce females.

Growth rate in Red-eared Sliders varies according to the availability and quality of food and the environmental temperatures. Males may reach sexual maturity in 2 to 5 years, at a minimum carapace length of about 12.5 cm (5 in). Females mature in 6 to 8 years at carapace lengths of about 18 to 20 cm (7 to 7.8 in). Captive Sliders have lived at least 42 years, but relatively few individuals reach their thirtieth birthday in the wild.

Conservation: Red-eared Sliders do not normally eat game fish, and in their natural habitat and range they pose no threat to human interests. Their former and, in some places, present abundance suggests that these adaptable turtles play an important role in aquatic ecosystems. However, this species has long suffered from staggering levels of human exploitation and destruction. Great numbers of these turtles are killed annually by automobiles, and the mistaken belief that they compete with humans for fish results in direct persecution by fishermen. Basking turtles are often used as targets by vandals with firearms. Adult Sliders are trapped for the biological supply trade and for human consumption. They are marketed domestically and shipped overseas as well. Unfortunately the larger female turtles bear the brunt of this demand. Slider eggs have been dug up and sold as fish bait; sometimes the collectors have killed gravid female turtles to obtain eggs rather than waiting for the turtles to nest.

Many thousands of hatchling and juvenile Sliders were once captured each year for the domestic and international pet trade, though few survived the often inadequate care offered them in captivity. Commercial turtle farms now produce several million baby Red-eared Sliders annually, although these farms still take large numbers of mature turtles from the wild to augment their breeding stock. Ironically, the hatchling turtles are mostly marketed overseas, since the sale of pet turtles under four inches (10.16 cm) in carapace length is presently prohibited in the United States. (Captive turtles raised or shipped under unsanitary conditions can become carriers of infectious bacteria, primarily *Salmonella* species. The "4-inch rule" is presumably an attempt to discourage people from buying the turtles as pets for small children.)

The international Slider trade has led to further irony—while some native Slider populations are declining or even disappearing due to continued exploitation and habitat loss, these turtles are beginning to establish themselves in many places outside their natural range due to the release of unwanted pets. Red-eared Sliders are reportedly established in California, France, South Africa, Bahrain, Japan, South Korea, Guam, Thailand, and probably elsewhere. There is concern that introduced Sliders could detrimentally compete with native species, but there is presently no evidence that the small, presumably introduced populations in the Great Lakes region have caused any ecological problems.

Softshell Turtles
Family Trionychidae

Twenty-two species of Softshell Turtles are found in North America, Africa, and temperate and tropical parts of Asia. They have broad, rubbery shells with the underlying bony elements greatly reduced and a complete lack of overlying scutes. These medium to very large turtles are well adapted for an aquatic existence, with strongly webbed feet and piglike, elongated noses that function as built-in snorkels in some species. One species occurs in the Great Lakes region.

Note: Most Softshell Turtles (including all North American softshells) were formerly placed in the genus *Trionyx* prior to a taxonomic study published in 1987, which established a number of new genera (Meylan 1987). Some herpetologists prefer to use the older name for North American species.

Eastern Spiny Softshell Turtle   *Apalone spinifera spinifera*

Description: This turtle is unmistakable with its smooth, flat, oval or round carapace and long, piglike snout. Both carapace and plastron lack scutes and are soft and rubbery, with flexible edges. The tan, brown, or olive carapace is decorated with black spots, flecks, and circles in juveniles and males, while adult females darken and become blotched or mottled with gray or brown. The name *spiny* refers to the short, often inconspicuous spines at the front of the carapace. Plastron coloration is white or pale yellow, with the underlying bones visible as gray patches. The head, very long neck, and legs are tan or olive above, speckled or mottled with black. All four feet are fully webbed and often streaked or mottled with yellow and black. There are usually two black-bordered yellowish stripes on each side of the head, behind the eye and jaw. Adult female carapace length: 24 to 48 cm (9.4 to 18.9 in). Adult male carapace length: 12.7 to 24 cm (5 to 9.4 in).

Besides being smaller than the female and retaining the juvenile color pattern, the male Spiny Softshell has a slightly granular (rougher) carapace surface and a longer, thicker tail that may project well beyond the rear carapace margin. Females have smoother carapaces and shorter tails that barely project beyond the rear edge of the carapace.

The hatchling is 3 to 4 cm (1.2 to 1.6 in) long, and has a circular, tan

Eastern Spiny Softshell Turtle

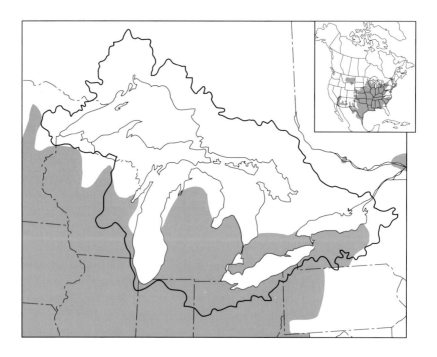

or olive brown carapace with a pattern of dark spots or circles and a light border. The new hatchling has a curled shell and a turned up nose, but these unfold within a day or two after emergence from the confinement of the egg shell.

Confusing Species: No other Great Lakes turtle has a flat, scuteless carapace and tubular nose. The Smooth Softshell Turtle *(Apalone mutica)* is known from the Ohio and Mississippi River systems in Ohio, Indiana, Illinois, and Wisconsin but is not known to occur within the Great Lakes basin. As its name implies, the Smooth Softshell lacks the short spines on the front of the carapace that are found on the Spiny Softshell.

Distribution and Status: This subspecies is found from western New York and southern Ontario west to Wisconsin and south to Tennessee, northern Alabama, and western Mississippi. There are disjunct populations in Vermont (Lake Champlain area), adjacent southern Quebec (Ottawa River), eastern New York, and southern New Jersey. It intergrades with other subspecies west of the Mississippi River and in the lower Mississippi valley. Spiny Softshells range across the lower Great Lakes region from the southern and western shores of Lake Ontario through southern Ontario and much of Michigan's Lower Peninsula, adjacent Ohio and Indiana, to the western Lake Michigan basin (north to Green Bay).

This turtle remains locally common in the western part of its Great Lakes range but is uncommon to rare and local in the east. Softshells have declined in some places due to pollution, exploitation, and elimination of nesting sites. It has been nearly extirpated from the western end of Lake Ontario, where it was reportedly common just a few decades ago.

Habitat and Ecology: Spiny Softshell Turtles inhabit rivers and the larger streams, inland lakes, reservoirs, and even protected bays and river mouth areas in the Great Lakes themselves. They tolerate a fairly swift current but prefer a sand or mud bottom and usually avoid streams with sharp-edged rocks or coarse gravel. Open habitats with little aquatic vegetation are favored over those with dense plant growth. Basking spots in the form of sloping banks or logs and open, preferably sandy, nesting areas close to the water are also important habitat components.

These highly aquatic turtles are fast and powerful swimmers that rarely leave the immediate vicinity of water. They spend much of their time basking, especially in late spring and summer, usually on a sloping bank or sandbar or on a low-floating log; they often sit at the shoreline facing the water, ready to dash in at any disturbance. Larger Softshells sometimes float at the surface in deeper water, especially on warm summer days. When not basking or actively foraging, these turtles spend much of their time buried in soft sand or silt. When in shallow water, they can use their long necks and snorkel-like noses to breathe with little effort. However, this species can remain submerged for long periods, obtaining oxygen by pumping water over the pharyngeal linings in the throat. The cloacal lining and skin also appear to function in underwater respiration. Softshells are inactive and largely dormant from early October to April or even May in the north, spending this time shallowly buried in the bottom substrate. They often enter dormancy earlier in fall and resume activity later in spring than most other turtle species sharing their habitats.

Spiny Softshell Turtles are mostly carnivorous, with a preference for crayfish, aquatic insects, and other invertebrates. Small fish and tadpoles are taken only occasionally. Plants and seeds are rarely consumed; much of the vegetable matter found in Spiny Softshell stomachs was probably ingested accidently. These turtles will actively seek food by probing along the bottom, beneath objects, or in clumps of vegetation, or they may conceal themselves in the mud or sand and ambush passing prey animals with quick thrusts of their long necks.

Many (probably most) Spiny Softshell nests are destroyed by raccoons, skunks, foxes, and other mammalian predators. Hatchlings and juveniles are particularly vulnerable to raccoons, herons, and large fish. Adult Spiny Softshell Turtles have few predators other than humans. They are extremely wary when basking and can swim faster than most fish. Nesting females on land are rarely far from water; they will usually abandon a nest site if disturbed prior to egg laying and can run with surprising speed. If attacked or restrained, a Spiny Softshell can bite, and its sharp-edged jaws are capable of causing severe lacerations, while the long neck gives it a wide striking range. A large, wet Softshell is difficult to hold. A firm grip on the rear portion of the carapace or hind legs is necessary, using care to avoid the flailing claws.

Reproduction and Growth: Eastern Spiny Softshells mate in April or May. Courtship and copulation behavior are poorly known, perhaps because most mating activities occur in deeper, offshore waters. The male will swim alongside the female while nosing her head and shell, perhaps to determine her willingness to mate. During copulation, the male reportedly rests on or swims just above the female's carapace, rather than cling-ing tightly with the claws as in most other turtle species

Most females lay their eggs in June or early July, often nesting on a warm, sunny morning. Some will produce a second clutch a few weeks after the first. Nesting is frequently a hurried process, with the female choosing a nest site, completing the nest cavity, laying her clutch, and covering the eggs within an hour or less. Most nests are in open, elevated sand or gravel banks or sandbars, as close to the water as possible. The nest cavity, which is dug with the hind feet, ranges from 9 to 25 cm (3.5 to 10 in) in depth, and from 7.6 to 12.8 cm (3 to 5 in) in diameter. The eggs number from 9 to 38 and are round, with a hard, calcareous shell. Larger females tend to lay larger clutches. Eggs range from 2.4 to 3.8 cm (0.9 to 1.5 in) in diameter.

Incubation requires between 55 and 85 days, with most hatchlings emerging in late August or September, although overwintering in the nest has been reported. The sex of Spiny Softshell Turtles is unaffected by nest temperature, and most clutches produce both males and females in roughly equal numbers.

Hatchling Spiny Softshells may double their length in their first year, but the growth rate gradually slows as they get older. Once they reach maturity, growth rate decreases significantly but remains greater for females than for males. Males may reach sexual maturity at an age of 4 to 5 years, while most females require 8 to 10 years to mature. An Eastern Spiny Softshell captured as an adult lived over 25 years in a zoo. It has been estimated that a female Spiny Softshell with a carapace length of 38 cm (15 in) would be about 30 years old, while a 43 cm (17 in) female could be over 50 years old. The maximum longevity is unknown.

Conservation: Spiny Softshell Turtles rarely eat game fish, and while they may compete with fish for food, it is unlikely that they significantly impact fish populations in the region. Due in part to their use of aquatic (pharyn-geal and cloacal) respiration, they are sensitive to pollutants that kill fish, particularly fish species requiring high dissolved oxygen levels. When fisheries biologists use the chemical rotenone to survey fish populations or to remove unwanted fish species, Softshells are sometimes sickened or killed during the operations. (Rotenone kills fish by interfering with oxy-gen absorption by the gills.) Spiny Softshell Turtles have disappeared from the more polluted sections of many rivers and lakes in the region. Other threats to this species include shoreline development (particularly the reduction or elimination of critical nesting sites), direct destruction by vandals with firearms, and injuries from boat propellers.

These turtles are often captured, and occasionally marketed, for human consumption. They are taken with traps and set hooks, by probing in sand or mud with poles or by hand, and with bow and arrow. A Spiny Softshell Turtle typically weighs less (and offers much less usable meat) than a Snapping Turtle of the same length. For example, a Softshell 33 cm (13 in) long would weigh about 3.2 kg (7 lbs), while a snapper of the same carapace length would be likely to weigh at least 7.7 kg (17 lbs). Since few male Softshells reach a size worthy of harvest, mature females inevitably bear the brunt of human exploitation. Some states and provinces regulate the harvest of this turtle with closed seasons, bag limits, and other controls.

Lizards (Order Squamata, Suborder Lacertilia)

Lizards are a very successful group of reptiles, with over 3,750 species in 383 genera distributed throughout the temperate and tropical parts of the world; one species even occurs above the Arctic Circle in northern Europe. Lizards are much more diverse in the tropics and subtropics and become progressively less so as one moves away from the equator. Only four species occur in the Great Lakes basin, and only one of these is widely distributed. It is thus not surprising that people living in the region are generally unfamiliar with lizards and often mistakenly apply the name to the superficially similar and more common salamanders. Salamanders are, of course, amphibians with typically smooth, moist skins and claw-less toes. Lizards are reptiles, with dry, scaly skins and clawed toes on their feet (if they have feet).

The majority of lizards have four limbs, but in some species (in at least seven families) the limbs are reduced in size or even absent altogether. One Great Lakes species, the Western Slender Glass Lizard, is legless. Although legless lizards are sometimes confused with snakes, their external ear openings and movable eyelids are features absent in snakes. All lizards have tails, which are often as long or longer than their bodies. The tail frequently serves as a part of a lizard's defensive strategy. If seized by a predator, many species can detach their tails at weak points, or "fracture-planes," in the vertebrae. The separated tail continues to wriggle for some time, possibly attracting the predator's interest and allowing the lizard to escape, to later regrow a new tail. Partly because many lizard specimens will have lost portions of their tails, herpetologists often note a lizard's body length (as measured from the tip of the snout to the vent) as well as the total length (from snout to tail tip).

Most lizards are predators. Small and moderate-sized species feed mostly on insects and other small invertebrates, while larger species also eat other vertebrates or their eggs. A few lizards are mostly herbivorous, though none of these inhabits our area. Lizards may locate food visually or by scent, or they may use their tongues to pick up chemical clues from the environment, as do snakes. These molecules are transferred to paired nerve-lined pits in the roof of the mouth called the vomeronasal (or Jacobson's) organ, which send information directly to the brain.

Lizards communicate with each other using body movements, odors (from glandular secretions), and color patterns. These can include specific head and body movements, tail waving, the display of crests or skin flaps, and seasonal color changes. Males (and less commonly, females) of many species advertise and defend territories to assure access to mates or feeding areas and may engage in direct combat when display and intimidation fail. Mating is often preceeded by a series of behaviors by the male that serve in mate recognition and in determining or inducing the female's receptivity. Fertilization is internal; during copulation the male inserts one of two copulatory organs called hemipenes into the female's cloaca, frequently while grasping the female's neck or body in his jaws.

The vast majority of lizards reproduce by laying eggs, which are usually oval in shape with leathery, flexible shells. There may be some embryonic development prior to egg laying, and a few species (generally from cooler climates) retain the eggs throughout development and give birth to fully developed young. Egg-laying lizards typically excavate a nest cavity in moist soil, sand, rotting wood, or leaf litter, or beneath a rock, log, or other shelter. After depositing their eggs, most abandon their nests, but females of a few species (including Five-lined Skinks and Slender Glass Lizards in our area) will stay often with their eggs until hatching. The temperature of the eggs during incubation can determine the sex of the hatchlings in some lizard species; males are usually produced at warmer temperatures, while females result from cooler temperatures—the opposite of the situation in most turtles.

Young lizards typically grow quickly and often mature and breed in the their first or second year. Compared to turtles, lizards typically have shorter lives and faster "turnover" in their populations. Few lizards (other than some of the large tropical species) live longer than 10 years.

Selected general references: Conant and Collins 1991, Halliday and Adler 1986, Mattison 1989, Smith 1946.

Skinks
Family Scincidae

This very large family, with 1,275 species in 85 genera, occurs through-out the warm-temperate and tropical parts of the world. Skinks are mostly small to medium-sized lizards with elongated bodies and short legs (some species are nearly or completely legless). Their shiny, overlapping scales are underlain by bony plates (osteoderms). North American skinks tend to prefer somewhat moister habitats than members of most other lizard families.

Five-lined Skink *Eumeces fasciatus*

Description: A shiny-scaled lizard named for the five yellowish or cream-colored stripes running from the snout down the back, sides, and tail. These stripes may darken and eventually disappear in older males. The background color is black in juveniles and young adult females but fades to brown, gray, or olive in older adults. Juveniles have bright metallic blue tails. Adult females often retain some bluish tail color, while the tails of males become gray. Adult total length: 12.7 to 21.6 cm (5 to 8.5 in). Maximum body (snout to vent) length: 8.6 cm (3.4 in).

In addition to losing the striped juvenile pattern and fading to a uniform color, adult males develop a widened head and reddish orange coloration on the snout and jaws. These features intensify in the spring breeding season. Females normally retain at least a hint of the striped pattern and bluish tail.

Young Five-lined Skinks, about 5 to 6.4 cm (2 to 2.5 in) long at hatching, have well-defined white or yellow stripes on a black background and brilliant blue tails.

Confusing Species: Coal Skinks are brownish and have a wide dark stripe on each side bordered by narrow light stripes, and no stripes on the top of the head. (The Five-lined Skink has two converging stripes on the head.) Northern Prairie Skinks have wide tan or brownish stripes separated by narrow black stripes on the back and wide dark stripes on the sides. Racerunners have six or seven dorsal stripes, and dull, granular (nonoverlapping) scales on the back and sides; their tails are encircled by rings of rough scales.

Five-lined Skink

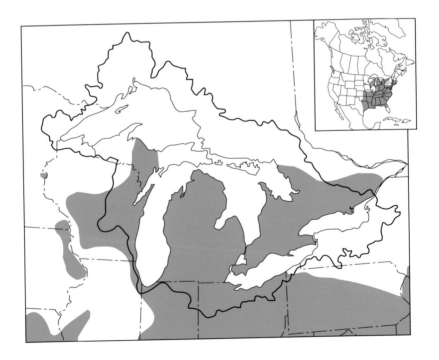

Distribution and Status: The Five-lined Skink ranges from eastern New York south to northern Florida and west to Wisconsin, Missouri, and eastern portions of Kansas, Oklahoma, and Texas. There are disjunct populations in west central Minnesota and northeastern Iowa and adjacent parts of southern Minnesota and Wisconsin. Within the Great Lakes basin this lizard occurs in southern Ontario (from the Lake Ontario region west to Georgian Bay, south to Point Pelee), Ohio, Indiana, throughout Michigan's Lower Peninsula, the western Lake Michigan basin (Indiana Dunes area north to Green Bay), and the central Upper Peninsula of Michigan (Menominee and Delta Counties north to Marquette County).

This species is locally common in some parts of its Great Lakes range, but its distribution is quite spotty and colonial in nature, particularly in the north.

Habitat and Ecology: Five-lined Skinks typically inhabit wooded or partially wooded areas with ample cover and basking sites in the form of stumps, logs, rock outcrops, wood and brush piles, sawdust piles, and slabs of loose or fallen bark. They are more abundant in ecotone areas (woodland openings or edges, cleared areas, partial burns, etc.) than in unbroken forest. Large skink populations are sometimes found among accumulations of driftwood along sandy Great Lakes beaches. Moist, but not wet, habitats are preferred over very dry ones. While less arboreal than some skink species, Five-lined Skinks will climb onto tree trunks and up the sides of abandoned buildings to bask in the sun or forage for food. Most individual skinks remain within small home ranges of about 9 to 30 m (30 to 100 ft) in diameter for much of their lives.

These lizards bask to raise their body temperature to preferred levels of about 28° to 34°C (82° to 93°F). They will forage and breed at temperatures somewhat lower, but not much higher, than these levels. If air temperatures are too cool or hot, they remain inactive and under cover. In the Great Lakes area these skinks are usually dormant between early October and late April or early May. Overwintering sites include mammal burrows, rotting stumps or logs, crevices in rock formations or building foundations, and piles of vegetation or sawdust.

Most of the diet is made up of invertebrates such as spiders, millipedes, termites, crickets, grasshoppers, beetles and beetle larvae, caterpillars, and snails. Larger skinks occasionally eat very small vertebrates such as newborn mice, frogs, and even smaller lizards. The blue tail color of juveniles may deter attacks by adult males. Captive skinks have reportedly eaten berries, and it is possible that wild ones would opportunistically do so as well.

Five-lined Skinks are eaten by various snakes, crows, hawks, shrews, moles, opossums, skunks, raccoons, and domestic cats. When warm these lizards are alert and fast moving and difficult to approach. If seized by a predator, a skink will disconnect a part or all of its tail, which continues to wriggle for several minutes, perhaps distracting the predator long enough to allow the lizard to escape. A new tail is later regrown, although it tends to be shorter and duller in color than the original. Skinks will also bite defensively, though only the largest males are able to inflict more than a firm pinch.

Reproduction and Growth: During the spring breeding season, males will aggressively defend their territories against intrusion by other males while tolerating the presence of juveniles and females. It is likely that potential mates and rivals are recognized in at least two ways—by chemical clues picked up by the flicking tongue and transferred to the vomeronasal organ, and by the presence or absence of bluish tail color (in females) and reddish jaw color (in males). A courting male will approach a receptive female from the side and grasp her neck with his jaws. He then wraps his tail around hers to align their cloacal openings, allowing insertion of one of the two hemipenes and effecting copulation, which lasts about four to eight minutes.

Egg laying occurs at least a month after mating, usually between mid-May and mid-July. The female seeks a secluded nest site in an old rodent burrow, a rotted log or stump, or beneath loose bark, a rock, or a board. There she clears a small cavity and lays from 5 to 18 thin-shelled eggs that vary in shape from nearly spherical to oval. Freshly laid eggs average about 1.3 cm (0.5 in) in length, but they absorb water and swell during incubation. Female skinks usually brood their eggs and defend them against small predators. They also maintain proper humidity by urinating in the nest and frequently turn the eggs, perhaps to discourage mold growth. Any spoiled eggs are eaten, and a displaced egg is retrieved by rolling it with the snout or body. By basking and then returning to the nest, the female may increase the nest temperature. Incubation requires from 24 to 55 days, and parental care ends when the hatchlings disperse from the nest, usually within a day or two after hatching.

Young Five-lined Skinks reach maturity in their second or third year of life and may live at least six years, based on captive longevity of related species.

Conservation: This species is harmless to human interests, and where abundant may help in controlling insect pests. Five-lined Skinks may benefit from selective logging operations that open the forest canopy and leave behind stumps, bark slabs, and sawdust piles. On the other hand, the clearing of woodlands for development or removal of fallen logs, stumps, or woody beach debris can be detrimental to these lizards. Since Five-lined Skinks in the Great Lakes area tend to exist in small, often isolated populations, even small-scale habitat disruptions could potentially lead to local extirpation of the species.

Northern Coal Skink   *Eumeces anthracinus anthracinus*

Description: This glossy-scaled skink has a brownish or greenish brown back and a wide black stripe on each side extending from the head onto the tail and bordered above and below by narrow white or yellow stripes. A very faint light brown middorsal stripe may be visible in some specimens, but there are no light stripes on top of the head. The belly is gray to bluish gray. Juveniles have blue to violet-blue tails; hints of the bluish tail color may persist into adulthood. Adult total length: 12.7 to 17.8 cm (5 to 7 in). Maximum body (snout to vent) length: 7 cm (2.75 in).

Males may develop orange or reddish orange coloration on the sides of the head and jaws during the spring breeding season.

Very young Northern Coal Skinks are usually colored much like the adults but have brighter blue tails. Total length at hatching is 4.8 to 5.6 cm (1.9 to 2.2 in).

Confusing Species: Five-lined Skinks usually have five light dorsal stripes and two converging stripes on top of the head. In older in-hand specimens lacking stripes, find the second broad scale behind the point of the chin (the postmental scale); it is usually single in the Coal Skink, but split into two in the Five-lined Skink (fig. 9).

Distribution and Status: This subspecies has a highly fragmented range that extends from western New York to North Carolina and eastern Ken-

Northern Coal Skink, male. (Photo by R. D. Bartlett.)

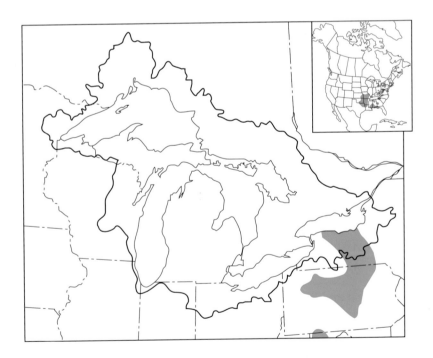

Fig. 9. Skink chins. In the Coal Skink (*left*), there is a single postmental scale (shaded). In the Five-lined Skink (*right*) and Prairie Skink, the postmental scale is divided.

tucky. Isolated colonies exist in Ohio and central Kentucky. This form intergrades with the Southern Coal Skink *(Eumeces anthracinus pluvialis)* in the western Carolinas, northern Georgia, and Alabama. Northern Coal Skinks occur in the Great Lakes basin in the vicinity of Rochester, New York, and surrounding counties.

These lizards are generally uncommon and local throughout their range and are rare and very localized in the Great Lakes area.

Habitat and Ecology: Coal Skinks typically inhabit damp forested areas, often near water, and with ample cover in the form of leaf litter, logs, boards, loose bark, or flat rocks. They may also occur on dry rocky hillsides, shale banks, and on standing dead trees. These lizards are difficult to approach during their frequent basking sessions and are most often found while turning cover objects. They are inactive in fall and winter and probably hibernate in burrows or crevices below the frost zone.

Small insects and spiders are the primary prey of the Coal Skink. In turn, these lizards fall prey to various snakes, birds, and mammalian predators. Coal Skinks are secretive and wary, and dart quickly beneath cover or even dive into a nearby stream if pursued. As in other skinks, they can detach a portion of the tail if seized, with the shed appendage perhaps distracting the enemy long enough to allow the lizard to escape.

Reproduction and Growth: Most mating occurs in May, with the male grasping the female in the neck region during copulation, as in the Five-lined Skink. Usually in June, the females deposit from 4 to 13 thin-shelled eggs in a cavity under a rock or log or other shelter. The newly laid eggs vary in length from 0.6 to 1.7 cm (0.24 to 0.67 in). Females attend and presumably protect their eggs during incubation, which requires four or five weeks. Growth and longevity in the Coal Skink is presently unknown but would probably be similar to that of related skink species.

Conservation: Removal of critical cover components of the Northern Coal Skink's habitat would be a serious threat to their survival. Due to the limited distribution of this lizard in the Great Lakes area, it can be assumed to be vulnerable to local extirpation should its habitat be disturbed or degraded by human activities. The effects of specific pesticides on these small insectivorous animals should evaluated and considered prior to implementing forest pest control programs.

Whiptails and Racerunners
Family Teiidae

The Teiids include over 220 species in 39 genera, restricted to the Western Hemisphere and reaching their peak of diversity in Central and northern South America. Most have small, granular body scales, rows of large rectangular scales on the belly, and broad platelike scales on the head. The majority of species are small to medium-sized and very active and fast moving, but a few are heavier bodied and larger; the South American Tegus (*Tupinambis* sp.) and the Caiman Lizards (*Dracaena* sp.) can exceed a meter (3.3 ft) in length. One genus, *Cnemidophorus,* inhabits North America and is particularly interesting in that several species exist only as unisexual (all-female) populations and reproduce by development of unfertilized eggs. The single Great Lakes area species, *Cnemidophorus sexlineatus,* is a "normal" bisexual species, however.

Six-lined Racerunner   *Cnemidophorus sexlineatus*

Description: This is a slim-bodied lizard with a very long tail and a pointed snout. There are usually six yellowish green or whitish stripes running down the upper back and sides, and often an indistinct brownish stripe down the middle of the back. The dorsal color between the stripes can be black, gray, brown, or olive; in adults (especially males) the neck and forward part of the body may be suffused with green or blue-green. The body scales are dull and granular (like tiny bumps), the head scales are large and platelike, and the belly scales are flat, rectangular, and arranged in straight rows. The tail is encircled by rings of rough scales. Adult total length: 15.2 to 26.7 cm (6 to 10.5 in). Maximum body (snout to vent) length: 8.6 cm (3.4 in).

The male typically has a more robust head and a wider vent than the female; in older males the stripes tend to be less distinct. During the breeding season, the male's chin and belly are tinged with blue, while the underparts of the female usually remain white or grayish.

Juvenile Racerunners have distinct light stripes on a dark ground color and bluish or bluish green tails. They measure about 3 cm (1.2 in) in body (snout to vent) length at hatching.

Note: There are two recognized subspecies of *Cnemidophorus sexlineatus:* the Six-lined Racerunner (*C. s. sexlineatus*) of the east (ranges are

Six-lined Racerunner, female. (Photo by R. D. Bartlett.)

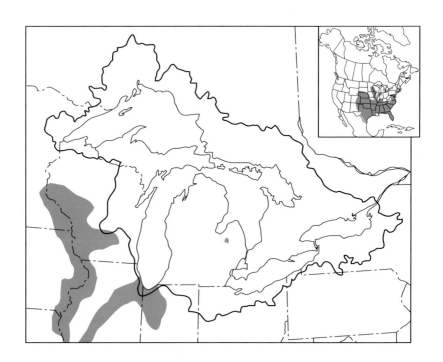

detailed below) has six clear light stripes down the back but typically lacks a medial back stripe and greenish color on the sides, while the Prairie Racerunner (*C. s. viridis*) of the west usually has a seventh (medial) back stripe and (particularly in males) bright green color on the forward part of the body. The Prairie Racerunner appears to be the subspecies present in the Great Lakes region, but some herpetologists consider the question unresolved in the absence of studies comparing the genetic affinities of the various regional and nearby populations.

Confusing Species: All other lizard species in our area have smooth, shiny, overlapping scales (skinks) or are legless (Slender Glass Lizard).

Distribution and Status: The western subspecies, the Prairie Racerunner, ranges from the Mississippi River west to eastern New Mexico and Colorado north to southern South Dakota and Missouri; it follows the Mississippi and Illinois River drainages to southeastern Minnesota, western Wisconsin, and (presumably) western Indiana. The eastern subspecies, the Six-lined Racerunner (which bears the same common name as the species), occurs from the Mississippi River east through southern Indiana and western Kentucky to Virginia and southern Maryland, south to Florida and the Gulf Coast. Racerunners enter the Great Lakes basin in northeastern Illinois and northwestern Indiana, including the coastal Indiana Dunes area (Lake, Porter, and LaPorte Counties, Indiana).

A disjunct colony of Racerunners exists in east-central Michigan (Tuscola County); although possibly introduced, the Michigan lizards, which display characteristics of the Prairie subspecies, may best be considered a natural relict population (in the absence of evidence to the contrary). These lizards could conceivably have entered Michigan during the warmer, drier postglacial time known as the xerothermic period.

These lizards are at the edge of their range in the Great Lakes region, but they can be locally common in isolated colonies.

Habitat and Ecology: Racerunners prefer sunny, well-drained habitats with areas of bare sand or loose sandy soil between clumps of low vegetation. They occur in both natural and human-modified habitats such as prairies, dune edges, oak savannas, riverbanks, abandoned fields, vacant lots, and road cuts. Shady forests are avoided, but they will inhabit drier, open woodlands, including those thinned by fire or logging. Most Racerunners spend their lives within a small home range, often an area of less than 800 square meters (0.2 acres) and in some places no more than about 160 square meters (0.04 acre), but they do not appear to defend territories.

These lizards prefer higher air temperatures than most temperate zone reptiles and are normally active only on warm days when the sun is shining. At night and on cloudy or cool days they remain in burrows that they dig themselves or are abandoned by other animals, or under surface cover (e.g., woody debris, leaf litter, rocks, boards). Racerunners have a relatively short activity season and are rarely observed (and are presumably dormant) between mid-August and late May, though juveniles may feed until late September and emerge slightly earlier in spring than adults.

Racerunners actively pursue a variety of invertebrate prey, including spiders, snails, beetles, flies, plant hoppers, crickets, grasshoppers, and moths. Young Racerunners may preferentially seek out larger food items more frequently than adults, perhaps to maximize energy intake as a proportion of the energy expended to obtain the food. As these lizards forage, they continuously "lick" the ground with their tongues, suggesting an important role for the vomeronasal organ in finding prey.

Predators of these lizards and their eggs include snakes (particularly Racers and Milk Snakes), birds, and small mammals. Racerunners, as their common name implies, are extremely fast runners and escape their enemies by dashing to their burrows or to nearby cover, often in a confusing stop-and-go manner. If seized, a Racerunner may drop all or a portion of its tail; later a new, though shorter, tail is regrown. However, this species does not appear to lose its tail as readily as do the skinks.

Reproduction and Growth: Courtship and mating occur after emergence from hibernation, in May or early June. A breeding male may display his bluish throat and chest and chase away potential rivals. The receptive female is straddled and nipped about the neck; eventually the male obtains a firm grip on her neck or back with his jaws and twists his tail beneath hers until their vents are aligned. He can then insert one of his hemipenes into the female's cloaca to effect copulation, which lasts only a few minutes.

In June, the female deposits from two to eight eggs in an underground burrow from 8 to 30 cm (3 to 12 in) deep; the eggs are oval, with thin, flexible shells, and average about 1.7 cm (0.7 in) long. Older females may lay a second clutch later in summer. Racerunners do not appear to brood or protect their eggs. Incubation requires about two months, with most hatchlings emerging in August or September.

Young Racerunners attain sexual maturity in their first or second year after hatching. Some females produce their first clutch late in their first full summer after hatching, when they are barely one year old. Natural longevity is unknown, but probably few Racerunners survive longer than four or five years.

Conservation: Racerunner populations in the Great Lakes area are localized and often isolated, and thus subject to rapid decline or extirpation if their open, sparsely vegetated habitats are modified or degraded. Natural vegetational succession that results in increased shade and ground cover could ultimately be as serious a threat as habitat loss caused by human development activities. Controlled use of fire resulting in maintenance of open habitat could benefit this species, particularly if burning occurred at a time of year when the lizards were inactive. Pesticide-spraying operations that reduce insect prey numbers predictably would be harmful to Racerunners.

Glass Lizards and Alligator Lizards
Family Anguidae

This family includes 75 species in eight genera distributed through the Americas, Europe, northwestern Africa, and Asia. Anguids are typically elongate and short-legged; many species are legless and snakelike. Their scales are reinforced with bony plates called osteoderms, making their bodies rather stiff and limiting their flexibility. A fold along each side of the body partly compensates for this stiffness by allowing expansion for respiration, feeding, or egg development. One legless species reaches the Great Lakes area.

Western Slender Glass Lizard *Ophisaurus attenuatus attenuatus*

Description: This lizard is sometimes called a "glass snake," and its legless, cylindrical body and very long tapering tail do give it a snakelike appearance. The tail, if complete and unregenerated, can make up about two-thirds of the animal's total length. The head is narrow (though relatively wider in males), with a pointed snout, movable eyelids, and visible ear openings. A deep skin groove or fold runs along each lower side, from the forward part of the body to the vent. Although Slender Glass Lizards can move quickly and gracefully, they lack the flexibility of snakes, due to their stiff body scales. The general coloration is brown, greenish brown, tan, or bronze. Young specimens usually have a dark brown stripe running down the middle of the back, another stripe above each lateral groove, and two or more thinner stripes below each groove. Striping extends onto the tail but fades about halfway to the tip. In mature adults the brown stripes often fade and break into spots or dashes and sometimes take the form of irregular crossbands. The belly is light yellow to white. Adult total length: 56 to 106.7 cm (22 to 42 in). Maximum body (snout to vent) length: 28.9 cm (11.4 in).

The sexes are similar and may be difficult to distinguish. Males are slightly longer on average and have wider heads than females and often develop white flecking mixed with black spotting on the upper sides, giving them a "salt and pepper" appearance.

Juvenile Slender Glass Lizards are similar to adults but have more vivid brown dorsal striping. They range from about 11.4 to 18.5 cm (4.5 to 7.3 in) in total length at hatching.

Western Slender Glass Lizard. (Photo by R. W. Van Devender.)

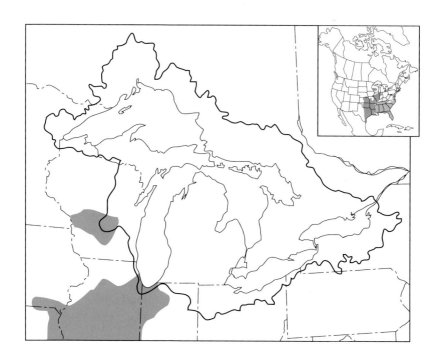

Confusing Species: This species is likely to be confused only with snakes, which lack the lizard's movable eyelids and external ear openings. Snakes have thin, overlapping scales and very flexible bodies. A Glass Lizard's scales are underlaid by hard bony plates (osteoderms), making its body less flexible. In addition, a snake has a single row of wide scales covering its belly, while a Glass Lizard has many small belly scales arranged in straight rows. When a Glass Lizard is grabbed by a predator (or a human hand), its tail easily breaks off, sometimes into several pieces. A snake does not easily lose its tail, and then only if it is subjected to severe trauma.

Distribution and Status: Western Slender Glass Lizards are found from northwestern Indiana west through Illinois and Missouri to eastern Kansas and south to coastal east Texas and western Louisiana. A disjunct population occurs in west-central Wisconsin. This lizard reaches the Great Lakes region in the extreme southern Lake Michigan basin, from Cook County, Illinois (where it is probably extirpated) to Lake and Porter Counties, in Indiana, where it still occurs in the Indiana Dunes area. Another subspecies, the Eastern Slender Glass Lizard *(Ophisaurus a. longicaudus)*, ranges through much of the southeastern United States.

This lizard can be locally common but is generally uncommon throughout much of its range; it is uncommon and local within its limited Great Lakes range.

Habitat and Ecology: Habitats used by Western Slender Glass Lizards include tallgrass and sand prairies, old fields, dunes, oak savannas, pine barrens, other open woodlands, and woodland/field ecotones. Dry, sandy soils are favored, but they can also be found where soils are fairly moist and loamy, though shaded sites are avoided. They will bask or actively forage throughout the day in spring and fall, but during the heat of summer are most active in early morning or late afternoon, or after rain. They are sometimes active at dusk or even after dark. This lizard is active over a wider range of air temperatures than many other native lizard species. By basking they can raise their body temperatures several degrees above that of the air; preferred body temperature appears to range between 26° and 31°C (78° to 88°F). During very cool or hot weather they take shelter in abandoned mammal burrows or other underground retreats, and hibernate in these places from October until April or May. Individual Slender

Glass Lizards tend to remain within small home ranges of about 0.4 hectares (1 acre) or less.

Slender Glass Lizards mostly eat invertebrates such as insects (especially grasshoppers, crickets, and beetle larvae), spiders, and snails. Larger ones will also eat small vertebrates, including frogs, snakes, other lizards, and occasionally young mice and bird's eggs.

Snakes such as the Racer are known to eat Slender Glass Lizards; other probable predators include hawks, raccoons, foxes, skunks, moles, and larger Glass Lizards. When active on the surface these lizards are wary and agile and difficult to capture. They often dash to cover in tall vegetation, under surface debris, or in mammal burrows. As their common name suggests, the ability to disconnect the tail when attacked is well developed in this species. Since much of the Glass Lizard's length is tail, a predator that seizes one is likely to find itself in possession of one or more writhing sections of tail, while the lizard itself escapes. Sometimes a startled lizard will break off its tail without having been physically contacted by the enemy. A new (but shorter) tail is eventually regrown. Slender Glass Lizards may bite if grabbed, but only the largest can inflict more than a hard pinch to a human hand.

Reproduction and Growth: Mating takes place mostly in May. During courtship, the male holds the female's head or neck with his jaws while attempting to bring their vents into contact.

In June or early July, the breeding female lays a clutch of 4 to 17 eggs in a small underground cavity or under a log, rock, or other shelter. The oval eggs have thin, flexible shells and vary from 1.6 to 2.2 cm (0.63 to 0.87 in) in length, though they absorb moisture and expand considerably during incubation. Females usually curl around their eggs and remain with them until they hatch, though it is not clear that they actively defend the nest against predators. Most hatchlings appear in August, after an incubation period of 50 to 60 days.

The young grow relatively quickly; growth slows considerably after maturity but continues throughout life. The females attain sexual maturity in three to four years, and potential longevity in the wild is at least nine years.

Conservation: Populations of this harmless lizard are threatened by human activities, such as agricultural, residential, and industrial development, and by natural succession, which may result in open, grassy habitats being taken over by shady woodland. Although natural or human-caused fires can help preserve open habitats, this lizard appears to be quite vulnerable to fire. Many instances of mass mortality of Glass Lizards have been reported following grass and brush fires, perhaps due to their habit of taking shelter beneath surface debris when frightened. Compared to other lizard species, Western Slender Glass Lizards are slower growing and take longer to reach sexual maturity; thus their populations predictably would take longer to recover from natural or human-caused disasters.

Snakes (Order Squamata, Suborder Serpentes)

Snakes are a highly specialized group of reptiles represented worldwide by over 2,400 species in about 400 genera. With their unique body form, snakes have adapted to a variety of habitat types (e.g., forests, prairies, deserts, streams, lakes, and oceans) and a wide variety of lifestyles (tree climbers, burrowers, swimmers, etc.). Although outnumbered by their squamate relatives, the lizards, in a count of species, snakes are notably better represented in temperate North America. At least 23 snake species inhabit, or recently inhabited, the Great Lakes basin, compared to only four confirmed native lizards.

The fragile nature of the snake skeleton has resulted in a rather poor fossil record for the group, but the available evidence indicates that they evolved from a lizard ancestor in the mid–Mesozoic era, during the reign of the dinosaurs. Although some of the more primitive living snake families retain vestigial hip and hind leg bones (e.g., boas, pythons, and worm snakes), all snakes show a number of unique adaptations to a legless way of life. Their elongated bodies contain from 150 to over 400 vertebrae that interconnect to offer extreme horizontal flexibility combined with vertical rigidity. Their internal organs are arranged to fit the available space; most snakes have only one functional lung (the right one being greatly elongated, while the left is vestigial or absent) and the kidneys are in-line rather than side by side.

Most snakes have a single row of wide belly scales (scutes) from head to vent that are important in locomotion. The scutes are attached internally to muscles, allowing them to be tilted outward and then pulled inward. If the snake wants to crawl forward, it extends and contracts its belly scutes in sequence along its body; the scutes grip the ground and then push against it, propelling the snake forward. This type of movement, called rectilinear motion, is usually used when the snake is not in a hurry. To move faster, a snake may throw its body into a series of curves, pushing against the ground with the back of each curve. This movement, called lateral undulation, is also used when a snake is swimming.

247

Although snakes appear to move very fast, this is largely an illusion—the Racer, probably the fastest Great Lakes area species, has a top speed of only about 6.5 kilometers per hour (about 4 miles per hour).

Most nonburrowing species of snakes appear to have reasonably good vision, at least for the detection of nearby motion, but their ability to see detail and to detect nonmoving objects may be limited. Snakes lack movable eyelids, but their eyes are protected by a transparent cap of skin called the brille.

All snakes periodically shed the keratinous outer skin layer (epidermis), including the eye cap, to accommodate growth and wear. Skin shedding (ecdysis) occurs from two to four or more times per year, depending on the snake's growth rate and condition. Prior to shedding, a special secretion loosens the outer skin layer, including the eye coverings. A snake in this pre-shed phase is dull colored and has opaque bluish eyes and will be particularly nervous and secretive due to its impaired vision. The skin is usually shed in one piece; starting at the snout or mouth, the snake catches the loosening skin on a rough object and literally crawls out of it, turning the shed skin inside out while moving slowly forward. A snake that has recently shed may look and feel glossy or velvety, and its coloration and markings will be at their greatest intensity.

Snakes do not have external ear openings but are able to sense low-frequency sounds and vibrations transmitted through their jawbones, and perhaps through the belly scutes and lungs as well. An important source of environmental information for snakes comes from the vomeronasal (Jacobson's) organ. This organ consists of two small adjacent structures in the roof of the snake's mouth; these contain sensory cells that are connected by nerves to the olfactory lobe of the brain. The constantly flicking forked tongue picks up chemicals from the ground or air and brings them into the mouth; there they are brought into contact with the vomeronasal organ, which sends the chemical information to the brain for analysis. This process might be compared to a combined sense of taste and smell and is used by the snake to detect potential food, mates, or enemies. The tongue of a snake is thus a harmless sensing organ, never a weapon.

A unique sense possessed by rattlesnakes, other pit vipers, and many boas and pythons, is the ability to detect heat (as infrared radiation). This is helpful in determining the position and distance of warm-blooded prey or predators. Nerve-lined openings ("pits") between the eye and nostril (in rattlesnakes) or along the jawline (in boas and pythons) are the externally visible parts of this system.

All snakes are predators and, lacking claws or chewing teeth, must swallow prey animals whole. Their teeth are curved backward to hold prey securely, and their jawbones and certain other skull bones are loosely connected and movable; thus a snake can swallow a prey item that is bigger around than its head or body. Many species have special adaptations to help in procuring food. Some species kill their prey before swallowing it. A constricting snake, such as a Black Rat Snake or Milk Snake, will seize a prey animal and quickly wrap coils of its body around it, continuously tightening and thus compressing its heart and lungs. A warm-blooded prey animal usually dies quickly from lack of blood circulation or suffocation. A rattlesnake injects venom (a specially modified form of saliva) into its prey through hollow fangs. It then trails the animal and waits until it dies and can be swallowed without fear of reprisal. On the other hand, most of the smaller snakes (such as Brown Snakes and garter snakes) simply seize their prey and swallow it alive; they are thus restricted to eating nonthreatening prey such as worms or amphibians.

Male snakes possess paired copulatory organs, the hemipenes—another trait shared with their lizard kin. Mating usually occurs in spring, soon after emergence from hibernation, but a few species also mate in fall. Females of most snake species are oviparous, laying thin-shelled eggs in a burrow or other protected place. However, many species in several families retain the developing embryos in their bodies and give birth to living young; at birth they often emerge from the female's cloaca in a thin membrane from which they soon wriggle free. Some highly advanced snakes, including our native water and garter snakes (e.g., genera *Nerodia, Regina, Thamnophis*), are truly viviparous; the developing embryos receive nourishment from the female's body through a placenta-like connection similar to that found in mammals. Live-bearing snakes are particularly successful in cool-temperate climates, and outnumber egg-laying species in the Great Lakes basin.

Several scale characters are useful in identifying snake specimens that can be examined closely or safely held in-hand, and may allow identification of a shed skin. (These are illustrated in figure 10 and are included in species descriptions.) First, look at the upper (dorsal) scales about midbody; are they smooth and shiny, or does each scale have a keel, or ridge, down the middle? (The Black Rat Snake has weakly keeled midbody scales that may appear smooth in juveniles.) Now count and record the number of dorsal scale rows at midbody, beginning with the row just above the wide belly scales on one side and continuing to the belly scales

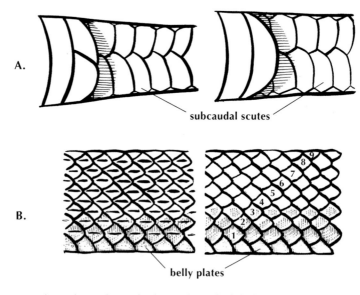

Fig. 10. Snake scales. *A*, base of tail in snake with (*left*) divided anal plate and (*right*) single anal plate. *B*, dorsal scales of snakes with (*left*) keeled scales and (*right*) smooth scales showing method of counting scale rows.

on the opposite side. Next, find the scale that covers the vent opening, called the anal plate. Is it single or divided into two parts? (The vent marks the beginning of the tail.) Note that unlike the belly scales, the scales under the tail, called subcaudals, are in two rows in all our native non-venomous snakes; the rattlesnakes have one row of subcaudals, except for a few near the tip. Finally, a count of the large "lip" (labial) scales just above the mouth on one side will sometimes help confirm an identification.

Selected general references: Conant and Collins 1991, Ernst and Barbour 1989, Halliday and Adler 1986, Mattison 1986, Parker and Grandison 1977, Seigel and Collins 1993, and Wright and Wright 1957.

Typical Snakes
Family Colubridae

The family Colubridae contains over 1,560 species, or about 65 percent of all snake species. Members of this group are often called "harmless" snakes, since the vast majority of species are indeed harmless to humans. However, some colubrids have enlarged teeth in the back of their mouths, and many have modified salivary glands (Duvernoy's glands) that produce toxic substances useful in subduing prey. A few tropical rear-fanged species, such as the African Boomslang *(Dispholidus typus)*, produce a venom sufficiently toxic to be dangerous to humans.

Many attempts have been made to divide this large family into a number of smaller groups, most often by studying similarities and differences in the structure of the vertebrae, the hemipenes, and teeth. Ongoing and future biochemical and genetics studies on snakes will surely result in changes to classification systems presently available. Colubrid snakes of the Great Lakes region have been placed in four subfamilies, listed below.

Subfamily Natricinae: Many members of this group are either small, terrestrial worm-eating snakes or larger semiaquatic snakes that eat mostly ectothermic vertebrates (e.g., fish and amphibians). Includes the water snakes *(Nerodia)*, Kirtland's Snake *(Clonophis kirtlandii)*, crayfish and Queen Snakes *(Regina)*, garter and ribbon snakes *(Thamnophis)*, and Brown and Red-bellied Snakes *(Storeria)*.

Subfamily Colubrinae: A group of active terrestrial snakes. Includes the Smooth Green Snake *(Opheodrys vernalis)* and the Racer *(Coluber constrictor)*.

Subfamily Lampropeltinae: Most species in this group use constriction to subdue their prey. Includes the Milk Snake *(Lampropeltis triangulum)*, Rat Snake *(Elaphe obsoleta)*, Fox Snakes *(Elaphe vulpina* and *E. gloydi)*, and the Bullsnake *(Pituophis catenifer)*.

Subfamily Xenodontinae: Some of these have enlarged teeth in the rear of the upper jaw and/or mildly toxic salivary secretions, but Great Lakes area representatives are harmless to humans. The Ring-necked Snake *(Diadophis punctatus)* and Eastern Hog-nosed Snake *(Heterodon platirhinos)* have traditionally been placed in this group, but some biologists doubt whether these species are actually closely related to each other or to the many xenodontine snakes found in Central and South America.

Northern Water Snake *Nerodia sipedon*

Description: This is a moderately large, dark-colored snake usually seen in or near water. The tan, brown, or gray background color is typically overlaid by a variable pattern of black, dark brown, or reddish brown crossbands and blotches on the back and sides. Complete crossbands usually predominate on the forward third of the body, breaking up into smaller, often alternating "saddles" and side blotches towards the tail. The blotched pattern may become obscured by dark pigment over time, and older adult Northern Water Snakes can appear solid brown or black, particularly when their skin is dry. At least a hint of the blotched pattern is often visible when they are wet. The white, yellowish, or orangish belly is usually marked with a pattern of reddish brown half-moon-shaped spots, sometimes interspersed with, or grading into, grayish or brownish speckling. There are 21 to 25 scale rows at midbody; the scales are keeled, and the anal plate is divided. Total adult length: 61 to 140.5 cm (24 to 55.3 in).

Males are, on average, smaller than females, and have proportionally longer tails. In males the subcaudal (undertail) scutes number from 66 to 84, with the tail length representing 23 percent to 29 percent of the total length; females have from 42 to 77 subcaudal scutes, and their tails make up 20 percent to 25 percent of their total length.

Newborn Northern Water Snakes range in length from 19 to 27 cm (7.5 to 10.6 in). They are more distinctly patterned than adults, with black or reddish brown bands and blotches on a grayish or tan background.

Note: The above description applies to the wide-ranging subspecies *Nerodia sipedon sipedon,* which retains the name Northern Water Snake. *Nerodia sipedon* inhabiting islands in western Lake Erie (the Put-In-Bay Archipelago) are recognized as a separate subspecies, the Lake Erie Water Snake *(Nerodia sipedon insularum).* Typical specimens of this subspecies are pale gray, grayish olive, or grayish brown in dorsal coloration and lack the dark-blotched pattern of a typical Northern Water Snake. The belly is white to yellowish. The average size is slightly larger than *N. s. sipedon* (maximum total length for a female = 144 cm; 56.7 in). Populations of water snakes on the various islands often contain a fairly high percentage of intergrade specimens (having varying degrees of pattern development), along with smaller percentages of the "pure" patternless form and still smaller numbers of the "typical" dark, banded form. The existence of this race may represent a classic example of natural selection, since it seems

Northern Water Snake

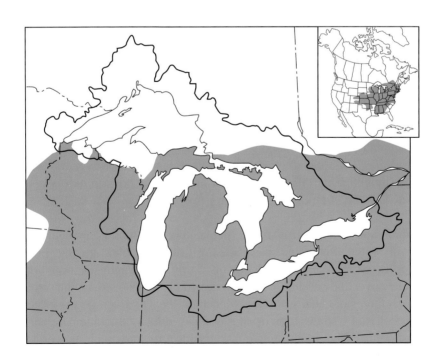

to more closely match the rocky (limestone) shoreline habitats in these islands (and may thus be less visible to predators, such as gulls) than the darker mainland form. However, the apparent ability of the snakes to move from the mainland to and between the islands and the high proportion of intergrade and "normal" patterned specimens on the islands has led some herpetologists to question the recognition of this subspecies.

Confusing Species: The Copper-bellied Water Snake has a plain red or orange belly, sometimes invaded by dark brown or black color along the edges of the ventral scales. Kirtland's Snake has a pink or red belly with a row of black spots down each side. Garter and ribbon snakes have lengthwise dorsal stripes and a single (undivided) anal plate. The Eastern Milk Snake has a black-on-white "checkerboard" belly pattern, smooth body scales, and a single anal plate.

Distribution and Status: The Northern Water Snake ranges from eastern Maine west through Nebraska and portions of eastern Colorado, south to Oklahoma and Arkansas and east to Virginia and the Carolinas. It occurs throughout the Great Lakes region, except for the northern and western portions of the Lake Superior drainage basin. The Lake Erie Water Snake is found on certain islands of western Lake Erie in Ontario and Ohio, from Pelee Island and East Sister Island south through the Bass Islands to Kelleys Island. They also occur sparingly on the Catawba-Marblehead Peninsula, in Ottawa County, Ohio. An additional subspecies (*Nerodia sipedon pleuralis*) extends the species' range from southern Indiana and Illinois to eastern Louisiana and the Florida panhandle.

Northern Water Snakes can be common to abundant in some places, though many local populations have been reduced or eliminated by persecution or pollution. The Lake Erie Water Snake, once locally abundant in its limited range, has experienced drastic reductions in numbers on many Lake Erie islands in recent years.

Habitat and Ecology: This snake will live in or near most permanent bodies of water, including rivers, streams, sloughs, lakes, ponds, bogs, marshes, swamps, and impoundments. Fairly open, sunny locations with ample cover and basking sites are preferred (e.g., low overhanging shrubbery, clumps of cattails or other vegetation, beaver and muskrat lodges, exposed root systems, logs, or piles of rocks, driftwood, or human-generated debris). They often frequent waterside structures such as wooden docks, boathouses, piers, bridge supports, earthen or rock dams and causeways, spillways, and flowing culverts.

Northern Water Snakes occasionally move overland (most often juveniles dispersing to new habitat) but are usually found in, or immediately adjacent to, water. These snakes are mostly active during daylight hours in spring and fall but may adopt nocturnal habits in summer. When not basking or foraging they tend to remain hidden beneath logs, flat rocks, boards, or other cover. Older juveniles and adults are often seen basking on shoreline debris but dive into the water at the slightest disturbance. A frightened snake will usually hide itself near the bottom for a few minutes, then resurface and swim parallel to the shoreline. If repeatedly threatened, however, most will eventually retreat to deeper water and may remain submerged for over an hour if necessary. Over most of their Great Lakes range these snakes hibernate from October to April, with the actual period of dormancy dependent on local climatic conditions. The colder months are passed (often with numbers of their own and other snake species) in mammal or crayfish burrows, rock crevices, overbank root systems, or other sheltered sites near their summer habitat.

Northern Water Snakes eat mostly "cold-blooded" prey; small fish make up the largest part of the diet, followed in frequency by frogs, tadpoles, aquatic salamanders, and crayfish. Insects and earthworms are occasionally consumed, particularly by young snakes, while small mammals (mice, shrews) are rarely taken. Food is located by sight (particularly moving objects) and by odor. They seek prey underwater by actively probing into clumps of vegetation or under rocks or other submerged objects and may charge open-mouthed into schools of small fish. On the other hand, they sometimes capture frogs or fish after a slow, deliberate stalk. These snakes will eat carrion, including partially decomposed fish. The Lake Erie Water Snake seems to feed mostly on dead and dying fish that wash into its rocky shoreline habitat.

Natural enemies of the Northern Water Snake include larger predatory fish, Bullfrogs, Snapping Turtles, other snakes (Racers, larger water snakes), hawks, herons (and other wading birds), raccoons, skunks, mink, and otters. Humans are the most serious enemies of these snakes in many places. A Northern Water Snake will try to escape from a potential predator whenever possible but can aggressively defend itself when necessary. If cornered or seized, it may flatten its head and body and strike out repeatedly at the perceived enemy. While not venomous, its tiny recurved teeth can cause pinpoint wounds or scratches that bleed freely and are, at least briefly, quite painful. In addition, this snake can release surprising quantities of a noxious, musky-smelling substance from its cloaca, which may discourage a predator (or human captor) not already deterred by its biting attack.

Reproduction and Growth: Courtship and mating occur in spring, typically mid-April to mid-June, and may take place on land or in water. A courting male will crawl over the female, matching her body position and movements, and rub his chin along her back, sometimes with occasional spasmodic jerks of his head or body. He must twine his tail around the female's and bring their cloacal openings into contact to effect copulation. It is not uncommon for two or more males to simultaneously court the same female; competing males may try to shove each other out of position but apparently do not bite or otherwise injure each other.

Most females give birth to their young in August or September. Reported litter size for the species ranges from 4 to 99 (most often 15 to 40), with larger females generally producing proportionally larger litters than smaller ones. Growth is rapid in the young snakes, some of which may nearly double their length in their first growing season (though the average increase is closer to about 50 percent per year). Growth rate slows considerably at sexual maturity, which is attained in two to three years. A Northern Water Snake lived over nine years and seven months in captivity, but the average life span in the wild is unknown.

Conservation: This is surely one of the most persecuted snake species in the Great Lakes region. People often kill Northern Water Snakes out of fear or ignorance, or in the belief that they reduce the numbers of game fish. Although these snakes will bite if cornered or seized, they are harmless if left alone. They are sometimes called "water moccasins" and erroneously assumed to be venomous. (The true "water moccasin" or Cottonmouth, *Agkistrodon piscivorus,* does not occur within the Great Lakes basin.)

Northern Water Snakes have little or no impact on sport fishing in natural bodies of water. They tend to eat smaller, slower-moving or injured fish, mostly species less desired by humans, and may actually improve fishing in some places by feeding on fish stunted by overpopulation, and by consuming dead or diseased fish. Being opportunistic feeders, Northern Water Snakes can be a problem in fish hatcheries and on fish farms, where their removal may be justified.

Unwarranted persecution, combined with shoreline development, has led to local extirpation of Northern Water Snakes in some areas. The Lake Erie Water Snake has proven particularly vulnerable to these problems, and they now are absent, or present only in low numbers, on many of the islands where they were once common. Public education programs, combined with legal protection, would greatly benefit remaining populations of this unique race.

Copper-bellied Water Snake   *Nerodia erythrogaster neglecta*

Description: This large water snake is typically a uniform black, gray, or dark brown when mature, though some individuals may retain a hint of the blotched juvenile pattern. The labial scales are orangish or reddish with dark edges, and the throat and chin may be whitish to orange. The plain, unmarked belly ranges in color from pale orange to red or coppery red, though the ventral scales are often tinged by the dark dorsal color along the edges; this effect tends to be more pronounced toward the rear of the snake. There are 19 to 23 scale rows at midbody; the scales are keeled, and the anal plate is usually divided (single in about 10 percent of specimens). Total adult length: 67 to 141.5 cm (26.4 to 56 in).

Males are generally smaller than females and have proportionally longer tails. In males the number of subcaudal scutes ranges from 71 to 81, and the tail comprises 23 percent to 30 percent of the total length. Females have 62 to 71 subcaudals, with tails making up 19 percent to 22 percent of their total length.

At birth Copper-bellied Water Snakes range in length from 21 to 27 cm (8.3 to 10.6 in). Newborn and juvenile specimens have a pattern of dark blotches on a reddish brown or grayish brown background color; the larger blotches on the back tend to alternate with smaller ones along the sides, though these markings may fuse into crossbands near the head. Juvenile belly color is often paler than that of the adult, varying from light yellow or orange to pinkish red.

Confusing Species: Northern Water Snakes have rows of dark spots (often half-moon shaped) on the belly, and usually retain at least a hint of a blotched pattern on the back and sides. Kirtland's Snakes and Queen Snakes also have conspicuous belly markings (rows of spots or stripes, respectively). The little Northern Red-bellied Snake rarely exceeds a length of 30 cm (12 in), and has only 15 midbody scale rows.

Copper-bellied Water Snake

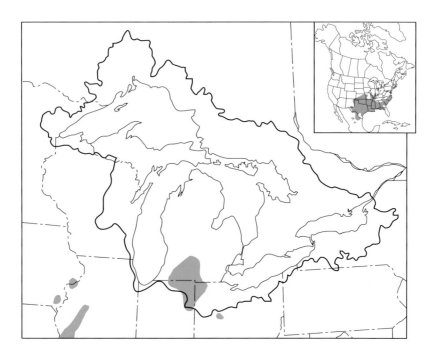

Distribution and Status: The range of the Copper-bellied Water Snake is presently centered near the confluence of the Ohio and Wabash Rivers in western Kentucky and adjacent southeastern Illinois and southwestern Indiana. Isolated (relict) populations occur, or recently occurred, in west-central Ohio, southern and eastern Indiana, northern Kentucky, northwestern Tennessee, and (within the Great Lakes basin) in south-central Michigan, northern Indiana, and northwestern Ohio. The northernmost confirmed records are in Eaton and Oakland Counties, in Michigan, where they are apparently extirpated; old unverified reports placed them as far north as Roscommon County, Michigan.

Three additional subspecies of *Nerodia erythrogaster* range from the Atlantic coast (Delaware and southern Virginia to Georgia) across the Deep South to Texas and northern Mexico, north to Kansas, Missouri, and the Mississippi valley as far as western Illinois and southern Iowa. Thus this is essentially a southern species that reaches its northern limit in the lower Great Lakes basin.

The Copper-bellied Water Snake is in decline throughout much of its limited range. Within the Great Lakes region, where it is presently recognized as endangered (Michigan and Ohio) or threatened (Indiana), it is very rare and restricted to a few isolated colonies. Many populations have been recently extirpated, and those that remain face continued threats from human activities. This snake's future existence in the region is precarious.

Habitat and Ecology: Copper-bellied Water Snakes typically occur in or near shrub swamps, ponds, lakes, oxbow sloughs, fens, and slow-moving streams, usually associated with either mature or second-growth woodlands, but occasionally in more open situations. In spring these snakes often inhabit the open edges of shallow ponds and buttonbush *(Cephalanthus occidentalis)* swamps and frequently bask on shoreline vegetation, muskrat lodges, or woody debris. When temperatures rise and these seasonal waters begin to dry up in early summer, the snakes migrate to permanent waters (lake and stream edges), often using fairly dry wooded or grassy upland corridors. They may become largely nocturnal during hot weather. Unlike the Northern Water Snake, this species may spend considerable periods of time in relatively dry habitats away from water, apparently by choice as well as necessity. They sometimes aestivate underground or beneath logs or debris piles during hot weather or drought. An individual Copper-bellied Water Snake may occupy a home range of 20 hectares (50 acres) or more, but the vast majority of its time will likely be spent in a few small areas within this range.

Declining temperatures in fall, especially several consecutive days with low temperatures below freezing, appear to trigger migration to hibernation sites. These snakes are typically dormant from late October or November until sometime in April, usually seeking shelter in burrows or debris piles that are higher than the nearby wetlands. Occasional individuals will overwinter in crayfish burrows or other lowland sites but risk death by flooding if water levels rise during dormancy.

Most reports on the diet of Copper-bellied Water Snakes in the Great Lakes area indicate a preference for amphibians (frogs, salamanders and their larvae) and crayfish, which may reflect this snake's habit of frequenting shallow ponds and swamps where fish are scarce or absent. Fish are readily eaten when available.

Natural predators of Copper-bellied Water Snakes (particularly juveniles) include the larger fish, Snapping Turtles, herons, hawks, opossums, raccoons, foxes, otters, mink, and skunks. They are also killed by humans and domestic animals (cats, dogs, pigs). This species may be especially vulnerable to attack by hawks and terrestrial mammals when moving through upland habitats; many individuals are found with injured tails, indicating unsuccessful predatory attempts. These are alert and agile snakes—they move quickly on land, and when frightened near water they can dive to the bottom and hide amid aquatic debris and vegetation. They can remain submerged for an hour or more. If cornered or seized, a "copperbelly" may flatten its head and body and strike repeatedly, while discharging copious amounts of feces and an odorous musk from its vent.

Reproduction and Growth: Most mating takes place between postwinter emergence in April and early June, with a peak of activity in May. At this time the adult snakes are still concentrated at basking sites along the edges of ponds and swamps. Courtship behavior has not been described in detail but appears to be similar to that of the Northern Water Snake.

Copper-bellied Water Snakes have a relatively long gestation period compared to most other viviparous snake species in the region. Females give birth to litters of 5 to 37 young (most often 8 to 20) from mid-September through mid-October. Growth and longevity data on this subspecies are lacking, but captive specimens of other subspecies have survived to known ages of 8 to nearly 15 years.

Conservation: The Copper-bellied Water Snake is at the northern periphery of its range in the Great Lakes region, which it may have entered during the postglacial "climatic optimum," when the climate was warmer and probably wetter than at present. It possibly was fairly common and widespread in swampy forested bottomlands during presettlement times, but the cutting of these forests and conversion of wetlands to agricultural uses over the last century have left the few remaining populations of this snake isolated in pockets of ever-shrinking habitat. Human persecution and road mortality are additional threats to already diminished populations.

Any attempt to create refuges for the Copper-bellied Water Snake must take into account its tendency to make seasonal migrations between shallow wetlands and permanent waters along upland corridors. Thus, preserving a fairly large and diverse block of habitat is desirable. These snakes may tolerate certain human activities in parts of their habitat, such as fishing, hiking, selective logging, livestock grazing (other than hogs), and harvest of forage crops, as long as use of vehicles and heavy equipment is restricted to times of the year when the snakes are inactive, and the snakes themselves are left alone. Where road mortality is a problem, the seasonal closing or even rerouting of roads should be considered. Public education, along with legal protection, can minimize the persecution of these snakes by people.

Queen Snake   *Regina septemvittata*

Description: The Queen Snake is a small-headed, slender, brown, olive, or gray snake with a light yellowish stripe on each side, on the second and upper half of the first scale row. These side stripes continue onto the labial scales and meet on the lower part of the rostral (nose) scale. Three dark dorsal stripes may be visible in young and some adult Queen Snakes. Striping often fades in old individuals, which may become practically unicolored. The chin and throat are yellow, and the belly is also yellowish, with four brownish lengthwise stripes that may merge or become obscured toward the tail. (Note that the two outer dark belly stripes occur on the lower half of the first scale row and the adjacent edges of the ventral scutes, and are flanked above by the yellow side stripes.) There are 19 scale rows at midbody; these scales are keeled, and the anal plate is divided. Total adult length: 34 to 92.2 cm (13.4 to 36.3 in).

Queen Snake

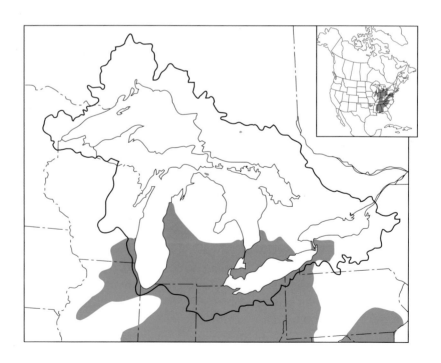

The sexes are often difficult to distinguish based on external characters. Male Queen Snakes have relatively longer tails than females. Males have from 65 to 89 subcaudal scutes (average = 76), with the tail from 23 percent to 34 percent of the snake's total length. Females have 54 to 87 subcaudals (average = 69), with tails equal to 19 percent to 27 percent of total length.

Young Queen Snakes range from 17.5 to 23 cm (6.9 to 9 in) in length and are colored much like the adults, although their markings (especially the belly stripes) are more distinct.

Confusing Species: Garter and ribbon snakes have an unstriped belly, a light stripe down the middle of the back, and a single (undivided) anal plate. In Graham's Crayfish Snake, the light side stripe is broader (on scale rows 1, 2, and 3), and the yellowish belly is either unmarked or with a single row of dark spots (or a faint dark line) down the center.

Distribution and Status: Queen Snakes range from the southern Great Lakes area south to the Gulf Coast (western Florida panhandle and adjacent Alabama) and eastward through the western Carolinas and central Virginia to southeastern Pennsylvania. There is a disjunct population in north-central Arkansas. Within the Great Lakes basin, this snake is known from the southeastern corner of Wisconsin and northeastern Illinois through northern Indiana, Ohio, and the southern and western portions of Michigan's Lower Peninsula (an isolated population occurs on Bois Blanc Island, in western Lake Huron). The range continues south from Lake Erie to western New York, and in Ontario from western Lake Erie north to Georgian Bay.

Queen Snake numbers have declined in many places due largely to habitat degradation, although they can be locally common where ideal habitat remains. This is generally an uncommon and local species throughout most of its Great Lakes range; it is considered to be endangered in Wisconsin.

Habitat and Ecology: Queen Snakes are most often found in or near warm, shallow, rocky-bottomed streams with an abundance of crayfish; they also inhabit the edges of ponds, lakes, marshes, ditches, and canals. The edges of inhabited bodies of water may be largely open or partially to mostly forested, but totally shaded sites are avoided. These snakes often bask on debris at the water's edge or in overhanging shrubbery or tree branches; if disturbed, they dive into the water and either hide near the bottom or swim along the shore for a short distance before emerging. When not basking or foraging, Queen Snakes often remain concealed beneath flat rocks or woody debris on the shoreline. They are usually inactive at night.

Queen Snakes in the Great Lakes area tend to be active from late April or early May until sometime in October or early November, depending on local climatic conditions. They reportedly hibernate near the water in mammal or crayfish burrows or other underground shelter.

The Queen Snake's primary food source is crayfish. Since large crayfish are protected by a hard exoskeleton and will defend themselves with their claws, the snakes prefer to eat those that have recently molted and are still "soft-shelled." Prey is sought by probing under rocks and other submerged objects, with the sense of smell (or, more precisely, the large tongue and vomeronasal organ) playing a major role in its detection. Occasionally (and opportunistically) a small fish or tadpole might be taken, but the Queen Snake can be considered a crayfish specialist.

Herons and raccoons are known to eat Queen Snakes; other likely predators include large fish and frogs, other snakes, hawks, otters, and mink. Ironically, crayfish are a potential danger to young Queen Snakes, since a small snake can drown if grasped in a crayfish's strong claws. Queen Snakes prefer to avoid confrontation with potential predators, but some individuals will bite if cornered or seized, and nearly all will smear an attacker with malodorous feces and anal musk.

Reproduction and Growth: Queen Snakes mate in spring, probably most often in May. Fall mating is suspected by some biologists but has apparently not been confirmed. A courting male will approach a female with much flicking of his tongue, probably seeking chemical cues to her identity and readiness to mate. He then crawls over the female, aligns his body with hers, and may (according to one observer) "bounce" the forward part of his body, in a rapid vertical oscillation, on that of the female. To copulate, the male must align his vent with that of the female.

In late summer or early autumn (late July to September) the female gives birth to 5 to 31 (usually about 10 to 12) young. The little snakes grow quickly, increasing in length by 50 percent to 80 percent in their first year, and perhaps nearly as much in the second year, after which time growth slows considerably. Both sexes may reach sexual maturity when two years old, but females probably do not actually breed until their third year. Longevity in the wild is unknown, but a zoo captive lived over 19 years.

Conservation: This very specialized snake is vulnerable to various forms of pollution and habitat alteration and is now scarce or absent in many Great Lakes area streams that once harbored healthy populations. Siltation from urban or agricultural runoff may reduce or eliminate the crayfish on which Queen Snakes depend. A preference for narrow streamside habitats makes these snakes particularly vulnerable to direct human persecution, and they are often killed by fishermen who erroneously believe that they consume game fish.

Kirtland's Snake *Clonophis kirtlandii*

Description: This small snake has four rows of alternating dark, rounded blotches running down the back and sides; these blotches are often faded and indistinct in very young and old adult individuals. The background color is reddish brown to grayish brown. A faint stripe is sometimes visible along the middle of the back. The small, narrow head (scarcely wider than the neck) is black or dark brown above, occasionally with some light mottling, while the labial scales and the chin and throat are a contrasting white, cream, or yellow. The belly is pink, red, or orange, with a row of black spots along each side, and there may be some irregular dark spotting between these lateral rows as well. There are 17 to 19 scale rows at midbody; the scales are keeled, and the anal plate is divided. Total adult length: 36 to 62.2 cm (14 to 24.5 in).

Adult males tend to be smaller (shorter and thinner-bodied) than females, and have proportionally longer tails (22 percent to 28 percent of total length, with 56 to 69 subcaudal scutes). The stouter females have tails 19 percent to 24 percent of total length and 44 to 61 subcaudals.

Newborn Kirtland's Snakes range in total length from 11 to 16.8 cm (4.3 to 6.6 in). They are darker above than the adults, with an indistinct (or sometimes nonexistent) blotch pattern, and have a deeper red color on the belly.

Confusing Species: Garter snakes have lengthwise dorsal striping, pale unspotted bellies, and a single anal plate. The smaller Red-bellied Snake lacks both dorsal blotching and rows of spots on the belly. Copper-bellied Water Snakes grow larger and also lack the two rows of belly spots.

Kirtland's Snake. (Photo by R. W. Van Devender.)

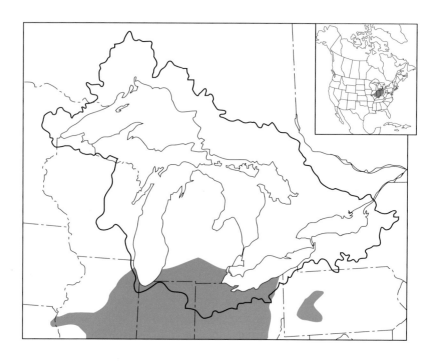

Distribution and Status: This species occurs in west and central Ohio, most of Indiana, southern Michigan, north-central Kentucky, and northeastern and central Illinois; they have also been recorded in western Pennsylvania and extreme southeastern Wisconsin. Much of its known range is within the postglacial "prairie peninsula." Most recent Great Lakes area records for Kirtland's Snake are clustered near the southern end of Lake Michigan (Cook County, Illinois, northwestern Indiana, and southwestern Michigan), and in Lucas County, Ohio (Toledo area).

This snake must be considered a rare and declining species throughout its range, despite its occasional occurrence in fairly dense local populations. It is presently recognized as "endangered" in Michigan and "threatened" in Indiana, and its future as part of the Great Lakes herpetofauna is precarious.

Habitat and Ecology: Kirtland's Snakes are usually found in damp habitats, often in the vicinity of streams, ditches, marshes, or ponds, but they are not truly aquatic. Open grassy habitats such as wet prairies, wet meadows, fens, swales, and pastures are preferred; they also occur in swampy woodlands, particularly in the unglaciated (southern edge) of its range. This species can be particularly abundant on undeveloped parcels of land in certain large metropolitan areas, but it is unclear whether these urban sites are preferred over more "natural" habitats, or whether the snakes are simply more accessible and easily found in these places (since they often hide under boards and other human-generated debris).

This is an extremely secretive species that spends much of its time below ground in burrows constructed by other animals, under leaf litter, or beneath logs, rocks, or other surface objects. Burrows of the chimney crayfish are a preferred retreat. Movement through subterranean habitats may be enhanced by this snake's ability to flatten its body to almost ribbonlike proportions. Kirtland's Snakes are active from late March or early April through late October or early November. The same burrows used as shelter during the active season undoubtedly serve as hibernation sites in winter. Most sightings of Kirtland's Snakes are in early spring or fall; they appear to be largely nocturnal, particularly in summer.

Earthworms are the preferred food for this species, although slugs and perhaps terrestrial leeches are also eaten. Captives reportedly have consumed these food items as well as chopped fish but refused to eat small frogs, toads, and salamanders.

Natural predation on Kirtland's Snake has not been reported in the

Great Lakes region. Since they spend little time exposed on the surface, they are probably most vulnerable to burrowing predators such as Eastern Milk Snakes, shrews, and weasels. During their brief aboveground forays, they are vulnerable to hawks and owls, larger mammalian predators (foxes, raccoons, skunks, cats), and (inevitably) automobiles and unappreciative humans.

When threatened (especially when suddenly exposed), a Kirtland's Snake can flatten its body to a remarkable degree and remain stiff and immobile. Upon further disturbance or if touched, it may violently writhe its body and attempt to hide its head, or suddenly dart into cover. Some individuals will strike and bite if cornered or grasped, but these little snakes are quite harmless to humans.

Reproduction and Growth: Mating has been observed in May under natural conditions. Females give birth to their young in late summer or early autumn (usually in August or September); litter size ranges from 4 to 15. At birth the young snakes are usually enclosed in a thin (chorionic) membrane from which they soon escape.

The little snakes grow rapidly, sometimes nearly doubling their lengths in the first full year. They probably reach sexual maturity within two years, with at least some females mating during their second spring after birth.

Conservation: Kirtland's Snake certainly lost the vast majority of its original habitat as the wet grasslands of the "prairie peninsula" were converted to agricultural use, beginning early in the nineteenth century. This species is now largely restricted to isolated colonies, often surrounded by intensively farmed or developed lands that offer little or no opportunity for dispersal or genetic interchange.

As noted, this snake has been able to thrive in vacant grassy habitats in and near some large cities; however, these places are extremely vulnerable to development, and many urban sites for *Clonophis* have completely disappeared in recent years. An additional problem is that these attractive and harmless little snakes are coveted by some reptile hobbyists, and surviving urban populations are often discovered and heavily exploited by collectors. This practice is particularly tragic since Kirtland's Snake is considered a "difficult" captive by most herpetologists and zoo professionals; few specimens survive more than a year in captivity.

Conserving this species will require identifying and protecting critical habitats, both in urban and rural areas. Legal protection by all states within its range would curtail pet trade exploitation, but a public-education campaign would be more effective in reducing incidental collecting and gratuitous killing.

Common Garter Snake   *Thamnophis sirtalis*

Description: This extremely variable snake typically has three light stripes on a background of black, brown, gray, or olive. The stripes may be yellow, greenish yellow, brown, bluish, or white. One stripe runs down the midline of the back, and another stripe extends along each lower side, covering scale rows 2 and 3. Occasionally the stripes are inconspicuous or even absent. Many individuals have two alternating rows of dark spots between the stripes, giving them a "checkered" appearance. The head is wider than the neck and is dark above, while the labial scales are yellowish, often edged in black, and the tongue is red with a black tip. The chin, throat and belly range in color from yellow, greenish yellow, or tan to white or pale blue; there may be one or two small black spots visible along the edges of some of the ventral scutes. There are 19 scale rows at midbody; the scales are keeled and the anal plate is single. Total adult length: 46 to 137 cm (18 to 54 in).

Males are generally smaller and thinner bodied than females and have proportionally longer tails. Tail length in males ranges from 21 percent to 30 percent of total length, while tail length in females equals 17 percent to 22 percent of total length.

Newborn Common Garter Snakes range in length from 12.5 to 23 cm (5 to 9 in) and are colored much like the adults.

Note: The Eastern Garter Snake, *Thamnophis sirtalis sirtalis,* is the subspecies of the Common Garter Snake found throughout most of the Great Lakes basin. Another subspecies, the Chicago Garter Snake *(Thamnophis sirtalis semifasciatus),* occurs at the southwestern end of Lake Michigan, from southeastern Wisconsin through northeastern Illinois to the Indiana Dunes area (Porter County, Indiana). It is distinguished by having the light side stripes on the anterior part of the body interrupted by vertical dark bars; the dorsal stripe may also be broken by dark markings. The validity of this subspecies has been frequently questioned, in part because snakes with this color pattern often turn up elsewhere in the region, and because it intergrades broadly with the Eastern Garter Snake. Another color variant common in Great Lakes area *T. sirtalis* is the presence of reddish color

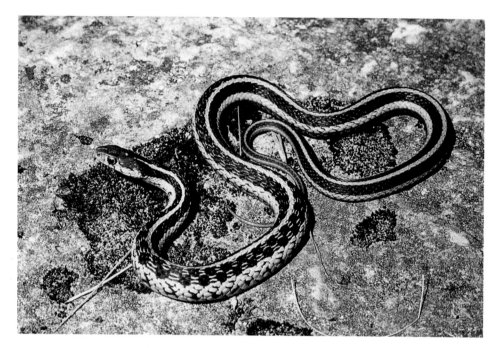

Eastern Garter Snake

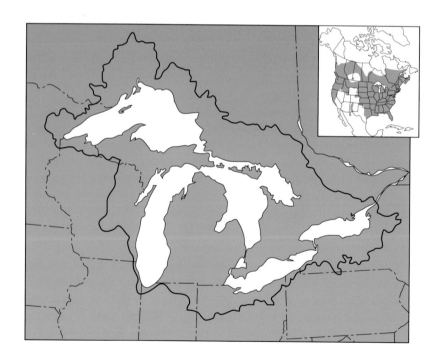

on the snake's neck and sides. A consistently red-sided subspecies, the Red-sided Garter Snake *(T. s. parietalis),* occurs in the prairies of the central and western United States and Canada, but no pure populations of this race are presently recognized in the Great Lakes basin.

Entirely black (melanistic) Eastern Garter Snakes are fairly common along portions of the Lake Erie coastline, particularly the Ohio coastal marshes between Toledo and Sandusky Bay, and at Point Pelee and Long Point, Ontario. Melanistic Eastern Garter Snakes also occur on some Great Lakes islands (e.g., Pelee Island, Ontario, and Isle Royale, Michigan), and, much more rarely, on the mainland. Melanistic individuals are entirely black except for some white on the chin and throat. This color phase is probably inherited as a simple Mendelian recessive trait.

Confusing Species: Ribbon Snakes and the Plains Garter Snakes have the side stripes on scale rows 3 and 4 (counting up from the belly scutes). Both Butler's and Short-headed Garter Snakes have small heads, barely or no wider than the neck. In Butler's Garter the side stripe on the neck usually extends onto scale row 4. The neck stripe on the Short-headed Garter may or may not touch the fourth scale row, but this species has only 17 scale rows (19 in Eastern Garter). To distinguish melanistic Common Garter Snakes from other black snakes, note that only the Garter Snakes have both heavily keeled scales and a single (undivided) anal plate.

Distribution and Status: The Common Garter Snake ranges from southern Ontario (extending well north of the Great Lakes) south to eastern Texas and the Gulf of Mexico and east to the Atlantic seaboard from New England to Florida. (See previous note on variation and subspecies in the Great Lakes area.)

Common Garter Snakes are generally common and locally abundant and are certainly the most familiar and frequently encountered snake in the Great Lakes region.

Habitat and Ecology: This snake has been found in nearly every natural habitat (and some fairly unnatural habitats) in the region. The largest populations tend to occur in moist grassy places, particularly near the edges of ponds, lakes, ditches, and streams, and in vacant urban and suburban lands with abundant cover in the form of scattered boards, metal sheeting, and piles of rocks or construction debris.

Common Garter Snakes are active over a wider range of temperatures than most other Great Lakes species. They generally hibernate from late October or early November until late March or early April, but may emerge to bask during warm spells in late fall or winter. Natural hibernation sites include rodent and crayfish burrows, stream banks, anthills, stumps, and tree roots. Human-made sites include road embankments, dams and cisterns, causeways, rock piles, postholes, and house or barn foundations. These snakes sometimes spend the winter in situations where they are partially or completely submerged in water. Fairly long migrations between summer feeding areas and suitable hibernation sites may occur in some populations, but yearly movements are more restricted in many others. Home range size for this species can vary between about 0.8 to 14 hectares (2 to 35 acres), presumably dependent on the productivity of the habitat.

Earthworms often constitute a large part of this snake's diet, especially in urban habitats, though amphibians, particularly newly metamorphosed frogs and toads, are avidly eaten when available. Common Garter Snakes will eat adult toads, apparently without suffering harm from the amphibians' toxic skin secretions. Other food items noted for this species include leeches, slugs, insects, crayfish, small fish, other snakes, and (rarely) nestling birds and rodents. Prey is located by sight and/or use of the tongue and vomeronasal organ and is simply grabbed and swallowed whole.

A great many predators will eat Common Garter Snakes; a partial list would include large fish, Bullfrogs, Snapping Turtles, various snakes (e.g., Milk Snakes, Racers, and Massasaugas), birds (including crows, turkeys, hawks, and herons), and many mammals, from shrews and rodents to foxes, raccoons, and bears. Domestic animals, such as dogs, cats, hogs, and chickens, can take a heavy toll in farming and suburban areas. Accidental and purposeful killing by humans is also a significant cause of mortality.

A Common Garter Snake's first line of defense is escape—its striped pattern makes it difficult to follow through grass or leaf litter. When seized, this snake invariably smears the attacker (or restraining human hand) with a foul-smelling anal musk. Some individuals will flatten their heads and bodies and attempt to bite, but most specimens tame quickly after brief handling. Garter snake saliva (in particular, secretions of the Duvernoy's gland) can be slightly toxic to some small animals and may help to quiet struggling prey. Allergic-like reactions to bites from this and related *Thamnophis* species have been reported in humans, but such instances are very rare, and the garter snake's long-standing reputation as a "harmless" snake is certainly deserved. Probably hundreds of people, including many children, are bitten by mishandled garter snakes each year with no medical effects beyond brief minor pain, bleeding, and embarrassment.

Common Garter Snakes are often found with portions of their tails missing. While many instances of "stub" tails are probably due to unsuccessful attacks by predators, these snakes are sometimes the victims of a parasitic nematode worm that resides in their tails. Damage to the host snake's tail reportedly occurs when the nematode larvae escape to the outside, causing a secondary infection. Intermediate hosts for this parasite are copepods and frog or salamander larvae; the parasitic cycle is thus perpetuated when the latter are eaten by the snakes.

Reproduction and Growth: Mating usually takes place in early spring before the snakes have dispersed from hibernation sites. Fall matings have been reported as well. Receptive females secrete chemical substances (pheromones) that attract the males. The courting male will move over the female's body, pressing his chin against her back and sides and rapidly flicking his tongue. Eventually he will lie over or adjacent to her and attempt to align his cloacal opening with hers; often at this point convulsive rippling movements will pass forward along his body. When ready, the female will lift her tail and expose her cloaca, allowing the male to insert a hemipenis. Copulation usually lasts from ten to fifteen minutes, and afterward the male may leave a plug of mucuslike material in the female's cloaca that prevents other males from mating with her for several days.

It is not uncommon for many males to court a female simultaneously, sometimes forming a writhing mass or "ball" of avid suitors around her. Some males can secrete femalelike odors, apparently to divert or confuse their rivals while they successfully mate with a real female.

Most Great Lakes area females give birth in August or early September (range from late July to early October). The young are usually born enclosed in a thin membrane, from which they soon wriggle free. Litter size ranges from 3 to 80 young (most often from 10 to 40) and is directly related to the size of the female. The newborn snakes may remain near their mother for several hours or even days, but there appears to be no intentional parental care or protection.

Young Common Garter Snakes grow quickly, and most will reach breeding size in their second or third year, at about 55 cm (22 in) in length for females and 46 cm (18 in) for males. Growth slows considerably after sexual maturity but probably continues throughout life. A captive individual was thought to have been about 20 years old at death, but few (if any) wild ones would approach such a life span.

Conservation: Common Garter Snakes are probably the most conspicuous and well-known of our native snakes, due largely to their ability to survive in urban and suburban settings. Although widely recognized as harmless, this species is nevertheless often persecuted by homeowners and park visitors. Domestic animals (especially dogs, cats, and pigs) also kill them in great numbers, and many others are killed by lawnmowers and automobiles. The use of persistent chlorinated-hydrocarbon pesticides during the mid–twentieth century is known to have reduced many local garter snake populations; newer pesticides used around homes and farms are less persistent in the environment, but more information is needed about their effects on reptiles. Although Common Garter Snakes are adaptable and relatively prolific, they are not immune to the effects of human activities. The above factors, combined with the destruction of wetland and meadow habitats for urban development, can lead to local or even regional population declines. It is essential to monitor the well-being of so-called common species, as they are important indicators of environmental health.

Butler's Garter Snake   *Thamnophis butleri*

Description: This is a rather small, stout-bodied garter snake with three distinct yellow or orange stripes on a background color of black, brown, or olive brown. Some individuals have two rows of black spots running down the back, between the dorsal and lateral (side) stripes. On the forward part of the body the lateral stripes are on scale row 3 and adjacent halves of rows 2 and 4. The black or olive head is small (barely wider than the neck), and there are often two tiny yellow spots on the large (parietal) scales at the back of the head. The labial scales are yellow, sometimes shaded or speckled with brown. The belly is pale green or greenish yellow, edged with brown, and there are often dark spots along the edges of the ventral scutes. There are 19 (occasionally 20 or 21) scale rows at midbody; the body scales are keeled and the anal plate is single. Total adult length: 38 to 73.7 cm (15 to 29 in).

Butler's Garter Snake

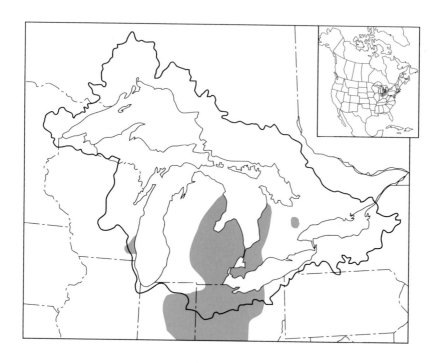

Male Butler's Garter Snakes tend to be slightly smaller and more narrow-bodied than females and have relatively longer tails. The subcaudal scale count in males ranges between 57 and 72; in females, from 49 to 64.

At birth the young of this snake range in length from 12.5 to 18.5 cm (5 to 7.3 in); they are colored like the adults but have proportionally larger heads.

Confusing Species: Other garter snakes and ribbon snakes have relatively larger, longer heads (except for the Short-headed). In the Common Garter Snake, the side stripes are restricted to scale rows 2 and 3, while in the Eastern Plains Garter and both ribbon snakes they are on rows 3 and 4. The Short-headed Garter Snake has only 17 midbody scale rows.

Distribution and Status: This snake's range is centered in the lower Great Lakes region, extending from western Ohio and northeastern Indiana through the eastern portion of Michigan's Lower Peninsula and adjacent southern Ontario. There is an isolated population in southeastern Wisconsin, centered in and near the Milwaukee area, and possible hybridization between this species and the Plains Garter Snake *(Thamnophis radix)* has been reported from this area. Another isolated population occurs in Ontario, in the Luther Marsh Conservation Area south of Georgian Bay (Wellington and Dufferin Counties). Although this population has been assigned to *T. butleri,* some individuals from this site appear to be closer to the Short-headed Garter Snake, *Thamnophis brachystoma* (based on scale counts and other features), while many others are intermediate between these two species.

Note: Butler's Garter Snake is a close relative of the Short-headed Garter Snake, and both of these are, in turn, closely related to the Plains Garter Snake. It is likely, based on available morphological and fossil evidence, that one or more disjunct eastern populations of the Plains Garter Snake gave rise to the other two species, perhaps during the mid-to-late Pleistocene, or possibly earlier. One suggested hypothesis is that an outlying population of *T. radix* was isolated south of the glacial front and evolved into *T. butleri* (which later dispersed northward after the ice receded), while another population, isolated on the unglaciated Allegheny Plateau, became *T. brachystoma.* A slight variant on this idea would derive *T. brachystoma* directly from an earlier-evolved *T. butleri.* Additional biochemical and fossil studies may clarify these relationships.

Within its known range Butler's Garter Snake has a somewhat erratic distribution, perhaps due in part to the concurrent creation and destruction of its preferred habitat by humans. This species is usually outnumbered by the Common Garter Snake, although dense local populations occur in some places, where it can outnumber or even replace its larger relative. It has been listed as a threatened species in Indiana.

Habitat and Ecology: This is a snake of wet meadows and prairies, marshy pond and lake borders, and other moist grassy places. Large colonies can occur along railroad embankments and in vacant lots in urban and suburban areas.

Butler's Garter Snakes have a relatively long annual activity period, generally from late March or early April into October or November. They hibernate below ground in winter, taking advantage of rodent or crayfish burrows or the loose soil of ant mounds. They are most often seen in early spring and in fall; they become highly secretive, perhaps even nocturnal, during the summer months. Much of their activity takes place underground or beneath sheltering objects or vegetation.

Earthworms are the most common prey of this little snake, though they will also eat leeches, salamanders, and small frogs. Captive Butler's Garter Snakes will take small fish.

This snake is surely preyed upon by most predators within its range; a list of known and likely enemies would include other snakes (such as Racers and Milk Snakes), various birds (e.g., crows, hawks, and owls), and mammals (including raccoons, skunks, weasels, shrews, foxes, and domestic cats and dogs). When discovered, Butler's Garter Snakes will attempt to escape into thick vegetation or under rocks or debris; when seized they expel a musky fluid from the cloaca but rarely attempt to bite. If surprised or uncovered in the open, these snakes have the odd habit of frantically throwing their bodies into side-to-side loops while making little forward progress. This thrashing behavior may possibly serve to confuse some predators, though from a human perspective it might appear to expose the snake to added risk.

Reproduction and Growth: Mating occurs soon after emergence from winter dormancy. The basic behavioral patterns by which males locate, court, and copulate with females are very similar to those described for the Common Garter Snake. As in the latter species, the male leaves a mucus plug in the cloaca of the female after copulation; this reportedly prevents or discourages other males from also trying to mate with her. From about half to three-quarters of the mature females will breed in any given year.

Females that have bred in spring will give birth in mid-to-late summer, most often in late July or August. Litter size ranges from 4 to 20, with larger females generally producing greater numbers of young. The young snakes grow rapidly at least until they attain sexual maturity, which can occur during their second spring after birth. Potential longevity is unknown; a wild-caught adult survived in captivity for two years.

Conservation: Some of the largest populations of Butler's Garter Snake have been found in grassy, litter-strewn vacant lots in urban areas, and it is likely that the species has benefited from the conversion of forests into open grassy habitats, both in urban and rural areas. However, it takes only a few minutes for a bulldozer to totally destroy a thriving colony, and the rapid development of urban and suburban lands has undoubtedly eliminated this little snake from many sites of former abundance. Many of these snakes are killed while crossing roads, particularly in the fall.

Short-headed Garter Snake   *Thamnophis brachystoma*

Description: A very short head, no wider or barely wider than the neck, should separate this snake from the other striped snakes in its restricted range. Background color above varies from brown to olive gray or black, while the dorsal and side stripes may be light brown, tan, or yellow. On the neck and forward part of the body the side stripes are on scale rows 2 and 3, sometimes extending onto row 4. There are usually no obvious large dark spots between the stripes, although the stripes may be bordered by black lines. The chin, throat, and labial scales are yellowish, buff, or gray; the upper labials may have dark edges. The belly can be greenish, grayish, or tan. There are usually 17 scale rows; the scales are keeled, and the anal plate is single. Total adult length: 36 to 56 cm (14 to 22 in).

External sex characters are not obvious. Male Short-headed Garter Snakes have slightly longer tails than females; subcaudal scale counts range from 57 to 75 for males, and 51 to 64 in females. Females tend to be thicker bodied, especially when gravid (pregnant) in summer.

Newborn Short-headed Garter Snakes range from 11.8 to 16 cm (4.6

Short-headed Garter Snake

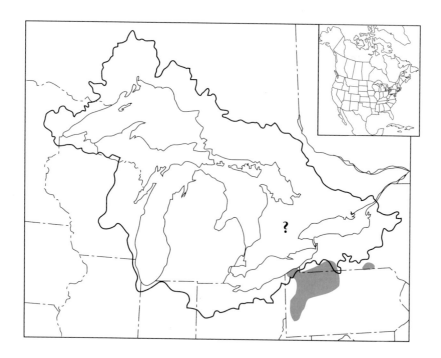

to 6.3 in) in length. They are patterned similarly to the adults but have darker background color and brighter striping.

Confusing Species: Common Garter Snakes and Ribbon Snakes have necks distinctly narrower than the head. In the former the side stripes are entirely on scale rows 2 and 3, and on rows 3 and 4 in the latter. Butler's Garter Snake often has large dark spots between the stripes, a head slightly wider than the neck, and (usually) 19 scale rows at the forward or middle part of the body.

Note: Snakes that appear intermediate in one or more characters between the Short-headed and Butler's Garter Snakes are sometimes found. It is probably best to identify questionable specimens by geographic location, since the two species are presently not thought to overlap in range. (A problematic population in the Luther Marsh area of southern Ontario has been historically assigned to Butler's Garter Snake but contains individuals close to the Short-headed Garter Snake, and many intermediate specimens; see discussion under Butler's Garter Snake.)

Distribution and Status: The Short-headed Garter Snake is found in southwestern New York and northwestern Pennsylvania, with its range centered on the unglaciated Allegheny Plateau. It enters the Great Lakes basin in Erie County, Pennsylvania, where it was presumably introduced, and possibly in southern Ontario (as noted above). Introduced populations also occur in the Pittsburgh area and south-central New York.

This snake is locally common to abundant within its limited range.

Habitat and Ecology: This species is usually found in grassy habitats such as meadows, old fields, pastures, marsh edges, and on hillsides and embankments, but rarely occurs in shady woodlands. They are most often discovered by turning natural objects (logs, bark, rocks) or human-generated debris (boards, roofing metal, tar paper, cardboard, etc.). Large colonies can occur on undeveloped or fallow land in urban and agricultural areas.

Short-headed Garter Snakes feed largely, if not entirely, on earthworms. In places where the this snake is abundant, other worm-eating species (such as Northern Brown Snakes and Common Garter Snakes) may be uncommon or even absent; this may be partly due to food competition, but climatic and habitat factors are also likely to be involved.

Like other small snakes, this species undoubtedly falls prey to a variety of predatory reptiles, mammals, and birds. Their primary defense is to escape into thick grass or other cover. They rarely, if ever, bite when first handled, but they will smear musk on the offending hand and make vigorous attempts to escape; a predator would probably elicit a similar reaction.

Reproduction and Growth: Short-headed Garter Snakes mate in early spring, while they are still concentrated around winter hibernation sites. Courtship and copulatory behaviors differ in only minor details from those described for the Common Garter Snake. At times several courting males will pursue and coil about one or more females, forming a "mating ball" of snakes.

Females give birth to their litters from late July through early September. Litter size ranges from 4 to 15, with the largest females producing the greatest number of young. The newborn snakes grow quickly, perhaps doubling their length during the first full growth year, and most probably reach sexual maturity in their second year. Growth continues, but much more slowly, after this point.

Conservation: Though locally common at present, the Short-headed Garter Snake has a small natural range and could become vulnerable in the future. This species may benefit from human activities that create or maintain open grassy habitats at the expense of woodlands, but urban development or agricultural land use changes can quickly remove this habitat and the snake colonies that depend on it.

Eastern Plains Garter Snake   *Thamnophis radix radix*

Description: In this moderate-sized garter snake, the side stripes usually cover scale rows 3 and 4. The background color above varies from black or gray to dark brown or olive. The middorsal stripe is yellow, orange, or orangish yellow, while the lateral stripes may be the same color or paler. There are usually two rows of dark spots above the lateral stripes, and another row of dark spots below them. The head is intermediate in size between the Eastern and Butler's Garter Snakes, being rather short but distinctly wider than the neck; the top of the head is dark (with two tiny light

Eastern Plains Garter Snake

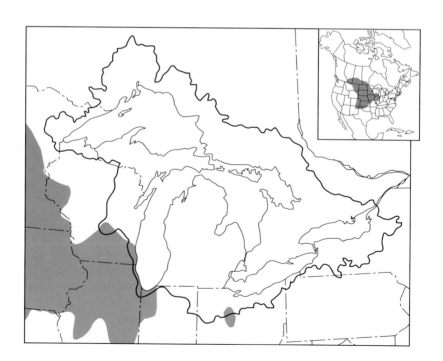

spots on the large parietal scales), while the upper labial scales are yellow to cream color with prominent dark lines along the scale edges. The belly is yellowish to greenish, often with black spots at the outer edges of the ventral scutes. There are 19 to 21 scales rows at midbody; the scales are keeled and the anal plate is single. Total adult length: 38 to 84.5 cm (15 to 33.3 in).

Males are considerably smaller, on average, than females and have relatively longer tails (23 percent to 25 percent of total length in males, 19 percent to 23 percent in females).

Juvenile Prairie Garter Snakes have a darker background color than adults, with less distinct spotting. At birth they range in length from 16 to 19 cm (6.3 to 7.5 in).

Confusing Species: The side stripe involves at least part of scale row 2 in the Common and Butler's Garter Snakes. Both the Northern and Western Ribbon Snakes have whitish or pale yellow labial scales without dark edges, and their tails (if undamaged) are usually 25 percent or more of their total length.

Distribution and Status: The Eastern Plains Garter Snake ranges from southeastern Minnesota and eastern Iowa through southern Wisconsin and northern Illinois to northwestern Indiana. There are isolated populations in north-central Ohio (Wyandot and Marion Counties), southwestern Illinois, and central Missouri. A western subspecies extends the range of *Thamnophis radix* to the eastern edge of the Rocky Mountain region, from southern Alberta to northeastern New Mexico. This snake enters the Great Lakes region along the southern shore of Lake Michigan (from southwest Wisconsin and the Chicago area to Porter County, Indiana); the relict Ohio population is on the extreme southern edge of the drainage basin.

This is a common snake in suitable habitat over most of its range, but it tends to be uncommon and local in the Great Lakes region.

Habitat and Ecology: As its name implies, this is mostly a snake of prairies and other open grassy habitats. They are often found in meadows near ponds, streams, ditches, and marsh edges, but can also occur in drier sites; vacant lots in cities and suburbs may support large populations. This species appears to prefer habitats on moist, black prairie soils (e.g., silt-loams and clay-loams), and is less common where the soil is sandy and well drained.

Eastern Plains Garter Snakes are active during daylight hours, though they spend much of their time hidden beneath rocks, logs, boards, and other natural or human-generated debris. Most individuals maintain a rather small home range, at least during the active season (usually early April to November). Winter hibernation sites include cracks in rock out-crops, mammal or crayfish burrows, and anthills, as well as in house and barn foundations, postholes, wells, and rock piles.

Eastern Plains Garter Snakes subsist largely on earthworms, though they will also eat leeches, snails, frogs, toads, and salamanders, and cap-tives will eat fish. They are, in turn, eaten by birds (herons, bitterns, hawks), mammals (raccoons, skunks, foxes, domestic cats), and probably snake-eating snakes such as Milk Snakes and Racers.

This snake is less likely to defend itself by biting than the Eastern Garter Snake, but temperament varies, and some individuals are rather aggres-sive. Like most garter snakes, they will release feces and musky secretions from the cloaca if grabbed by a predator or a curious human.

Reproduction and Growth: Males locate females by following their scent trails; courtship and mating behaviors are very similar to those described for the Common Garter Snake. It is likely that most mating takes place in early spring, soon after emergence from hibernation, though fall matings have also been noted.

Females give birth to litters of 5 to 60 (one record of 92) young, between late July and mid-September. The young snakes grow quickly during their first two years, although females may grow faster than males. Both sexes probably reach maturity by their second spring, with growth then slowing. A captive Plains Garter Snake survived for over eight years.

Conservation: Though still abundant in or near some cities and suburbs, many urban populations of Eastern Plains Garter Snakes have been elim-inated by land development. They have largely disappeared from areas converted to intensive agricultural use. These snakes are frequent victims of cars or mowing equipment, especially while moving between over-wintering sites and summer habitats in spring and fall. Large numbers of these inoffensive creatures are killed by fearful or ignorant people.

Northern Ribbon Snake   *Thamnophis sauritus septentrionalis*

Description: This is a slim-bodied, striped snake with a very long tail that equals at least a quarter, and sometimes nearly a third, of the snake's total length. The three yellow, greenish yellow, or white stripes contrast sharply with a background coloration of dark brown or black. (The dorsal stripe is sometimes brownish or tan.) Each side stripe is on scale rows 3 and 4; below this stripe (on scale rows 1 and 2 and the adjoining edges of the ventral scutes) is a brown stripe. The head is distinctly wider than the neck, and the large eyes are edged in front by a light bar; the seven (occasionally eight) upper labial scales are bright white or pale yellow, without dark edges. There may be two faint light spots on the large parietal scales on the back of the head. The belly is an unmarked pale green, yellow, or white. There are 19 scale rows at midbody; the scales are keeled, and the anal plate is single. Total adult length: 46 to 86.2 cm (18 to 34 in).

The sexes are often difficult to distinguish based on external characters, but females are, on average, slightly larger and thicker bodied than males (especially noticeable when they are gravid in summer).

Newborn Northern Ribbon Snakes range in length from 16 to 24 cm (6.3 to 9.4 in) and are colored like their parents.

Confusing Species: The thin body, long tail, and unmarked labial scales will distinguish the ribbon snakes from all garter snakes in the region. The Northern Ribbon Snake overlaps with the Western Ribbon Snake *(Thamnophis p. proximus)* in the Indiana Dunes area and, potentially, in southern Wisconsin. The latter species usually has eight upper labial scales and prominent (often fused) parietal spots, and its dorsal stripe is often a bright orange or orangish yellow.

Distribution and Status: The Northern Ribbon Snake ranges from southern Maine west through New York, southern Ontario, northern Ohio, northern and central Indiana, and all of Michigan's Lower Peninsula. Isolated (relict) populations occur in eastern and southern Wisconsin. Other subspecies of *Thamnophis sauritus* occur from New England south to Florida and the Gulf states, and northward east of the Mississippi River to Kentucky and southern Illinois and Indiana. This snake is largely absent from the more mountainous parts of the eastern United States.

Northern Ribbon Snakes can be quite common in the appropriate

Northern Ribbon Snake

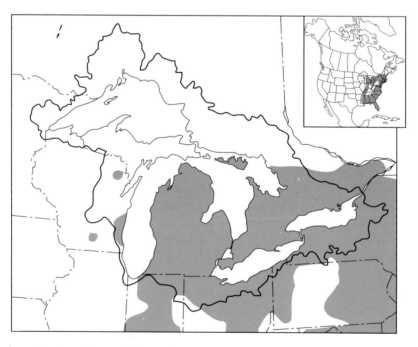

Note: Northern Ribbon Snake intergrades with Eastern Ribbon Snake *(Thamnophis s. sauritus)* in southeast portion of this map.

habitat, but they tend to be uncommon to rare and local at the periphery of the range.

Habitat and Ecology: Look for Northern Ribbon Snakes along the edges of lakes, ponds, bogs, streams, and marshes, especially where there are clumps of grasses or sedges and scattered low shrubbery. Sunny sites are preferred over shaded ones, but they sometimes occur in the more open portions of swamps or near woodland ponds. In the Indiana Dunes area and southern Wisconsin, where this species overlaps with the Western Ribbon Snake, it seems to prefer bog edge habitat, while the latter is more common in open marshland.

These are active, rather nervous snakes that are usually seen moving through vegetation near or at the water's edge, though they sometimes move into nearby upland meadows in late spring and summer, perhaps in pursuit of dispersing amphibian prey. Northern Ribbon Snakes often climb into low shrubs to bask. They are active from April into October in most years and spend the colder months hibernating in burrows of other animals (e.g., crayfish, voles, muskrats) or in anthills, either close to the water or in higher, better-drained sites.

Frogs and salamanders and their larvae make up the bulk of this snake's diet; small fish are also taken. Unlike other eastern *Thamnophis*, Northern Ribbon Snakes rarely, if ever, eat earthworms. Prey is either stalked slowly or actively pursued and is simply seized in the jaws and swallowed alive.

Northern Ribbon Snakes are eaten by many predators of wetland edges, particularly herons, hawks, mink, and raccoons. Juveniles are vulnerable to large fish and frogs. These snakes can dart through the dense vegetation with great agility and do not hesitate to swim to escape an enemy. They prefer to glide along the surface parallel to the shoreline, but if closely pursued they may dive to the bottom and hide in vegetation or debris. Many specimens are found with portions of the tail missing, perhaps attesting to close encounters with predators; lost tails are not regrown. If cornered or seized, a Northern Ribbon Snake may flatten its head and bite (although many do not) and will almost invariably thrash about, smearing musky anal secretions upon its tormentor.

Reproduction and Growth: Most courtship and mating takes place in early spring, often soon after emergence from winter dormancy, but fall mating may also occur.

Gravid females may move short distances away from water before giving birth, since they and newborn young are sometimes observed in nearby upland habitats. Most young are born in late July or August in the Great Lakes region; litters range in size from 3 to 26 for the species, though 10 to 12 is more usual.

The young snakes grow quickly at first, with many maturing by their second year, and the rest the following (third) year. Growth slows for both sexes after maturity, though females seem to continue growing at a faster rate than males. Average longevity in the wild would probably be less than the 10 years attained by one Northern Ribbon Snake in captivity.

Conservation: The fate of this species is certainly tied to the availability and health of wetland and littoral habitats, and to the numbers of amphibian prey that these habitats support. Populations invariably decline where frequent human activity results in degradation of shoreline vegetation, and thus loss of cover and food. Direct persecution and road mortality are further threats.

Western Ribbon Snake *Thamnophis proximus proximus*

Description: This slender, striped snake has a very long tail that, when undamaged, equals at least a quarter to nearly a third of the animal's total length. Of the three lengthwise stripes, the dorsal stripe is usually a bright orange or yellow, while the side stripes (on scale rows 3 and 4) are a paler yellow or greenish white. The background color is black or dark brown, including the narrow dark stripe that usually covers scale rows 1 and 2 and the edges of the ventral scutes. The remainder of the belly is an unmarked pale yellow or greenish white. There are typically eight unmarked white or cream-colored upper labial scales. The eyes are large, and there are usually two bright yellow parietal spots (often fused together) on the back of the otherwise dark head. There are 19 scale rows at midbody; the scales are keeled and the anal plate is single. Total adult length: 51 to 107.5 cm (20 to 42.3 in).

Males are, on average, smaller and slimmer than females and have slightly longer tails, but sex is often difficult to determine based on external characters.

Newborn Western Ribbon Snakes are 19 to 29 cm (7.5 to 11.4 in) long and are colored like the adults.

Western Ribbon Snake

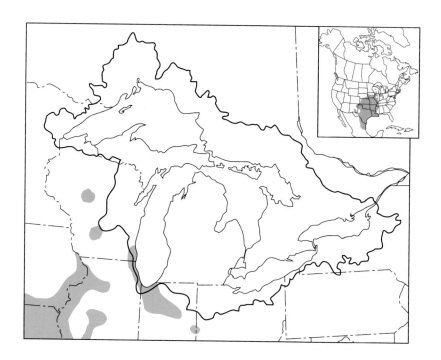

Confusing Species: Garter snakes have shorter tails (less than a quarter of total length) and usually have some dark markings on the labial scales. The Northern Ribbon Snake is similar, but typically has seven upper labial scales, and paler, unfused parietal spots. (In the Great Lakes region the two species of ribbon snakes overlap only in the Indiana Dunes area and possibly in southern Wisconsin.)

Distribution and Status: The primary range of the Western Ribbon Snake extends from southwestern Wisconsin and western Illinois south to Louisiana and Texas and west to eastern Nebraska, Kansas, and Oklahoma. Records in or near the Great Lakes basin (in southeastern Wisconsin, northeastern Illinois, and northwestern Indiana) may represent an eastern disjunct population, or perhaps a series of isolated relict populations, perhaps resulting from postglacial dispersal via the "prairie peninsula." Other subspecies occur in portions of Texas, New Mexico, and northern Mexico.

This snake is common in suitable habitat throughout its primary range and in the Indiana Dunes area; it is rare and very local in Wisconsin and the Chicago area.

Habitat and Ecology: The Western Ribbon Snake is usually seen in vegetation adjacent to ponds, lakes, marshes, sloughs, or streams. It seems to prefer more open, drier sandy sites (though close to water) in Wisconsin and northern Indiana, compared to the moister bog-edge habitats used by Northern Ribbon Snakes in the same area.

The annual period of activity generally runs from mid-April to sometime in October but varies with local climatic conditions. Western Ribbon Snakes hibernate in rodent burrows, anthills, decaying stumps and logs, drainpipes, and other shelters and may share hibernation sites with other snake species.

Frogs, toads, salamanders, and small fish make up most of the diet. Western Ribbon Snakes may depend, at least locally, on the annual "crop" of tadpoles and newly metamorphosed frogs, and a failure in amphibian breeding success (as in a drought year) may be detrimental to their survival. These snakes have been seen swimming with open mouths, clamping down whenever small fish were contacted.

The natural enemies of this snake include herons and bitterns, hawks, mink, weasels, raccoons, and other wetland birds and mammals. Reptiles such as Snapping Turtles, Racers, and Milk Snakes probably eat them on occasion, and large frogs and fish would pose a danger to juveniles. Western Ribbon Snakes are alert, quick-moving creatures and often elude capture by dashing (or swimming) into thick shoreline or emergent vegetation. Most individuals do not bite when handled (though occasional ones will bite aggressively), but they often smear malodorous anal secretions on the handler.

Reproduction and Growth: Mating takes place soon after emergence in early spring. In late summer (July through September) the females give birth to litters of 4 to 27 (usually around 12) young. The young snakes grow rapidly and may increase in length by 50 percent or more prior to their first winter. Most will reach sexual maturity in two years or less, with males maturing earlier than females. Some females may not breed until their third year.

Conservation: Western Ribbon Snakes presumably extended their range into the western Great Lakes area postglacially by following the "prairie peninsula" eastward, and their present scarcity in the region may reflect the loss of prairie wetlands to natural succession and agricultural development. Other threats include continued wetland drainage and degradation of existing habitats by groundwater pollution (e.g., pesticides, livestock waste) and recreational activities.

Brown Snake   *Storeria dekayi*

Description: This is a very small brown, grayish brown, or tan snake with two parallel rows of dark spots down the back. The spots may be connected across the back by dark crossbars, forming a ladderlike pattern; occasionally the spots are faint or entirely lacking (see the following note on subspecies differences). The area between the dorsal spots is usually lighter in color than the sides, giving the impression of a single wide dorsal stripe. Some individuals have scattered dark spots along the sides. The head is small and dark above; there is often a vertical dark bar at the back of the jawline, a dark spot (sometimes two) beneath the eye, and a dark blotch on each side of the neck. The belly varies in color from cream to buff or light pink, and there may be small dark dots at the edges of the ventral scutes. There are usually 17 scale rows at midbody; the scales are keeled and the anal plate is divided. Total adult length: 23 to 52.7 cm (9 to 20.7 in); very few Brown Snakes exceed a length of 38 cm (15 in).

Northern Brown Snake

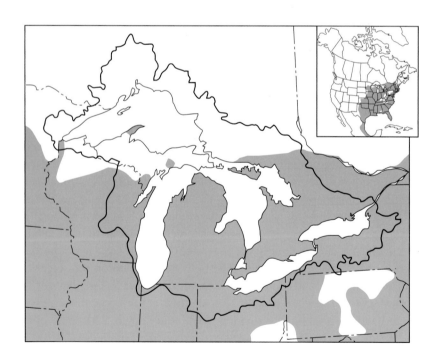

Males are slightly smaller, on average, than females and have relatively longer tails; the male's tail is usually 23 percent to 26 percent of total length (subcaudal scutes number 46 to 73), and the female's tail is 17 percent to 23 percent of total length (with 36 to 66 subcaudals).

The newborn young measure 7 to 11.7 cm (2.7 to 4.6 in) in length and are darker than their parents, but with a light band or "collar" around the neck.

Note: Two subspecies of the Brown Snake meet in the Great Lakes region. The Northern Brown Snake *(Storeria dekayi dekayi)* enters our area from the east. This form typically has few or no dark crossbars linking the dorsal spots across the back. The Midland Brown Snake *(Storeria d. wrightorum),* the dominant form from the Lake Michigan basin southward along the Mississippi drainage, has numerous crossbars linking the dorsal spots. A third subspecies, the Texas Brown Snake *(S. d. texana)* approaches the Great Lakes area in central and western Wisconsin. It has thin dorsal crossbars and a conspicuous dark blotch on each side of the neck. The first two subspecies intergrade broadly over the region from southern Ontario through Ohio and Michigan's Lower Peninsula; in this area the assignment of a particular Brown Snake to one subspecies or the other will be often be difficult or impossible, and (except for taxonomic studies) unnecessary.

Confusing Species: Northern Red-bellied Snakes usually have red or pink bellies and 15 scale rows at midbody. Garter snakes have light stripes along the sides and a single anal plate. Northern Ring-necked Snakes lack spots or stripes on the back and have yellow or orange bellies and smooth scales.

Distribution and Status: This species ranges from southern Maine, Quebec, and Ontario to Florida and the Gulf Coast and west to Minnesota, eastern Nebraska, Kansas, Oklahoma, and eastern Texas southward into Mexico and Honduras. It occurs throughout the Great Lakes region except for the area north of Georgian Bay and Lake Superior; it is sparsely distributed in northern Wisconsin and Michigan's Upper Peninsula.

Brown Snakes are locally common but become considerably less common toward the northern periphery of their range.

Habitat and Ecology: Brown Snakes occur in a great variety of habitats, from dense woods and shrublands to open prairies, meadows, and marshes. Moist soils are preferred, but they are sometimes found on dry hillsides, railroad embankments, and in pine woods. This species is tolerant of human-modified habitats and can be common in agricultural, urban, and suburban areas, particularly in weedy fields and dump sites strewn with sheltering debris such as boards, bricks, tar paper, sheet metal, or cardboard.

These secretive little snakes spend much of their active season below ground or under leaf litter or surface debris, although a heavy rain will sometimes induce them to move about in the open. Brown Snakes are largely nocturnal, especially in summer. Most surface activity occurs in fall (October and November) and in early spring (late March and April), when they are moving to or away from hibernation sites. They overwinter in animal burrows and abandoned anthills, beneath stumps and logs, and in crevices in rock ledges and house and barn foundations. Individual Brown Snakes typically return to the same hibernacula used the previous winter, sites often shared with other small snake species such as various garter, Red-bellied, and Smooth Green Snakes.

Earthworms and slugs form the greatest part of the diet, although snails, pill bugs, soft-bodied insects, and small amphibians are also eaten on occasion. Brown Snakes have specializations of the jaws and teeth that assist them in pulling snails from their shells. Since most prey is taken underground and/or at night, it is likely that food is located largely by use of the tongue and vomeronasal organ.

Brown Snakes are readily eaten by a host of predators, including large frogs and toads, larger snakes, crows, hawks, shrews, weasels, and domestic cats and dogs. Ground-feeding birds that sift through leaf litter, such as jays, thrushes, and thrashers, probably take many of these snakes. This is a docile species that rarely attempts to bite; in any case the tiny teeth would be an ineffective defense against most enemies. When cornered or seized a Brown Snake may flatten its body and assume a threatening posture and often releases a musky fluid from the cloaca.

Reproduction and Growth: Courtship and mating occur in early spring, with the males undoubtedly taking advantage of the presence of females prior to dispersal away from group hibernacula. The male locates a potential mate by following a pheromone (odor) trail left by the female. The female is approached and identified with numerous tongue-flicks; the male then moves over or alongside the female, aligning his body with hers. The male attempts to keep his chin on the female's neck and align his cloacal region with that of the female; at this point a succession of ripplelike movements may travel up the male's body, from tail to head. Eventually the male inserts a hemipenis into the female's cloaca to effect fertilization. Sometimes two or more males may court the same female; they may engage in mild shoving to gain the best position, but there is no actual fighting among the rivals.

Most females give birth to their litters in late July or August (range, late June through September). Litter size ranges from 3 to 41, but 10 to 14 young is most typical. There is no parental care, but newborn Brown Snakes often remain in close association for some time after birth.

Growth can be rapid, and some young Brown Snakes will nearly double in length by the end of their second summer, when they are probably sexually mature. A captive Brown Snake lived over seven years in captivity.

Conservation: Despite their local abundance in the less intensively developed city parks and residential areas, these secretive snakes often remain undetected (and unappreciated) by their human neighbors. Brown Snake colonies in urban and agricultural settings are in constant danger of rapid extirpation by development activities or exposure to toxic chemicals. They are harmless to human interests and may help control slug damage in gardens. These interesting little snakes are worthy of consideration in urban and suburban park and open-space conservation planning efforts.

Northern Red-bellied Snake   *Storeria occipitomaculata occipitomaculata*

Description: This is a very small, brown, reddish brown, or gray snake with a narrow neck and small head. (In a given population the brown and gray phases may be equally common, or one phase may predominate.) The upper surface may be unmarked or have two or four thin dark stripes running down the back and/or sides; there is sometimes a suggestion of a light middorsal stripe. The top of the head is usually dark brown or reddish brown, while the chin and throat are white. There often is a light spot behind and below the eye (on the fifth upper labial scale), and three light tan or yellow spots on the neck—one at the nape and another on each side of the neck; these spots may fuse to form a light collar, or, alternatively, may be absent. As the common name implies, the belly is usually

Northern Red-bellied Snake

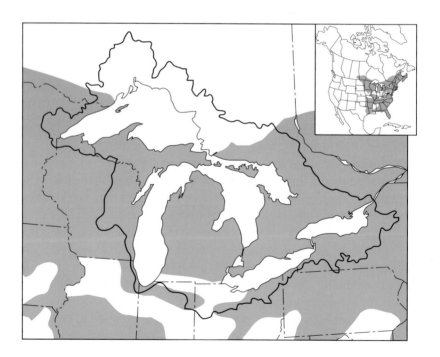

bright red, though it can also be pink, orange, light yellow, or (rarely) gray or black. There are 15 scale rows at midbody; the scales are keeled and the anal plate is divided. Total adult length: 20.3 to 40.6 cm (8 to 16 in).

The sexes are similar and often difficult to distinguish based on external characters, except when females are gravid and thus heavier-bodied than males. Males have proportionally slightly longer tails (21 percent to 25 percent of total length) than females (17 percent to 22 percent of total length).

Newborn Red-bellied Snakes are 7 to 11 cm (2.8 to 4.3 in) in total length at birth. They tend to be darker above and paler below than their parents and have a prominent light spot or collar on the neck.

Confusing Species: Brown Snakes have paler (cream or buff colored) bellies and 17 scale rows at midbody. Kirtland's Snakes have two rows of black spots down each side of the belly. Garter and ribbon snakes have paler bellies and undivided (single) anal plates. Northern Ring-necked Snakes have smooth, unkeeled scales.

Distribution and Status: Northern Red-bellied Snakes range from Nova Scotia south to northern Georgia and Tennessee, west to eastern Oklahoma and Kansas, and north to southeastern Saskatchewan, Minnesota, and southern Ontario; they are rare or absent in large portions of the former "prairie peninsula." They occur throughout most of the Great Lakes region but are absent from the northeastern Lake Superior basin and are known from only a few scattered localities between the western end of Lake Erie and the southeastern end of Lake Michigan (northwestern Ohio, northern Indiana, and extreme southern Michigan). A southern subspecies, the Florida Red-bellied Snake *(Storeria occipitomaculata obscura)*, extends the range into the Gulf coastal region, from north Florida to eastern Texas. A relict population in the Black Hills of South Dakota and adjacent Wyoming has been designated as a third subspecies, *Storeria o. pahasapae*. Red-bellied Snakes in Iowa, Minnesota, the Dakotas, and adjacent Canada may show genetic influence from this race, in which the light spots on the neck and fifth upper labial scale are faint or lacking.

The Northern Red-bellied Snake is locally common in the Great Lakes region.

Habitat and Ecology: This snake inhabits deciduous or mixed woodlands as well as adjacent fields, pastures, road embankments, marshes, and sphagnum bogs. A moist substrate is preferred, but they do turn up in drier sites. This species is sometimes found hiding under boards and other trash in urban or suburban parks and vacant lots, along with Brown Snakes and garter snakes. Even in more natural situations much of their time is spent hiding under bark, logs, rocks, or in leaf litter. They occasionally bask in the open, particularly in spring, sometimes climbing into low shrubs, vines, and grass clumps. They may become nocturnal during hot weather. Surface activity in summer and fall is often associated with heavy rainfall. Their abundance in northern parts of the Great Lakes basin suggests that they are quite cold-tolerant.

The yearly activity period extends from April or May into October or November, depending on local conditions. Mass migrations toward and away from hibernation sites may occur in fall and spring, respectively. These snakes often hibernate in groups of their own and other small snake species, taking refuge in anthills, abandoned animal burrows, old building foundations, and other shelters.

Northern Red-bellied Snakes feed mostly on slugs and earthworms, with snails, pill bugs, soft-bodied insect larvae, and perhaps small salamanders rounding out the diet. Like the Brown Snake, this species has jaw and tooth adaptations that assist the extraction of snails from their shells.

These little snakes are eaten by a variety of predators, including other snakes (Milk Snakes, Racers), hawks, crows, shrews, ground squirrels, raccoons, and domestic animals (dogs, cats, chickens). They rarely, if ever, bite in self-defense, and their tiny jaws and teeth would be ineffective against all but the tiniest predator. When threatened they sometimes flatten their bodies and curl their upper "lips" outward in a gesture that might be interpreted as a warning, however futile it might be. As with most area snakes, they can excrete a musky-smelling substance from the cloaca. A few "red-bellies" will, when handled, suddenly stiffen their bodies and roll onto their backs—a behavior that could be interpreted as "playing dead" (but may as well be a type of seizure brought on by stress); this does serve to expose the red belly, possibly startling the potential predator.

Reproduction and Growth: Mating occurs most often in spring, sometimes in late summer and fall. In our region most females give birth between late July and early September. From 1 to 21 (usually about 7 or 8) young are produced per litter.

The young snakes may double their length in the first year of growth, and most become sexually mature in their second year. A captive Red-bellied Snake survived over four years, but the average and potential life span in the wild are unknown.

Conservation: Northern Red-bellied Snakes are often most easily found by turning boards, tar paper, sheet metal, and other debris at the edges of trash dumps or abandoned buildings in or near wooded areas; they can sometimes be quite abundant in these situations. It is unclear whether the availability of such artificial cover leads to higher populations, or whether it simply makes them easier to find. Human activities that create open edges in and around woodlands probably benefit this species. However, when roads separate wintering sites and summer feeding areas, large numbers may be killed during spring and fall migrations. This harmless and inoffensive little snake should be welcomed around yards and vegetable gardens, due to its slug-eating habits.

Smooth Green Snake   *Opheodrys vernalis*

Description: This is the only Great Lakes area snake that is entirely bright green on its upper surfaces. The head, only slightly wider than the neck, is green above, with yellowish or white on the labial (lip) scales, chin, and throat. The belly is white, ivory, or pale yellow. Occasional specimens are light brown, tan, or bronze instead of green; this variant is most common in Wisconsin, Illinois, and Michigan. There are 15 scale rows at midbody; the scales are smooth and the anal plate is divided. Total adult length: 30 to 66 cm (11.8 to 26 in).

Males are smaller, on average, than females but have relatively longer tails. Subcaudal scute counts range from 74 to 96 for males and 60 to 84 for females.

Newly hatched Smooth Green Snakes range in length from 8.3 to 16.5 cm (3.25 to 6.5 in). Hatchlings and small juveniles tend to be duller in color than the adults, typically olive green, brownish, or bluish gray.

Confusing Species: This is the only bright green snake in the region. The green color fades to pale blue or bluish gray after death, leading to pos-

Smooth Green Snake

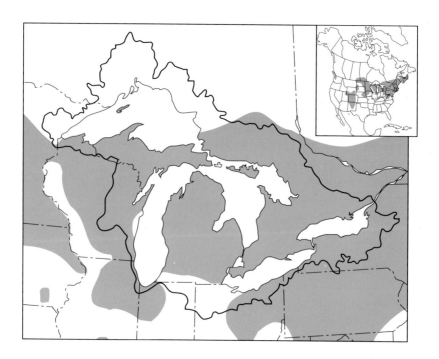

sible confusion of dead or preserved specimens with the Blue Racer; however, a Racer the size of the largest Smooth Green Snake would retain at least a hint of its spotted juvenile pattern. Brown-phase Green Snakes can be recognized by their smooth (unkeeled) scales and lack of stripes, spots, or other markings on the head and back.

Distribution and Status: This snake is found from Nova Scotia west to southeastern Saskatchewan and south to Illinois, Ohio, and northwestern Virginia. This range includes most of the Great Lakes basin, except for the area north of Lake Superior and northeastern Indiana and northwestern Ohio. There are scattered disjunct populations from Iowa and Missouri to Utah, Wyoming, and Colorado, south into New Mexico, Texas, and Chihuahua, Mexico.

Smooth Green Snakes remain locally common in portions of the Great Lakes region, but their numbers have declined drastically in many areas. They appear to be increasingly rare and locally extirpated over much of the southern Lower Peninsula of Michigan and northwestern Indiana.

Habitat and Ecology: This is largely a snake of moist grassy places such as prairie remnants and savannas, meadows, old fields, pastures, roadsides, and marsh and lake edges. They also occur in open deciduous or pine woodlands and along woodland borders. Most activity is on or near the ground (on occasion they will forage in stumps or low shrubbery), and they often bask or hide beneath logs, bark, flat rocks, and human-generated debris such as boards, concrete, or tar paper.

Green Snakes are generally active from mid-April to late October (probably May to September in the northern Great Lakes basin). In winter they may hibernate communally with other small snake species, taking refuge in underground shelters such as anthills and abandoned rodent burrows. They are active during daylight hours, though they appear to confine their activities to morning and early evening during hot weather.

This is the only Great Lakes area snake that is predominantly an insect eater. They have a preference for crickets, grasshoppers, and hairless caterpillars but also take beetles (and their larvae), spiders, centipedes, millipedes, snails, slugs, and (rarely) small amphibians. Green Snakes often feed sparingly or not at all in captivity and are generally a poor choice for laboratory study, educational exhibits, or hobbyists.

Though well camouflaged in their grassy habitats, Smooth Green Snakes are undoubtedly eaten on occasion by hawks and other birds, various mammals, and reptile-eating snakes. They depend on their cryptic coloration and rapid escape for defense and rarely strike or bite when seized or handled; in any case they are too small to do any harm to humans or most predators. They will smear musky-smelling cloacal fluids on a restraining hand.

Reproduction and Growth: Smooth Green Snakes have been observed mating in spring and in late summer. Females produce from 3 to 13 cylindrical, thin-shelled white eggs that range in length from 1.9 to 3.4 cm (0.75 to 1.3 in). The eggs are laid in shallow burrows, rotting wood, or plant material, or under logs, rocks, boards, and similar shelters. Several females may deposit their eggs in the same nest site. The egg-laying period extends from late June into September, with the later dates usually occurring toward the northern parts of the region.

Most Smooth Green Snake eggs hatch in August or September. This species has a relatively short incubation period ranging from 30 days to only 4 days, and one anecdotal account suggests that the young may occasionally be born alive. The ability of this snake to retain its eggs for long periods during embryonic development (and, presumably, to hasten development by basking) may be an adaptation to the cool-temperate climate (and relatively short growing season) that prevails over much of its contiguous range.

The young snakes probably mature in their second year. Average and potential life spans are unknown, but one individual survived for six years in captivity.

Conservation: Decreasing numbers and local extirpation of the Smooth Green Snake, particularly in the southern Great Lakes basin, have been blamed on the conversion of its habitat to intensive agricultural use, and on the widespread application of pesticides. The insectivorous diet of this species would be likely to increase its vulnerability to direct and indirect effects of certain pesticides. This distinctively colored little snake is often recognized and tolerated by persons who generally fear or persecute other equally harmless and potentially beneficial snake species.

Racer *Coluber constrictor*

Identification: Racers are large, active snakes with smooth, shiny scales and (in mature individuals) a uniform black, bluish, gray, olive, or brownish dorsal coloration. The head is relatively narrow, though wider than the neck, and the large eyes are bordered above by distinct brow ridges. The upper labial (lip) scales, chin, and throat are whitish or yellowish, grading to a belly color that varies from black or dark gray to light blue, white, cream, or light yellow. There are 17 scale rows at midbody (15 rows near the tail); the scales are smooth and the anal plate is divided. Total adult length: 90 to 190 cm (35 to 75 in).

Males have slightly longer tails (on average) than females; the base of the male's tail is nearly as wide as the body at the vent, or may even bulge slightly (due to the presence of the hemipenes). In contrast, the female's tail usually tapers more abruptly from the body.

At hatching Racers range in length from 19 to 35.5 cm (7.5 to 14 in). They are colored very differently than the adults, having a pattern of black-bordered gray, brown, or maroon dorsal blotches on a grayish or brownish background. There are also numerous dark spots on the head, sides, and belly. This pattern gradually fades as the snake grows, with the belly spots often persisting the longest. Most young Racers have lost all traces of the juvenile pattern by the time they reach a length of 70 to 90 cm (27.5 to 35 in), in their second or third summer.

Note: Two subspecies of the Racer are recognized in the Great Lakes region. The Northern Black Racer *(Coluber constrictor constrictor)* occurs in the eastern portion of the basin to the south of Lake Ontario and eastern Lake Erie (New York, Pennsylvania, and eastern Ohio). This subspecies is black above and dark gray on the belly; the chin and throat are white, sometimes speckled with dark spots.

The Blue Racer *(Coluber constrictor foxi)* ranges from the western end of Lake Erie across northern and western Ohio, northern Indiana, and the southern and western portions of Michigan's Lower Peninsula, to eastern Iowa and central Wisconsin; an isolated population occurs in Menominee County, in Michigan's Upper Peninsula. Blue Racers can be gray, bluish gray, turquoise, olive, or brownish above; the head may be slightly darker than the body, and most have a black "mask" behind the eye. The belly is usually bluish, white, or cream but may be yellowish, especially in Illinois and Wisconsin, where the range of this subspecies approaches that of the Eastern Yellow-bellied Racer *(Coluber c. flaviventris)*, a sub-

Nothern Black Racer.
(Photo by R. D. Bartlett.)

Juvenile Blue Racer

species found largely west of the Mississippi River. Areas of intergradation may be expected wherever the ranges of two subspecies meet (e.g., northeastern Ohio, western Wisconsin).

Confusing Species: The Racer's smooth scales and rounded body shape (in cross section) will distinguish it from Black Rat Snakes and both Fox Snakes, which have weakly keeled dorsal scales and a squarish cross-sectional body shape. Young Black Rat Snakes have a black stripe angling from the eye to rear edge of the jawline. Entirely black (melanistic) Eastern Garter Snakes have heavily keeled scales and a single anal plate.

Distribution and Status: This wide-ranging species is found from southern Maine and the southern Great Lakes basin south to Florida and the Gulf Coast states into eastern Mexico and northern Guatemala, and west through the central and southern plains states to southern British Columbia, Oregon, and California. They are largely absent (or restricted to isolated colonies) in the northern coniferous forest zone, the arid southwest, and higher altitudes in the Rocky Mountain region. Eleven subspecies have been recognized, two of which occur in the Great Lakes region and are described above.

Racers are generally to locally common in our area. Populations have declined in some areas (e.g., southern Michigan, northern Indiana), while the species may be expanding its range elsewhere (e.g., northern Michigan).

Habitat and Ecology: Racers generally prefer dry, sunny habitats with access to cover, including old fields, hedgerows and shrubby fence-lines, thickets, open woodlands, and woods edges; however, damper sites, such as grassy lake borders and marshes, are also used in some areas. These alert animals forage with head and neck raised and often bask in the open, stretched out or loosely coiled on clumps of vegetation or in the branches of low shrubs. When inactive they seek shelter in mammal burrows or under flat rocks, logs, fallen bark, boards, and other objects. This species is diurnal and tolerates warmer temperatures than most other snakes of this region; body temperatures of active Racers typically range from 22° to 38°C (72° to 100°F).

Racers occupy summer home ranges that vary in size from about a hectare (2.5 acres) to 10 hectares (25 acres) or larger, depending on the diversity and productivity of the habitat. They often seem to know their home area quite well and to have favorite foraging routes and places of refuge. This may explain at least some of the alleged instances of these snakes "chasing" people, for a startled Racer will frequently head directly for a preferred shelter, even if this route takes it directly toward its presumed attacker.

The active period for this species in the Great Lakes region generally lasts from early to mid-April until sometime in October. Hibernation takes place in mammal or crayfish burrows, rock crevices, rotted stumps, old building foundations, and other sites that provide refuge from subfreezing temperatures. Very cold winters, especially those with little snow cover, can result in the deaths of many hibernating Racers. When necessary, Racers may make lengthy migrations between summer ranges and over-wintering sites and often share hibernacula with numbers of their own and other snake species.

Racers probably have the most diverse diet of any Great Lakes snake. Included on the menu are insects (especially crickets, grasshoppers, large moths and their larvae), spiders, frogs, salamanders, small turtles, lizards, snakes (including smaller Racers and venomous species), birds and bird eggs, and mice and other small mammals. Juvenile Racers probably depend more on insects, small frogs, and other young snakes, while adults favor larger prey, especially rodents. Food is probably detected mostly by sight, although chemical cues (using the tongue and vomeronasal organ) probably play a part as well. Most prey animals are simply chased down, seized, and swallowed; these snakes are attracted to movement, and a potential victim that remains still may avoid detection. Racers do not constrict their prey (contrary to the implication of their scientific name), but larger or more active animals may be held down by a coil of the body and "chewed" into submission.

Racers, particularly the juveniles, are eaten by many predators, including larger Racers and other snake-eating snakes, hawks, crows, and mammals such as skunks, raccoons, foxes, and domestic dogs and cats. Racer eggs are sought by some of these same enemies. Shrews and mice may threaten these snakes during winter dormancy or other periods of inactivity.

A Racer's first line of defense is its speed and agility, and the vast majority will attempt to escape a potential predator (or approaching human) if given an opportunity to do so, darting into a burrow, thick vegetation, or rock crevice, or even climbing into a tree or shrub. They are relatively fast-moving animals, though human observers tend to overestimate the Racer's actual speed, which probably does not exceed about 6.5 kilometers per hour (4 mph)—or about the rate of a fast walk for a human.

If cornered, a typical Racer will coil and strike, while vibrating its tail nervously. The Racer is nonvenomous, but the slashing bite and sharp recurved teeth can leave scratches on human skin that may bleed freely for several minutes. They will also release a foul-smelling anal musk, particularly after being seized or injured. Racers rarely become tame or accept confinement and are poor candidates for pets or captive study.

Reproduction and Growth: Mating takes place in spring, from late April into early June. During this season the males may appear quite nervous and excitable, and perhaps become somewhat territorial, although there is little evidence that they actually defend areas or females against other males. Occasional reports of Racers "holding their ground" or even acting aggressively toward people may be based in part on encounters with feisty territorial males.

Males probably locate prospective mates by following their pheromone (chemical scent) trails, and two or more males may end up courting the same female. During courtship the male attempts to move over or alongside the female; rippling movements may travel down his body at this time. The pair often entwine their bodies, or at least their tails, as the male tries to align his vent with that of the female; a receptive female will raise her tail to assist copulation.

In June or early July the female Racer will lay from 3 to 32 (usually 8 to 20) eggs in a hidden nest site such as an old mammal burrow, a rotted stump or log, under a rock or board, or in a new cavity in sand, sawdust, or leaf litter. Two or more females sometimes share a nest site. The oval, white eggs range in length from 2.5 to 3.9 cm (1 to 1.5 in) and, when freshly laid, have leathery, flexible shells with a rough granular texture (appearing as though they were sprinkled with salt). As incubation progresses, the eggs swell and become firmer and may nearly double in size by hatching, which usually occurs in August or early September.

The hatchling Racers grow quickly, with some individuals increasing in length by 50 percent or more prior to their first winter. Males become sexually mature in 1 to 2 years, females in 2 to 3 years, after which growth continues at a slower rate. Racers are comparatively long-lived snakes, sometimes exceeding an age of 10 years in the wild.

Conservation: These large, active snakes require relatively large areas of habitat, and their populations quickly decline in the face of intensive agriculture or suburban/urban development. Pesticide residues pose a danger, particularly to the insectivorous young Racers. Additional problems include road mortality and direct killing of snakes by people. The tendency of Racers to converge in numbers on a few favored winter dens makes them vulnerable to mass destruction by intolerant humans. These snakes undoubtedly have economic value as destroyers of rodent and insect pests. Despite their occasional displays of bravado, Racers are harmless to people willing to leave them alone.

Black Rat Snake   *Elaphe obsoleta obsoleta*

Description: This is the largest snake in the Great Lakes region. Adult Black Rat Snakes are mostly black and/or dark brown above, with white on the labial scales, chin, and throat. An indication of the blotched juvenile color pattern often persists well into adulthood (or throughout life in some populations); most older specimens show at least a trace of white, yellow, or orange flecking, especially on the skin between the body scales. The head is distinct from the neck, rather elongated and flattened, and widest behind the eyes. The belly may be whitish or yellowish, marked with a dark checkerboard pattern on the forward part of the body but becoming clouded by gray or brown toward the midbody and tail. The body is squarish in cross section, with fairly straight sides and a flat belly. There are 23 to 27 scale rows at midbody; the upper-body scales are weakly keeled, and the anal plate is divided. Total adult length: 100 to 256.5 cm (40 to 101 in).

The sexes are difficult to distinguish based on external characters. Males have slightly longer tails relative to total length; the female's tail tends to taper quite rapidly from the body (particularly noticeable in gravid females), while the male's tail tapers more gradually from the body.

Newly hatched young Black Rat Snakes are strongly patterned, with a dorsal row of dark gray or brown saddles alternating with smaller side blotches on a pale gray background. There is a black band just in front of (and connecting) the eyes, and a black stripe slanting from behind the eye to the rear edge of the jawline. Hatchlings range in length from 27 to 37 cm (10.6 to 14.5 in).

Black Rat Snake

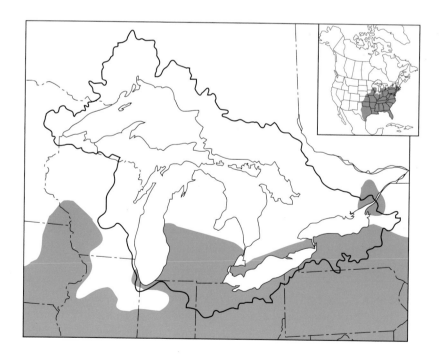

Confusing Species: Racers have smooth scales and a rounded body in cross section; juvenile Racers lack the stripe from the eye to the rear edge of the mouth. Western and Eastern Fox Snakes have 216 or fewer ventral scutes (221 or more ventral scutes in Black Rat Snakes).

Distribution and Status: Black Rat Snakes are found from northeastern New York and New England east to Wisconsin and southeastern Minnesota and south to Oklahoma, Louisiana, and northern Georgia. In the Great Lakes region they occur south of Lake Ontario and west through the Lake Erie basin and western Lower Michigan to the southern end of Lake Michigan. A disjunct population occurs near the eastern end of Lake Ontario (Ontario and New York). Other subspecies extend the range of *Elaphe obsoleta* south into Florida, the Gulf Coast region, and southern Texas.

This species is uncommon to rare and local over most of the Great Lakes region. Many populations have been greatly reduced or extirpated in recent decades, particularly in the western and northern Lake Erie watershed in Ontario and southeastern Michigan.

Habitat and Ecology: Black Rat Snakes typically occur in or near woodlands but also use adjacent open habitats such as shrubby fields, pastures, hedgerows, and marsh and bog edges. They often forage or seek shelter in or around barns, outbuildings, old foundations, trash dumps, and abandoned cars or farm machinery. They are quite arboreal, sometimes climbing as high as 9 to 12 meters (30 to 40 ft) and are capable of scaling vertical surfaces such as tree trunks, fence posts, and the sides of buildings.

These snakes are usually active from late April through October. They are largely diurnal in spring and fall but may forage in the early evening or even at night during hot summer weather. In fall they move to den sites that offer refuge from freezing temperatures, such as mammal burrows, root systems, or deep rock crevices. Rat Snakes often hibernate communally with other large snakes such as Racers and Timber Rattlesnakes. (This species was formerly called the "pilot black snake" due to the erroneous belief that they lead Timber Rattlesnakes and Copperheads to winter dens.)

Black Rat Snakes may occupy specific home ranges for much of their lives; an average home range would be about 600 m (2,000 ft) in diameter, based on studies outside the Great Lakes area. There is no evidence that these snakes actually defend territories against others of their kind, but males will engage in ritualized combat behavior, probably to establish social dominance related to reproduction. During combat episodes, a male attempts to pin his rival down using his head and body. The efforts of each male to "top" the other results in considerable twining, jerking, and occasional biting; eventually one combatant will tire and try to escape the confrontation.

Small mammals make up the largest part of this snake's diet, followed by birds and bird's eggs. Mice, rats, chipmunks, shrews, moles, rabbits, opossums, and other large prey animals are killed by constriction prior to being swallowed. Most birds are taken as nestlings, which, along with eggs and other small, nonthreatening prey, may be simply seized and swallowed. Juvenile Black Rat Snakes (and occasionally the adults) will also eat small frogs, reptiles, and reptile eggs.

Adult Black Rat Snakes appear to have relatively few enemies other than people. Large hawks and owls are probably the most important natural predators, though they could also be attacked by mammals such as raccoons, coyotes, dogs, and swine. The list of enemies for juvenile Rat Snakes would be longer and could include shrews, weasels, and other snakes. The defensive attitude of this snake varies considerably between individuals. They are a relatively slow-moving species compared to most other large snakes, and many adults will "freeze" when confronted by danger, perhaps to reduce the chances of being detected. Some individuals (especially older adults) refuse to defend themselves even when handled. However, most juveniles and many adults will coil, vibrate their tails, and strike if cornered or seized. They can also release a foul-smelling musk from the cloaca.

Reproduction: Mating occurs in spring, mostly in May and early June. Black Rat Snake courtship is similar in many respects to that of the Racer but is comparatively more of a slow-motion affair, in keeping with this species' more placid demeanor. The male presses his chin on a receptive female's back and moves forward, aligning his body with hers; waves of rippling muscular contractions often move forward along the male's lower body, and he may also grasp the female's neck or body with his jaws. Cloacal contact is accomplished after much tail twitching and twining, with copulation lasting about 20 minutes on average.

Females lay their eggs in late June or July. Typical nest sites include burrows in loose soil or leaf mold, rotted stumps or logs, manure or sawdust piles, or cavities under rocks or boards. At times, two or more females will share a nest site. The eggs number from 5 to 44 (usually about a dozen) per clutch, have flexible, granular shells, and may stick to each another in a clump. They are oval to almost spherical in shape and range in length from 3.5 to 5.5 cm (1.4 to 2.1 in).

Incubation takes from 60 to 75 days, with most hatchlings emerging in late August or September. The young snakes grow relatively quickly at first, but most probably do not reach sexual maturity until their fourth year. This is a potentially long-lived snake, with a known life span (in a captive) of nearly 23 years.

Conservation: Black Rat Snakes are harmless to humans and are economically useful in the destruction of rodent pests around farms and gardens. The fact that they also eat birds may be objectionable to some people, but their impact on bird numbers would be insignificant compared to that of more abundant bird predators.

This species requires a comparatively large living area and certainly has suffered from the loss of forest and forest-edge habitats to intensive agriculture and urbanization. However, it can benefit when logging and low-intensity agriculture or livestock grazing create a mosaic of wooded and open land. There are many areas in the lower Great Lakes region that could (and, in many cases, once did) support healthy Black Rat Snake populations, and the species' scarcity or absence in such places suggests that additional problems exist. This conspicuous, slow-moving snake is a frequent victim of human persecution, road mortality, and collection by hobbyists; these and similar factors may be serious threats to a population already stressed by habitat degradation.

Western Fox Snake *Elaphe vulpina*

Description: This fairly large, stout-bodied snake has a row of brown or black blotches running down the back and onto the tail, alternating with smaller dark blotches on the sides. The background color is yellowish brown, grayish brown, or tan, sometimes grading to orangish on the tail. The head is distinct from the neck and widest behind the eyes, and the snout is bluntly rounded. The head varies in color from a yellowish or reddish brown to coppery orange; many (especially younger) individuals have a dark band between the eyes that continues behind the eye to the end of the jawline (a vestige of the darker juvenile pattern). The belly is

Western Fox Snake

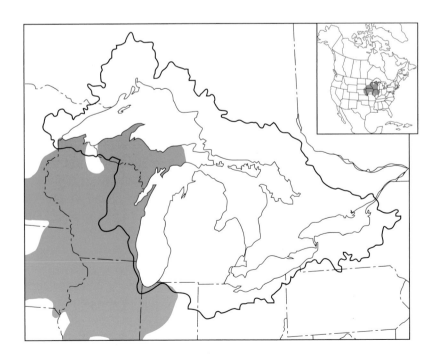

yellowish to cream color with scattered squarish dark spots. The tail is stout, tapering to a spinelike tip. There are 23 to 27 scale rows at mid-body; the scales are keeled on the upper back, becoming smooth on the sides, and the anal plate is divided. Total adult length: 90 to 155 cm (35.4 to 61 in).

Male Western Fox Snakes attain a slightly larger body size than females and have comparatively longer tails. Males have 52 to 71 subcaudal scutes, while females have 45 to 60 subcaudals.

Young Western Fox Snakes range in length from 23 to 31 cm (9 to 12.2 in) at hatching. They have gray or brown, black-bordered blotches on a light gray background; the head markings are distinct, with a dark band in front of the eyes, and a stripe slanting from the back of each eye to the end of the jawline.

Confusing Species: Eastern Milk Snakes have smooth scales and single anal plates. Juvenile Racers have smooth scales and lack the stripe from eye to end of jaw. Bullsnakes have more heavily keeled scales, single anal plates, and rather pointed snouts (bluntly rounded in Western Fox Snake). Juvenile Black Rat Snakes are similar but have more than 220 ventral scutes (216 or less in both Fox Snakes). The range of the Eastern Fox Snake does not overlap that of the Western Fox Snake, but captives of unknown origin could be confusing. Easterns have fewer but larger dorsal blotches on the body (range 28 to 43, average 34) and tail, while Westerns have a greater number of smaller dorsal body blotches (range 32 to 52, average 41).

Distribution and Status: This species ranges from the central Upper Peninsula of Michigan through most of Wisconsin to southern Minnesota, Iowa, southeastern South Dakota, and eastern Nebraska, and south to northern Missouri, Illinois, and the northwestern corner of Indiana. Its Great Lakes range extends from upper Michigan through the western Lake Michigan basin in eastern Wisconsin and Illinois to the Indiana Dunes area.

Western Fox Snakes are locally common in their Great Lakes range.

Habitat and Ecology: This is a snake of prairie, pasture, and farmland in the southern and western parts of its range, but it inhabits open woodland and forest-edge habitats farther north. In northern Michigan and Wisconsin they occur in pine/oak woodlands and adjacent farm fields and stumpy, brush-covered clear-cuts. (People in upper Michigan and Wisconsin often call this species "pine snake.") They occur in dry habitats as well as moister sites near streams or ponds.

Western Fox Snakes are less arboreal than the Black Rat Snake but occasionally climb into low shrubs, stumps, and abandoned buildings. Although most active during the day, much of their foraging occurs out of sight in rodent burrows or under rock or trash piles. They sometimes move about on warm rainy nights. They hibernate, often communally, from late October until mid-April in dens that offer refuge from freezing temperatures, such as mammal burrows, rock crevices, and old wells and barn foundations. In some den sites the snakes successfully overwinter while submerged in water.

Small mammals such as mice, voles, chipmunks, ground squirrels, gophers, and baby rabbits are this snake's favored prey, but bird eggs and nestlings are also eaten when available. Juveniles will also eat insects, earthworms, frogs, and small reptiles. Prey animals are killed by constriction prior to swallowing

The natural enemies of adult Western Fox Snakes undoubtedly include the larger birds of prey and predatory mammals, while their eggs and young would be vulnerable to snake-eating snakes, shrews, weasels, and many other small predators. These snakes are relatively sluggish in their movements, but most will attempt to escape into the closest cover when threatened. If cornered they will coil and raise their heads, vibrate their tails, and sometimes strike; younger individuals seem more willing to bite than older ones. The musky-smelling anal secretions that this species produces when disturbed or handled supposedly smell foxlike, hence the common name.

Reproduction and Growth: Male Western Fox Snakes will engage in ritualized combat, similar to that described for the Black Rat Snake. During these "wrestling matches," each combatant attempts to "top" and "pin" his rival by twining around him and pushing down on his head and body. The winners of these bouts appear to maintain a temporary dominance over the losers, and to have better success at mating with nearby females.

Mating usually takes place in April or May while the snakes are still near the winter dens but also occurs later in spring after dispersal to summer feeding areas. A courting male will vigorously pursue his intended mate for some time until she finally accepts him. The male then attempts to align his body with the female's, at which time both snakes may begin jerking their heads and bodies in a forward movement that may continue throughout mating. The pair eventually twine their tails together, bringing the anal openings together and allowing the male to insert a hemipenis into the female's cloaca. The male may grasp the female's neck with his jaws during copulation.

In late June or early July the female seeks a nest site in loose soil, a decaying log or stump, or under a rock, board, or other surface litter. She produces a clutch of from 7 to 27 elliptical, flexible-shelled eggs that average about 4.5 cm (1.7 in) in length. The eggs often stick to each other and may tear if forcibly pulled apart. Incubation requires from 35 to 75 days, with most hatchlings emerging between mid-August and early September.

Natural growth patterns for this species are in need of study. If Western Fox Snakes have growth rates similar to those reported for related North American *Elaphe,* they would attain sexual maturity in three to four years. Potential longevity is unknown; a captive specimen survived for over six years.

Conservation: Populations of this snake can persist in areas largely devoted to agriculture, and this species undoubtedly benefits when densely forested tracts are opened up by timber harvest or creation of grazing and crop lands. However, agricultural trends that favor intensive "shoulder to shoulder" cultivation at the expense of hedgerows, shrubby fence-lines, and fallow fields can lead to declines and local extirpation. Its rodent-eating habits make this a beneficial species to the farmer and gardener.

Western Fox Snakes are frequent highway victims, and many others are needlessly killed by fearful people. Due to its often reddish colored head and habit of vibrating its tail when frightened, this harmless snake is sometimes mistaken for a Copperhead *(Agkistrodon contortrix),* a venomous snake not native to the Great Lakes region, or for a rattlesnake.

Eastern Fox Snake   *Elaphe gloydi*

Description: This is a robust yellowish or light brown snake with a row of large black or dark brown middorsal blotches alternating with smaller dark blotches on the sides. The head varies in color from light brown to a coppery reddish brown, and there is usually an indistinct dark band

Eastern Fox Snake

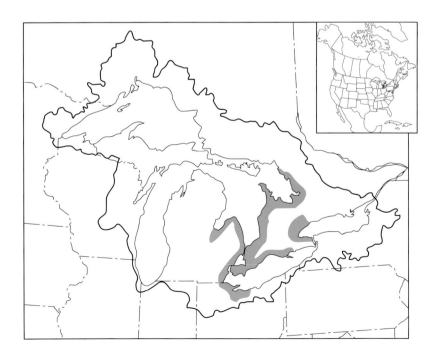

between the eyes, another band extending downward from the eye to the mouth, and another slanting back from eye to the corner of the mouth; these markings may fade completely in old adults. The belly has irregular rows of dark squarish spots on a yellowish background. The tail is rather short and has a spinelike tip. There are usually 23 to 25 scale rows at mid-body; the upper-body scales are weakly keeled, and the anal plate is divided. Total adult length: 90 to 170.5 cm (35.4 to 67 in).

External sex differences are not obvious; males may be, on average, slightly larger and have proportionally longer tails than females. When gravid in summer, adult females are noticeably thicker-bodied than males, with more abruptly tapering tails (males have gradual body-to-tail taper).

Juvenile Eastern Fox Snakes are paler in background color than adults, with more distinct head markings and gray or brown dorsal blotches edged in black. They range from 26 to 31 cm (10.2 to 12.2 in) in total length at hatching.

Confusing Species: Eastern Milk Snakes have smooth scales and single (undivided) anal plates. Racers also have smooth scales and no slanting line from eye to corner of mouth. Black Rat Snakes, with similar juvenile coloration, have 221 or more ventral scutes (216 or fewer in Eastern Fox Snake). Differences between Eastern and Western Fox Snake (which do not overlap in range) are noted under the latter species' account.

Distribution and Status: This snake's range is entirely within the Great Lakes basin. It inhabits coastal marshes and other near-shore habitats along Lake Huron from Saginaw Bay (Michigan) and Georgian Bay (Ontario) south to Lake St. Clair and the Detroit River, then east along the northern Lake Erie shore to Long Point Bay (Norfolk County, Ontario), and along the southern Lake Erie shore to Erie County, Ohio. This snake also occurs on Pelee Island as well as on some of the smaller Lake Erie islands. Isolated records for Buffalo, New York, and the western end of Lake Ontario (in Ontario) may be valid but are in need of verification.

The Eastern Fox Snake is now uncommon or rare in many areas where it was once abundant but can be locally common where ample habitat remains.

Habitat and Ecology: This is a snake of the Great Lakes shoreline marshes and vegetated dunes and beaches, although it sometimes wanders into nearby farm fields, pastures, and woodlots. Rocky areas and open woodlands are occupied on the Lake Erie islands. This snake will bask or forage on raised dikes, muskrat houses, and road embankments but only rarely climbs into trees or shrubbery. Although not strictly aquatic, they are good swimmers capable of moving considerable distances over open off-shore waters and between islands.

In a typical year Eastern Fox Snakes are active from mid-April until late October but are most often seen abroad during May and June. Whether they are truly inactive during the summer or simply become more nocturnal in response to warmer temperatures is unclear. They hibernate during the winter months in abandoned mammal burrows or other frost-free shelters.

Small mammals, particularly meadow voles *(Microtus)* and deer mice *(Peromyscus),* make up the largest part of this snake's diet. They will also eat bird eggs and nestlings. Smaller prey items and eggs are simply seized and swallowed, but larger prey are killed by constriction. Young Eastern Fox Snakes may possibly eat "cold-blooded" animals such as earthworms and frogs.

Potential predators of Eastern Fox Snakes include egrets, herons, hawks, raccoons, foxes, and mink; the juvenile snakes would be vulnerable to a longer list of predators that could include large fish and frogs, turtles, shrews, weasels, and even rodents. When threatened, this harmless snake will vibrate its tail, which can sound quite "rattlerlike" if it is in contact with dry leaves. Some individuals, especially younger ones, will strike, but older snakes are often reluctant to bite even when handled, though they will spray a musky-smelling (supposedly foxlike) anal secretion on the offender.

Reproduction and Growth: The mating habits of this snake are little known but are presumably similar to those of the Western Fox Snake and other *Elaphe.* Females lay their eggs during late June and July, depositing clutches of 7 to 29 eggs in rotted stumps or shallow burrows, or under logs, boards, or mats of decaying vegetation. At times several females will lay their eggs in one nest site. The white, leathery-shelled eggs are elongated and range from 2.9 to 5.8 cm (1.2 to 2.3 in) in length. They often adhere together in one or more clumps.

Incubation requires from 50 to 65 days, with most hatching occurring in late August or September. The young snakes probably reach maturity in three or four years. An Eastern Fox Snake obtained as an adult lived for over seven years and five months in a zoo.

Conservation: The Eastern Fox Snake is harmless to humans, and its rodent-eating habits make it an economically useful species in agricultural areas. Unfortunately this snake's reddish head color and tail-buzzing habits can lead uninformed persons to mistake it for a venomous species, and many are killed out of needless fear.

Over most of its limited range, the fate of the Eastern Fox Snake is tied to the fate of the coastal marshlands. Considerable portions of this habitat has been ditched and drained for agriculture and residential and industrial development, and remaining marshland often suffers from pollution and other forms of degradation. Even where the marsh is protected (and on the offshore islands) local snake populations are vulnerable to depletion by the aforementioned persecution and by collecting for the commercial pet trade. The Eastern Fox Snake is presently given legal protection in Michigan and Ontario.

Eastern Milk Snake *Lampropeltis triangulum triangulum*

Description: Eastern Milk Snakes are slender, medium-sized snakes with a dorsal row of brown or reddish brown blotches on a gray or tan (occasionally pinkish) background. The saddlelike blotches are edged in black and alternate with one or two rows of smaller dark blotches along each side. The head is rather small but slightly wider than the neck; there is usually a light marking on the back of the head shaped like a Y or V. The belly is white, cream, or pale yellow with an irregular checkerboard pattern of rectangular black spots; much of the belly pattern may be obscured by dark pigment in some older individuals. There are usually 21 (19 to 23) scale rows at midbody; the scales are smooth and the anal plate is single. Total adult length: 61 to 132 cm (24 to 52 in).

There are no generally reliable external characteristics that separate the sexes. Gravid females in summer will have thicker bodies posteriorly that quickly taper at the start of the tail (anal plate), while males have no abrupt narrowing where the body meets the tail.

Very young Eastern Milk Snakes are more brightly colored than adults, with black-bordered red or maroon blotches on a pale gray background. At hatching they range in length from 16.8 to 28.0 cm (6.6 to 11 in).

Confusing Species: Water snakes have distinctly keeled scales and divided anal plates. Juvenile Racers, Black Rat Snakes, and Eastern and Western Fox Snakes also have divided anal plates.

Eastern Milk Snake

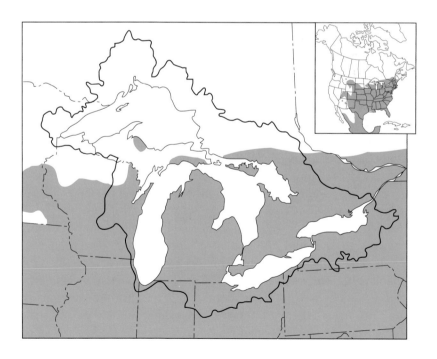

Distribution and Status: The Eastern Milk Snake ranges from southern Maine and Quebec west to Minnesota and south to the uplands of Tennessee and South Carolina. It occurs throughout much of the Great Lakes region but appears to be absent from the northern and western Lake Superior watershed and is rare and local in Michigan's Upper Peninsula. Additional subspecies of *Lampropeltis triangulum* extend the species' range west to Montana and Utah, south to Florida and Texas, and into Mexico and Central America to Ecuador.

This snake is locally common throughout most of its Great Lakes range.

Habitat and Ecology: This snake is found in a wide variety of habitats, from open woodlands, bogs, swamps, and woods edges, to marshes, lakeshores, old fields, pastures, farmyards, and suburban parks and gardens. In some areas they make seasonal migrations between higher, drier winter hibernation sites and moister summer habitats. They often occur in or near farm outbuildings, barns, and sheds, and are attracted to piles of rocks, logs, firewood, or building materials—or virtually any place that offers shelter to the snakes and their rodent food.

This snake's predilection for foraging around barns probably earned it the name "milk snake," since it became associated with an absurd (and today, rarely believed) myth that certain snakes can steal milk from cows. Some people call this snake the "house snake, " which is more reasonable than another vernacular name, "spotted adder," since this is a nonvenomous species.

Eastern Milk Snakes are secretive and remain underground or under cover much of the time. They appear to be largely nocturnal, particularly during the warm summer months. Adults are most often seen on the surface in late spring, while new hatchlings and small juveniles are frequently observed in September and October. (Late summer often brings a flurry of calls to zoos, nature centers, and college biology departments from people wondering if the "little red-spotted snakes" in their yards and garages are dangerous!)

Milk Snakes typically hibernate, often communally, from late October or November until mid-April. Suitable hibernacula include rodent burrows, rock or soil crevices, cavities under rotted stumps, rock-filled road embankments, old wells and root cellars, house foundations and crawl spaces. (Additional worried telephone calls to the above-mentioned institutions are often generated by Milk Snakes that fall into poorly sealed basements while seeking winter den sites.)

Small mammals (mice, voles, young rats, shrews) make up about 70 percent of the Eastern Milk Snake's food, with snakes, lizards, birds, and reptile and bird eggs rounding out the diet. Very young Milk Snakes may feed largely on smaller snakes, switching to rodents as they grow. Larger prey animals are killed by constriction, while helpless prey (e.g., baby mice) and eggs are simply seized and swallowed.

Eastern Milk Snakes are undoubtedly eaten on occasion by various predatory birds and mammals, but their secretive habits may make them less vulnerable than snake species that spend more time exposed on the surface. Underground hunters such as weasels and shrews would pose a danger to young or dormant Milk Snakes and eggs. Milk Snakes are known to feed on smaller individuals of their own species.

This species prefers flight to confrontation; when closely chased or cornered an Eastern Milk Snake may vibrate its tail, hiss, and strike, or coil tightly into a ball and attempt to hide its head under its body. Although most individuals seem to tame down quickly when handled, they often remain nervous and unpredictable and may turn and bite a restraining hand without warning. This habit, along with a reluctance to feed when confined, makes this snake a poor choice for captive study or display.

Reproduction and Growth: Mating may take place in early spring, prior to dispersal from winter den areas, or later in May and June; males can locate females by following their scent trails. The courting male will press his chin on the female's back and twine around her body and tail, attempting to bring their cloacas into contact. During copulation the male may grasp the female's neck in his jaws.

Females produce from 5 to 24 eggs in late June or early July. Typical nest sites include rotted stumps or logs, piles of vegetation, manure, or compost, shallow burrows in soil or sand, or cavities under rocks, bark, boards, or other surface litter. The eggs are white, cylindrical or oval in shape, and range in length from 2.5 to 4.2 cm (1 to 1.7 in). They often adhere to each other, forming one or more clusters. Most eggs hatch in late August or September, after an incubation period of six to nine weeks.

The young snakes reach maturity in their third or fourth year. A zoo specimen captured as an adult lived over 21 years, but 7 to 10 years would be a more normal longevity in the wild.

Conservation: The Eastern Milk Snake's tendency to remain out of sight and to forage mainly after dark are useful adaptations for living near humans. While intense agricultural or urban development has surely eliminated some local populations, Milk Snakes remain common in many farming and suburban areas. Unfortunately, many people are still needlessly frightened by their startling color pattern and tail-buzzing habit and kill them on sight. However, increasing numbers of farmers and homeowners now recognize the value of having these harmless rodent-eating snakes as neighbors. Milk Snakes are often fatally attracted to the lingering warmth of black-topped roads at night.

Northern Ring-necked Snake   *Diadophis punctatus edwardsii*

Description: This is a small, dark, shiny-scaled snake with a bright orange or yellow ring around its neck. Coloration on the back and sides is a solid bluish black, gray, or brownish gray. The head may be darker than the body, and is slightly flattened and wider than the neck. The belly is yellow or yellowish-orange, either unmarked or with a few small black dots scattered along the mid-line. There are usually 15 scale rows at midbody; the scales are smooth and the anal plate is divided. Total adult length: 25.4 to 70.6 cm (10 to 27.7 in); very few exceed 50 cm (19.7 in) total length.

Mature males have ridges on the scales in the anal area and have slightly longer tails (as a percentage of total length) than females.

Hatchlings typically range from 9 to 14 cm (3.5 to 5.5 in) in length and are similar in color to their parents, though somewhat darker on the back and paler on the belly.

Confusing Species: Very young Brown Snakes and Northern Red-bellied Snakes are also dark colored with a light neck blotch or collar, but the former has at least a hint of dorsal spotting, while the latter usually has a pink or red belly. Both have keeled scales.

Distribution and Status: Northern Ring-necked Snakes are found from Nova Scotia west to northeastern Minnesota and south through New England and the Appalachian highlands to northern Georgia and west to southern Illinois. They occur throughout the Great Lakes region excepting the northern Lake Superior watershed (in Ontario); they also appear to be scarce or absent in the former prairie and "prairie peninsula" portions of

Northern Ringnecked Snake

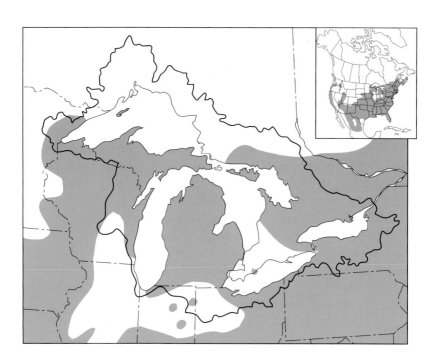

northern Illinois, Indiana, and Ohio. Several other recognized subspecies extend the species' range south to Florida and west to Mexico and the Pacific coast of the United States.

Its secretive habits make this a difficult species to survey—in some places Ring-necked Snakes may be locally common but overlooked, while elsewhere they may be presumed to be common (based on old records) when in actuality the local populations have declined or even disappeared. Northern Ring-necked Snakes tend to exist in small localized colonies throughout much of the central and western Great Lakes basin; within these colonies they can be numerous. The species remains notably common on several of the larger islands in northern Lake Michigan (e.g., Washington Island, Wisconsin; Beaver Island, North and South Manitou Islands, Michigan).

Habitat and Ecology: The Northern Ring-necked Snake is usually characterized as a woodland inhabitant and indeed is one of the few snake species that regularly occurs in moist, shady woodlands, although flood-prone bottomlands are avoided. They also use more open habitats close to the woods, such as clear-cuts, old fields, grassy (stabilized) dunes and beaches, and trash dumps. They are rarely seen on the surface but instead remain under leaf litter or cover objects such as flat rocks, logs, pieces of bark, or boards, or within the tunnels of small mammals, earthworms, or insects. This snake is largely nocturnal, but heavy rains may stimulate daylight activity on the surface.

The annual activity period depends on local climatic conditions, but probably extends from early April to late October in the southern parts of the region, and late April or early May to mid- or late September in the north. Ring-necked Snakes hibernate underground, in burrows made by other animals, in deep rock crevices, or in anthills. They often move to higher ground when seeking winter den sites, which are frequently shared with numbers of their own or other snake species.

Northern Ring-necked Snakes feed on a variety of small animals, including smaller snakes, lizards, frogs, salamanders, earthworms, slugs, and insect larvae. However, local populations may specialize in certain types of prey; in the northern Great Lakes region Red-backed Salamanders seem to make up a large portion of this snake's diet, followed in frequency by small snakes and earthworms. Most food items are simply seized and swallowed, but larger prey may be held tightly until they stop moving. This species has a pair of slightly enlarged teeth at the back of the upper jaw, and its saliva may be mildly toxic to small animals. By any measure, however, Northern Ring-necked Snakes are completely harmless to humans.

The tendency of the Northern Ring-necked Snake to remain underground or under cover reduces their vulnerability to many predators. During their occasional surface forays, they risk being eaten by owls, hawks, foxes, domestic cats, and other surface hunters. Predators willing to enter burrows or dig, such as Eastern Milk Snakes, Racers, shrews, weasels, and skunks, are a more constant threat. A Northern Ring-necked Snake rarely attempts to bite, even when seized by a predator or held in the hand, but instead will usually writhe vigorously and release a foul-smelling musky substance from its cloaca.

Reproduction and Growth: Mating may occur in either spring, late summer, or fall. Females that mate late in the year can store active sperm in their oviducts over winter to fertilize their eggs in spring.

Females deposit from 1 to 10 (usually 3 or 4) eggs in late June or early July. Nests may be in rodent burrows, beneath flat rocks or boards, or within rotted logs or stumps; several females will often share a particularly favored spot, which may be used for several consecutive seasons. The eggs are thin-shelled and elongate, sometimes tapered or even slightly curved in shape, and measure from 2.2 to 3.6 cm (0.9 to 1.4 in) in length. Incubation time varies from four to nine weeks, with most hatching occurring between mid-August and early September.

Growth is rapid during a young Ring-necked Snake's first summer and gradually tapers off as it approaches sexual maturity during its third or fourth year. Males tend to mature slightly earlier than females. This seems to be a fairly long-lived snake considering its small size; average life span may approach 10 years in some populations, with occasional individuals reaching 20 years or more.

Conservation: Northern Ring-necked Snakes require moist woodland and woodland edge habitats; large-scale clear-cutting or even selective logging could be detrimental to its survival. The colonial nature of this snake's distribution would make it particularly vulnerable to rapid local extirpation when its habitats are disturbed. The apparent decline of Ring-necked Snake populations in many areas (e.g., southern Michigan) may be due largely to habitat loss, but the widespread use of persistent pesticides during the mid–twentieth century could also have played a role.

Ring-necked Snakes are occasionally killed while crossing roads at night.

Eastern Hog-nosed Snake   *Heterodon platirhinos*

Description: This moderate-sized snake is thick bodied, with a short tail and a flattened, upturned snout. Its unique defensive behavior (described below) is also a good identifying characteristic. Coloration is extremely variable—some individuals have a distinct pattern of irregular dark blotches down the back, alternating with dark spots on the sides, on a mottled background of gray, brown, tan, olive, orange, yellow, or pinkish. Others lack the dorsal blotching and are a plain gray, brown, or olive; occasional ones are melanistic (entirely black). Many specimens are intermediate in pattern, with indistinct, faded blotches. Elongated dark neck blotches are present in all but the darkest individuals. The head is wide and slightly distinct from the neck (unless the neck is flattened during defensive display); the rostral (nose) scale is upturned and keeled above. Well-patterned individuals usually have a dark band between the eyes and another extending from each eye to the back of the jawline. The belly can be yellowish, cream, gray, or pinkish, often mottled with darker color; the chin, throat, and subcaudal (undertail) scales are usually lighter than the rest of the underside. There are usually 25 (range 23–27) scale rows at midbody; the scales are keeled and the anal plate is divided. Total adult length: 50 to 115.6 cm (20 to 45.5 in).

Males are somewhat smaller and less robust, on average, than females and have relatively longer tails. A male's tail length is typically 17 percent to 22 percent of its total length, while a female's tail is usually 12 percent to 17 percent of total length.

Very young Eastern Hog-nosed Snakes have dark dorsal blotches and lateral spots on a light gray or brown, or occasionally pinkish, background; this pattern is evident even in those destined to be unpatterned and unicolored as adults. The belly of the hatchling is dark gray or black, though the throat and undersurface of the tail are white or yellowish. Total length at hatching ranges from 12.5 to 25.4 cm (5 to 10 in).

Confusing Species: This snake is likely to be confused only with the Eastern Massasauga or the Timber Rattlesnake, both of which have rattles on the tail, elliptical eye pupils, and facial pits (visible as an opening

Eastern Hog-nosed Snake

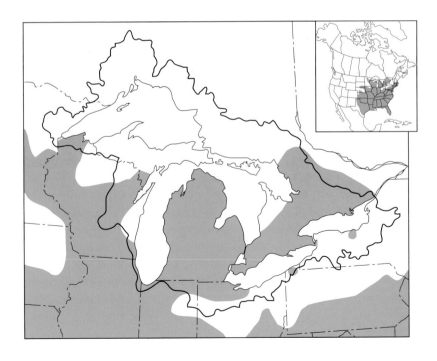

between eye and nostril). In addition, rattlesnakes lack the Hog-nosed Snake's upturned snout and neck-spreading ability.

Distribution and Status: The Eastern Hog-nosed snake is found from southern New England south through Florida, west to central Texas, and north to southeastern South Dakota, southern Iowa, and eastern Minnesota, and east to southern Ontario. Its Great Lakes range includes much of Wisconsin (except for the north-central counties and the Door Peninsula), Michigan's Lower Peninsula and Menominee County in the Upper Peninsula, northern Indiana, northwestern Ohio (east to Erie County), and southern Ontario (north to the Algonquin Park area). It appears to be absent from the Lake Superior basin and much of the area south of Lake Ontario and eastern Lake Erie. There is an isolated population near the Lake Erie shore in northwestern Pennsylvania.

This species can be locally common in suitable habitat, particularly where human activity is minimal, but this has become an uncommon-to-rare snake in many parts of the region where it was reasonably common only a decade or two previously.

Habitat and Ecology: Eastern Hog-nosed Snakes inhabit nearly all types of terrestrial habitats, from open pine or deciduous woodlands to old fields, meadows, and pastures. Although occasionally found along wetland edges, they have a decided preference for habitats with sandy, well-drained soils. These snakes are largely diurnal but tend to be most active in the morning and in early evening during the warm summer months.

When not foraging or basking in the open, Eastern Hog-nosed Snakes remain underground or (less commonly) beneath logs or other surface debris. They are excellent burrowers—the broad, sloping "forehead" and upturned snout are used to push downward, with a side-to-side motion, into the soil or sand. While capable of making their own burrows, they also use or enlarge burrows made by other animals. The colder months (typically late October to early April) are spent hibernating in a deep burrow or under a rotted stump or similar shelter.

Food items recorded for the Eastern Hog-nosed Snake include toads, frogs, salamanders, small reptiles, reptile eggs, small mammals, birds, and insects; however, toads are by far the most frequent food taken. This snake has a number of adaptations for finding and consuming toads—its digging abilities facilitate the search for burrowing amphibians, and its wide gape, flexible jaws, and recurved teeth aid in holding and swallowing chunky-bodied toads (which often inflate themselves with air when seized). Hog-nosed Snakes have a pair of enlarged teeth at the back of the mouth. It has been suggested that these teeth are used to puncture the lungs of inflated toads, but there is little direct evidence for such a function. This snake's enlarged adrenal glands secrete hormones that may help to counteract toxic toad skin secretions.

Hog-nosed Snakes have specialized salivary glands (Duvernoy's glands) that produce a substance that is toxic to some amphibians, but its effects are so mild and slow-acting that it would appear to be of limited use in subduing struggling prey. One person accidentally bitten on the arm while handling an Eastern Hog-nosed Snake suffered subsequent pain and discoloration near the wound, leading to speculation that this snake's saliva could be toxic to humans. However, this writer was firmly bitten and chewed on the thumb while handling a large female Hognosed Snake (which was undoubtedly responding to the smell of a previously handled toad) and suffered only minor pinprick wounds (and considerable humiliation). Some people might be hypersensitive to this snake's saliva, but its traditional designation as a harmless species appears fully justified. This snake rarely bites defensively, even when handled.

Hawks and snake-eating snakes are known to kill and eat Eastern Hognosed Snakes, but reports of natural predation on these slow-moving and conspicuous snakes are surprisingly rare. This snake is well-known for its exaggerated defensive display, which probably discourages many wouldbe natural predators (but, as noted below, may be less successful in confrontations with humans). An alarmed Hog-nosed Snake will raise its head and neck, slowly flick its oversized tongue in and out, and inhale deeply while flattening its head and neck into a cobralike "hood." The dark neck blotches suddenly become quite conspicuous, perhaps resembling large eyes to a predator. The snake then exhales slowly, producing a series of loud hisses, and may strike at the presumed enemy—though most often with the mouth closed. The tail may be repeatedly coiled and uncoiled, and odorous anal secretions and feces are often smeared over the snake's body.

If the snake continues to be harassed, or is physically attacked, it may then go into convulsions and show signs of extreme distress—writhing violently, dragging its everted cloaca and open mouth in the dirt, and sometimes vomiting its last meal. Eventually its writhing movements slow, and it turns upside down, lying limp with mouth open, covered in dirt and musk and feces, looking (and smelling) thoroughly disgusting and quite dead. If at this point the snake is turned right side up, however, it belies its supposed death by promptly twisting onto its back again. Once the enemy leaves (or the curious human observer withdraws to a hidden position) the snake eventually raises its head, flicks its tongue, and (if all seems quiet) flips over and goes on its way. It should be noted that there is much individual variation in defensive behavior; some individual snakes will skip portions of the "typical" display, while others go right into writhing and death feigning at first threat. Captive Hog-nosed Snakes soon cease this "bluff and death" display and become tame, but a preference for a toad diet makes this species a poor choice for captive display or study.

Reproduction and Growth: Most mating probably occurs in April or May but has also been reported in September. In June or July the female deposits a clutch of from 4 to 61 eggs in a shallow burrow in sand or soil, or under a log or rock. The thin-shelled eggs are broadly oval, sometimes nearly spherical, and range in length from 2.1 to 3.9 cm (0.8 to 1.5 in), though they expand considerably in size during incubation. Hatching typically occurs in late August or September, after an incubation of about 50 to 65 days. The newly hatched young will hiss, expand their necks, and "play dead," even before they are totally free of their eggshells.

Growth is rapid at first, then slows as the young snake approaches sexual maturity in its second or third year. A captive Eastern Hog-nosed Snake lived for eleven years, but average longevity in the wild is unknown.

Conservation: Eastern Hog-nosed Snakes are harmless to humans, but their defensive bluffing behavior gives them the appearance of being dangerous. Many local names have been applied to this snake, most of which imply that it is a venomous species (e.g., puff adder, hissing adder, sand adder, spreading viper, blowing viper, blow snake, spreadhead, etc.). It is an unfortunately safe assumption that many (perhaps most) confrontations between humans and Hog-nosed Snakes end up being fatal for the snakes. When we add in the numerous snakes killed on roads and by farm and recreational equipment, it is not surprising that their populations are declining over much of their Great Lakes range—even where their preferred sandy woodland habitats are still available. Reported local declines in toad populations in parts of the region would, if sustained over time, present an additional challenge to Hog-nosed Snake survival.

Pit Vipers and Vipers
Family Viperidae

Snakes in this family of about 190 species have a pair of hollow fangs at the front of the very short upper mouth (maxilla) bones, connected to venom glands on either side of the head. When the snake strikes, the gaping of the mouth causes the fangs to rotate forward (from a normally folded position) to stab into the target animal; powerful muscles then squeeze the venom glands, injecting venom (a greatly modified saliva) into the wound. Most viperids strike their prey and then wait until the animal dies before attempting to swallow it.

The so-called true vipers (subfamily Viperinae) are found in Europe, Asia, and Africa. All North and South American viperids are "pit vipers" (subfamily Crotalinae, also represented in Eurasia), so named because they possess heat-sensitive organs called pits; these pits are visible as an opening on each side of the head, between (and slightly lower than) the eye and nostril. Each pit contains a membrane lined with nerve cells that are extremely sensitive to infrared radiation (i.e., heat). Using these pits, the snake can detect the heat given off by a nearby endothermic ("warm-blooded") animal that may be a potential predator or prey and determine its exact location.

Species in two genera of American pit vipers (*Sistrurus* and *Crotalus*) are called rattlesnakes, with one representative of each genus occurring in the Great Lakes region. The rattle is a series of loosely connected hollow buttonlike segments on the tail tip, formed from thick scale material; when the tail is vibrated, a buzzing sound is produced that can warn away possible enemies. A new segment is added each time the snake sheds its skin, replacing older ones that break off the end. (Thus, the number of segments does not indicate the age of the snake, despite a popular belief.) All rattlesnakes are stout-bodied snakes with vertically elliptical eye pupils in bright light. *Sistrurus* (which includes the Massasauga and the Pygmy Rattlesnakes) is considered by some herpetologists to be the more primitive rattlesnake genus, in part because its members have nine large scales on the crown of the head as in most nonvenomous snakes. It was possibly ancestral to *Crotalus* (which includes all other rattlesnakes), in which the head is largely covered by numerous small, irregular scales (fig. 11).

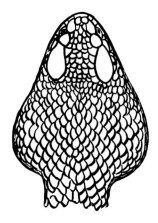

Fig. 11. Rattlesnake heads. The Massasauga (*left*) has nine enlarged scales on top of the head. The Timber Rattlesnake (*right*) has many small scales on top of the head.

Eastern Massasauga   *Sistrurus catenatus catenatus*   Venomous

Description: This is a medium-sized, thick-bodied snake with a segmented rattle on the tail tip, an opening ("pit") between eye and nostril, and elliptical ("catlike") pupils. A row of 21 to 40 large, dark brown, black-edged blotches runs down the back; these are sometimes outlined with thin white or yellowish margins. Two or three additional rows of dark spots alternate along the sides, the lowest of these contacting the ventral (belly) scutes, and there are alternating dark and light bands around the tail. The background color is gray, gray-brown, or brown. The head is widened toward the back and distinct from the neck. A dark stripe extends back from the eye, bordered below by a white stripe, and there are two dark stripes on the back of the head extending onto the neck. The belly is usually black with gray, yellowish, or white mottling. Occasional individuals are entirely black (melanistic) except for light markings on the chin, throat, and "lip." The subcaudal (undertail) scutes are undivided except for a few near the rattle. There are usually 25 (19–27) scale rows at midbody; the scales are keeled and the anal plate is single. Total adult length: 47 to 100.3 cm (18.5 to 39.5 in).

Males have relatively longer tails than females. Tail length is usually equal to or greater than 10 percent of the total length in males, but less than 10 percent of total length in females.

Eastern Massasauga

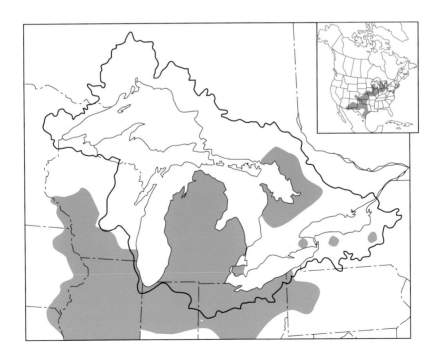

Newborn Eastern Massasaugas range in length from 18 to 25.6 cm (7 to 10 in). They are similar to adults, but with a lighter background color; the tail is yellowish below, and the rattle is represented by a single "button." The spotted pattern is present even in young Massasaugas that will be melanistic as adults. Fangs and venom glands (and the ability to use them) are present at birth.

Confusing Species: All nonvenomous snakes in the region have round (not elliptical) eye pupils in daylight, and do not have a "pit" between eye and nostril or rattles on the tail—though many species will vibrate the tail tip when alarmed. Timber Rattlesnakes have many small scales on the head between the eyes, and the tail is usually all-black; Massasaugas have enlarged head scales and banded tails.

Distribution and Status: This snake ranges from western New York, western Pennsylvania, and southern Ontario west to eastern Iowa and eastern Missouri. Western subspecies extend the species' range from western Missouri and southeast Nebraska south to the Texas Gulf Coast and west to Arizona, with isolated colonies in east-central Colorado and northern Mexico.

Eastern Massasaugas were once common across much of the lower Great Lakes basin but are now restricted to scattered and often isolated colonies. Only two populations are known to remain in the Lake Ontario drainage of New York. They are locally common in southern Ontario (e.g., on some Georgian Bay islands and the Bruce Peninsula, and scattered shoreline sites along Lake Erie and Lake St. Clair), and are uncommon and local, but widely distributed, across Michigan's Lower Peninsula; they have not been reported on the Upper Peninsula mainland but are present on Bois Blanc Island (which is part of Mackinac County in the Upper Peninsula). They occur very locally across northern Ohio and northern Indiana, including the Indiana Dunes area but are nearly (if not completely) extirpated in the Lake Michigan drainage of Illinois and Wisconsin.

The Eastern Massasauga is considered endangered, threatened, or a "special concern" species throughout its range.

Habitat and Ecology: Eastern Massasaugas are usually associated with damp lowlands, including river bottom woodlands, shrub swamps, bogs and fens, marsh borders, sedge meadows, and moist prairie. The preferred habitat is reflected in the name *massasauga,* which means "great river mouth" in the Chippewa language. Such lowland habitats are occupied from early fall into late spring (typically from late September or October into June). In early summer many Massasaugas move into adjacent well-drained uplands to spend the warmer months foraging in shrubby fields and grasslands, including pastures and hay fields. (Farmers often report seeing these snakes—and occasionally baling them up—while harvesting forage crops in summer.)

These snakes usually overwinter singly in crayfish or mammal burrows, often close to the groundwater level, and emerge in April as water levels rise. Although they swim well when necessary, they spend much time in spring basking on whatever high ground is available, such as sedge and grass clumps, muskrat and beaver lodges, or the edges of dikes and other embankments. At this time, and in fall, Massasaugas are most active during daylight hours. Later in the heat of summer their periods of activity shift to the early morning, late evening, and night. The total area utilized by a Massasauga during a year can be quite small, frequently encompassing less than 1 or 2 hectares (2.5 to 5 acres).

Small mammals make up the bulk of this snake's diet, with voles *(Microtus)* being the favorite prey, followed in frequency by deer mice *(Peromyscus),* jumping mice *(Zapus),* and shrews. Nonmammalian prey taken on occasion includes other snakes, frogs, birds, bird eggs, and insects. Young Massasaugas are particularly inclined to eat smaller snakes and may lure prey animals (especially frogs) within range by twitching their yellowish tail tips. Massasaugas usually strike and release adult rodents and shrews, then wait for the venom to immobilize the animal before swallowing it; nonthreatening prey (e.g., frogs, baby mice) may be simply seized and swallowed without envenomation.

Large snakes such as Racers are known to eat Massasaugas, and it is likely that some birds (herons, hawks) and mammals (raccoons, foxes) are able to kill them at times. Deer are said to trample these (and other) snakes, and domestic hogs, well known for their tendency to kill snakes, have been used by people to eliminate rattlesnakes from certain areas. (According to local legend, Belle Isle, now a park in the Detroit River in southeast Michigan, was cleared of a once-abundant rattlesnake fauna in the eighteenth century using this method.) There is little doubt that humans are this snake's most important enemy.

The Massasauga's first line of defense is to avoid being seen, and its earth-toned color pattern offers excellent camouflage. Most will "freeze" when approached and frequently remain undetected by people passing close by. Should a potential enemy come too close or even touch a Massasauga, it may try to flee into thick vegetation or choose to stand its ground—at which time it may vibrate its rattle as a warning (which in this species usually sounds like a high-pitched hiss or an insectlike buzz, with little carrying power). Many Massasaugas seem hesitant to strike unless actually seized or stepped on, while others are more nervous and strike out immediately at any threatening object, at times without rattling in advance.

Accidental bites to humans are rare and sometimes result from efforts to kill or handle the snakes. Despite having a potent venom, massasaugas can deliver only small amounts at a time through relatively short fangs that often fail to penetrate loose clothing and leather footwear. Curious dogs are far more frequently bitten than people and most survive the experience. Symptoms of envenomation include pain, swelling, and discoloration (due to rupturing of blood vessels) at the bite site, as well as possible systemic reactions (nausea, sweating, fainting). Massasauga bites should always receive prompt medical treatment but serious complications and fatalities are extremely rare.

Reproduction and Growth: Eastern Massasaugas mate in both spring and fall. A courting male will align his body with that of the female while rubbing his chin on her head and body; he may also twitch or jerk his body and head. At the same time he attempts to loop his tail around the female's tail and thus bring their cloacas into contact, allowing copulation to occur.

The females give birth to litters of 5 to 20 young in August and early September, usually while they are still in their drier summer habitats. The young are born enclosed in a thin membrane from which they soon emerge. They may remain near their mother for several days before dispersing. Many females reproduce only every other year.

The young snakes reach sexual maturity in their third or fourth year. Captive Massasaugas have lived over 20 years, but the normal life span in the wild is unknown.

Conservation: Populations of the little "swamp rattler" have declined rapidly over the last few decades, as its habitats have been converted to human uses, while incessant persecution has reduced their numbers even in the small pockets of remaining habitat. This snake prefers shrubby or marshy lowlands that are immediately adjacent to open uplands. Thus, conservation efforts that focus on preserving wetlands while ignoring contiguous upland will fail to preserve this species.

This rattlesnake is generally shy and unaggressive and offers little danger to reasonably cautious people willing to leave them alone. The gratuitous killing of Massasaugas encountered in their natural habitat is needless and regrettable, although their removal from the vicinity of human dwellings is justified. Ironically, Massasaugas found in residential areas are often simply seeking traditional habitats that have been lost to recent development.

Timber Rattlesnake *Crotalus horridus* VENOMOUS

Description: This large, thick-bodied snake has a prominent segmented rattle on the tail tip, an opening ("pit") between eye and nostril, and elliptical eye pupils. Background color of the head, back, and sides may be yellow, tan, brown, olive brown, or gray, whereas the tail is black with a yellowish or tan rattle. A dorsal series of irregular black or brown crossbands runs from neck to tail; these are often broken into saddlelike blotches and spots on the forward third of the body. These bands and blotches may have yellow or white borders, one scale wide. The banded pattern is less prominent in individuals with a darker background color; melanistic (all-black) specimens are occasionally found. The head is broadly triangular and distinct from the neck, with numerous small scales between the eyes. The belly may be yellowish, tan, white, or gray, often with dark gray or black speckles that become heavier towards the tail. The subcaudal (undertail) scales are undivided except for a few near the rattle. There are usually 23 (19 to 26) scale rows at midbody; the scales are keeled and the anal plate is single. Total adult length: 90 to 188 cm (35.4 to 74 in); few specimens exceed 140 cm (55 in).

The sexes are difficult to distinguish based on external characters; males are, on average, longer than females, although gravid females will appear proportionally bulkier and more robust. Males tend to have longer tails relative to body length, but there is considerable overlap in numbers of subcaudal scutes (18 to 30 in males, 13 to 26 in females).

At birth, Timber Rattlesnakes range in length from 20 to 41 cm (7.9 to 16 in); they are colored much like their parents, except that the banded pattern may be more distinct against a lighter background, and the tail is

Timber Rattlesnake. (Photo by R. D. Bartlett.)

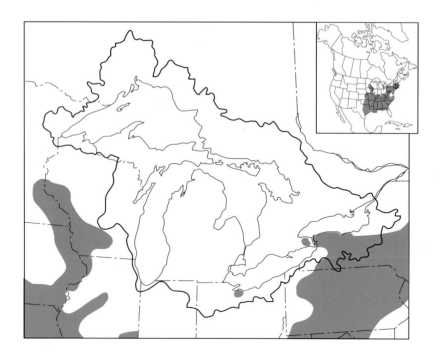

often banded instead of solid black. The rattle is represented by a single button. Some juveniles have a reddish stripe down the back. Young rattlesnakes can strike and inject venom at birth.

Confusing Species: All nonvenomous snakes in the region have round eye pupils and lack facial pits and rattles. The Eastern Massasauga has nine enlarged scales on the crown of the head, while the Timber Rattlesnake has mostly small scales on the head.

Distribution and Status: The Timber Rattlesnake ranged historically from southern Maine and New England west through southern New York, Pennsylvania, and the Ohio River valley to eastern Minnesota, Iowa, and Nebraska, south to Texas, the Gulf states, and northern Florida, and north along the Atlantic seaboard to Virginia. Within the Great Lakes basin it has been found in New York State (southern Lake Ontario drainage), southern Ontario (Niagara Glen and the western end of Lake Ontario), and northern Ohio (the Lake Erie islands and the Catawba and Marblehead Peninsulas, Ottawa County). An old record for Kalamazoo County, Michigan, is probably unverifiable; Timber Rattlesnakes have not been a part of the Michigan fauna for a very long time, if they ever were.

Populations of the Timber Rattlesnake are in decline nearly rangewide, and many states list it as a threatened or endangered species. Within the Great Lakes region this snake has probably been eliminated from Ontario (last reported in 1941) and northern Ohio (not confirmed since the late 1950s) and is rare and local in western New York State, with a few recent records for Wyoming, Livingston, and Ontario Counties.

Habitat and Ecology: Timber Rattlesnakes are found in and near forested upland habitats, particularly those associated with rock outcrops, ledges, and talus slopes. Most local populations are centered around communal winter den sites usually situated on rocky south-facing hillsides. The den itself is typically in a deep rock fissure, but mammal burrows, root systems, and other underground retreats are also used and are often shared with other snake species. Formerly hundreds of rattlesnakes could return to ancestral dens that may have been used continuously for hundreds, perhaps thousands, of years, but persecution and habitat destruction have destroyed most of these congregations.

The snakes move to their den sites in September and October, though they spend much time basking, at least on warmer, sunnier days. They retreat underground for the winter and emerge again in late April or early May. They may remain near the den area, basking but apparently not actively feeding, for several days or weeks before dispersing (usually by mid-May) into nearby woodlands for the summer. Timber Rattlesnakes are diurnal for much of the year, but hot summer weather may restrict their activities to the evening or night. When conditions are not conducive to foraging or surface basking, they remain under cover, beneath rocks, logs, other debris, or underground in rock crevices or mammal burrows. Though usually seen on the ground in fairly dry habitats, these snakes occasionally climb into shrubs or trees and also swim well when the need arises.

Male Timber Rattlesnakes tend to disperse farther and to occupy more densely wooded terrain than females. Gravid females, in particular, seem to prefer more open, sunny locations and often remain closer to their den sites during the summer. Males sometimes engage in "wrestling matches" in which they twine the forward parts of their bodies and attempt to throw and pin their opponents against the ground. The winner is determined when one combatant tires and retreats from the scene. The purpose of these aggressive encounters is unclear, but they probably serve to establish social dominance, perhaps increasing reproductive or feeding opportunities for dominant individuals.

Small to moderate-sized mammals are the preferred food of the Timber Rattlesnake, although birds, eggs, and (more rarely) amphibians and reptiles are also eaten. Common prey animals include shrews, mice, squirrels, chipmunks, and rabbits, but many others are taken opportunistically, including young woodchucks and skunks, weasels, mink, bats, quail, grouse, song birds, and other snakes. Timber Rattlesnakes will either actively forage for prey or conceal themselves in a likely spot (e.g., next to a fallen log or other natural prey corridor) and wait for prey to come to them. They can strike and then relocate prey animals at night by using their heat-sensitive facial pits.

Fully grown Timber Rattlesnakes appear to have few enemies other than humans, but their young are undoubtedly eaten by various thick-feathered and furred predators (e.g., hawks, owls, raccoons) as well as by other snakes (Racers, Milk Snakes, Black Rat Snakes). It is probable that even the adults are vulnerable when slowed or immobilized by cold temperatures. Deer and hogs are known to kill rattlesnakes, and the latter have been used purposefully by people to eliminate snakes from settled areas. Though individual temperament is variable, this species is generally shy and unaggressive. When approached by a potential enemy, a typical Timber Rattlesnake will either "freeze" and attempt to go unnoticed, or move toward the nearest cover, often rattling a warning as it goes. If cornered, it will likely coil and continuously buzz its rattle and perhaps hide its head under its body. However, they do not hesitate to strike if closely harassed or attacked.

This is a large and potentially dangerous snake, with the ability to deliver a potent venom through fangs that are long enough to penetrate clothing and standard footwear. Symptoms of envenomation can include localized pain, swelling, bleeding, and discoloration (from the breakdown of blood vessels and cells), as well as nausea, fainting, paralysis, and respiratory and circulatory difficulties. Perhaps up to a quarter of bites are "dry," with no venom being injected. Human fatalities are very rare, but prompt medical attention, including use of antivenin therapy when appropriate, is indicated for any bite from this species. The best way to avoid being bitten is to use reasonable caution when hiking in known habitat and to maintain a respectful distance from any rattlesnake that is encountered.

Reproduction and Growth: Mating probably can occur at any time during the active season but is observed most often from mid-July through September, when the snakes are concentrating near their den sites. Courtship behavior is similar to that described for the Eastern Massasauga.

Female Timber Rattlesnakes may produce young only every third or fourth year in the northern parts of the range. Gravid females seek sunnier habitats where basking can raise body temperature; feeding may be infrequent or cease completely during pregnancy. Litters of 3 to 19 young are born between late August and early October. Although there is no demonstrated period of intentional parental care, the newborn snakes are able to follow the scent trails of older snakes and presumably use this ability to locate communal overwintering sites.

Young female Timber Rattlesnakes reach sexual maturity at 6 to 11 years of age, depending on individual growth rates; males mature somewhat earlier, at ages of 4 to 7 years. A captive lived over 30 years, and many individuals survive 20 years or more in the wild.

Conservation: Despite the loss of much former habitat to agricultural and urban development, viable populations of Timber Rattlesnakes can (and in a very few places, still do) persist even in close proximity to humans by occupying wooded rocky bluffs and ridges that are poorly suited to farming or housing. Incessant killing and exploitation of this snake has led to its decline and extirpation over much of its former range. Not surprisingly, the few remaining areas that support larger numbers of Timber Rattlesnakes are fairly distant from human activity centers. Unfortunately, persistent (and often systematic) persecution and commercial collecting are threats to even the most remote populations.

Until quite recently, bounties were paid in several states (including Minnesota and Wisconsin) to encourage the extermination of rattlesnakes. Such control efforts were ill advised from a wildlife management standpoint and wasteful of taxpayer dollars. In any case, people have rarely needed a monetary incentive to destroy rattlesnakes. Demands for Timber Rattlesnakes by hobbyists, zoos, venom researchers, and the leather trade have provided reptile collectors with new financial incentives to exploit this species; as the snakes are protected or regulated in many of the states where they occur, much of the recent collecting activity is illegal.

The tendency of Timber Rattlesnakes to gather in large numbers at a few winter den sites makes them particularly vulnerable to organized efforts at destroying or exploiting them. In addition, this snake has several biological traits (such as slow maturation rates, low reproductive output, low juvenile survival, and slow population replacement rate) that reduce its ability to recover from large-scale losses of adult animals in a population. In this regard it is perhaps less like many snake species and similar to certain turtle species. For this reason, persistent or large-scale killing or collecting of rattlesnakes, even when perpetrated by only small numbers of people, can drastically reduce or eliminate local populations.

Conserving a potentially deadly animal clearly presents a challenge to wildlife managers, biologists, and environmental educators. In can be emphasized that Timber Rattlesnake prefer to avoid confrontation with humans and can utilize rugged habitats that humans often spurn, at least for wholesale development. Many people find them beautiful, a symbol of wilderness and "untamed nature," though one to be admired from a safe distance. Preserving remaining populations will require a combination of public education, careful land use planning, and the elimination of commercial exploitation and unwarranted persecution.

Marginal and Questionable Species

A number of amphibian and reptile species have ranges that closely approach the Great Lakes drainage basin or are represented therein only by isolated specimens, but they are not presently known to have breeding populations within the basin. These species are described briefly below, so that biologists and naturalists will recognize the possible significance of new discoveries. Extralimital (out-of-range) specimens of amphibians and reptiles may represent previously overlooked populations, recent natural dispersal, or intentional or accidental introductions by humans.

Eastern Hellbender *Cryptobranchus alleganiensis alleganiensis*

A very large gray, olive, or brown salamander with a broad, flattened head and body and wavy folds of skin along the sides. They are completely aquatic, though adults lack external gills. Maximum total length: 74 cm (29 in). Hellbenders inhabit fast-flowing, rocky-bedded rivers and streams, and historically range from southern New York to northern Alabama and Missouri. They occur in the upper Allegheny River and its tributaries (in northern Pennsylvania and southwestern New York); old records for the Great Lakes (Lake Erie) drainage are probably erroneous.

Eastern Hellbender. (Photo by R. W. Van Devender.)

Long-tailed Salamander

Long-tailed Salamander   *Eurycea longicauda longicauda*

This is a slender, long-tailed, yellow or orange salamander with dark spots scattered over the upper surface, irregular dark bars on the sides of the tail, and 13 or 14 costal grooves. Maximum total length: 19.7 cm (7.75 in). Long-tailed Salamanders inhabit cool, shady woodlands near small streams, springs, or seepages and are usually found under flat rocks or logs. They range from southern New York south to the Gulf Coast and west to Missouri and Oklahoma. They may enter the Great Lakes basin in extreme northeastern Ohio, but their presence in the Lake Erie drainage is in need of verification.

Plains Leopard Frog

Plains Leopard Frog *Rana blairi*

Similar to Northern Leopard Frog, but stockier and nearly always brown or tan, with a light spot on the tympanum and yellowish color on the groin. The dorsolateral folds are "broken" over the hind legs, with the posterior portions displaced toward the midback. Maximum body length: 11.1 cm (4.37 in). A prairie species that breeds in marshes, ponds, and small streams, this frog ranges from western Indiana west to eastern Colorado, eastern New Mexico, and central Texas; it approaches the Great Lakes area in northeastern Illinois (southern Cook and Will Counties) and northwestern Indiana (south of the Kankakee River).

Eastern Mud Turtle

Eastern Mud Turtle   *Kinosternon subrubrum subrubrum*

Similar to the Common Musk Turtle but has a relatively larger plastron with two flexible transverse hinges. The smooth, oval carapace is brown, olive, or black, and the robust head is usually mottled or streaked with light color. Maximum carapace length: 12.4 cm (4.87 in). A semiaquatic turtle of shallow ponds, marshes, and ditches, ranging from Long Island, New York, south to Florida and west to the Mississippi River drainage in southern Illinois and Indiana. An isolated (and nearly extirpated) population occurs south of the Kankakee River in northwestern Indiana, the species' closest approach to the Great Lakes region.

Yellow Mud Turtle. (Photo by R. W. Van Devender.)

Yellow Mud Turtle   *Kinosternon flavescens*

Similar to the Common Musk Turtle but with a relatively larger plastron with two transverse hinges. Lacks distinct yellow head stripes. Smooth, oval carapace is dark brown to olive brown with a maximum length of 14.5 cm (5.7 in). The ninth marginal scute on each side (counting from the front of the carapace) is distinctly higher than previous marginals; this is not true in the Eastern Mud Turtle. This turtle feeds in shallow, often temporary, waters and often wanders or burrows on land. It ranges from Nebraska south into northern Mexico. A disjunct population in north-western Illinois and adjacent Iowa and Missouri is recognized by some herpetologists as a distinct subspecies, the Illinois Mud Turtle, *Kinosternon flavescens spooneri*. One specimen is known from the Illinois Dunes area (Lake County, Illinois), but evidence of a breeding population in the Great Lakes region is presently lacking.

Ornate Box Turtle

Ornate Box Turtle   *Terrapene ornata ornata*

This is a small land turtle with a domed carapace and hinged plastron. It is similar to the Eastern Box Turtle but differs in having a slightly flattened, unkeeled carapace that is dark brown or black with narrow, radiating yellow lines on each scute. The large plastron is also conspicuously marked with light lines and streaks. Maximum carapace length: 15.4 cm (6.1 in). This turtle typically inhabits sandy grasslands and open savannas. It approaches the Great Lakes region in relict prairie in northwestern Indiana but apparently does not occur north of the Kankakee River; its numbers in Indiana have greatly declined in recent years, due mostly to land use changes resulting from agricultural development.

False Map Turtle

False Map Turtle   *Graptemys pseudogeographica*

This medium-sized turtle is sometimes called "sawback" due to the distinct, pointed or knobby vertebral keel on the midline of its brown or olive carapace. The dark legs, head, and neck have numerous yellow stripes; two upper head stripes usually angle downward to form a bar, crescent, or blotch behind each eye. Maximum carapace length: 27.7 cm (10.9 in); females grow larger than males. Compare to Common Map Turtle. This turtle inhabits larger rivers and adjacent sloughs, and is often seen basking but is wary and difficult to approach. They range from the Dakotas, eastern Minnesota, and central Wisconsin south to the Gulf Coast. There is a disjunct population in southern Ohio, and scattered extralimital specimens have been found in eastern Wisconsin (Green Bay, Oconto County), northern Indiana (Kankakee River, St. Joseph County), southern Michigan (Grand River, Ingham County), and probably elsewhere. Hatchling False Map Turtles were once collected and sold in the pet trade, along with greater numbers of the Red-eared Slider; thus, escaped pets may account for at least some out-of-range sightings.

Northern Prairie Skink. (Photo by R. W. Van Devender.)

Northern Prairie Skink *Eumeces septentrionalis*

This is a smooth-scaled, olive brown or tan lizard with six or eight dark stripes down the back and sides. The two dark stripes nearest the midline of the back are very narrow (occasionally broken or missing), and there are one or two broad dark stripes on each side, extending onto the tail. Juveniles have metallic blue-black tails; adult males in the breeding season have reddish orange on the sides of the head. Maximum total length: 22.4 cm (8.8 in). Compare to Five-lined Skink. A lizard of open, sandy grasslands, savannas, and pines barrens, often found along stream or riverbanks or road embankments. This skink ranges from northern Minnesota south to central Kansas, with a disjunct population in southern Manitoba. It closely approaches the Lake Superior drainage basin in northwestern Wisconsin (Douglas and Bayfield Counties).

Graham's Crayfish Snake. (Photo by R. W. Van Devender.)

Graham's Crayfish Snake   *Regina grahamii*

This olive or brown snake is very similar to the Queen Snake, but the yellow stripe on each side is on scale rows 1, 2, and 3, and its yellowish belly is either unmarked or has a single medial dark stripe or series of dots (most evident on the posterior part of the belly). The body scales are keeled and the anal plate is divided. Maximum total length: 119.4 (47 in); rarely exceeds 71 cm (28 in). A largely aquatic snake of marshes, ponds, sloughs, and slow-moving streams and rivers. It ranges from central Illinois and Iowa south through Kansas and Oklahoma to the Texas and Louisiana coast, and northward along the Mississippi drainage to southern Missouri. At some point this snake apparently followed the Illinois River system eastward and established a presence in the Chicago area. Local, isolated populations occur in Cook and Will Counties (Illinois); at least one specimen is also known from Lake County.

Bullsnake

Bullsnake *Pituophis catenifer sayi*

This is a large, yellow or light brown snake with a strong dorsal pattern of dark squarish blotches and spots that are often black near the head and tail and brownish at midbody. The snout is rather pointed, the labial scales are marked with black bars, and there is a black band in front of the eyes and another slanting from each eye to the back of the mouth. The body scales are keeled, and the anal plate is single. Maximum total length: 254 cm (100 in). It is a snake of sandy prairie, grassland, savannas, and pastures, and considered beneficial to agriculture due to rodent-eating habits. This subspecies ranges from western Illinois, Wisconsin and southern Minnesota, west through the Great Plains from southern Alberta to northern Mexico. Like the Ornate Box Turtle, this species has an isolated population in the remnant prairie of northeastern Illinois and northwestern Indiana; recent specimens from Lake and Porter Counties (Indiana) suggest that the Bullsnake has recently extended its range (or was introduced) north of the Kankakee River and into the Great Lakes basin.

Resources

Bibliography and Information Sources

Adler, K. 1968. Turtles from archeological sites in the Great Lakes region. *Michigan Archaeologist* 14 (3–4): 147–63.

———. 1970. The influence of prehistoric man on the distribution of the box turtle. *Annals of the Carnegie Mus.* 41: 263–80.

Banks, R. C., R. W. McDiarmid, and A. L. Gardner, eds. 1987. *Checklist of the Vertebrates of the United States, the U.S. Territories, and Canada.* Resource Publ. 166. Washington, D.C.: U.S. Fish and Wildlife Service.

Bishop, C. A., and K. E. Pettit, eds. 1992. *Declines in Canadian amphibian populations: Designing a national monitoring strategy.* Occ. Pap. No. 76. Ottawa: Canadian Wildlife Service.

Bishop, S. C. 1941. *The salamanders of New York.* New York State Mus. Bull. No. 324. Albany.

Bishop, S. C. 1943. *Handbook of Salamanders.* Ithaca, N.Y.: Cornell Univ. Press.

Boundy, J. 1995. Maximum lengths of North American snakes. *Bulletin of the Chicago Herpet. Soc.* 30 (6): 109–22.

Breckinridge, W. J. 1944. *Reptiles and Amphibians of Minnesota.* Minneapolis: Univ. Minnesota Press.

Breden, F. 1988. Natural history and ecology of Fowler's Toad, *Bufo woodhousei fowleri* (Amphibia, Bufonidae), in the Indiana Dunes National Lakeshore. *Fieldiana (Zoology)* 49:1–16.

Brooks, R. J., D. A. Galbraith, E. G. Nancekivell, and C. A. Bishop. 1988. Developing management guidelines for snapping turtles. In R. C. Szaro, K. E. Severson, and D. R. Patton, eds., *Management of amphibians, reptiles, and small mammals in North America,* 174–79. USDA Forest Service, Gen. Tech. Rep. RM-166.

Brown, W. S. 1993. *Biology, status, and management of the Timber Rattlesnake (Crotalus horridus): A guide for conservation.* Herpet. Circular No. 22. Soc. Study Amph. and Rept.

Burton, T. M., and G. E. Likens. 1975. Salamander populations and biomass in the Hubbard Brook Experimental Forest, New Hampshire. *Copeia* 1975: 541–46.

Bury, R. B. 1979. *Review of the ecology and conservation of the bog turtle, Clemmys muhlenbergii.* U.S. Dept. of the Interior. Fish and Wildlife Service. Special Sci. Report—Wildlife No. 219.

Carr, A. F. 1952. *Handbook of Turtles.* Ithaca, N.Y.: Cornell Univ. Press.

Casper, G. S. 1996. *Geographic Distributions of the Amphibians and Reptiles of Wisconsin.* Milwaukee Public Museum.

Cleland, C. E. 1966. *The prehistoric animal ecology and ethnozoology of the upper Great Lakes Region.* Univ. of Michigan, Museum of Anthropology. Anthro. Pap. No. 29.

Collins, J. T. 1991. Viewpoint: A new taxonomic arrangement for some North American amphibians and reptiles. *Herpet. Review* 22 (2): 42–43.

Collins, J. T. 1993. *Amphibians and Reptiles in Kansas.* 3d ed. Lawrence: Univ. Kansas Mus. Nat. Hist.

Conant, R. 1938. *The Reptiles of Ohio.* Notre Dame, Ind.: Univ. Notre Dame Press. Reprint *Amer. Midl. Nat.* 20 (1): 1–200.

———. 1951. *The Reptiles of Ohio: Revisionary Addenda.* Notre Dame, Ind.: Univ. Notre Dame Press. Reprint. *Amer. Midl. Nat.* 20 (1): 200–284.

Conant, R., and J. T. Collins. 1991. *A Field Guide to Reptiles and Amphibians: Eastern and Central North America.* 3d. ed. Boston: Houghton Mifflin.

Congdon, J. D., A. E. Dunham, and R. C. van Loben Sels. 1993. Delayed sexual maturity and demographics of Blanding's Turtles *(Emydoidea blandingii):* Implications for conservation and management of long-lived organisms. *Conserv. Biol.* 7 (4): 826–33.

———. 1994. Demographics of Common Snapping Turtles: Implications for conservation and management of long-lived organisms. *Amer. Zool.* 34: 397–408.

Cook, F. R. 1984. *Introduction to Canadian Amphibians and Reptiles.* Ottawa: National Mus. Nat. Sciences.

Curtiss, J. T. 1959. *The Vegetation of Wisconsin.* Madison: Univ. Wisconsin Press.

Daniel, G., and J. Sullivan. 1981. *A Sierra Club Naturalist's Guide: The North Woods of Michigan, Wisconsin, Minnesota, and Southern Ontario.* San Francisco: Sierra Club Books.

Denny, G. L. 1990a. *Ohio's Amphibians.* Ohio Dept. Nat. Res.

———. 1990b. *Ohio's Reptiles.* Ohio Dept. Nat. Res.

Dickinson, W. E. 1949. *Lizards and Snakes of Wisconsin.* Pop. Sci. Handbook Ser. No. 2. Milwaukee Public Mus.

Duellman, W. E., and L. Trueb. 1986. *Biology of Amphibians.* New York: McGraw-Hill.

Ernst, C. H., and R. W. Barbour. 1989. *Snakes of Eastern North America.* Fairfax, Va.: George Mason Univ. Press.

Ernst, C. H., J. E. Lovich, and R. W. Barbour. 1994. *Turtles of the United States and Canada.* Washington, D.C.: Smithsonian Inst. Press.

Evers, D. C., ed. 1994. *Endangered and Threatened Wildlife of Michigan.* Ann Arbor: Univ. Michigan Press.

Ewert, M. A., D. R. Jackson, and C. E. Nelson. 1994. Patterns of temperature-dependent sex determination in turtles. *J. Exper. Zool.* 270: 3–15.

Feder, M. E., and W. W. Burggren. 1992. *Environmental Physiology of the Amphibians.* Chicago: Univ. Chicago Press.

Froom, B. 1972. *The Snakes of Canada.* Toronto: McClelland and Stewart.

———. 1976. *The Turtles of Canada.* Toronto: McClelland and Stewart.

Gibbons, J. W., ed. 1990. *Life History and Ecology of the Slider Turtle.* Washington, D.C.: Smithsonian Inst. Press.

Green, N. B., and T. K. Pauley. 1987. *Amphibians and Reptiles in West Virginia.* Pittsburgh: Univ. Pittsburgh Press.

Halliday, T. R., and K. Adler, eds. 1986. *The Encyclopedia of Reptiles and Amphibians.* New York: Facts on File.

Harding, J. H., and J. A. Holman. 1990. *Michigan Turtles and Lizards: A Field Guide and Pocket Reference.* Publ. E-2234. East Lansing: Michigan State Univ. Coop. Extension Serv.

———. 1992. *Michigan Frogs, Toads, and Salamanders: A Field Guide and Pocket Reference.* Publ. E-2350. East Lansing: Michigan State Univ. Coop. Extension Serv.

Harless, M., and H. Morlock. 1979. *Turtles: Perspectives and Research.* New York: John Wiley and Sons.

Heyer, W. R., M. A. Donnelly, R. W. McDiarmid, L. C. Hayek, and M. S. Foster, eds. 1994. *Measuring and Monitoring Biological Diversity: Standard Methods for Amphibians.* Washington, D.C.: Smithsonian Inst. Press.

Holman, J. A. 1995a. *Ancient Life of the Great Lakes Basin.* Ann Arbor: Univ. Michigan Press.

———. 1995b. *Pleistocene Amphibians and Reptiles in North America.* New York: Oxford Univ. Press.

Holman, J. A., J. H. Harding, M. M. Hensley, and G. R. Dudderar. 1989. *Michigan Snakes: A Field Guide and Pocket Reference.* Publ. E-2000. East Lansing: Michigan State Univ. Coop. Extension Serv.

Hunter, M. L., J. Albright, and J. Arbuckle, eds. 1992. *The Amphibians and Reptiles of Maine.* Orono: Maine Agricul. Exp. Station. Bull. 838.

Johnson, B. 1989. *Familiar Amphibians and Reptiles of Ontario.* Toronto: Natural Heritage/Natural History.

Johnson, B. K., and J. L. Christiansen. 1976. The food and food habits of Blanchard's Cricket Frog, *Acris crepitans blanchardi,* in Iowa. *J. Herpet.* 10 (2): 63–74.

Karns, D. R. 1986. *Field Herpetology: Methods for the Study of Amphibians and Reptiles in Minnesota.* Occ. Pap. No. 18. J. F. Bell Mus. Nat. Hist., Univ. Minnesota.

Kaufmann, J. H. 1992. The social behavior of wood turtles, *Clemmys insculpta,* in central Pennsylvania. *Herpet. Monographs* 6:1–25.

Klemens, M. W. 1993. *Amphibians and Reptiles of Connecticut and Adjacent Regions*. Bull. 112. Hartford: State Geol. and Nat. Hist. Survey of Connecticut.

Kraus, F., and G. W. Schuett. 1982. A herpetofaunal survey of the coastal zone of northwest Ohio. *Cleveland Mus. Nat. Hist.:* Kirtlandia 36.

Kurta, A. 1995. *Mammals of the Great Lakes Region*. Ann Arbor: Univ. Michigan Press.

Levell, J. P. 1995. *A Field Guide to Reptiles and the Law*. Excelsior, Minn.: Serpent's Tale Nat. Hist. Book Dist.

Logier, E. B. S. 1952. *The Frogs, Toads, and Salamanders of Eastern Canada*. Toronto: Clark, Irwin.

———. 1958. *The Snakes of Ontario*. Univ. Toronto Press.

Martin, P. S., and R. G. Klein, eds. 1984. *Quaternary Extinctions: A Prehistoric Revolution*. Tucson: Univ. Arizona Press.

Mattison, C. 1986. *Snakes of the World*. New York: Facts on File.

———. 1987. *Frogs and Toads of the World*. New York: Facts on File.

———. 1989. *Lizards of the World*. New York: Facts on File.

———. 1992. *The Care of Reptiles and Amphibians in Captivity*. 3d ed. New York: Sterling Publ.

McCoy, C. J. 1982. *Amphibians and Reptiles in Pennsylvania: Checklist, Bibliography, and Atlas of Distribution*. Spec. Publ. No. 6. Pittsburgh: Carnegie Mus. Nat. Hist.

Meylan, P. A. 1987. The phylogenetic relationships of soft-shelled turtles (Family Trionychidae). *Bull. Amer. Mus. Nat. Hist.* 186: 1–101.

Minton, S. A., Jr. 1972. *Amphibians and Reptiles of Indiana*. Indianapolis: Indiana Academy of Science.

Moriarty, J. J. 1987. *Distribution Maps for Reptiles and Amphibians of Minnesota*. Minneapolis: Minnesota Herpet. Soc.

Moriarty, J. J., and D. G. Jones. 1988. *An Annotated Bibliography of Minnesota Herpetology, 1900–1985*. J. F. Bell Mus. Nat. Hist., Univ. Minn.

Morris, M. A., R. S. Funk, and P. W. Smith. 1983. An annotated bibliography of the Illinois herpetological literature, 1960–1980, and an updated checklist of species of the state. *Illinois Nat. Hist. Survey Bull.* (Champaign) 33, art. 2: 123–37.

Murphy, J. B., K. Adler, and J. T. Collins. 1994. *Captive Management and Conservation of Amphibians and Reptiles*. Soc. Study Amph. Rept.

Obst, F. J. 1986. *Turtles, Tortoises, and Terrapins*. New York: St. Martin's Press.

Oldfield, B., and J. J. Moriarty. 1994. *Amphibians and Reptiles Native to Minnesota*. Minneapolis: Univ. Minnesota Press.

Parker, H. W., and A. G. C. Grandison. 1977. *Snakes—A Natural History*. Ithaca, N.Y.: Cornell Univ. Press; London: British Mus.—Nat. Hist.

Pentecost, E. D., and R. C. Vogt. 1976. *Environmental Status of the Lake Michigan Basin*. Vol. 16: *Amphibians and Reptiles of the Lake Michigan Drainage Basin*. Argonne, Ill.: Argonne Nat. Lab.

Pfingsten, R. A., and F. L. Downs, eds. 1989. Salamanders of Ohio. *Bull. Ohio Biol. Survey* 7 (2).

Pope, C. H. 1947. *Amphibians and Reptiles of the Chicago Area*. Chicago: Chicago Nat. Hist. Mus. Press.

Rossman, D. A., N. B. Ford, and R. A. Seigel. 1996. *The Garter Snakes: Evolution and Ecology*. Norman: Univ. of Oklahoma Press.

Ruthven, A. G., C. Thompson, and H. T. Gaige. 1928. *The Herpetology of Michigan*. Handbook Ser. No. 3. Ann Arbor: Museums, Univ. Michigan.

Schmidt, K. P. 1938. Herpetological evidence for the postglacial eastward extension of the steppe in North America. *Ecology* 19 (3): 396–407.

Seigel, R. A., and J. T. Collins, eds. 1993. *Snakes: Ecology and Behavior*. New York: McGraw-Hill.

Shaffer, L. L. 1991. *Pennsylvania Amphibians and Reptiles*. Harrisburg: Penn. Fish Comm.

Smith, H. M. 1946. *Handbook of Lizards: Lizards of the United States and Canada*. Ithaca, N.Y.: Cornell Univ. Press.

———. 1978. *A Guide to Field Identification: Amphibians of North America*. New York: Golden Press.

———. 1982. *A Guide to Field Identification: Reptiles of North America*. New York: Golden Press.

Smith, P. W. 1957. An analysis of post-Wisconsin biogeography of the prairie peninsula region based on distributional phenomena among terrestrial vertebrate populations. *Ecology* 38 (2): 205–18.

———. 1961. The amphibians and reptiles of Illinois. *Illinois Nat. Hist. Survey Bull.* (Urbana) 28, art. 1.

Snider, A. T., and J. K. Bowler. 1992. *Longevity of Reptiles and Amphibians in North American Collections*. 2d ed. Herpet. Circular No. 21. Soc. Study Amph. and Rept.

Sommers, L. M., ed. 1977. *Atlas of Michigan*. East Lansing: Michigan State Univ. Press.

Stearns, F., and N. Kobriger. 1975. *Environmental status of the Lake Michigan region*. Vol. 10: *Vegetation of the Lake Michigan Drainage Basin*. Argonne, Ill.: Argonne Nat. Lab.

Stebbins, R. C., and N. W. Cohen. 1995. *A Natural History of Amphibians*. Princeton: Princeton Univ. Press.

Sullivan, B. K., K. B. Malmos, and M. F. Given. 1996. Systematics of the *Bufo woodhousii* complex (Anura: Bufonidae): advertisement call variation. *Copeia* 1996 (2):274–80.

Tyning, T. F. 1990. *Stokes Nature Guides: A Guide to Amphibians and Reptiles.* Boston: Little, Brown.

U.S. Department of Agriculture. Forest Service. 1988. *Management of Amphibians, Reptiles, and Small Mammals in North America: Proceedings of the Symposium.* Gen. Tech. Report RM-166. Fort Collins, Colo.

Vogt, R. C. 1981. *Natural History of Amphibians and Reptiles of Wisconsin.* Milwaukee: Milwaukee Public Mus.

Watermolen, D. J. 1995. *A Key to the Eggs of Wisconsin's Amphibians.* Research Rep. 165. Wisconsin Dept. Nat. Res.

Watermolen, D. J. and H. Gilbertson. 1996. *Key for the Identification of Wisconsin's Larval Amphibians.* Wisconsin Endangered Resources Report 109. Madison: Wisconsin Dept. Nat. Res.

Williams, K. L. 1988. *Systematics and Natural History of the American Milksnake, Lampropeltis triangulum.* 2d ed. Milwaukee: Milwaukee Public Mus.

Wilsmann, L. A., and M. A. Sellers. 1988. *Clonophis kirtlandii* rangewide survey. Final report (unpubl.) to U.S. Fish and Wildlife Service, Region 3. Office of Endangered Species. Twin Cities, Minnesota.

Wright, A. H., and A. A. Wright. 1949. *Handbook of Frogs and Toads of the United States and Canada.* Ithaca, N.Y.: Comstock Publ.

———. 1957. *Handbook of Snakes of the United States and Canada.* 2 vols. Ithaca, N.Y.: Cornell Univ. Press.

Wright, H. E., Jr., ed. 1983. *Late-Quaternary Environments of the United States. Vol. 2: The Holocene.* Minneapolis: Univ. Minnesota Press.

Wright, H. E., Jr., and S. C. Porter, eds. 1983. *Late-Quaternary Environments of the United States. Vol. 1: The Late Pleistocene.* Minneapolis: Univ. Minnesota Press.

Recordings of Frog and Toad Vocalizations

Bogert, C. M. 1958. *Sounds of North American Frogs: The Biological Significance of Voice in Frogs.* New York: Folkways Records. Distributed by Rounder Records, Cambridge, Massachusetts, and Smithsonian Folkways Records, Rockville, Maryland. (92 calls of 50 species, with informative booklet.)

Elliot, L. 1992. *The Calls of Frogs and Toads: Eastern and Central North America.* Post Mills, Vt.: Chelsea Green Publ. (42 species, with cassette and booklet.)

Kellogg, P. P., A. A. Allen, and T. Wiewandt. 1982. *Voices of the Night: The Calls of the Frogs and Toads of Eastern North America.* Ithaca, N.Y.: Library of Natural Sounds, Cornell Laboratory of Ornithology. (36 species, record or cassette.)

Herpetological Organizations

National/International

Note: Addresses for membership or correspondence for these organizations change frequently but can be obtained by consulting their recent publications or by contacting the information desks in most public and college libraries.

Herpetologist's League
    Publications: *Herpetologica; Herpetological Monographs*
Society for the Study of Amphibians and Reptiles
    Publications: *Journal of Herpetology; Herpetological Review; Catalogue of American Amphibians and Reptiles, Contributions to Herpetology, Facsimile Reprints in Herpetology, Herpetological Circulars, Herpetological Conservation*
American Society of Ichthyologists and Herpetologists
    Publication: *Copeia*

Regional

There are a number of smaller, regional herpetological societies in the Great Lakes area. Traditionally, these local societies have largely focused on captive husbandry and breeding of amphibians and reptiles, but some groups place considerable emphasis on field studies and surveys and on conservation issues. Information on contacting or joining these local groups can often be obtained through zoological parks, nature centers, or libraries. The two listed below have larger, broader-based memberships and particularly notable publications.

Chicago Herpetological Society
    Publication: *Bulletin of the Chicago Herpetological Society*
    Correspondence: 2060 North Clark Street
        Chicago, IL 60614 USA
Northern Ohio Association of Herpetologists
    Publications: *Notes from NOAH; Journal of the Northern Ohio Association of Herpetologists*
    Correspondence: Department of Biology
        Case Western Reserve University
        Cleveland, OH 44106 USA

State and Provincial Regulatory Agencies

Contact these agencies for information on laws and regulations concerning amphibians and reptiles in their respective jurisdictions.

Illinois

Illinois Department of Conservation
Lincoln Tower Plaza
524 S. Second Street
Springfield, IL 62701
(217) 782-6302

Indiana

Indiana Division of Fish and Wildlife
Nongame Wildlife Program
402 W. Washington Street
Room 273-W
Indianapolis, IN 46204-2748
(317) 232-4080

Michigan

Michigan Department of Natural Resources
Fisheries Division
Box 30446
Lansing, MI 48909
(517) 373-1280

Minnesota

Minnesota Department of Natural Resources
500 Lafayette Road
St. Paul, MN 55155
(612) 296-6157

New York

New York State Department of Environmental Conservation
Division of Fish and Wildlife
50 Wolf Road
Albany, NY 12233
(518) 457-5691

or:
New York State Department of Environmental Conservation
Wildlife Resources Center
Endangered Species Unit
Delmar, NY 12054-9767
(518) 439-7635

Ohio

Ohio Department of Natural Resources
Division of Wildlife
1840 Belcher Drive
Columbus, OH 43224-1329
(614) 265-6300

Ontario

Ontario Ministry of Natural Resources
Natural Heritage Information Center
P.O. Box 7000
Peterborough, Ontario K9J 8M5 Canada

Pennsylvania

Pennsylvania Fish Commission
P.O. Box 1673
Harrisburg, PA 17105
(717) 787-4250

Wisconsin

Wisconsin Department of Natural Resources
P.O. Box 7921
Madison, WI 53707
(608) 266-7012 or
(608) 267-0849 (Bureau of Endangered Resources)

Glossary

Note that the definitions given are based on usage in this book and may not include all possible meanings of these words or terms.

Aberrant: Deviating from the normal form or coloration of a species.

Aestivation: A state of dormancy or inactivity during hot or dry weather. Sometimes spelled *estivation*.

Algae: Primitive, mostly aquatic, one-celled or colonial plants that lack true stems, roots, and leaves.

Amnion: A membrane that forms a fluid-filled sac surrounding the embryo in reptiles, birds, and mammals. These three vertebrate groups thus form a larger natural group, the *amniotes*.

Amplexus: A reproductive behavior in frogs and toads in which the male grasps the female's body from above with his forelegs. From this position the male can fertilize the female's eggs externally as they are laid.

Anal plate: The enlarged scale that precedes and partly covers the vent (anal or cloacal opening) in snakes; depending on species, it can be single (entire) or divided into two parts.

Annuli: The concentric ridges ("growth rings") on the scutes of certain turtles that are formed during periods of growth and separated by indentations indicating periods of little or no growth. In some Great Lakes species, the annuli (singular = *annulus*) may be used to estimate the age, or at least a minimum age, of a specimen.

Anterior: Toward the front (head) of an animal.

Anuran: A frog or toad.

Aquatic: Living in water.

Arboreal: Living in or climbing trees.

Arthropod: A member of the phylum of invertebrate animals with jointed legs; includes the insects, spiders, crustaceans, and other groups.

Band: A marking or contrasting strip of color that goes across an animal's body, from side to side.

Bar: A short, contrasting stripe or band.

Barbel: A fleshy, often pointed projection of skin on the chin, throat, or neck of some turtles.

Blotch: An irregular large spot or patch of color contrasting with the background color.

Calorie: A unit used to measure heat energy, especially the energy available in food after digestion.

Carapace: The upper part of a turtle's shell.

Carnivore: An animal that eats other animals.

Carrion: The remains of a dead animal.

Caruncle: A temporary horny toothlike structure on the snout of a hatchling turtle; it may help the hatchling slice or break the eggshell during hatching.

Caudal: Referring to the tail (e.g., *caudal scutes,* the scales under a snake's tail).

Centimeter: A metric measure of length, equal to 0.01 meter, or about 0.39 inch. (There are 2.54 cm per inch.)

Chromosomes: Structures in each body cell composed of hereditary material (genes). Most sexually reproducing animals have two sets of chromosomes per cell (the diploid, or 2N, number), one derived from the father and the other from the mother.

Cirri (singular = *cirrus*): Downward projections of the upper lip, extending from the nostrils, in some plethodontid salamanders. They serve to extend the naso-labial groove and are especially prominent in mature males of certain species.

Cloaca: An internal chamber in amphibians, reptiles, and birds that receives and discharges both reproductive materials and body waste products. It opens to the outside at the vent, or anus.

Clutch: A complement of eggs in a nest.

Colony: A small, local population of an animal species, usually separated from other populations of the same species.

Concave: Curved inward; bowl-like.

Convex: Curved outward.

Costal grooves: Vertical grooves or creases along the sides of some salamanders that correspond to the positions of ribs; numbers vary between species and are thus useful in identification.

Cryptic: Tending to remain concealed; inconspicuous; camouflaged.

Dermal: Growing on, or originating in, the skin.

Disjunct: Separated from the main range of the species.

Diurnal: Active in the daytime.

Dorsal: Referring to the upper surface or back.

Dorsolateral fold (= *dorsolateral ridge*): A ridge of glandular skin extending backward from the eye along the lower back in some frogs (esp. genus *Rana*).

Ecdysis: The shedding of the outer layer of skin.

Ecotone: An edge or transitional area between two habitat types.

Ectotherm: An animal that obtains most of its body heat from the surrounding environment (e.g., amphibians, reptiles).

Elliptical: Oval in shape.

Endotherm: An animal that generates much of its body heat internally (e.g., birds and mammals).

Extirpated: Extinct within a localized area or a portion of a species' range; use of this term often implies a local extinction caused by human activities.

Extralimital: Occurring outside of a species' accepted or previously known range.

Gelatinous: Jellylike.

Globular: Rounded like a ball; spherical.

Granular: Appearing like small bumps or grains.

Gravid: Carrying mature eggs or embryos in the body; i.e., pregnant.

Habitat: Where an animal lives. An animal's habitat is largely defined by the vegetation and physical characteristics of the area it inhabits.

Hectare: A metric measure of land area, equal to 10,000 square meters or about 2.47 acres.

Hemipenes: The paired copulatory organs in male lizards and snakes.

Herbivore: An animal that feeds largely on plants and plant products.

Herpetofauna: The amphibians and reptiles occurring in a defined geographical area.

Herpetology: The scientific study of amphibians and reptiles.

Hibernaculum: The place where an animal hibernates in winter.

Hibernation: An extended period of dormancy or inactivity during the coldest part of the year. Some herpetologists use the word *brumation* for winter dormancy in amphibians and reptiles.

Hinge: A flexible connection between sections of a turtle's plastron, usually allowing partial or complete closure of the shell.

Home range: The area in which an animal spends most or all of its time.

Hybrid: Offspring resulting from the mating of two different species.

Intergrade: An animal that is genetically and/or morphologically intermediate between two or more races or subspecies.

Invertebrate: An animal that does not have an internal skeleton of true bone or cartilage (e.g., insects, spiders, mollusks, worms, etc.).

Juvenile: An immature animal, especially one that has grown beyond the newborn or hatchling stage (or, in amphibians, one that has metamorphosed but is not yet sexually mature).

Keel: A raised ridge. Examples include the keeled scales of some snakes and the central keel on the carapace of certain turtle species.

Keratin: A tough, fibrous protein material that makes up the horny (keratinous) outer covering of reptilian scales and claws as well as mammalian hair and bird's feathers.

Labial: Referring to the lips; such as the *labial scales* around the mouths of lizards and snakes.

Larva (plural = *larvae*):The immature aquatic (usually gilled) form of an amphibian (after hatching and prior to metamorphosis to the adult form); the larvae of frogs and toads are called "tadpoles."

Lateral: Referring to the side or sides of an animal.

Littoral: Pertaining to a shoreline of a lake, river, or other water body.

Medial: Occurring at the middle or midline.

Melanistic: Refers to an animal that is darker in color than normal for its species (sometimes entirely black) due to an abundance of the pigment melanin.

Mental gland: A glandular area under the chin of some male salamanders, sometimes visible as a conspicuous bump.

Metamorphosis: The physical changes that occur when a larval amphibian (e.g., a tadpole) transforms into the adult form. (Note that most newly transformed amphibians are not yet sexually mature.)

Meter: A metric measure of length equal to 100 centimeters, or about 39.37 inches (3.28 feet).

Mollusk: A phylum of invertebrate animals that includes the snails, slugs, clams, and squids.

Morphological: Referring to the form, structure, or appearance of an animal.

Mortality: A measurement of deaths in a population; death rate.

Mottled: Covered with irregular spots or streaks of different colors or shades of colors.

Naso-labial groove: A groove or slit running from the nostril to the upper lip in metamorphosed plethodontid (lungless) salamanders.

Neotenic: Attaining sexual maturity and breeding while retaining larval characteristics (a condition seen in certain salamander species).

Niche: An animal's function and role in the ecosystem, often largely defined by what and how it eats.

Nocturnal: Active at night.

Omnivore: An animal that eats both plants and other animals.

Organism: A living thing, such as an animal or plant.

Oviparous: Egg-laying.

Parotoid glands: The large wartlike glandular lumps located behind the eyes in toads and some salamanders.

pH: In chemistry, a measurement of acidity and alkalinity, with a range from 0 to 14. A pH of 7.0 is neutral; above this point is increasingly alkaline, below is increasingly acid.

Pheromone: A chemical substance given off by an animal that can influence the behavior or physical condition of another individual of its own species.

Plankton: The community of very tiny (usually microscopic) plants and animals that moves or floats through the water column in a pond, lake, or other body of water.

Plastron: The bottom part of a turtle's shell.

Pleistocene: A geological time period beginning about 1.8 million years ago and ending 10,000 years ago, during which continental glaciers intermittently advanced and retreated over portions of North America and Eurasia.

Population: All individuals of a species living in a certain (defined) area at a certain point in time.

Posterior: Toward the back (tail end) of an animal.

Predator: An animal that kills and eats other animals.

Prey: An animal that is hunted or eaten by a predator; also used as verb meaning "to attack, kill, and eat" (another animal).

Recruitment: The addition of new individuals to an animal population by natural reproduction or immigration.

Relict population: A surviving population of animals that is isolated from the main portion of the species' range after all adjacent populations of the same species have disappeared.

Reticulate: A netlike pattern of criss-crossing lines or streaks.

Savanna: A habitat type intermediate between forest and prairie; a grassland with a few scattered trees or isolated small woodlands.

Scute: A large scale (e.g., the scutes on a turtle's shell); sometimes these scutes are called *plates* or *laminae*.

Sedimentary rock: Rocks that formed from the settling or consolidation of sediments such as soil, sand, mud, organic matter, or salts.

Serrated: Having pointed projections or indentations along the edge.

Spermatophore: A cylindrical or cone-shaped gelatinous mass capped with sperm, discharged from the cloaca of the male of some salamander species during or after courtship.

Spherical: Rounded in shape, like a ball or globe.

Spiracle: In a tadpole, the funnel-like opening that connects the opercular (gill) chamber to the outside.

Stripe: A narrow strip of color that usually occurs in the long dimension of part of an animal's body (e.g., head to tail, hip to knee, etc.).

Tadpole: The aquatic larval stage of a frog or toad (from Middle English *taddepol,* meaning "toad head"); occasionally called "polliwog" (also from Middle English, *polwygle,* meaning a "wiggling head").

Terminal: On the end; the tip.

Terrestrial: Living primarily on land.

Territory: An area that is defended by an animal against others of its own species (often part of, but not necessarily equivalent to, the animal's home range).

Tetraploid: An individual (or species) having four sets of chromosomes in each body cell (4N), or twice the number of chromosomes as its parents (or its ancestral species). See *chromosome.*

Tetrapod: A four-footed animal, or an animal that directly descended from four-footed animals; i.e., amphibians, reptiles, birds, and mammals.

Tibia: the portion of the leg between the knee and the ankle; also, one of two bones in the lower leg of most tetrapods.

Tortoise: Any member of the family Testudinidae, a family of turtles adapted for a terrestrial lifestyle. (North American usage; in Britain and Australia this word is often used for freshwater turtles.)

Trill: A type of anuran call in which a series of notes is repeated very rapidly in succession.

Triploid: An animal with three sets of chromosomes in each body cell (3N). See *chromosome.*

Tympanum: The rounded eardrum visible behind the eye in most anurans and turtles.

Vent: The external opening of the cloaca; the anal opening.

Ventral: Referring to the lower surface, or belly, of an animal.

Viviparous: Retaining developing embryos in the female's body until birth; bearing the young "alive." In true viviparity, the embryo usually obtains some direct nourishment from the mother's blood stream.

Index

This section combines a general index to selected topics discussed in the Introduction with an index to common and scientific names of amphibians and reptiles found throughout the book. Use common names when seeking complete text references to particular species or subspecies. Go to the general category (i.e., "salamanders," "turtles," etc.) and find the species/subspecies in question below. Species accounts and illustrations are in **bold** type (photos of Great Lakes species occur within each account).